CW00502618

This book comes with access to more content online.

Quiz yourself, study with flashcards,
and score high on test day!

Register your book or ebook at
www.dummies.com/go/getaccess.

Select your product, and then follow the prompts
to validate your purchase.

You'll receive an email with your PIN and instructions.

GMAT® Prep
2024/2025

GMAT® Prep 2024/2025

with Online Practice

by Lisa Zimmer Hatch, MA, Scott A. Hatch, JD, and Sandra Luna McCune, PhD

A Wiley Brand

GMAT® Prep 2024/2025 For Dummies® with Online Practice

Published by: **John Wiley & Sons, Inc.,** 111 River Street, Hoboken, NJ 07030-5774, www.wiley.com

For general information on our other products and services, please contact our Customer Care Department within the U.S. at 877-762-2974, outside the U.S. at 317-572-3993, or fax 317-572-4002. For technical support, please visit https://hub.wiley.com/community/support/dummies.

Wiley publishes in a variety of print and electronic formats and by print-on-demand. Some material included with standard print versions of this book may not be included in e-books or in print-on-demand. If this book refers to media such as a CD or DVD that is not included in the version you purchased, you may download this material at http://booksupport.wiley.com. For more information about Wiley products, visit www.wiley.com.

Library of Congress Control Number: 2023935196

ISBN 978-1-394-18336-4 (pbk); ISBN 978-1-394-18338-8 (ebk); ISBN 978-1-394-18340-1 (ebk)

Printed and bound by CPI Group (UK) Ltd, Croydon, CR0 4YY

C9781394183364_190923

Contents at a Glance

Table of Contents

Introduction

You're merrily skimming through the admissions requirements for your favorite MBA programs when all of a sudden, you're dealt a shocking blow. Your absolute top choice program — you'll die if you don't get in — requires that you take the Graduate Management Admission Test (GMAT). And you thought your days of speed-reading passages and solving for *x* were over.

Many MBA programs include the GMAT as an admissions requirement, so you'll be in good company. But how do you prepare for such a comprehensive test? What are you going to do? Get out your spiral notebooks from undergraduate courses and sift through years' worth of doodles? Many years may have gone by since you encountered an algebra problem, and we bet your reading proficiency has gotten a little rusty since English 101.

Clearly, you need a readable, concisely structured resource. Well, you've come to the right place. *GMAT Prep 2024/2025 For Dummies,* with Online Practice, puts at your fingertips everything you need to know to conquer the GMAT. We offer beneficial quantitative and verbal reviews that will assist you in pinpointing areas for improvement. In addition, we provide insights into how to avoid the pitfalls that the GMAT creators want you to fall into. We also try to make this book as enjoyable as a book that devotes itself to setting up equations and critiquing arguments can be.

About This Book

We suspect that you aren't eagerly anticipating sitting through the GMAT, and you're probably not looking forward to studying for it, either. Therefore, we've attempted to make the study process as painless as possible by giving you clearly written advice in a casual tone. We realize you have a heap of things you'd rather be doing, so we've broken down the information into easily digested bites. If you have an extra hour before work or Pilates class, you can devour a chapter or even a particular section within a chapter. (If these eating metaphors are making you hungry, feel free to take a snack break.)

In this book, you can find

» Plenty of sample questions so you can see just how the GMAT tests a particular concept. Our sample questions read like the actual test questions, so you can get comfortable with the way the GMAT phrases questions and expresses answer choices.

» A handy pre-assessment to help you define your areas of strength and weakness and tips for tackling a study plan based on your timeframe.

» Detailed explanations of the strategies for mastering all three sections of the GMAT. Enjoy an in-depth reading review for the verbal reasoning section, an extensive math lesson to help you with the quantitative reasoning section, and a how-to on reading and interpreting all kinds of graphs for the data insights section.

» Three practice tests. Two sections of one practice test appear in this book in Chapter 18. You can find the complete Practice Test from Chapter 18, including the interactive data insights section, and two other complete practice tests online.

>> Time-tested techniques for improving your score. We show you how to quickly eliminate incorrect answer choices and make educated guesses.

>> Tips on how to manage your time wisely.

>> Suggestions for creating a relaxation routine to employ if you start to panic during the test.

We've included all kinds of information to help you do your best on the GMAT.

You should find this book easily accessible, but a few things may require explanation. A few of the chapters may contain sidebars (a paragraph or two in a shaded box) with quirky bits of information that we think may interest you but aren't essential to your performance on the GMAT. If you're trying to save time, you can skip the sidebars.

Foolish Assumptions

Although we guess it's possible that you picked up this book just because you have an insatiable love for math, reading, and argument analysis, we're betting it's more likely that you're examining this book particularly because you've been told you need to take the GMAT. (We have been praised for our startling ability to recognize the obvious!) And because we're pretty astute, we've figured that this means that you intend to apply to MBA programs and probably are considering working toward a Master of Business Administration.

Generally, MBA programs are pretty selective, so we're thinking that you're really motivated to get into the program of your choice. Some of you are fresh out of college and may have more recent experience with math and verbal skills. Others of you probably haven't stepped into a classroom in over a decade but possess work and life experience that will help you maximize your GMAT score despite the time that's passed since college.

If math and verbal skills are fresh in your mind and you just need to know what to expect when you arrive at the test site, this book has that information for you. If you've been out of school for a while, this book provides you with all the basics as well as advanced concepts to give you everything you need to know to conquer the GMAT with flying colors.

Icons Used in This Book

One exciting feature of this book is the icons that highlight especially significant portions of the text. These little pictures in the margins alert you to areas where you should pay particularly close attention.

This icon highlights really important information that you should remember even after you close the book.

REMEMBER

Throughout the book, we give you insights into how you can enhance your performance on the GMAT. The tips give you juicy timesavers and point out especially relevant concepts to keep in mind for the test.

TIP

Your world won't fall apart if you ignore our warnings, but your score may suffer. Heed these cautionary pointers to avoid making careless mistakes that can cost you points.

WARNING

Whenever you see this icon in the text, you know you're going to get to practice the particular area of instruction covered in that section with a question like one you may see on the test. Our examples include detailed explanations of how to most efficiently answer GMAT questions and avoid common pitfalls.

EXAMPLE

Beyond the Book: The Online Practice

In addition to what you're reading right now, this book comes with a free access-anywhere Cheat Sheet that includes tips to help you prepare for the GMAT. To get this Cheat Sheet, simply go to www.dummies.com and type "GMAT For Dummies Cheat Sheet" in the Search box.

You also get access to three full-length online practice tests and approximately 100 flashcards. To gain access to the online practice, all you have to do is register. Just follow these simple steps:

1. Register your book or ebook at Dummies.com to get your PIN by going to www.dummies.com/go/getaccess.

2. Select your product from the drop-down list on that page.

3. Follow the prompts to validate your product and then check your email for a confirmation message that includes your PIN and instructions for logging in.

If you don't receive this email within two hours, please check your spam folder before contacting us through our Technical Support website at http://support.wiley.com or by phone at 877-762-2974.

Now you're ready to go! You can come back to the practice material as often as you want — simply log on with the username and password you created during your initial login. No need to enter the access code a second time.

Your registration is good for one year from the day you activate your PIN.

REMEMBER

Where to Go from Here

We know that everyone who uses this book has different strengths and weaknesses, so this book is designed for you to read in the way that best suits you. If you're a math whiz and need to brush up only on your verbal skills, you can skim Part 4 and focus on Parts 1 and 3. If you've been writing proposals every day for the last ten years, you can probably scan Part 3 and focus your attention on the math review in Part 4. Because the data insights section differs so significantly from other standardized test questions, you'll benefit from delving into Part 5 regardless of your math prowess or verbal genius. The pre-assessment in Part 2 can help you figure out where to focus if you aren't sure.

We suggest that you take a more thorough approach, however. Familiarize yourself with the general test-taking process in the first two chapters, take the pre-assessment, and then go through the complete GMAT review, starting with the verbal section and working your way through the math and data insights sections. You can skim through information that you know more about by just reading the Tips and Warnings and working through the examples in those sections. When you've finished pouring through the entirety of Parts 1 through 5, you can take practice tests from

Part 6 and the online content. As you complete your practice tests, compare your scores. This way, you can see just how much you improve with practice. And whatever you do, don't go skipping over the oh-so-helpful advice tucked away in Part 7.

TIP

This book provides you with a bunch of practice tests and lots of online practice, but you can never get enough. So, if after taking all the practice tests provided at dummies.com, you still crave more, visit the official GMAT website at www.mba.com and download the free GMATPrep software from there. This software mimics the computerized format of the test and gives you practice on the types of mouse-clicking and eye-straining skills you need to succeed on the exam. That way, you can experience using the same software you'll see on the exam. Plus, you can purchase the current editions of *GMAT Official Guide*, *GMAT Official Guide Quantitative Review*, *GMAT Official Guide Verbal Review*, and *GMAT Official Guide Data Insights Review*, all published by John Wiley & Sons, Inc., for thousands of additional official practice questions.

We're confident that if you devote a few hours a week for at least six weeks to practicing the skills and tips we provide for you in this book, you'll be thoroughly ready to excel when you sit in front of that computer on GMAT test day. We wish you the greatest success on your ultimate GMAT score!

REMEMBER

The GMAT, developed in 1953, was originally designed to forecast the performance of MBA candidates in business and management courses. Over time, the test has undergone various transformations to align with the evolving requirements of business schools and the business community. Notably, in 2023, the Graduate Management Admission Council (GMAC), responsible for managing the GMAT, introduced the GMAT Focus Edition. This edition introduces a comprehensive revision to the test's format and content, aiming to bolster its pertinence and address the dynamic demands of business schools and employers. This publication is written to adhere to the specifications of the GMAT Focus Edition, herein and hereafter referred to as simply the GMAT. Delve into Chapter 1 to acquire a complete understanding of the new GMAT, as it provides a thorough breakdown of everything you need to know.

1

Getting Started with the GMAT

IN THIS PART . . .

Familiarize yourself with the test structure.

Find out how to maximize your score by organizing your time and streamlining your approach.

Discover what you can and should do to gain admission to the business school of your choice.

IN THIS CHAPTER

» Finding out how MBA programs use your GMAT score

» Deciding when and how to take the GMAT and having the right supplies

» Examining the structure of the GMAT

» Understanding how the GMAT is scored

» Considering whether you should retake the GMAT

Chapter **1**

The Lowdown on the GMAT

Congratulations on deciding to take a significant step in your business career! More than 100 countries offer the Graduate Management Admission Test (GMAT), and according to the Graduate Management Admission Council (GMAC), more than 7,700 programs at 2,400 universities and organizations in 110 countries use the GMAT to make admissions decisions. That said, you're probably not taking the GMAT because you want to. In fact, you may not be looking forward to the experience at all! But the GMAT need not be a daunting ordeal. A little knowledge can help calm your nerves, so this chapter shows you how admissions programs use your test score and addresses the concerns you may have about the GMAT's format and testing and scoring procedures.

Knowing Why the GMAT Is Important

If you're reading this book, you're probably thinking about applying to an MBA program. And if you're applying to an MBA program, you probably need to take the GMAT. Many MBA programs require that you submit a GMAT score for the admissions process. (Some may require other tests or no test at all, so make sure you check each program's admissions checklist.) Even if your program doesn't require a GMAT score through a test-optional or test-flexible policy, a strong GMAT score can significantly support your application.

Your GMAT score gives the admissions committee another tool to use to assess your skills and compare you with other applicants. But if you're seeking a career in business, you're probably resigned to being continually assessed and compared. The GMAT doesn't attempt to evaluate any particular subject area that you may have studied, but instead it gives admissions officers a standardized idea of how you'll likely perform in the classes that make up a graduate business curriculum. Although the GMAT doesn't rate your experience or motivation, it does provide an estimate of your academic preparation for graduate business studies.

REMEMBER

Not every MBA applicant has the same undergraduate experience, but most applicants take a standardized test. Other admissions factors, like college grades, work experience, the admissions essay or essays, and a personal interview, are important, but the GMAT is a tool that admissions committees can use to directly compare you with other applicants and confirm your academic qualifications.

The most selective schools primarily admit candidates with solid GMAT scores, and good scores will certainly strengthen your application to any program, but you shouldn't feel discouraged if your practice tests don't put you in the 90th percentile. Very few students achieve anything near a perfect score on the GMAT. Even if you don't score as high as you want to, you undoubtedly have other strengths in your admissions profile, such as work experience, leadership ability, good college grades, motivation, and people skills. You may want to contact the admissions offices of the schools you're interested in to see how much they emphasize the GMAT. While the weight of the GMAT in the admissions process varies by institution, it can often be a significant factor. Therefore, you should take all necessary measures to ensure you perform your best!

Planning It Perfectly: When and How to Take the GMAT

Which MBA programs to apply to isn't the only decision you have to make. After you've figured out where you want to go, you have to make plans for the GMAT. You need to choose which format works best for you, determine the ideal time to take the test, and know what to have with you when you do. The following sections can help you out.

Choosing between taking the GMAT online or at a test center

You have two options of delivery method of the GMAT: online at home or at a designated testing center, the choice is yours. Regardless of where you take it, the GMAT e-content and interface are the same. Which method is best for you depends on several considerations. For many, the advantage of testing in a familiar environment outweighs the challenges of creating a secure testing environment. Others prefer the stability of taking the computerized exam at a testing center.

The GMAT online exam

You may choose to take the GMAT online exam in the comfort of your home on your own computer. Before you take the exam, you download the special secure software and set up your test space. A human proctor virtually oversees the online exam throughout the testing experience, and you're responsible for meeting the stringent specifications for setting up the testing environment. Here are the advantages of taking the online exam:

>> **The online format is available even more often than the options provided at testing centers.** You can take the online GMAT 24 hours a day, 7 days a week, and you can register 24 hours before an open slot.

>> **The testing environment is familiar.** As long as you set up the testing environment along the required guidelines, you can test from any location.

>> **You don't have to worry about traffic or other commuting issues.** It's hard to get lost when you're commuting from your bedroom to your home office.

The GMAT at a testing center

You can also opt to take the GMAT at a testing center. Although testing at home may seem more desirable, you may choose the testing center for the following reasons:

>> **The testing center provides all supplies.** You don't have to worry about a reliable Internet connection or purchasing your own whiteboard for notes.

>> **You aren't responsible for securing your environment.** To maintain the integrity of the home testing experience, you must follow stringent guidelines. Testing at a center guarantees that you won't be penalized for an interruption by a family member or fail to pass a room scan.

When to register for and take the GMAT

When is the best time to take the GMAT? With the computerized and online testing procedures, this question has become more interesting than it was in the days of paper-based tests. When the exam was a paper-and-pencil format with a test booklet and an answer sheet full of bubbles, you had a limited choice of possible test dates — about one every two months. Now you've got much more flexibility when choosing the date and time for taking the test. You can pick just about any time to sit down and click answer choices with your mouse.

Registering when you're ready

The first step in the GMAT registration process is scheduling an appointment, but don't put off making this appointment the way you'd put off calling the dentist (even though you'd probably like to avoid both!). Depending on the time of year, appointment times can go quickly. You may have to wait at least a month for an open time. To determine what's available, you can go to the official GMAT website at www.mba.com. From there, you can choose an online test appointment or testing location and find out what dates and times are available. When you find a date and time you like, you can register online or over the phone.

REMEMBER

The best time to take the GMAT is after you've had at least six to eight weeks of quality study time and during a period when you don't have a lot of other things going on to distract you. Of course, if your MBA program application is due in four weeks, put this book down and schedule an appointment right away! Be sure to come right back, though. You need to start studying — and now! If you have more flexibility, you should still plan to take the GMAT as soon as you think you've studied sufficiently. All the following circumstances warrant taking the GMAT as soon as you can:

>> **You want to start your MBA program right away.** If you're confident that you want to begin business school within the next few semesters, you should consider taking the GMAT in the near future. After you know your score, you'll be better able to narrow down the business schools you want to apply to. Then you can focus on the other parts of your application, and you won't have to worry about having an application due in four weeks and no GMAT score.

>> **You're considering attending business school.** Maybe you don't know whether you want to pursue an MBA. Even so, now's a good time to take the GMAT. Your GMAT score may help you decide that you have the skills to succeed academically in graduate business school. You may think that you don't have what it takes, but your performance on the GMAT may surprise you! If you do decide to apply to an MBA program, you'll already have one key component of the application under wraps.

>> **You're about to earn (or have just earned) your bachelor's degree.** If you're nearing graduation or have just graduated from college and you think you may want to get an MBA, it's better to take the GMAT now than wait until later. You're used to studying. You're used to tests. And your math and verbal analytical abilities are probably as fresh as they'll ever be.

You don't have to start an MBA program right away. Your GMAT scores are valid for up to five years, so you can take the test now and take advantage of your current skills as a student to get you into a great graduate program later.

REMEMBER

Giving yourself about six to eight weeks to study provides you with enough time to master the GMAT concepts but not so much time that you forget what you've studied by the time you sit for the test.

Scheduling for success

Whenever you register, you want to consider your own schedule when picking a test date and time. Take advantage of the flexibility allowed by the computer format. The GMAT is no longer just an 8 a.m. Saturday morning option. You can take the test any day of the week except Sunday, and, depending on the test center, you may be able to start at a variety of times. Many centers offer 8 a.m. testing times, but some have other options, even 6:30 at night — great for those night owls who consider 8 a.m. a good bedtime rather than a good exam time. Your options for the online test may be even more abundant. You have a little bit of control over making the test fit into your life instead of having to make your life fit the test!

If you're not a morning person, don't schedule an early test if you can help it. If you're better able to handle a nonstop, two-and-a-quarter-hour barrage of questions after the sun hits its highest point in the sky, schedule your test for the afternoon or evening. By choosing the time that works for you, you'll be able to comfortably approach the test instead of worrying whether you set your alarm. We're guessing that you have enough to worry about in life as it is without the added stress of an inconvenient test time.

TIP

Check the GMAT website for the available testing times at the test centers near you or at home. Then study for the test at the different available times of the day to see when you're at your best. Schedule your test session for that time. Even if you have to take a few hours away from work or classes, being able to take the test at a time that's best for you is worth it. And you may end up picking a test center based on its available times rather than its proximity to you.

While you're thinking about the time that's best for the test, you should think about days of the week, as well. For some people, Saturday may be a good day for a test. For others, the weekend is the wrong time for that type of concentrated academic activity. If you're used to taking the weekends off, scheduling the test during the week may make more sense for you.

REMEMBER

Choosing the time and day to take the GMAT is primarily up to you. Be honest with yourself about your habits, preferences, and schedule, and pick a time and day when you'll excel.

Things to take to the GMAT testing center (or to have at home)

The most important thing you can bring to the GMAT is a positive attitude and a willingness to succeed. However, if you don't have your admission voucher or your photo ID, you won't get the chance to apply those qualities! It's also important to bring a list of up to five schools where you want your Official Score Report to be sent. Sending your official report to these schools for free is possible at the test center or from home, and you'll be able to see your GMAT scores before you make any selections.

Additionally, you have the option to send your score report for free from your GMAT online account within 48 hours of completing your exam. You can, of course, list fewer than five schools, but if you decide to send your report to additional schools later, you'll have to pay. Therefore, if you have five schools in mind and feel confident about your abilities, it's best to send your official report for free. Finally, it's worth noting that the schools you select will receive only your scores from the exam you just completed, not all the scores you've received in the last five years, as was previously the case.

TIP

Because you can take one optional ten-minute break, we recommend you have access to a quick snack, like a protein bar, and a bottle of water. You can't have food or drink in the testing area, but at the centers you're provided a secure locker that you can access during a break. For the online test, you can leave the room during the break to use the restroom or eat a quick snack, but you need to leave your camera on while you're gone.

That's really all you need to bring to the testing center. You can't use a hand-held calculator, and the test center provides a booklet of five erasable noteboards and a special black marker (but no eraser), which you're required to use instead of pencil and paper. You can ask for another booklet if you fill yours up.

If you test at home, you'll likely want to purchase your own whiteboard to use for notes during the test. The software provides you with an online whiteboard, but you can't use a stylus, so the online version is awkward to use. The erasable whiteboard can be no bigger than 12 by 20 inches. You can have up to two erasable markers and one whiteboard eraser.

Forming First Impressions: The Format of the GMAT

The GMAT is a standardized test, and by now in your academic career, you're probably familiar with what that means: lots of questions to answer in a short period of time, no way to cram for them or memorize answers, and very little chance of scoring 100 percent. The skills tested on the GMAT are those that leading business schools have decided are important for MBA students: data insights, quantitative reasoning, and verbal reasoning.

The GMAT "Select Section Order" option allows you to complete the three sections in any order you choose:

- ≫ data insights→quantitative→verbal
- ≫ data insights→verbal→quantitative
- ≫ quantitative→verbal→data insights
- ≫ quantitative→data insights→verbal
- ≫ verbal→data insights→quantitative
- ≫ verbal→quantitative→data insights

Pick the order that's most comfortable for you. You may want to lead with your strength or get the section you like least out of the way in the beginning.

Examining the structure of the GMAT

The following table presents a summary of the structure of the GMAT by Sections:

Section	Data Insights	Quantitative	Verbal
Time	45 min.	45 min.	45 min.
Number of questions	20	21	23
Question type(s)	Data Sufficiency Table Analysis Two-Part Analysis Graphics Interpretation Multi-Source Reasoning	Basic Arithmetic Algebra Data Interpretation Probability and Statistics	Reading Comprehension Critical Reasoning
Avg. time/question	2 min. 15 sec.	2 min. 9 sec.	1 min. 57 sec.

Getting familiar with what the GMAT tests

Standardized tests are supposed to test your academic potential, not your knowledge of specific subjects. The GMAT focuses on the areas that admissions committees have found to be relevant to MBA programs. The sections that follow are an introduction to the three GMAT sections. We devote the majority of the rest of this book to telling you exactly how to approach each one.

Leveraging your data literacy skills

The GMAT data insights section has 20 questions consisting of two question types: data sufficiency questions and integrated reasoning questions.

Data sufficiency questions present you with two statements and ask you to decide whether the problem can be solved by using the information provided by the first statement only, the second statement only, both statements, or neither statement. We show you exactly how to tackle these unusual math questions in Chapter 17.

Integrated reasoning (IR) questions test your ability to read and evaluate charts, graphs, and other forms of presented data. You'll examine a variety of data representation and answer questions based on the information. Turn to Chapters 15 and 16 to get prepared to respond to these questions with confidence.

The IR questions are of four basic question types: table analysis, two-part analysis, graphics interpretation, and multi-source reasoning. Table analysis and graphics interpretation questions are self-explanatory: You analyze tables and interpret graphs — simple enough, right? The two-part analysis questions present a problem and related data, provided in two columns. You choose a piece of information from each column to solve the problem. Multi-source reasoning questions provide you with a bunch of information from which you have to decide what piece or pieces of data actually give you what you need to know to solve the problem.

Quizzing your quantitative skills

The GMAT quantitative section consists of 21 questions and assesses your proficiency in arithmetic, algebra, data interpretation, and probability and statistics. This section is comparable to other standardized math assessments in terms of its format and question type. To succeed on this section, you will need to employ your problem solving skills to answer multiple-choice questions, choosing the best response from five possible options.

Validating your verbal skills

The GMAT verbal section consists of 23 multiple-choice questions of two general types: the ubiquitous reading comprehension questions and critical reasoning questions. Reading comprehension requires you to answer questions about written passages on a number of different subjects. Critical reasoning questions require you to analyze logical arguments and understand how to strengthen or weaken those arguments. For all questions in this section, you must choose the best response from five possible options.

Understanding the computerized format

All three sections of the computerized GMAT are available only in *computer-adaptive test* (CAT) format. The first question of each section is of medium difficulty. The CAT adjusts to your skill level by presenting you with questions of various difficulty, based on your responses to previous questions. If you consistently answer questions correctly, the computer will challenge you with more difficult questions to gauge the limits of your impressive intellect. Conversely, if you're having a tough day and many of your answers are wrong, the computer presents you with easier questions to determine the appropriate level of difficulty for you.

With the CAT format, your score isn't based solely on how many questions you answer correctly or incorrectly, but also on the average difficulty level of the questions you answer correctly. Theoretically, you could miss several questions and still get a very high score, so long as the questions you missed were among the most challenging in the question bank.

At the conclusion of each section, you are assigned a level of ability, which is used to score your performance. This method of evaluation is designed to ensure that test takers are assessed based on their individual capabilities.

Answering in an orderly fashion

With the CAT format, the first question in a section is preselected for you, and the order of subsequent questions depends on how well you've answered this question. So if you do well on the first question, Question 2 will reflect your success by being more challenging. If you do poorly on the initial questions, you'll get an easier Question 2. The computer program continues to take all previous questions into account as it feeds you question after question.

WARNING

The CAT format is distinctive in several ways, but — because each question is based on your answers to previous questions — you can't skip questions, and you must answer each question as it appears. Additionally, neither can you return to a previous question to revise your answer, although there is a chance to review and edit your responses after you have completed the section. This review and edit feature permits you to change up to three answers in a section, but only if time allows (see the next chapter for a full discussion of the review and edit feature). If you realize several questions later that you made a mistake, try not to worry about it. If time permits, you might be able to revisit the question after you complete the section. Even if you don't have the chance to take advantage of that opportunity, it's reassuring to know your score isn't solely determined by the number of correct or incorrect answers, but also takes in account the difficulty level of the questions.

Observing time limits

The time limit for each section is 45 minutes. This time limit has important implications for your test strategy. As we discuss later in this chapter, your GMAT score depends on the number of questions you're able to answer. If you run out of the allotted time and leave questions unanswered at the end of a section, you'll essentially reduce your score by the number of questions you don't answer. In addition, you won't have time to revisit questions you may have struggled with. In Chapter 2, we present you with an efficient, workable strategy for managing your time and maximizing your score.

Honing your computer skills for the GMAT

Technically challenged, take heart! You need to have only minimal computer skills to take the computerized GMAT. In fact, the skills you need for the test are far fewer in number than those you'll need while pursuing an MBA. All that is required is that you know how to select answers by using either the mouse or the keyboard.

Knowing Where You Stand: Scoring Considerations

Okay, you know the GMAT's format and how many questions it has and so on. But what about what's really important to you, the crucial final score? Probably very few people take standardized tests for fun, so we give you the lowdown on scoring in the following sections.

How the GMAT testers figure your score

The GMAT is divided into three sections: Data insights, quantitative reasoning, and verbal reasoning. Each section of the GMAT is scored on a scale from 60 to 90, in 1-point increments, and contributes equally to the GMAT total score. The GMAT total score is on a scale of 205 to 805, in 10-point increments. So, the maximum total score you can earn on the GMAT is 805.

However, it is important to note that the GMAT is a computer-adaptive test, meaning that your section scores are determined by more than just the number of questions you get right. In fact, the scores you earn take into account three factors:

>> **The difficulty of the questions you answer:** The questions become more difficult as you continue to answer correctly, so getting tough questions means you're doing well on the test.

>> **The number of questions you answer:** If you don't get to all the questions in a section, your score is reduced by the proportion of questions you didn't answer. So, if you failed to answer 5 of the 21 quantitative questions, for example, your raw score would be reduced by about 24 percent: After converting the raw score to the scaled measure, this loss could significantly decrease your percentile rank.

>> **The number of questions you answer correctly:** In addition to scoring based on how difficult the questions are, the GMAT score also reflects your ability to answer those questions correctly.

How the GMAT testers report your score

When you're finished with the test — or when your time is up — the computer immediately calculates your unofficial scores for the data insights, quantitative reasoning, and verbal reasoning sections, as well as your total score and displays them on-screen to you in an unofficial score report.

You will receive an email notification when your Official Score Report is available in your online GMAT account, usually within 7 business days (but it could take up to 20 business days in some cases). The report will include your individual section scores, total score, and percentile rank. It will also provide detailed graphical data that can offer a more comprehensive understanding of your performance.

Official scores, including the data insights, quantitative reasoning, and verbal reasoning scores, and total score a re sent to the schools that you've requested to receive them, free of charge. If you wish to send your score report to additional schools, you can do so for a fee, up to five years after the test.

What about canceling your GMAT scores?

Thanks to the GMAT's policy of letting you preview your scores before you decide which schools will receive your Official Score Report, you'll never have to worry about canceling your scores. By selecting the schools you wish to receive your official report, you have full control over the process. Any schools you do not designate will not have access to your report. It will remain confidential and secure in your online GMAT account.

WARNING

Be aware that once you send your Official Score Report to a program, GMAC cannot cancel that action or disable the school's ability to view your report.

Repeating the Process: Retaking the GMAT

If you're not satisfied with your GMAT score, retaking the test may be advantageous, especially as most selective MBA programs prioritize high scores. Fortunately, the GMAT administrators let you take the test quite a few times if you want (that's pretty big of them, considering you have to pay for it every time). Having multiple opportunities to take the test increases your chances of improving your score, thereby enhancing your prospect of getting accepted into your desired program.

WARNING

Each time you attempt the GMAT, it counts toward your five attempts during a 12-month period and eight total lifetime attempts.

IN THIS CHAPTER

» **Checking out guessing strategies**

» **Managing your time like a pro**

» **Knowing how to recognize a wrong answer**

» **Avoiding worthless activities that minimize your score**

» **Quieting your nerves with reliable relaxation techniques**

Chapter **2**

Maximizing Your Score on the GMAT

You enter the test center and stare down the computer. For the next two hours and fifteen minutes, that machine is your adversary. The GMAT loaded on it is your nemesis. All you have to aid you in this showdown is a booklet of noteboards or a whiteboard and your intellect. The questions come quickly, and your reward for answering a question correctly is another, usually more difficult question! Why did you give up your precious free time for this torture?

By the time you actually take the GMAT, you'll have already given up hours and hours of your free time studying for the test, researching business schools, and planning for the future. That two hours and fifteen minutes alone with a computer represents a rite of passage that you complete to accomplish the goals you've set for yourself. And because you've invested so much of yourself, you may as well get the highest score you're capable of achieving!

This chapter contains techniques you need to apply to pull together a winning strategy for the GMAT. You already have the brains. In this chapter, we share with you the other tools you need to maximize your score.

Discovering Strategies for Boosting Your Score

It may seem counterintuitive that we start this discussion by acknowledging that guessing plays a significant role in achieving a high score on the GMAT. Your ideal GMAT test-day scenario probably involves knowing the answers to most of the questions right away rather than randomly guessing! The reality is that even the most prepared test-takers will encounter questions that stump them. Think back: Did you have to guess at any questions on the ACT or SAT? We bet you did!

In the upcoming sections, you will find valuable suggestions to enhance your GMAT score, including reliable strategies for guessing, which can improve your chances of answering questions correctly, even if you otherwise have no clue of the right answer.

Forcing yourself to guess so you can move on

Remember that standardized tests aren't like tests in your undergraduate college courses. If you studied hard in college, you may not have had to do much guessing on your midterms and finals. On the GMAT, however, the software won't allow you to skip questions. So, if you stumble upon some really difficult questions that you're not sure how to answer, you have to guess and move on.

If a question is taking too much time, you can use the bookmark feature to flag the question for review and edit after you complete the section (provided you have time remaining).

Don't fall into thinking that you must know the correct answer for each question to do well on the GMAT. The GMAT is designed to test the potential of a wide range of future MBA students, so some of the questions have to be ridiculously difficult to challenge that one-in-a-million Einstein who takes the GMAT. Almost everyone incorrectly answers a few questions in each section, and almost everyone has to guess on those really difficult questions. Don't worry if you have to guess; just figure out how to guess effectively!

With the computer-adaptive test (CAT) format, developing a strategy for successful guessing is actually more important than ever. As you answer questions correctly, the level of difficulty continues to increase. so be sure to apply the guessing strategies we discuss in this chapter to all three sections (verbal, quantitative, and data insights) of the test. Even if you do really, really well on the test, you'll probably find yourself guessing on some questions. On the GMAT, almost *everyone* guesses!

Taking advantage of the review and edit feature

The GMAT allows you to review and edit answers for up to three questions in each section before the section time runs out. Also, while you're working through a section, you can use the bookmark feature to flag as many questions as you like, giving you the freedom to move on to other questions and return to flagged ones to review — provided you've submitted an answer for every question in the section (including those you've flagged) and have time remaining.

After you confirm your answer for the final question in a section, a "Question Review & Edit" screen will pop up (this screen will not appear if your time has run out). On that screen, you'll see a numbered list of the questions in the section, and you'll also see a bookmark icon in the list on any question you flagged. You click on a question number to return to that question to review and, possibly, change your answer. Knowing that you can change answers to at most three questions, you must be strategic in deciding which questions are the most promising candidates to consider.

Don't change an answer unless you have a good reason to do so! You should change an answer only if you are confident that your initial answer was incorrect and you have a good reason to believe that your new answer is correct. Generally, it is better to trust your instincts and stick with your initial choice unless, for example, you made a wild guess on a question or you realize that you misread the question or made a careless mistake.

Understanding the importance of completing each section

To get the optimum score for the questions you answer correctly, you must respond to all the questions in each section. If you don't have time to complete the questions at the end of each section, your score is reduced in proportion to the number of questions you didn't answer. Therefore, it's important to move at a pace that allows you to get to all the questions.

WARNING

One of the ways you can get into real trouble with the CAT format is by spending too much time early on trying to correctly answer questions that are more difficult. If you're reluctant to guess and, therefore, spend more than a minute or two on several difficult questions, you may not have time to answer the relatively easy questions at the end.

TIP

Answer every question in each section! If you notice that you have only three or four minutes remaining in a section and more than five questions left, spend the remaining minutes marking an answer for every question, even if you don't have time to read them. You always have a 20 percent chance of randomly guessing the correct answer to a five-option multiple choice question, which is better than not answering the question at all. If you have to guess randomly at the end of the section, mark the same bubble for each answer. For example, you may choose to mark the second bubble from the bottom. Chances are that at least one in five questions will have a correct answer placed second to the end. Marking the same bubble also saves time because you don't have to choose which answer to mark for each question; you already have your guessing strategy in mind, so you don't have to think about it.

Even the GMAT folks warn of a severe penalty for not completing the test. They claim that your score will decrease significantly with each unanswered question, which could make a huge difference in your admissions chances!

Winning the Race against the Clock

Random guessing as the clock runs out serves you better than leaving the remaining questions in a section unanswered, but it's not a good way to approach the test in general. Instead, adopt a strategy of good time management that combines proper pacing, an active approach to answering questions, and appropriate guessing. We discuss all these time-management strategies in the following sections.

Giving each question equal treatment

You may have heard that you should spend a lot of time on the first ten questions because your performance on them determines your ultimate score. Although your performance on the first ten questions *does* give the computer an initial estimate of your ability, in the end, these first questions don't carry greater significance than any other questions. You'll still encounter all the questions in the section eventually, so you really have no reason to spend an unreasonable length of time on the first ten.

WARNING

If you spend too much time on the first ten questions and answer them all correctly, you'll have a limited amount of time in which to answer the remaining questions in the section. The software program would give you a high estimated score after those first ten questions, but that initial estimate would then most likely fall steadily throughout the section as you would hurry through questions and, at the end, guess at those you didn't have time to answer properly. The worst outcome of all would be if you were unable to finish the section and had your score reduced in proportion to the questions you couldn't answer. You can't cheat the system by focusing on the first few questions. If you could, the very intelligent, highly paid test designers would find a way to adjust the format to thwart you.

Making time for the last ten questions

A much better approach than lavishing time on the first ten questions is allowing ample time to answer the *last* ten questions in the sections. Because the best way to score well is to give adequate time to each question, guess when necessary, and complete the entire test, you shouldn't spend a disproportionate amount of time answering the early questions.

Here are the steps to follow for this approach:

1. **Work through the first 22 minutes and 30 seconds of each section at a good pace.**

   Allocate a little over two minutes per quantitative question, slightly under two minutes per verbal question, and precisely two minutes and 15 seconds per data insights question.

2. **Don't spend more than three minutes on any question during the first 25 minutes of a section.**

3. **When you have ten questions remaining in the section, check the time remaining and adjust your pace accordingly.**

   Ten questions remain when you hit Question 11 of the quantitative section, Question 13 of the verbal section, or Question 10 of the data insights section.

TIP

   For instance, let's say you have managed to answer the first 11 quantitative questions in just 20 minutes. With 25 minutes remaining, you have the opportunity to allocate more time to each of the remaining ten questions. By doing so, you can avoid resorting to random guessing for the unanswered questions towards the end of the section. These additional seconds per question could be crucial in improving your accuracy when addressing the final ten questions. Moreover, you might even have surplus time to review and edit your answers for up to three questions.

WARNING

We're not suggesting that you rush through the first 20 or so minutes of each section so you can spend lots of time on the last ten questions. Instead, you should stick to a pace that allows you to give equal time to all the questions in a section. You can't spend five or six minutes on a single question without sacrificing your performance on the rest of the test, so stick to your pace.

TIP

If you happen to have additional time when you get to the last ten questions, by all means, use it. There's a severe penalty for not finishing a section but no prize for getting done early.

When you work steadily and carefully through the first 75 percent of each section, you're rewarded with a score that stabilizes toward the higher end of the percentile and that may rise to an even higher level at the end of the section as you spend extra time getting the last questions right. Talk about ending on a high note!

Keeping track of your pace

You may think that keeping an even pace throughout the test means a lot of clock watching, but this isn't the case if you go into the test with a plan. You can conceal the clock on the computer to keep from becoming obsessed with time, but you should periodically reveal the clock to check your progress. For example, you may plan to check your computer clock after every five questions you answer. This means revealing the feature about four times during each section. You'll spend a second or two clicking on the clock and glancing at it, but knowing that you're on pace will be worth it.

If you time yourself during practice tests, you'll probably begin to know intuitively whether you're falling behind. During the actual exam, you may not have to look at your clock as frequently. However, if you suspect that you're using too much time on a question (more than three minutes), you should check the clock. If you've spent more than three minutes, mark your best guess from the choices you haven't already eliminated and move on.

Getting Rid of Wrong Answers

We've stressed that the key to success is to move through the test steadily so you can answer every question and maximize your score. Keeping this steady pace will probably require you to make some intelligent guesses, and intelligent guesses hang on your ability to eliminate incorrect answers.

Eliminating answer choices is crucial on the verbal and quantitative sections of the GMAT. These questions come with five answer choices, and usually one or two of the options are obviously wrong (especially in the verbal section). As soon as you know an answer choice is wrong, eliminate it. After you've eliminated that answer, don't waste time reading it again. By quickly getting rid of choices that you know are *wrong*, you'll be well on your way to finding the *right* answer! In the following sections, we show you a few elimination strategies that help you cross off wrong answers so you can home in on the right ones.

Keeping track of eliminated answer choices for the computer test format

You may be thinking that eliminating answer choices on a computerized test won't work. In truth, doing so is more difficult than on a paper test where you can actually cross off the entire answer in your test booklet. However, you can achieve the same results on the computerized test with a little practice. You must train your mind to look only at the remaining choices and not read every word that your eyes fall upon. You can't afford to waste time rereading a choice after you've eliminated it. That's why you need a system.

You can use the booklet of noteboards you're given at the test site or the whiteboard if you take the online version to help you eliminate answers. The test administrators will replenish your noteboard supply if you fill them up, and you have unlimited space to write on the online whiteboard, so don't be afraid to write all over your noteboards or whiteboard.

Here are some simple steps to help you keep track of which answers you've eliminated:

1. **At the beginning of the section (especially the verbal one, where eliminating answer choices is easier), quickly write down "A, B, C, D, and E" (or 1, 2, 3, 4, and 5 if you prefer numbers) in a vertical row on your noteboard or whiteboard.**

   A stands for the first answer choice, B for the second, C for the third, and so on, even though these letters don't appear on your computer screen.

2. **When you eliminate an answer choice, cross out the corresponding letter on your noteboard or whiteboard.**

   For example, if you're sure that the second and fifth answers are wrong, mark a line through B and E on your board.

3. **If you look at your noteboard or whiteboard and see only one remaining answer letter, you've zeroed in on the right answer.**

    You don't need to reread the answer choices to remember which one was correct. It's listed right there on the board.

4. **If you can't narrow down your choices to just one answer, eliminating three incorrect choices gives you a good chance of guessing correctly between the two options that remain.**

5. **Quickly rewrite the five letters (or numbers) for the next question and repeat the process.**

Practice this technique when you're taking your practice tests. The hard part isn't crossing out the letters on your board; it's training your eyes to skip the wrong answers on the computer screen. Your brain will want to read through each choice every time you look at the answers. With the paper test booklet, you'd simply cross out the entire answer choice and then skip that choice every time you came to it. With the computerized test, you have to mentally cross out wrong answers. Developing this skill takes time. Mastering it is especially important for the verbal section, which has some long answer choices.

Recognizing wrong answers

So, maybe you've mastered the art of the noteboard answer-elimination system, but you may be wondering how you know which answers to eliminate. Most of the verbal questions are best answered by process of elimination because answers aren't as clearly right or wrong as they may be for the math questions. For many math questions, the correct answer is obvious after you've performed the necessary calculations, but you may be able to answer some math questions without performing complex calculations if you look through the answers first and eliminate choices that don't make sense. So, by using your common sense and analyzing all the information you have to work with (we show you how to do both in the next sections), you can reach a correct answer without knowing everything there is to know about a question.

Using common sense

Reading carefully reveals a surprising number of answer choices that are obviously wrong. For problem solving questions, you may know before you even do a math calculation that one or two of the answers are simply illogical. During the verbal section, it's possible to encounter critical reasoning questions with answer choices that are unrelated to the argument's topic. You can swiftly eliminate these incongruous choices from contention. If an answer is outside the realm of possibility, you don't ever have to read through it again. For example, consider the following sample critical reasoning question.

EXAMPLE

Most New Year's resolutions are quickly forgotten. Americans commonly make resolutions to exercise, lose weight, quit smoking, or spend less money. In January, many people take some action, such as joining a gym, but by February, they are back to their old habits again.

Which of the following, if true, most strengthens the preceding argument?

(A) Some Americans do not make New Year's resolutions.

(B) Americans who do not keep their resolutions feel guilty the rest of the year.

(C) Attempts to quit smoking begun at times other than the first of the year are less successful than those begun in January.

(D) Increased sports programming in January motivates people to exercise more.

(E) People who are serious about lifestyle changes usually make those changes immediately and do not wait for New Year's Day.

Chapter 8 gives you a whole slew of tips on how to answer critical reasoning questions, but without even looking closely at this one, you can eliminate at least two choices immediately. The argument states that people usually don't live up to New Year's resolutions and the question asks you to strengthen that argument. Two of the answer choices have nothing to do with keeping resolutions, so you can discard them right away: Choice (A) provides irrelevant information — the argument is about people who make resolutions, not those who don't — and Choice (D) brings up a completely different topic (sports programming) and doesn't mention resolutions.

Without even taxing your brain, you've gone from five choices down to three. Psychologically, dealing with three answer choices is much easier than dealing with all five. Plus, if you were short on time and had to quickly guess at this question, narrowing your choices to only three would give you a much better chance of answering it correctly.

Relying on what you know

TIP

Before you attempt to solve a quantitative problem, you can use what you know to eliminate answer choices.

For example, if a quantitative question asks for a solution that's an absolute value, you can immediately eliminate any negative answer choices, because absolute value is always nonnegative. (For more about absolute value, see Chapter 10.) Even if you don't remember how to solve the problem, you can at least narrow down the choices and increase your chances of guessing correctly. If you eliminate one or two choices and if you have the time, you may be able to plug the remaining answer choices back into the problem and find the correct answer that way. So, if you approach questions with a stash of knowledge, you can correctly answer more questions than you realize.

Letting the question guide you

If you've ever watched a certain popular TV game show, you know that the clue to the answer can sometimes be found in the question. Although the answers to most GMAT questions aren't as obvious as the answer to "in 1959, the United States said 'aloha' to this 50th state," you can still use clues from the GMAT questions themselves to answer them.

In the earlier critical reasoning example on New Year's resolutions, you were left with three answer choices. Paying attention to the wording of the question can help you eliminate two more.

The question asks you to *strengthen* the argument that Americans quickly forget their New Year's resolutions. Choice (B) seriously *weakens* the argument by indicating that instead of forgetting their resolutions, Americans are haunted by failed resolutions for the rest of the year. Likewise, Choice (C) indicates that a resolution to quit smoking at the beginning of the new year may be more successful than the same resolution at other times. Because these answers weaken the argument rather than strengthen it as the question asks, you can eliminate them, too. By process of elimination, you know that Choice (E) is the correct answer to the question, and you haven't yet seriously considered the logic of the argument!

Quickly recognizing and eliminating wrong answers after only a few seconds puts you on the path to choosing a right answer. This strategy works in the quantitative section as well. Consider this problem solving question example.

EXAMPLE

If $\frac{1}{2}$ of the air in a balloon is removed every 10 seconds, what fraction of the air has been removed from the balloon after 30 seconds?

(A) $\frac{1}{8}$

(B) $\frac{1}{6}$

(C) $\frac{1}{4}$

(D) $\frac{5}{6}$

(E) $\frac{7}{8}$

$$\frac{1}{2} + \frac{1}{2} \times \frac{1}{2} + \frac{1}{2} \times \frac{1}{2} \times \frac{1}{2}$$
$$= \frac{1}{2} + \frac{1}{4} + \frac{1}{8} \Rightarrow E$$

You can immediately eliminate any choices with fractions smaller than one-half because the problem tells you that half the air departs within the first ten seconds. So, you can discard Choices (A), (B), and (C). Without performing any calculations at all, you've narrowed down your choices to just two!

TIP

Another benefit of eliminating obviously wrong answer choices is that you save yourself from inadvertently making costly errors. The GMAT offers choices (A), (B), and (C) to trap unsuspecting test-takers. If you mistakenly tried to solve the problem by multiplying $\frac{1}{2} \times \frac{1}{2} \times \frac{1}{2}$, you'd come up with $\frac{1}{8}$. But if you've already eliminated that answer, you know you've done something wrong. By immediately getting rid of the answer choices that can't be right, you may avoid choosing a clever distractor. By the way, $\frac{1}{8}$ is the amount of air remaining in the balloon after 30 seconds. After the first 10 seconds, $\frac{1}{2}$ of the air remains. After 20 seconds, $\frac{1}{2}$ of that, or $\frac{1}{4}$, remains. After 30 seconds, the balloon still has $\frac{1}{2}$ of $\frac{1}{4}$ of its air, which is $\frac{1}{8}$.

So, the amount of air removed in 30 seconds is Choice (E), $\frac{7}{8}$, because $1 - \frac{1}{8} = \frac{7}{8}$.

Dealing with questions that contain Roman numerals

The GMAT presents a special type of question that pops up from time to time. This question gives you three statements marked with the Roman numerals I, II, and III and asks you to evaluate their validity. You'll find these questions in the quantitative and verbal reasoning sections. You're supposed to select the answer choice that presents the correct list of either valid or invalid statements, depending on what the question is looking for.

TIP

To approach questions that contain statements with Roman numerals, follow these steps:

1. **Evaluate the validity of the first statement or the statement that seems easiest to evaluate.**

2. **If the first statement meets the qualifications stated by the question, eliminate any answer choices that don't contain Roman numeral I; if it doesn't, eliminate any choices that have Roman numeral I in them.**

3. **Examine the remaining answer choices to see which of the two remaining statements is best to evaluate next.**

4. **Evaluate another statement and eliminate answer choices based on your findings.**

   You may find that you don't have to spend time evaluating the third statement.

Here's an example to show how the approach works.

EXAMPLE

If *x* and *y* are different integers, each greater than 1, which of the following must be true?

   i. $x + y > 4$

   ii. $x - y = 0$

   iii. $x - y$ results in an integer

(A) II only

(B) I and II

(C) I, II, and III

(D) I and III

(E) III only

[handwritten notes:]
x and $y > 1$
i $x + y > 4$
     $x = 2$ $x + y > 4$ ✓
     $y = 3$
ii $x - y = 0$ ✗
     $x \neq y \rightarrow x - y \neq 0$ $\rightarrow$ D

Consider the statements one by one. Start with Roman I and determine whether the expression $x + y > 4$ is true. Because *x* and *y* are greater than 1, they must be positive. The smaller of the two integers must be at least 2, and the other number can't be less than 3. So, because $2 + 3 = 5$, $x + y \geq 5$, so their sum has to be greater than 4.

Don't read Roman II yet. Instead, run through the answer choices and eliminate any that don't include Roman I. Choice (A) and Choice (E) don't include Roman I, so cross out those letters on your noteboard or whiteboard. The remaining choices don't give you any indication which statement is best to evaluate next, so proceed with your evaluation of Roman II, which states that $x - y = 0$. This statement can't be correct because *x* and *y* have different values. The only way one number subtracted from another number can result in 0 is when the two numbers are the same. The difference of two different integers will always be at least 1.

Because Roman II isn't correct, eliminate choices that include Roman II. You can cross out Choice (B) and Choice (C), which leaves you with Choice (D). By process of elimination, Choice (D) has to be right. You don't even need to read Roman III because you know the correct answer. Not all Roman numeral questions are so helpful, but many are, and in those cases, the strategy is a real timesaver!

Playing It Smart: A Few Things You Shouldn't Do When Taking the Test

Most of this chapter focuses on what you *should* do to maximize your score on the GMAT. However, there are also a few things you *shouldn't* do, which we discuss in the following sections. Avoid these mistakes, and you'll have an advantage over many other test-takers!

Don't lose your focus

You may be used to the fast-paced world of business or the cooperative world of group presentations that is popular in many business classes. Don't be surprised if 135 minutes of answering questions gets a little boring. We know the prospect is shocking!

Don't allow yourself to lose focus. Keep your brain on a tight leash, and don't let your mind wander. This test is too important. Just remind yourself how important these two hours and fifteen minutes are to your future. Teach yourself to concentrate and rely on the relaxation tips we give you later in this chapter to avoid incessant mind wandering. You'll need those powers of concentration in that MBA program you'll soon be starting!

Don't read questions at lightning speed

We hate to break it to you, but you probably aren't a superhero named "Speedy Reader." You'll be anxious when the test begins, and you may want to blow through the questions at record speed. Big mistake! You don't get bonus points for finishing early, and you have plenty of time to answer every question if you read at a reasonable pace. You may take pride in your ability to speed-read novels, and that skill may help you with the reading comprehension passages, but don't use it to read the questions. You need to read questions carefully to capture the nuances the GMAT offers and understand exactly what it asks of you.

Many people who get bogged down on a few questions and fail to complete a section do so because of poor test-taking techniques, not because of slow reading. Do yourself a favor: Relax, read at a reasonable pace, and maximize your score!

Don't waste all your time on the hardest questions

Although you shouldn't try to work at lightning speed, remember not to get held back by a few hard questions, either. The difficulty of a question depends on the person taking the test. For everyone, even the high scorers, a few questions on a test are just harder than others. When you confront a difficult question on the GMAT, do your best, eliminate as many wrong answers as you can, and then make an intelligent guess. Even if you had all day, you might not be able to answer that particular question. (However, if you believe you may have a shot at it, you can bookmark it in case you have time to return to it later.) If you allow yourself to guess and move on, you can work on plenty of other questions that you'll answer correctly.

Don't cheat

We aren't sure how you'd cheat on the computerized GMAT, and we won't be wasting our time thinking of ways! Spend your time practicing for the test and do your best. Cheating is futile.

Tackling a Case of Nerves with Relaxation Techniques

All this talk about time management, distracting answer choices, blind guessing, and losing focus may be making you nervous. Relax. After you've read this book, you'll have plenty of techniques for turning your quick intellect and that whiteboard or packet of noteboards into a high GMAT score. You may feel a little nervous on the day of the test, but don't worry about it, because a little nervous adrenaline can actually keep you alert. Just don't let anxiety ruin your performance.

You may be working along steadily when suddenly, from out of the blue, a question appears that you don't understand at all. Instead of trying to eliminate answer choices and solve the problem, you may stare at the question as if it were written in a foreign language. You may start to second-guess your performance on the test as a whole. You panic and think that maybe you're just not cut out for a graduate business degree. You're on the verge of freaking out — help!

REMEMBER

Because much of the GMAT is in CAT format, encountering a super-hard question probably means you're doing pretty well. Besides, if you do miss a question, you'll just get an easier question next — unless you're on the last question, in which case you needn't freak out at all. Heck, you're nearly done!

If you do find yourself seizing up with anxiety partway through the test, and if these facts about the CAT format don't ease your tension, try these techniques to get back on track:

>> **Inhale deeply and exhale slowly.** When you stress out, you take shallow breaths and don't get the oxygen you need to think straight. Breathing deeply and exhaling slowly can calm you and supply the air you need to get back to doing your best.

>> **Stretch a little.** Anxiety causes tension, and so does working at a computer. Do a few simple stretches to relax and get the blood flowing. Try shrugging your shoulders toward your ears and rolling your head from side to side. You can put your hands together and stretch your arms above your head or stretch your legs out and move your ankles up and down (or both!). Last, shake your hands as though you've just washed them and don't have a towel.

>> **Give yourself a mini massage.** If you're really tense, give yourself a little rubdown. The shoulders and neck usually hold the most tension in your body, so rub your right shoulder with your left hand and vice versa. Rub the back of your neck. It's not as great as getting a full rubdown from a professional, but you can book that appointment for after the test!

>> **Think positive thoughts.** Give yourself a quick break. The GMAT is tough, but don't get discouraged. Focus on the positive; think about the questions you've done well on. If you're facing a tough question, remind yourself that it's only temporary, and it will get better.

>> **Take a little vacation.** If nothing else is working and you're still anxious, picture a place in your mind that makes you feel comfortable and confident. Visit that place for a few moments and come back ready to take charge!

Chapter **3**

Mastering Business School Admissions

I f you're reading a book about the GMAT, you're probably considering an MBA. Well, get ready for a great adventure. Applying to business school can be a challenge, not to be attempted by the lukewarm or ambivalent. If you're truly committed to acquiring an MBA, though, the application process may be sort of exciting. You may end up living someplace new and broadening your opportunities in ways you never considered.

In this chapter, we discuss the ins and outs of evaluating business programs and applying for admission, as well as the importance of the GMAT in this process.

Choosing a Business School

Selecting the right business school is not unlike choosing the right car or home — you're faced with numerous considerations, and what works best for, say, your sister or friend may not be the best option for you. Just as cars and houses are major investments, so is a business school education, so just as you would likely test-drive a new car before buying it and have a home inspection performed on a house before sinking your life savings into it, you ought to conduct extensive research before deciding where to pursue that MBA.

Not all MBA programs are created equal. You may still be able to get a fine business education at most of them but understand that different programs have different characteristics. Some are extremely competitive, while others are easier to get into. Most require attending classes on campus, but a growing number of colleges offer programs that can be completed entirely online or through a blend of online and on-campus coursework. Some have excellent practical career-oriented programs while others present a more theoretical approach to business. You need to decide what you want in a school before you let schools decide whether they have the privilege of accepting you.

As you build your application list, consider the following factors:

>> **Prestige:** School prestige falls first on this list, and that isn't by accident. In a *Forbes* survey of about 750 GMAT test-takers, prospective students were asked which consideration was most important to them when selecting a business school. Prestige was the most common answer, and the best measure of prestige at a given school was said to be the proven success of its alumni. Why does prestige get so much credit? Primarily, because students believe that being affiliated with a particular high-ranked school will give them a foot up in many areas and help them stand out from the crowd. To be more specific, students tend to associate higher-prestige business schools with enhanced opportunities for career and business networking, and in many ways the association is justified. For example, Wall Street firms generally recruit from the top-ranked East Coast MBA programs, so if you want to join one of these corporations, you need to apply to the programs they favor. Checking the top five rankings of MBA programs — *Forbes*, *Businessweek*, *U.S. News & World Report*, *The Economist*, and the *Financial Times* — provides you with an indication of which programs are most prestigious. An MBA school's rank may not matter to you, however, if you're already employed or are self-employed and primarily want to acquire skills to enhance your professional standing.

>> **Affordability:** Obviously, it makes sense to borrow as little money as possible for business school, as you'll more than likely be committed to paying it all back, plus interest, somewhere down the line. MBA programs generally aren't cheap, however, so the trick is to not only find a school that you can afford, but also uncover one that offers the biggest return on investment (ROI). To get a sense of what that ROI may ultimately be, you'll want to take a comprehensive look at all costs associated with attending a particular institution. In addition to tuition rates, review any additional fees that contribute to the total cost of attendance, such as room and board (if applicable), textbooks and technology needs (for example, laptops and so on), and personal living expenses. Carefully assess the likelihood of receiving financial aid and merit scholarships to help offset expenses. Also, consider the wages you give up while you attend a full-time program. Ultimately, ROI comes down to whether the amount you spend for your MBA, including the lost wages, will be less than the salary increase you receive as a result of enhancing your academic credentials.

>> **Selectivity:** You have to get into an MBA program before you can graduate from it. Check with admissions to determine a school's mid 50 percent and top 25 percent qualifications regarding accepted GPA and GMAT scores. Your application list should include at least one or two programs where your numbers — grades and test scores — fall within the top 25 percent. With that assurance, you can toss your hat in the ring for more selective schools.

>> **Concentrations and specialties:** As with undergraduate programs, some MBA programs specialize in a particular business concentration. Do your research. If your focus is finance, apply to programs with a strong finance curriculum. If your goal is to increase your management opportunities, find programs that specialize in business management. Some universities offer dual-degree programs. You can earn an MBA and a law degree in four years at some or combine an MBA with an MD. Master's degrees in a variety of areas, such as education, public policy, journalism, and so on, may be paired with an MBA. If gaining more than one degree excites you, look for schools that offer these options.

>> **Special programs:** While traditional MBA programs consist of a full-time, two-year commitment, you'll find a variety of options that stray from this model. Some schools offer part-time programs that allow you to work while you earn your degree. Other programs may integrate online learning or may be offered entirely online to accommodate different schedules. You may seek a program that offers more practical application opportunities, or you may be more interested in a program with a more theoretical approach. Investigate programs to find the ones that best fit your schedule and goals.

- **Location:** Geography plays a big role in deciding where you pursue your MBA. Do you want to be near your family? Do you want to be able to drive to the beach or the mountains to get a break from your studies? Do you feel more comfortable on the East Coast or West Coast? Or are you more at home in the Midwest or South? Location may also be a factor in overall cost; living in Palo Alto, California, is more expensive than residing in Columbus, Ohio.

   If you're fresh out of college and don't yet have a family, you may have more flexibility choosing a business school than you might if you own property and have children or other responsibilities that require you to stay close to your home base. Additionally, it's wise to think beyond graduation when determining where to attend business school. Often, MBA programs have tight links within their communities, meaning your best bet at landing a job through networking, interning, or networking with alumni may be in the same neighborhood as the institution. Choosing a business school may also mean choosing your future hometown.

- **Public or private:** MBA programs may be found at state university systems or in private universities. Many public schools charge less for tuition than private ones, especially for in-state residents, but more financial aid and scholarship possibilities may exist at private universities.

- **Average starting salary:** You're probably considering business school at least in part because you hope an MBA will boost your ability to secure gainful employment or command a higher salary. The ROI of MBA programs varies greatly, and (here's where "prestige" again factors in) attending a big-name school really can help you bring home the bacon, so to speak. An MBA from a highly ranked, selective business school, such as Stanford, Harvard, or Wharton, can considerably boost your ability to earn a substantial income. The average MBA starting salary is also important if you are accruing interest on student loans. Checking program rankings based on starting salary may help give you a rough idea of how long you'll be indebted.

- **Quality of life:** Some business schools are known for being competitive, even cutthroat; others embrace a more collaborative atmosphere. Examine your personality and be honest with yourself. Does competition challenge you or defeat you? Are you more comfortable working in groups or individually? Talk with current students and alumni to get an accurate assessment of a program's character to make sure it fits with yours.

- **Alumni network:** You're going to spend much more of your life as a business school graduate than as a business school student. The connections you make as you earn your MBA may last a lifetime, and a strong alumni network can be a valuable resource throughout your career. Consider the depth and breadth of a program's alumni when you draw up your application list.

REMEMBER

When it comes to selecting a business school, there is no "one size fits all" approach. Therefore, do your due diligence to find the programs that best fit you. Once you have your list, your next step is to create a memorable, effective application that leaves a lasting impression.

Lining Up Your Ducks — Applying to Business Schools

Applying to MBA programs is an expensive and time-consuming process not to be entered into lightly. Each school has its own admissions requirements and components you must gather and submit according to instructions. Be sure to check each program's admissions web page thoroughly, and carefully follow the instructions. Despite slight differences, most MBA admissions expect to receive by a designated deadline the application, GMAT (or GRE) scores, college transcripts, a personal essay, a list of activities and/or a resume, letters of recommendation, and the application fee.

TO GMAT OR TO GRE? THAT'S THE QUESTION

A growing trend among business schools is to accept either the GRE or the GMAT for admissions. This practice may leave you wondering which to choose. The GRE is used for most graduate programs other than the MBA, so if you aren't sure whether you want an MBA or, say, a masters in finance, or you have your heart set on a dual-degree program, it may seem that the GRE is a more efficient option. Be careful, though; some business schools may view your GRE score as a lack of surety on your part regarding your dedication to an MBA. Choosing the GMAT over the GRE may help your admissions chances because it indicates a commitment to the MBA path. If an MBA is your one and only goal, the GMAT is likely a better option, and that choice may serve you well even after you graduate with potential employers who are more familiar with GMAT results in job applications.

When to apply

Most traditional MBA programs begin in the fall semester, and the application season begins the prior fall. More flexible schedules may accommodate entry at several times throughout the year, each with its own application deadline. Some schools have rolling admissions, reviewing applications as they come in and cutting off applications after a certain date. A relatively common application practice is to accept applications in two or three rounds with separate deadlines and notification dates. This practice cuts down on the time it takes for you to receive a decision.

TIP

Whether your program has one deadline or three, rolling admissions or not, it's best to get your materials in as early as possible. Early applications cut down on your competition and may make you eligible for additional scholarships and financial aid. To ready yourself for applying early, take the GMAT as soon as you decide to pursue an MBA.

What to submit

Many programs expect to see the following:

>> A completed, signed application form

>> GMAT (or GRE) score

>> Transcripts of your prior academic record

>> Letters of recommendation, at least one from an immediate supervisor

>> A personal statement — an essay usually explaining why you want to earn an MBA

>> For some programs, additional essays, usually defining why you want to study at that institution

>> A hefty application fee, which can vary from around $50 to $250 at some selective universities

You may also have to send in documentation of state residency, financial aid forms, or other relevant information.

WARNING

If one required component of your application isn't in place by the deadline (or whenever the admissions committee stops considering applications), no one will read any of it. So if one of your recommenders forgets to send in a letter or you neglect to order an official transcript from a college you attended during the summer, your application may be jeopardized or thrown out.

REVIEW OF APPLICATIONS

Many MBA programs receive far more applicants than they have spaces for in an entering class. Obviously, the first thing admissions committees look at is academic credentials and then GMAT scores, but numbers aren't everything. Every year competitive business schools admit some students with comparatively low scores and grades and reject some with stellar numbers.

MBA programs want to create classes that represent a diversity of backgrounds and interests and have the potential to bring them fame and fortune as successful alumni. Therefore, these factors may also contribute to a successful application:

- Geography (where students come from); schools like to get people from all over the world

- Diverse background

- Unique activities or work experience

You can highlight your individual contributions in your personal statement, which is why this essay can be a very important component of your application.

Crafting Effective Business School Essays

More people apply to MBA programs than any other post-graduate degree, which results in a large number of business school graduates seeking positions. This fact poses a problem for business school administrators who want to boast about their alumni's high employment rates. Therefore, MBA programs are much more likely to accept you when they see the potential for your future success. This support comes to them in your academic record, for sure, but it's also conveyed in the case you make in your personal statement.

Before you sit down to write your essay, outline your future plans. Define exactly why you want to earn an MBA and clarify specific career goals. The personal statement should not only convey what you've achieved so far, but it should also link your past accomplishments to concrete future goals, ones that require an MBA to fulfill. The essay is your chance to show admissions the unique contributions you can make to their program. To this end, here is a summary of what an appropriate personal statement is *not*:

>> **The essay isn't a summary of your past education, activities, and accolades.** Your resume fulfills this task. Use the personal statement to provide deeper insight into who you are as well as what you do.

>> **The essay isn't a university fan letter.** Resist the temptation to fill your personal statement with boundless praise. Your discussion of the business school should reveal your knowledge of its strengths as they relate to your particular goals. Don't tell a school about its unique concentrations and experiences; show how these opportunities align with your goals and abilities.

>> **The essay isn't poetic license.** The personal statement provides an opportunity for you to convey your story in creative ways. By all means, use stories and sensory description to reveal your qualities in a very real way. But avoid overstepping the boundaries. Observe word or page limits and follow directions. An attempt to dazzle with difference may just show admissions that you have trouble following rules.

>> **The essay isn't a philosophical treatise.** Focus on what's true for you rather than what's true for the world.

» **The essay isn't a personality assessment.** Perhaps the biggest mistake applicants make in writing their personal essays is over-generalization and under-substantiation. You don't convince others of your personal characteristics by simply telling them you're awesome or hardworking. *Show* who you are through carefully chosen stories that unfold through specific details. Allow the reader to draw conclusions about who you are from reading about how you interact with the world.

» **The essay doesn't have to sugarcoat.** Don't be afraid to express some vulnerability. You aren't good at everything. If you were, you wouldn't need an advanced degree. Sometimes the best way to endear your reader is to acknowledge a shortcoming.

2

Creating a GMAT Study Plan

IN THIS PART . . .

Discover the value of taking a practice assessment and how to use it.

Sample several quantitative, verbal, and data insights question types so you know what to expect when you take the GMAT.

Receive full explanations of the correct answers to the sample questions and know where to find help for trouble spots.

Chapter **4**

Planning Your Approach

You're gearing up to take the GMAT, but starting your studies can be daunting. However, starting with the pre-assessment in Chapter 5 is a great way to kickstart your study plan. This helpful resource consists of 24 questions, divided evenly among quantitative, verbal, and data insights. While not comprehensive, the pre-assessment serves as a scaled-down version of the actual GMAT, which includes a total of 64 questions. Keep in mind that the pre-assessment won't cover every topic that appears on the exam, but it can give you a sense of which areas you need to focus on the most. By taking advantage of this useful tool, you can gain a better understanding of your strengths and weaknesses and develop a study plan tailored to your specific needs.

Using the Pre-assessment: The How-To

Start with Chapter 5. After you finish the questions in Chapter 5, check your answers in Chapter 6. We include a quick scoring key at the end of that chapter. Discover which questions you missed. Then read the explanations for those questions and any others that you find challenging. The end of each explanation directs you to the chapter or chapters where you can find the information relevant to understanding that question type.

Evaluating Section 1: Quantitative

Section 1 in Chapter 5 tests your ability to apply your foundational mathematical knowledge to solve problems. The GMAT quantitative section contains problem solving questions that test number properties and other prealgebra concepts, algebra, and probability and statistics. We offer you a sampling of these areas in the assessment.

Review Chapter 10 if you miss Questions 1, 4, 5, or 6. Chapter 11 provides the concepts necessary to solve Questions 7 and 8. Chapter 12 covers Questions 2 and 3.

Evaluating Section 2: Verbal

Section 2 in Chapter 5 tests your reading and verbal reasoning abilities. The GMAT verbal section contains two general types of questions:

>> Reading comprehension

>> Critical reasoning

Chapter 7 provides the background for answering Questions 4, 5, and 6, associated with a reading passage. Questions 1, 2, 3, 4, and 8 are critical reasoning questions. Read Chapter 8 to discover how to approach this potentially unfamiliar question type that tests your ability to form and analyze logical arguments.

Evaluating Section 3: Data insights

Section 3 in Chapter 5 tests your ability to analyze and make decisions about data. The GMAT data insights section contains two types of questions:

>> Integrated reasoning

>> Data sufficiency

Even though the quantitative section prohibits calculator use, you have access to a simple on-screen calculator during the data insights section.

The interactive integrated reasoning questions in the GMAT's data insights section test your reasoning ability in a variety of circumstances using multiple tools. Most of the integrated reasoning questions have at least two parts. You must answer each part correctly to get credit for the question. The GMAT offers no partial credit for integrated reasoning questions.

The assessment presents an example of each of the four integrated reasoning question types. Question 1 is of the multi-source reasoning variety, Question 2 requires graphics interpretation, Question 3 presents a two-part analysis question, and Question 4 is a table analysis question. For tips for success on all integrated reasoning types, read Chapter 15. If you need help reading graphs for these questions, refer to Chapter 16.

In addition to standard math questions like those in the quantitative section that give you a problem to solve, the GMAT also has math-based data sufficiency questions. These questions are presented in the data insights section. They ask you to determine whether bits of provided information supply enough data to solve a problem.

These data sufficiency questions are unique to the GMAT, and Questions 5, 6, 7, and 8 in Section 3 provide examples. If you have trouble answering these questions or need precise instructions on how to approach the data sufficiency question type, follow the steps to solving data sufficiency questions in Chapter 17. In addition to suggesting helpful tips to avoid common traps associated with these questions, this chapter provides a step-by-step approach to efficiently solving this question type.

Devising a Plan of Attack

After you examine your performance on the pre-assessment, you're ready to form a GMAT study plan. The best way to avoid freaking out on exam day is to be fully prepared. So, make sure you have a strategy that fits your preparation timeline. Table 4-1 references suggested resources to include in your study plan based on your schedule.

TABLE 4-1 **Following a GMAT Preparation Schedule**

Resource	Preparation Time		
	More than 3 Months	2 to 3 Months	Less than 2 Months
GMAT Prep 2024/2025 For Dummies Chapter 5 pre-assessment	X	X	X
GMAT Prep 2024/2025 For Dummies Chapter 18 timed practice test	X	X	
Focused study in *GMAT Prep 2024/2025 For Dummies* Parts 3–6 based on evaluation of pretest results	X	X	X
Extensive practice question quizzes in the online material accompanying *GMAT Prep 2024/2025 For Dummies*	X	X	
Practice questions from current print or online edition of *GMAT Official Guide*	X	X	
Practice questions from current print or online editions of *GMAT Official Guide Quantitative Review, GMAT Official Guide Verbal Review, and GMAT Official Data Insights Review*	X		
Practice questions from print or online *GMAT Official Advanced Questions*	X		
Full-length computer-adaptive Practice Tests 1 and 2 available free in the Official GMAT Starter Kit from www.mba.com	X	X	X
Full-length computer-adaptive Practice Tests 3, 4, 5, and 6 available for purchase from www.mba.com	X		

When you have more than three months

About three to four months before your test day, map out a regular study schedule:

>> **Week 1:** Grab a general GMAT overview, such as this book.

1. Read Chapters 1 and 2 of this book to get an overview of the test format and scoring considerations. Choose your preferred format and schedule your test date.

2. Take the pre-assessment in Chapter 5 and analyze your results using the guidelines in "Using the Pre-assessment: The How-To" in this chapter.

3. Download The Official GMAT Starter Kit from www.mba.com. This free kit provides you with online practice questions and two full-length GMAT practice exams.

>> **Week 2:** Run through reading comprehension questions.

1. Study Chapter 7.

2. Create and answer a practice set of reading comprehension questions in the GMAT Starter Kit.

>> **Week 3:** Prepare for critical reasoning questions and practice the verbal section.

   1. Study Chapter 8.

   2. Answer a practice set of critical reasoning questions in the GMAT Starter Kit.

   3. Answer the practice verbal section questions in Chapter 9.

>> **Weeks 4 and 5:** Review math concepts and format.

   1. Study Chapters 10–13.

   2. Answer the math practice questions in Chapter 14.

   3. Answer a set of math practice questions in the GMAT Starter Kit.

>> **Weeks 6, 7, and 8:** Prepare for the data insights section.

   1. Study Chapters 15 and 16 to get familiar with integrated reasoning questions.

   2. Answer a set of integrated reasoning questions in the GMAT Starter Kit.

   3. Read Chapter 17 to get familiar with data sufficiency questions.

   4. Answer a set of data sufficiency questions in the GMAT Starter Kit.

>> **Week 9:** First, complete the quantitative and verbal sections of the first practice test, which are available in Chapter 18. Afterward, thoroughly study the corresponding answer explanations provided in Chapter 19. Following that, access the online platform to complete and score the entire first practice test, as well as the two additional online practice tests available there. After you score your efforts, examine the questions you answered incorrectly to determine your errors. Then check the answer explanations for more insight.

>> **Weeks 10 and 11:** Test your skills by answering official GMAT practice questions in the timed practice tests 1 and 2 in the GMAT Starter Kit.

   1. Reserve two hours and fifteen minutes of time to take full-length GMAT Practice Exam 1. Based on your results, review the appropriate concepts and strategies in this book.

   2. Take GMAT Practice Exam 2 adhering to the same time limit of two hours and fifteen minutes.

>> **Weeks 12 through exam day:** Hone your exam knowledge and refine your skills by regularly answering official GMAT practice problems. Try to spend an hour a day at least three to four times a week in GMAT practice questions.

   Supplement your practice with the most current official GMAT materials: *The Official Guide for GMAT Review, The Official Guide for GMAT Quantitative Review, The Official Guide for GMAT Verbal Review,* and *The Official Guide for GMAT Data Insights Review.* These publications are available for purchase in print form or as ebooks from www.mba.com. You can also purchase additional online practice tests and practice questions on the site. Use official practice tests 3–6 to test your study results.

When you have fewer than two months

But what if you don't have months to prepare? What if you need a GMAT score in eight weeks or fewer? Here is a plan to optimize your study time using this book and other resources when time is tight.

>> **Week 1:** Grab a general GMAT overview, such as the one in this book.

   1. Read Chapters 1 and 2 of this book to get an overview of the test format and scoring considerations. Choose your preferred format and schedule your test date.

2. Take the pre-assessment in Chapter 5 and analyze your results using the guidelines in "Using the Pre-assessment: The How-To" in this chapter.

3. Download The Official GMAT Starter Kit from www.mba.com. This free kit provides you with online practice questions and two full-length GMAT practice exams.

>> **Week 2:** Based on your preassessment scores, read the chapters in this book that correspond to those areas where you need the most improvement.

If your verbal score is lower than your math, focus on improving your reading comprehension and critical reasoning skills in Part 3. If your math score is closer to your total number of fingers and toes than to the measure of your height in inches, open up the math review in Part 4. If you are perplexed by integrated reasoning or data sufficiency questions, review Part 5 for a better understanding. Then answer relevant practice questions in the Official GMAT Starter Kit.

>> **Week 3:** Based on your practice results, answer more question types in your areas of weakness.

Use the questions provided in the three practice tests available in the online material that accompanies this book. Try to spend several hours each day involved in practice. After you score your efforts, examine the questions you answered incorrectly to determine your errors. Then check the answer explanations for more insight.

>> **Week 4:** Follow the same approach to studying your areas of strength.

If you've spent the previous week focusing on the math in Part 4, focus on the verbal approach offered in Part 3. If you've concentrated on the verbal questions, set your sights on the math chapters.

>> **Week 5:** When you've mastered the verbal and math questions, revisit Part 5 to sharpen your skills in tackling data insight questions.

>> **Weeks 6 to 8:** Test your skills on actual GMAT questions and get used to the online test format.

Supplement your practice with the most current print or online versions of official GMAT materials: *The Official Guide for GMAT Review, The Official Guide for GMAT Quantitative Review, The Official Guide for GMAT Verbal Review,* and *The Official Guide for GMAT Data Insights Review.* Reserve two hours and fifteen minutes of time to take full-length GMAT Practice Exam 1 in the Official GMAT Starter Kit. Based on your results, review concepts and strategies in this book. Then take the other full-length Practice Exam 2 in the starter kit adhering to the same time limit. If you have time, you can also purchase additional online practice tests from the official website. Set aside at least an hour each day to improve your GMAT testing abilities.

TIP

You can download a copy of the 8-week Official GMAT Exam Study Planner from www.mba.com. This two-page flier outlines a plan for using official GMAT exam preparation tools over an 8-week period.

REMEMBER

Regardless of how much study time you have, stick to your practice schedule. Create space in your calendar four or more times a week for at least 30 minutes to an hour of GMAT practice. Regular practice will reinforce the concepts you learn in *GMAT Prep 2024/2025 For Dummies* and familiarize you with GMAT questions to help increase your test-taking efficiency.

REMEMBER

Take the GMAT as soon as you're ready. You'll lose momentum and intensity if you prepare for more than four months prior to your test date.

Chapter **5**

GMAT Practice Assessment

E mbarking on a GMAT practice schedule may seem daunting. To get started, take this GMAT pretest. This step will provide you with an overview of the question types that you can expect on the actual exam and will assist you in prioritizing which concepts to study. Take this mini-GMAT. Then head over to Chapter 6 for an answer key and answer explanations for each of the questions and directions on which chapters and sections of *GMAT Prep 2024/2025 For Dummies* contain the tools to beef up your skills.

Because this pretest is designed to alert you to particular concepts for study and to direct you to particular portions of this book to find those concepts, you don't need to set a timer. Work through the questions at your own pace. Additionally, this mini-GMAT contains fewer questions than the real thing. For information on the structure of the actual GMAT, see Chapter 1.

Section 1: Quantitative

Sample problem solving questions with these 8 questions.

Put down your calculator for these questions; the GMAT doesn't allow one in the quantitative section.

DIRECTIONS: Choose the best answer from the five choices provided.

1. Section A and section B comprise $\frac{1}{3}$ and $\frac{1}{5}$ respectively in the figure below. What fraction of the circle is comprised by section C?

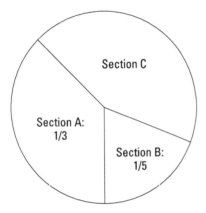

(A) $\frac{1}{4}$

(B) $\frac{2}{5}$

(C) $\frac{2}{15}$

(D) $\frac{7}{15}$

(E) $\frac{8}{15}$

2. If $S = \{3,4,0,2,11,10\}$, how much greater than the median of the numbers in S is the mean of the numbers in S?

(A) 0.5

(B) 1

(C) 1.5

(D) 2

(E) 2.5

3. Fatim is playing a video coin game in which she has a collection of virtual coins composed of p pennies, d dimes, n nickels, and q quarters. If Fatim adds an additional 3 pennies, 2 dimes, and 1 nickel to her collection, what is the probability that she will pick a penny when she randomly removes a single coin from the collection?

(A) $\frac{p}{d+n+q}$

(B) $\frac{p}{p+d+n+q}$

(C) $\frac{p+3}{d+n+q+3}$

(D) $\frac{p+3}{p+d+n+q+3}$

(E) $\frac{p+3}{p+d+n+q+6}$

4. The positive integer x is divisible by 15. If $\sqrt{x} < 15$, which of the following could be the value of $\frac{x}{15}$?

(A) 14

(B) 15

(C) 16

(D) 17

(E) 18

5. If n is an integer and $11 \times 10^n < \frac{1}{10}$, which of the following is the greatest possible value of n?

(A) -4

(B) -3

(C) -2

(D) -1

(E) 0

6. What is the value of $\frac{32+32^2}{32}$?

(A) 33

(B) 34

(C) 64

(D) 1,024

(E) 1,056

7. Machine X produces 1,050 components in 5 hours when working alone at a constant rate. Machine Y produces the same number of components in 7.5 hours when working alone at a constant rate. How many components does Machine Y produce if both devices operate simultaneously for T hours and produce 1,050 components?

(A) 140

(B) 210

(C) 420

(D) 525

(E) 630

8. Which of the following equations have both 3 and -3 in the solution set?

I. $x = \sqrt{9}$

II. $x^2 = 9$

III. $x^4 = 81$

(A) I only

(B) II only

(C) III only

(D) II and III only

(E) I, II, and III

Section 2: Verbal

Sample verbal question types with these 8 questions.

DIRECTIONS: Follow these directions for each of the two question types:

- **Questions 5, 6, & 7 are reading comprehension questions:** Choose the best answer to every question based on what is stated or implied in the passage.

- **Questions 1, 2, 3, 4, & 8 are critical reasoning questions:** Pick the answer choice that best answers the question about the argument provided.

1. The Earth's magnetic field has reversed a number of times in its history. Before the poles actually flip, the magnetic field weakens and the magnetic poles drift away from "true" north and south. On average, the magnetic North and South Poles flip about once every 200,000 years. The last time the poles flipped was 780,000 years ago. Therefore, the poles are in the process of reversing.

   Which of the following, if true, would most strengthen the argument above?

   (A) Magnetic north has recently been moving toward closer alignment with "true" north.
   (B) Sometimes the magnetic fields go for over one million years without reversing.
   (C) The Earth's atmosphere has warmed by about one degree Celsius over the past century.
   (D) The strength of the magnetic field has declined by over 10 percent since 1845, the first year it was measured.
   (E) The location of the magnetic poles has remained unchanged for as long as magnetic compasses have been in use.

2. Many names that people think of as Irish were actually brought to Ireland by the Anglo-Norman invasion of Ireland in the 12th century. Names like Seamus, Patrick, and Sean are so widespread because of the Catholic Church's requirements that Irish sons and daughters be named after saints. *Seamus* is the Gaelic version of *James*, and *Sean* is the Gaelic version of *John*. Criminal laws in Ireland from the 1500s to the 1900s forbade parents from giving their children traditional Irish names like Cathal, Aodh, and Brian. Nowadays parents are free to give their children these long-forgotten, truly Irish names.

   Which of the following inferences can be drawn from the statements above?

   (A) Only Irish names used in Ireland before the 12th century are "traditional."
   (B) Irish parents prefer to give their children names that are as traditionally Irish as possible.
   (C) Parents in Ireland should now give their children names like Cathal, Aodh, and Brian.
   (D) Even after hundreds of years of use, names like Seamus, Patrick, and Sean are still not "truly Irish."
   (E) Criminal laws in Ireland are unnecessarily punitive.

3. The Springfield Junior Philharmonic (SJP) has cemented its reputation as the premier children's musical organization due in large part to major donations from former members who enjoy attending the annual holiday concert. Although the SJP is widely regarded as being the best organization of its kind, the holiday concert was canceled this year; so SJP will experience a resulting reduction in donations.

The argument above relies on which of the following assumptions about SJP?

(A) SJP's reputation as the premier children's musical organization is enhanced by the amount of money it receives from donors.

(B) SJP alums will have at least as much money to donate next year as they did this year.

(C) The SJP holiday concert will likely be canceled next year as well.

(D) Some SJP alums contribute to the organization because they enjoy attending the annual holiday concert.

(E) Contributions from alums are necessary for SJP to be able to play its annual holiday concert.

4. Following a route already taken by other industrialized countries, the Food and Drug Administration recently unveiled nine new graphic warning labels that will soon adorn all cigarette packs sold in the United States. Although the addition of the new labels marks the first time in a quarter-century that the warnings have included imagery of the dangerous effects of smoking, heated debate arose over just how graphic the images should be, with the FDA ultimately withdrawing a number of images deemed too graphic. Some, however, argue that _____.

Which of the following most logically completes the passage?

(A) Including warning labels will be ineffective, because the primary issue is not one of awareness but physical addiction.

(B) No substantial evidence indicates that pictorial warning labels are effective.

(C) The addition of the new pictorial warning labels are just another way the government is encroaching on the rights of Americans.

(D) The images ultimately selected are too tame, and if the FDA is to go as far as including images at all, it should not hold back from showing the full effects of smoking, however ugly they may be.

(E) If such imagery will be added to cigarette packs, then images of drunk driving accidents and liver disease should be added to all alcoholic products.

GO ON TO NEXT PAGE

Questions 5–7 refer to the following passage, which is from *Applied Turfgrass Science and Physiology,* by Jack Fry and Bingru Huang (John Wiley & Sons, Inc.).

Plant injury resulting from high light intensity is due not to the light per se but to an excess of light energy over that utilized by photosynthesis. When light reaching the leaves is not used for photosynthesis, the excess energy triggers production of free radicals that can damage cells (oxidative damage). This often occurs when light intensity is high but photosynthesis is inhibited due to stress from temperature extremes, drought, or excessive soil water. When light intensity is at a low level where photosynthesis and respiration reach equilibrium and the net carbon gain is zero, no plant growth will occur. This light level is the light compensation point (LCP). Leaves exposed to light levels below the LCP for an extended period of time will eventually senesce. . . . LCP var[ies] among turfgrass species and with temperature and CO_2 concentration.

Under high irradiance, warm-season grasses maintain a higher rate of photosynthesis than cool-season grasses. However, cool-season grasses have a lower LCP and exhibit higher photosynthetic rates under low light levels compared to warm-season grasses. Photosynthetic rates of both warm-season and cool-season grasses exhibit a diurnal pattern on clear, sunny days, increasing from sunrise, reaching a maximum around noon, and then decreasing to the lowest levels by sunset.

Photosynthesis is affected by light duration because it occurs only during daylight. Increasing light duration may not increase the rate of carbon fixation, but the total amount of carbon fixed by photosynthesis will increase due to increased light exposure. Sunlight has all the colors of visible light and is composed of different wavelengths. Not all wavelengths are equally effective in driving photosynthesis, however. Most photosynthetic activity is stimulated by blue and red wavelengths — chlorophylls absorb blue and red light and carotenoids absorb blue light. Green light is reflected, thus giving plants their green color. Green-yellow and far red are transmitted through the leaf.

5. The authors of the passage are primarily concerned with

(A) discussing the impacts of light energy and photosynthesis on warm-season and cool-season grasses.

(B) arguing in favor of warm-season grasses, which are less prone to oxidative damage than cool-season grasses.

(C) exploring the important role of photosynthesis in sustaining turfgrass production.

(D) comparing different kinds of turfgrasses according to their responses to various levels of light energy.

(E) clarifying the scientific details of recent research into the photosynthesis of turfgrass.

6. According to the passage, which of the following is an important difference between warm-season and cool-season grasses?

(A) Cool-season grasses can better withstand higher light intensities such as those found nearer the equator, while warm-season grasses are better suited to northern climates.

(B) Warm-season grasses can handle the higher light levels of summer, while cool-season grasses can grow during the lower light conditions of winter.

(C) Most of the photosynthesis in warm-season grasses takes place during the day, while cool-season grasses usually photosynthesize at night.

(D) Warm-season grasses use only the blue and red spectrums of light for photosynthesis, while reflecting harmful green light.

(E) Excess light reaching cool-season grasses can be responsible for damage to the plant's cells, while warm-season grasses are unharmed.

7. Which of the following can be inferred from the discussion on oxidative damage in the first paragraph?

(A) Oxidative damage most frequently occurs about one hour after sunrise and one hour before sunset.

(B) Homeowners should water their lawns as often as possible because damage to grass is caused by drought and not simply by light intensity.

(C) Oxidative damage to grass occurs when light reaching the leaves is not used for photosynthesis and, therefore, forms carbon fixation.

(D) Damage to grass occurs because of the high intensity of light and homeowners can do nothing to preserve their lawns.

(E) Both overwatering and underwatering a lawn can inhibit photosynthesis and damage grass.

8. I bought a pair of glasses from an optometrist. One of the lenses regularly pops out of the frame. Therefore, this optometrist doesn't know how to make a good pair of glasses.

The reasoning in the argument is most vulnerable to criticism on the grounds that the argument

(A) does not allow the optometrist a chance to offer a defense.

(B) does not consider the possibility that other optometrists also make defective frames.

(C) criticizes the optometrist's use of a particular technique when making glasses.

(D) jumps to the conclusion that the defect in the glasses must be due to the optometrist's lack of skill.

(E) accuses the optometrist of deliberately sabotaging the glasses.

Section 3: **Data Insights**

Sample data insights question types with these 8 questions.

The following four integrated reasoning questions have been modified to work on paper. Their online format contains some features that cannot be duplicated exactly in this pretest, but these questions provide you with enough similarity to gain an understanding of the approach they require. Each question has multiple parts; you must answer every part correctly to receive credit for the question. If needed, you can use a simple calculator to answer these questions.

DIRECTIONS: Follow these directions for each of the four integrated reading question types:

1. The multi-source reasoning Question Set #1 presents you with several different sets of data. Read through the data and examine the information you need to answer the questions.

2. The two-part analysis Question Set #2 has two solutions. Make one selection in the first column and one selection in the second column from a list of options in the third column of a three-column response table. You must pick one correct answer in the first column and one correct answer in the second column to get credit for the question.

3. For graphics interpretation Question Set #3, examine the graph and select the answer from the list that most accurately completes the statement.

4. Analyze the data in the table analysis Question Set #4 to determine which of the two opposing answer choices most clearly defines the accuracy of the statements.

Question Set 1

> *Email #1 from Caroline Zion, client, to John Barry, attorney at law*
>
> Mr. Barry,
>
> As I'm sure he plans to make this request, please inform my soon-to-be ex-husband or his representative that I will not consent to any custody arrangement that involves removing my children from the state of Virginia for any length of time. I'm taking this stance because my job is here, their schools are here, and Mia's doctors are here. (As you know, Mia has a serious medical condition that requires frequent medical care.) The great distance of interstate travel would obviously conflict considerably with these aspects of my children's lives and my own life. This decision is not to "get back at him" for his marital transgressions, as I'm sure he will maintain. I'm simply looking out for the best interests of my children.
>
> Thank you,
>
> Caroline Zion

Email #2 from John Barry, attorney at law, to Mark Turner, attorney at law

Dear Mr. Turner,

In preparing for the deposition, please be aware that Mrs. Zion will not consent to any custody agreement that involves taking the minor children out of the state of Virginia. A number of factors are involved, the most critical being the location of the children's schools, the children's desire to maintain relationships with their friends, and the need to be in close proximity to Mia's doctors. Mrs. Zion fears Mr. Zion will argue that her request constitutes retribution for past indiscretions, but she maintains that staying in-state is necessary in order to keep the children safe and make the divorce transition for them as painless as possible.

Sincerely,

John Barry, J.D.

Email #3 from Mark Turner, attorney at law, to John Barry, attorney at law

Dear Mr. Barry:

Louis Zion has stipulated that in order to maintain his current standard of living and continue to be able to provide for his children after his divorce from Caroline, he will need to relocate to West Virginia, where there are higher-paying jobs in the mines. He stresses that although he would reside out of state, the town is still less than an hour away from Caroline's residence and many places within the state of Virginia are substantially farther away than an hour by car.

Sincerely,

Mark Turner, Esquire

GO ON TO NEXT PAGE

DIRECTIONS: Consider each statement and determine whether the information in the three emails allows you to make the specific inference. Place a check mark under *Inferable* if it can be inferred that the statement is true. Otherwise, place a check mark under *Not Inferable*.

Inferable	Not Inferable	
		1A. Louis and Caroline's divorce is likely due to acts of infidelity.
		1B. West Virginia has, on average, higher-paying jobs than Virginia does.
		1C. Caroline's attorney does not consider her place of employment to be as crucial an issue in deciding the custody matter as Caroline does.

Question Set 2

Automobile gasoline consumption is directly related to pollutant emissions. The following graph represents how gasoline mileage is affected by freeway driving speeds of 50, 60, and 70 miles per hour (mph) for three different types of cars: compact, mid-size, and full-size.

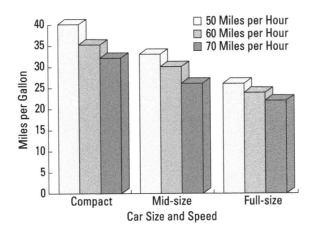

DIRECTIONS: Complete the sentences based on this information.

2A The _____ will emit the most pollutants on a 100-mile trip.

(a) compact car driven at 50 mph

(b) mid-sized car driven at 70 mph

(c) full-sized car driven at 50 mph

(d) full-sized car driven at 60 mph

2B The best estimate of average miles per gallon for a full-size car driven at 55 mph is _____.

(a) 20

(b) 23

(c) 25

(d) 32

(e) 37

Question Set 3

Two different animal populations can be approximated with different equations. Let x represents the number of years since 1950; $x = 0$ when the year is 1950; and let y represent the animal population in thousands. The relationship between the number of years since 1950 and population numbers for the first animal population can be described by the quadratic equation $y = (4 - x)^2$. The relationship between the number of years since 1950 and population for the second animal population can be described by the linear equation $y = 6x + 3$.

DIRECTIONS: In the table, place a check mark for the first year when the two animal populations were equal in the first column and a check mark for the next year the two animal populations were equal in the second column. Mark only one answer in each column.

Questions 3A: First Year	Question 3B: Next Year	
		1944
		1951
		1957
		1963
		1968

Question Set 4

A water bottle manufacturer produces a line of water bottles. The following table shows the characteristics of the water bottles.

	Capacity (mL)	Weight (g)	Retail Price	Production Cost	Popularity Rank
Basic Plastic	946	110	$10	$6	5
Stainless Steel	650	230	$35	$20	1
Wide Mouth	946	100	$12	$7	6
One-handed	750	172	$14	$8	3
Vacuum Insulated	502	300	$60	$45	4
Graphic Design	946	110	$15	$9	2

DIRECTIONS: For each of the following statements, place a check mark under *Consistent* if the statement is consistent with the information provided. Otherwise, place a check mark under *Inconsistent*.

Consistent	Inconsistent	
		4A. The profit percentage for the Basic Plastic bottles is the same as for the Graphic Design bottles.
		4B. The average capacity for the line of water bottles is 800 mL.
		4C. The two least popular designs are also the cheapest to produce.

DIRECTIONS: Follow these directions for each of the data sufficiency questions:

For each data sufficiency problem examine the question and two statements, labeled (1) and (2), decide whether the statements given are sufficient for answering the question, and select one of the answer choices that follow.

5. Mateo and Tristan each received a salary increase. Which one received the greater dollar increase?

 (1) Mateo's salary increased 4.5 percent.

 (2) Tristan's salary increased 7.5 percent.

 (A) Statement (1) *alone* is sufficient, but Statement (2) *alone* is *not* sufficient.

 (B) Statement (2) *alone* is sufficient, but Statement (1) *alone* is *not* sufficient.

 (C) *Both* statements *together* are sufficient, but *neither* statement *alone* is sufficient.

 (D) *Each* statement *alone* is sufficient.

 (E) Statements (1) and (2) *together* are *not* sufficient.

6. What is the value of the prime number p?

 (1) $11 < p - 2 < 17$

 (2) $p^2 = 289$

 (A) Statement (1) *alone* is sufficient, but Statement (2) *alone* is *not* sufficient.

 (B) Statement (2) *alone* is sufficient, but Statement (1) *alone* is *not* sufficient.

 (C) *Both* statements *together* are sufficient, but *neither* statement *alone* is sufficient.

 (D) *Each* statement *alone* is sufficient.

 (E) Statements (1) and (2) *together* are *not* sufficient.

7. At a summer camp, all 200 campers play soccer or tennis or both. If 50 of the campers do not play tennis, how many campers play both tennis and soccer?

 (1) A total of 170 of the campers play soccer.

 (2) Less than 50 of the campers do not play soccer.

 (A) Statement (1) *alone* is sufficient, but Statement (2) *alone* is *not* sufficient.

 (B) Statement (2) *alone* is sufficient, but Statement (1) *alone* is *not* sufficient.

 (C) *Both* statements *together* are sufficient, but *neither* statement *alone* is sufficient.

 (D) *Each* statement *alone* is sufficient.

 (E) Statements (1) and (2) *together* are *not* sufficient.

8. A supermarket sells mangos for $1.50 each and cantaloupes for $2.00 each? How many mangos did the supermarket sell today?

 (1) The number of mangos sold today is 20 more than twice the number of cantaloupes sold.

 (2) Today the supermarket received a total of $155 from the sale of mangos and cantaloupes.

 (A) Statement (1) *alone* is sufficient, but Statement (2) *alone* is *not* sufficient.

 (B) Statement (2) *alone* is sufficient, but Statement (1) *alone* is *not* sufficient.

 (C) *Both* statements *together* are sufficient, but *neither* statement *alone* is sufficient.

 (D) *Each* statement *alone* is sufficient.

 (E) Statements (1) and (2) *together* are *not* sufficient.

Chapter **6**

Scoring and Interpreting the Practice Assessment

Y ou've finished the pretest, but you're not done yet. Reading through the following explanations may be the most important part of taking the practice assessment. Examine the information for the questions you missed as well as those you answered correctly. You may find tips and techniques you haven't thought of before in one of the answer explanations. If you're short on time or just want to quickly check your answers, head to the end of this chapter for an abbreviated answer key.

Section 1: Quantitative Reasoning

1. **D.** $\frac{7}{15}$

   Finding the fractional area of section C, call it x, is as easy as adding up sections A and B and subtracting that total from the whole circle.

   1. **Find the common denominator of the fractions for A and B; then add the fractions.**

   $$\frac{1}{3} + \frac{1}{5} = x$$
   $$\left(\frac{1}{3}\right)\left(\frac{5}{5}\right) + \left(\frac{1}{5}\right)\left(\frac{3}{3}\right) = x$$
   $$\frac{5}{15} + \frac{3}{15} = x$$
   $$\frac{8}{15} = x$$

2. Subtract that total from the whole circle.

The whole circle is designated by the fractional equivalent of 1. So subtract the combined value of sections A and B from a fraction that's equivalent to 1.

$$\frac{15}{15} - \frac{8}{15} = \frac{7}{15}$$

The answer is Choice (D).

For more about how to solve problem solving questions, read Chapter 13. To review fractions, read Chapter 10.

2. C. 1.5

To solve this problem, you need to know the mean and median of the set of numbers. Find the mean by adding up the numbers in the set and dividing this sum by 6, the number of values in the set. The sum of the numbers is 30, and 30 divided by 6 is 5. The mean of the set is 5.

Next, find the median. The median is the middle value for an odd number of values and the average of the two middle values for an even number of values.

1. Order the values in the set from least to greatest.

For this problem, that order is 0, 2, 3, 4, 10, 11.

2. Find the two middle values.

The middle values of the list in Step 1 are 3 and 4.

3. Calculate the mean of the middle values in Step 2 to get the median.

$$(3+4) \div 2 = 3.5$$

After you know the mean and median, subtract them to get the final answer: $5 - 3.5 = 1.5$. Choice (C) is correct.

For more about how to solve problem solving questions, read Chapter 13. To review mean, median, and other statistical concepts, read Chapter 12.

3. E. $\dfrac{p+3}{p+d+n+q+6}$

To solve this problem, you need to find the ratio of the number of pennies in Fatim's collection to the number of all coins in the collection. Because Fatim initially has p pennies in her collection and then adds 3 more pennies, you can say the number of pennies is $p+3$. The total number of virtual coins in the collection is the sum of all the coins in the collection initially $(p+d+n+q)$ plus the coins she adds $(3+2+1)$. So Fatim has a total of $p+d+n+q+6$ virtual coins in her collection. Thus, the probability of selecting a penny at random is this:

$$\frac{\text{Total Number of Pennies}}{\text{Total Number of All Coins}} = \frac{p+3}{p+d+n+q+6}$$

That's Choice (E).

If working through this problem makes doing laundry sound fun, try assigning values to the variables and calculate the answer choices to see which one fits. Sometimes, the quickest and easiest way to answer a math question is to analyze each answer choice to see which one works.

Say Fatim has 2 pennies $(p = 2)$, 3 dimes $(d = 3)$, 5 nickels $(n = 5)$, and 4 quarters $(q = 4)$. Write these values on your noteboard. When Fatim adds the new coins to the stash, she has 5 pennies, 5 dimes, 6 nickels, and 4 quarters. The probability that Fatim will select a penny at random is 5 out of 20 or $\frac{1}{4}$. Then see which answer equals $\frac{1}{4}$ when you substitute your values for the variables. You can easily see that the numerator is $p + 3$ rather than p, so try Choice (D) first:

$$\frac{2+3}{2+3+5+4+3} = \frac{5}{17}$$

The denominator has to be bigger, which leads you to try Choice (E). When you add 6 to the denominator instead of 3, you get $\frac{5}{20}$.

For more about how to solve problem solving questions, read Chapter 13. To review probability, read Chapter 12.

4. **A. 14**

To solve this problem, transform the inequality $\sqrt{x} < 15$ to make it look more like $\frac{x}{15}$, the expression you're asked about. First, square both sides of $\sqrt{x} < 15$ to get $x < 225$. Next, divide both sides of the resulting inequality by 15 to get $\frac{x}{15} < \frac{225}{15}$, or $\frac{x}{15} < 15$.

The only value in the answer choices that's less than 15 is 14. The correct answer is Choice (A).

For more about how to solve problem solving questions, read Chapter 13. To review exponents and radicals, check out Chapter 10.

5. **B. −3**

The easiest way to approach this exponent question may be to substitute the possible values of n in the answer choices into the inequality. If −2 makes the value too big, consider −3 and −4; if it makes the value too small, consider −1 and 0.

If n equals −2, you get 11×10^{-2}, or 0.11 (just move the decimal point two places to the left). Then you have to ask yourself whether the inequality is true. If you use the decimal value of 0.10 for $\frac{1}{10}$, the inequality becomes $0.11 < 0.10$, which is clearly not true. Therefore, you have to move the decimal point one more place to the left, which means that n has to equal −3 to make 11×10^n less than $\frac{1}{10}$. The answer is −3, Choice B.

−4 also makes 11×10^n less than $\frac{1}{10}$, but the problem asks for the *greatest* possible value, and −3 is greater than −4.

For more about how to solve problem solving questions, flip to Chapter 13. To review exponents and radicals, read Chapter 10.

6. **A. 33**

You have two relatively easy routes to solving this question:

1. **You can split the fraction into two fractions with the same denominator.**

$$\frac{32 + 32^2}{32} = \frac{32}{32} + \frac{32^2}{32}$$
$$= 1 + 32$$
$$= 33$$

2. You can factor 32 from each term in the numerator, reduce, and simplify.

$$\frac{32 + 32^2}{32} = \frac{32(1 + 32)}{32}$$
$$= (1 + 32)$$
$$= 33$$

Either way, the answer is Choice (A).

For more about how to solve problem solving questions, read Chapter 13. To review exponents, read Chapter 10.

7. C. 420

1. First, determine T, the time, in hours, that it will take the two machines working simultaneously to produce 1,050 components.

The portion of the 1,050 components that Machine X can produce in one hour is $\frac{1}{5}$, and the portion that Machine Y can produce in one hour is $\frac{1}{7.5} = \frac{10}{75} = \frac{2}{15}$. Thus, in one hour, the two machines can produce

$$\left(\frac{1}{5} \times 1,050\right) + \left(\frac{2}{15} \times 1,050\right) = 210 + 140 = 350 \text{ components.}$$

So, $T = 1,050$ components $\div 350$ components per hr $= 3$ hours.

2. Next, determine how many components Machine Y produces in 3 hours.

Because Machine Y produces 140 components per hour, at the end of 3 hours, it produces $140 \times 3 = 420$ components, Choice (C).

For more about how to solve problem solving questions, read Chapter 13. To review word problems, read Chapter 11.

8. D. II and III only

The square root symbol $\left(\sqrt{\ }\right)$ always returns the principal square root, which is nonnegative, so the solution set of $x = \sqrt{9}$ is 3. Hence, the correct answer does not contain Roman I. Eliminate choices (A) and (E). The solution set of $x^2 = 9$ is 3 and -3. Thus, the correct answer contains Roman II. Eliminate Choice (C). The solution set of $x^4 = 81$ contains 3 and -3. Eliminate Choice (B). Therefore, the correct answer is Choice (D), II and III only.

For more about how to solve problem solving questions, read Chapter 13. To review algebra, read Chapter 11. To learn how to deal with questions that have Roman numerals, read Chapter 2.

Section 2: Verbal

1. D. The strength of the magnetic field has declined by over 10 percent since 1845, the first year it was measured.

For this question, you need to strengthen the conclusion that the poles are currently in the process of reversing. To support the conclusion, the author presents the case that magnetic fields weaken and the poles drift apart from true north and south before the poles reverse and that the poles reverse about once every 200,000 years. The author has already provided evidence that the latter requirement has occurred. It's been more than 200,000 years since the last reversal. Look for an answer that relates to the first premise about the weakening magnetic fields.

Approach the answers systematically. Eliminate answers that are irrelevant. Choice (C) concerns temperature rather than magnetic fields, so it's out. You already know that we're past due for a pole reversal, so Choice (B) isn't particularly helpful. Cross out choices that weaken the argument rather than support it. Choice (A) weakens the conclusion by indicating that the North Pole is getting closer to rather than farther from true north. Choice E also weakens the conclusion, because it again suggests stability in the poles. Choice (D) is the only answer choice that indicates a weakening in the strength of the magnetic field and a trend toward a reversal of the poles.

For more about how to answer critical reasoning questions, read Chapter 8.

2. **D. Even after hundreds of years of use, names like Seamus, Patrick, and Sean are still not "truly Irish."**

This critical-reasoning argument provides reasons for the choosing of Irish boys' names. The author explains that many "Irish" names were actually imposed on the Irish by Anglo-Norman invaders. The question asks you to make an inference based on the statements.

Choice (A) just reiterates information that the author states directly, so it can't be an inference. Choice (C) also mentions a fact that is stated directly in the premises. Choice (B) and Choice (E) have the opposite problem; their information isn't stated in the premises, but you also don't have enough information to infer them from the premises. Concluding that Irish parents prefer the most traditional names available is too far-fetched, as is concluding that the criminal laws are unnecessarily punitive. The only answer choice that works is Choice (D). If the author of the argument speaks of traditional names as those that were Irish before the 12th century, the author must think that Seamus, Patrick, and Sean are not traditional names.

For more about how to solve critical reasoning problems, read Chapter 8. To review how to approach questions that ask for inferences, read "Using your noggin to make inferences" in the same chapter.

3. **D. Some SJP alums contribute to the organization because they enjoy attending the annual holiday concert.**

This critical reasoning question asks for an underlying assumption. Generally, the best answer for an assumption question is the choice that links an element of the last premise to the author's conclusion.

The last premise of this argument is that the holiday concert was canceled. The conclusion is that donations will go down. So find the answer choice that links the canceled concert to a decrease in donations.

Eliminate Choice (A) right away because it simply restates one of the premises. An assumption by definition isn't a direct assertion. Cross out Choice (B) and Choice (C) because both reference next year. Nothing in the argument points to events that will happen next year. It's concerned only with this year's possibilities. Choice (E) is backwards. It links donations to the holiday concert rather than the other way around. The only answer that connects the occurrence of the holiday concert to donation amounts is Choice (D). If donations will decrease as a result of the lack of holiday concert, at least some segment of the donor population must give to the organization based on the occurrence of the concert.

For more about how to solve critical reasoning problems, read Chapter 8.

4. **D. The images ultimately selected are too tame, and if the FDA is to go as far as including images at all, it should not hold back from showing the full effects of smoking, however ugly they may be.**

The key word for answering this complete-the-idea question is *however*. You know you're looking for an answer that's related to how graphic the images are because that's the argument that comes right before the *however* statement. You also know that the answer will contrast the idea that the images are too graphic to be displayed on labels. Look for an answer that argues for the label images.

The only answer that addresses the graphic nature of the images is Choice (D). It's also the one that opposes the argument that the images are too graphic by stating that they're ultimately too tame. Choice (A), Choice (B), and Choice (C) argue against the warning labels, so they agree with the decision to yank them and don't offer an opposing opinion. Choice (E) goes off on a tangent, so it can't be right. Pick Choice (D).

For more about how to solve critical reasoning problems, read Chapter 8.

5. **A. discussing the impacts of light energy and photosynthesis on warm-season and cool-season grasses.**

This question asks you to identify the author's primary concern in writing the passage. This question type extends the main idea to relate to why the author wrote the passage. As is typical for science passages, the author is mainly concerned with putting out some information, not advancing a position, so you can eliminate Choice (B) right off the bat just based on its first word, arguing. The author doesn't argue a specific point in this passage.

You know that the passage is discussing light energy, photosynthesis, and turfgrass. On closer inspection, you'll find that the author is primarily concerned with educating people so that they know the difference between warm-season and cool-season turfgrass and they understand the factors that damage grass. Choice (C), Choice (D), and Choice (E) deal with specific parts of the passage but not the passage as a whole. Neither Choice (C) nor Choice (E) deals with light energy (and the passage doesn't mention anything about the research being recent), and Choice (D) neglects photosynthesis. The only answer that encompasses all three ideas is Choice (A).

For more about how to answer reading comprehension questions, read Chapter 7.

6. **B. Warm-season grasses can handle the higher light levels of summer, while cool-season grasses can grow during the lower light conditions of winter.**

This specific-information question asks you to identify an important difference between cool-season and warm-season grasses. The second paragraph discusses the two kinds of turfgrasses. Warm-season grasses do better in the summer because they can withstand higher light intensities. Cool-season grasses don't die back as much in the winter because they can survive on a lower amount of light energy. Eliminate Choice (C) because the passage says that all plants that photosynthesize do so during the day. Choice (D) is also incorrect because green light is never characterized by the passage as harmful. Choice (E) isn't correct because the first paragraph suggests that both cool-season and warm-season grasses are harmed by excess light levels. That leaves you with Choice (A) and Choice (B). Both address the important difference in light level tolerance between the two types of grasses, but Choice (A) states that cool-season grasses can withstand higher light intensities, and the opposite is true. Choice (B) is the answer that properly states the actual difference between the two grasses.

For more about how to answer reading comprehension questions, refer to Chapter 7.

7. **E. Both overwatering and underwatering a lawn can inhibit photosynthesis and damage grass.**

The question asks you to make an inference regarding the discussion of oxidative damage. In the first paragraph, you find out that oxidative damage occurs not only because of high light intensity but also because more light energy arrives than photosynthesis can use. Anything that hinders photosynthesis can contribute to oxidative damage.

Choose an answer that you can logically deduce from the information in the passage without making wild assumptions. Choice (A) is incorrect because light intensity is greatest at noon, not at sunrise and sunset. And because overwatering can impede photosynthesis and damage grass, Choice (B) is out.

Eliminate Choice (C) because oxidative damage results from the formation of free radicals, not carbon fixation. Choice (D) is wrong because homeowners and any actions they might take with regard to their lawns are not mentioned in the passage. Because the passage states that both drought and excessive soil water can inhibit photosynthesis, Choice (E) is the best answer.

For more about how to answer reading comprehension questions, read Chapter 7.

8. **D. jumps to the conclusion that the defect in the glasses must be due to the optometrist's lack of skill.**

The conclusion is that the optometrist is incompetent; the evidence is that one lens pops out regularly. But there's no evidence that occurs because of the optometrist's lack of skill. Choice (A) is wrong. Although giving the optometrist a chance to offer a defense would be nice, it's not a fault of the argument that the speaker doesn't provide one. Choice (B) is wrong because other potentially unskilled optometrists have no bearing on the skills of the one in question here. Choice (C) doesn't work. The authors don't mention any particular techniques. Choice (D) may be the answer. The authors do jump to a conclusion here without making a connection between the glasses and the optometrist's skill. Choice (E) is wrong because the author doesn't suggest that sabotage played a role in the bad glasses. Choice (D) is the best answer.

For more about how to solve critical reasoning questions, read Chapter 8.

Section 3: Data Insights

1A. **Not inferable.**

Caroline refers to Louis's "marital transgressions," and her attorney mentions Louis's "past indiscretions." This language strongly implies that Louis was in some way unfaithful in his marriage, but knowing that information is not sufficient to determine that unfaithfulness was the reason for the divorce. Making guesses informed by experience isn't enough to draw reasoned inferences on the GMAT.

1B. **Not inferable.**

Just because Louis's attorney states that a certain town in West Virginia has higher-paying jobs in a certain field, mining, doesn't mean that that particular line of work in that particular town is representative of all of West Virginia. You have to make way too big of a logical leap to get to this statement.

1C. **Inferable.**

In her email, Caroline lists three "most important" reasons for her opposition to Louis's move. In his email to Mr. Turner, Mr. Barry also lists three of the "most crucial" reasons. Two of his reasons mirror Caroline's, but he leaves out one: the fact that her job is in Virginia. Therefore, you can reasonably assume that Caroline's attorney places less importance on her place of employment than Caroline does.

For more about how to solve multi-source reasoning questions, read Chapter 15.

2A. **Full-size car driven at 60 mph.**

The car that emits the most pollution is the one that uses the most gasoline, and the car that uses the most gasoline is the one that gets the worst gas mileage. According to the graph, the full-size car driven at 60 mph is the one that guzzles the most gas.

2B. **25.**

Because 55 comes between 50 and 60, the answer has to be between the miles per gallon for a full-size car driven at 50 miles per hour and one driven at 60 miles per hour. The set of bars on the right side of the graph represents the full-size car. The 50-miles-per-hour bar ends at about 26 miles per gallon. The 60-miles-per-hour bar ends at about 24. So, the answer has to be between 24 and 26. You know that it can't be 32 or 37 because the graph shows that better gas mileage is achieved at lower speeds.

For more about how to solve graphics interpretation questions, read Chapter 15.

3A. **1951.**

3B. **1963.**

The problem gives you two equations for the two animal populations. You're looking for the years when y is the same value in both equations, so set them equal to each other. Then you can solve for x.

Set the two equations equal to each other (because both are equal to y) and plug in values for x as gathered from the answer options to see which values fulfill the condition of $(4-x)^2 = 6x + 3$. Disregard 1944 because it occurred before the year that $x = 0$ (1950).

In 1951, $x = 1$ because $1950 + 1$ year is 1951 and $0 + 1 = 1$. Substitute 1 for x in the equation: $(4-1)^2 \overset{?}{=} 6(1) + 3$; $3^2 \overset{?}{=} 6 + 3$; $9 = 9$. That works! The first year that the populations were equal was 1951. Mark it in the first column. Keep going.

The next option is 1957, the year that $x = 7$: $(4-7)^2 \overset{?}{=} 6(7) + 3$; $(-3)^2 \overset{?}{=} 42 + 3$; $9 \ne 45$. That's not right.

In 1963, $x = 13$: $(4-13)^2 \overset{?}{=} 6(13) + 3$; $(-9)^2 \overset{?}{=} 78 + 3$; $81 = 81$. That's true. The next possible year that the two populations were equal was 1963. Mark it in the second column.

For more about how to solve two-part analysis questions, read Chapter 15.

4A. **Consistent**

The integrated reasoning online format allows you to sort tables by column heading. You don't have that option in this practice assessment, so evaluating the data will be easier online.

Statement 1: The profit percentage for the Basic Plastic bottles is the same as for the Graphic Design bottles. To calculate the profit percentage, you'll need to subtract the production cost from the retail price, and then divide this amount by the production cost. *Warning:* Be sure to divide by the production cost and not the retail price when calculating profit percentage. Profit is based on how much it costs the company to make the product.

For the Basic Plastic bottles, the profit percentage is $\frac{10-6}{6} = \frac{4}{6} = 0.\overline{6} = 66.\overline{6}\%$

For the Graphic Design bottles, the profit percentage is $\frac{15-9}{9} = \frac{6}{9} = 0.\overline{6} = 66.\overline{6}\%$

You've found that these products both have the same profit percentage. The statement is consistent with the data. Check *Consistent*.

4B. **Inconsistent**

Statement 2: The average capacity for the line of water bottles is 800 mL. To find the average capacity of the line of water bottles, you'll have to add up each of the capacities and then divide by the total number of water bottles in the line, which is 6. So, the average capacity is

$$\frac{940+650+946+750+520+946}{6} = \frac{4740}{6} = 790 \text{ ml}$$

Thus, the statement is inconsistent with the data. Check *Inconsistent*.

4C. **Consistent**

Statement 3: The two least-popular designs are also the cheapest to produce. Looking at the table, you can see which two designs are least popular by checking out the popularity ranking. The two least-popular designs are the Basic Plastic bottle and the Wide Mouth bottle. Looking at the prices to produce these bottles, you can see that the Plastic Bottle costs $6 to produce and the Wide Mouth bottle costs $7 to produce. These production costs are the lowest of any of the water bottles in the product line. The data is consistent with the statement. Check *Consistent*.

For more about how to solve table analysis questions, read Chapter 15.

5. **E. Statements (1) and (2)** *together* **are not sufficient.**

Evaluate the question.

1. **Find out what to solve for.**

   This data sufficiency question asks you to evaluate what data you need to figure out whether Mateo or Tristan received a greater dollar increase.

2. **Examine Statement (1).**

   Statement (1) tells you the percentage of Mateo's increase. Without knowing Mateo's original salary, you can't use the percentage to figure out the dollar amount of the increase. Write (1) is *no*. Statement (1) by itself isn't sufficient, which means that the answer can't be Choice (A) or Choice (D).

3. **Examine Statement (2).**

   Statement (2) offers the same kind of information about Tristan's increase that Statement (1) provides for Mateo's. Again, because you don't know Tristan's original salary, knowing the percentage increase doesn't tell you how much the salary increased by dollars. Write (2) is *no*. Statement (2) isn't sufficient by itself, so the answer is either Choice (C) or Choice (E). To decide which it is, consider whether you can figure out the greater dollar increase using both statements.

4. **Check out what you've written.**

   You have double *no*s, so look at all of the information provided by both statements.

5. Evaluate the two statements together.

Because neither statement allows you to figure out the dollar amount, you can't use them together to answer the question, so you have to choose Choice (E).

On the GMAT, you can't assume information that isn't expressly stated. If you were tempted to pick Choice (C) because the two statements together indicated that Tristan received a greater percentage increase than Mateo, you assumed that both individuals had the same original salary. However, it could have instead been the case that Mateo's original salary was much higher than Tristan's, in which case Mateo's smaller percentage increase could still correspond to a larger dollar increase.

6. **D. *Each* statement *alone* is sufficient.**

    Evaluate the question.

    1. Find out what to solve for.

    The question asks for the value of the prime number *p*.

    2. Examine Statement (1).

    From Statement (1) you have $11 < p - 2 < 17$, which implies that $13 < p < 19$. Thus, *p* is 17, because 17 is the only prime number that falls between 13 and 19. Therefore, Statement (1) is sufficient. Write (1) is *yes,* and eliminate choices (B), (C), and (E).

    3. Examine Statement (2).

    Statement (2) lets you know that $p^2 = 289$, which means that *p* equals 17 because –17 is not a prime number. Thus, Statement (2) is sufficient. Write (2) is *yes.* Therefore, both statements are sufficient, so the answer is Choice (D).

For more about how to solve data sufficiency problems, refer to Chapter 17. To review variables, inequalities, and other algebraic concepts, read Chapter 11.

7. **A. Statement (1) *alone* is sufficient, but Statement (2) *alone* is *not* sufficient.**

    Evaluate the question.

    1. Find out what to solve for.

    Visualizing this problem may be easier if you draw a Venn diagram such as the one below.

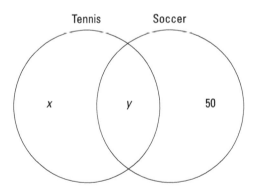

    The *x* stands for the number of campers that play tennis only, and *y* represents the number of campers that play both tennis and soccer. The two circles comprise all 200 campers. Because 50 of the 200 campers don't play tennis, they must play soccer only. You can see from the Venn diagram that $200 = x + y + 50$.

2. **Examine Statement (1).**

   Statement (1) tells you that the total number of members in the soccer circle is 170. So, to find out how many campers play both tennis and soccer, you just subtract 50 from 170. You don't have to actually perform the calculation to know that Statement (1) provides a definite answer to the question. Write (1) is *yes*. The answer is either Choice (A) or Choice (D).

3. **Examine Statement (2).**

   From Statement (2) you know that x is less than 50 campers, but without additional information, you cannot determine an exact number for y, the number of campers who play both tennis and soccer. so Statement (2) is not sufficient to answer the question. Write (2) is *no*. Eliminate Choice (D).

Therefore, Statement (1) *alone* is sufficient, but Statement (2) *alone* is *not* sufficient. Select Choice (A).

For more about how to solve data sufficiency problems, read Chapter 17. To review sets and Venn diagrams, read Chapter 12.

8. **C.** *Both* statements *together* are sufficient, but *neither* statement *alone* is sufficient.

Evaluate the question.

1. **Find out what to solve for.**

   You need to determine the number of mangos sold today. The problem tells you that mangos sell for $1.50 each and cantaloupes sell for $2.00 each. Let M = the number of mangos sold today and C = the number of cantaloupes sold today.

2. **Examine Statement (1).**

   From Statement (1), you have $M = 2C + 20$, which is one equation with two unknowns. Without additional information, you cannot determine an exact value of M. Write (1) is *no*. You've just eliminated choices (A) and (D).

3. **Examine Statement (2).**

   From Statement (2) you have $1.50M + 2.00C = 155.00$, which is one equation with two unknowns. Without additional information, you cannot determine an exact value of M. Write (2) is *no*. You've eliminated Choice (B).

4. **Evaluate what you've written on your noteboard.**

   You have double *no*s, so you have to consider both statements together.

5. **Evaluate the two statements together.**

Taking (1) and (2) together yields a system of two equations, $M = 2C + 20$ and $1.50M + 2.00C = 155.00$, with two variables. You can find the simultaneous solution of the two equations and determine an exact value of M, The two statements together provide enough information to answer the question asked. Choose Choice (C).

For more about how to solve data sufficiency problems, read Chapter 17. To review how to solve word problems, read Chapter 11.

Answers at a Glance

Section 1: Quantitative Reasoning

1.	D	3.	E	5.	B	7.	C
2.	C	4.	A	6.	A	8.	D

Section 2: Verbal

1.	D	3.	D	5.	A	7.	E
2.	D	4.	D	6.	B	8.	D

Section 3: Data Insights

1A.	Not Inferable	2A.	Full-size car driven at 60 mph	3B.	1963	5.	E
1B.	Not inferable			4A.	Consistent	6.	D
1C.	Inferable	2B.	25	4B.	Inconsistent	7.	A
		3A.	1951	4C.	Consistent	8.	C

3

Vanquishing the Verbal Section

Chapter **7**

Not as Enticing as a Bestseller: Reading Comprehension

f you find yourself reading approximately 350 words about white dwarfs in space, you're not encountering a sci-fi fable about the seven companions of an astronomical Snow White. You're more likely tackling a reading comprehension problem on the GMAT. The GMAT test-makers present yet another way to poke and prod your intellect with several paragraphs of fascinating reading material and a few questions to test your comprehension of it. The questions may be specific and focus on highlighted portions of the passage, or they may concern general themes, like the author's main idea.

Reading comprehension questions are designed to test how well you understand unfamiliar reading material. But you're probably less concerned with the reason these passages are included on the GMAT than you are with getting through all that reading and question-answering with enough time left over to confront those pesky critical reasoning questions. What you need is a proven strategy. And in this chapter, we deliver by introducing you to the types of passages and questions you'll encounter and telling you how to deal with them.

Judging by Appearances: What Reading Comprehension Questions Look Like

The verbal section of the GMAT mixes reading comprehension questions with critical reasoning questions. About one-half of the 23 questions in the verbal section are reading questions. You'll see a split screen with an article passage on the left and a question with five answer choices on the right.

Although every passage has more than one question (usually, passages have about three to four questions), only one question pops up at a time. You read the passage (which contains about 350 words), click on the choice that best answers the question, and confirm your answer. As soon as you confirm your answer, another question pops up on the right side of the screen. The passage remains on the left. Sometimes a question refers to a particular part of the passage. For these questions, the GMAT highlights the portion of the passage you need to focus on to answer the question.

Approaching Reading Passages

Reading comprehension questions don't ask you to do anything particularly unfamiliar. You've probably been reading passages and answering multiple-choice questions about them since you were in elementary school. If you're having difficulty answering reading comprehension questions correctly, don't worry: Your reading skills are likely fine. You're probably just not familiar with the specific way you have to read for the GMAT.

REMEMBER

You have about two minutes to answer each reading comprehension question, and that includes reading the passage. Generally, you shouldn't spend more than five minutes reading a passage before you answer its questions, so you have to read as efficiently as you can. You need a plan for getting through the passage in a way that allows you to answer questions correctly and quickly. When you read a passage, focus on the following elements:

>> The passage's general theme

>> The author's tone

>> The way the author organizes the passage

TIP

Unless you have a photographic memory, you won't be able to remember all of a passage's details long enough to answer the questions. Don't try to figure out the passage's minutiae while you're reading it. If you encounter a question about a little detail, you can go back and reread the relevant section. Instead of sweating the small stuff, make sure you understand the author's main point, the author's tone, and the overall way the author presents the information.

Mastering the message: The main point

Generally, people write passages to inform or persuade. Most of the passages on the GMAT are informative rather than argumentative, and even the argumentative ones are pretty tame.

REMEMBER

The main point of GMAT passages is often *to discuss a topic, to inform the reader about a phenomenon, or to compare one idea to another.* Rarely does a GMAT passage seek to condemn, criticize, or enthusiastically advocate a particular idea or position.

Because most authors present the main theme in the first paragraph or two, you'll probably figure it out in the first few seconds of your reading. If it's not clear in the first paragraphs, it probably appears in the last paragraph, where the author sums up the ideas. After you've figured out the author's overall theme, quickly jot down on your noteboard a word or two to help you remember the theme. For a passage that describes the differences between the flight patterns of houseflies and horseflies, you can write *compare flight — house/horse.* Your notation gives you something to refer to when you're asked the inevitable main theme synthesis question (which we discuss in greater detail in the later section, "Getting to the point: Main-idea questions").

Absorbing the ambiance: Author's tone

In addition to understanding the author's main point, you need to know how the author feels about the issue. You get clues to the authors' tone or mood by the words they use. GMAT passages either inform the reader about something or try to persuade the reader to adopt the author's viewpoint. Informative passages are often more objective than persuasive ones, so the author's tone is usually neutral. Authors of persuasive passages may exhibit more emotion. You may sense that an author is critical, sarcastic, pessimistic, optimistic, or supportive. When you figure out how the author feels about the topic, write a short description on your noteboard, like *objective, hopeful,* or *mildly critical.* Knowing the tone of a passage helps you choose answers that exhibit the same tone or level of bias.

WARNING

Regardless of the author's mood, don't let your personal opinions about a passage's subject matter influence your answer. Getting emotionally involved with the content of the passage can cloud your judgment. You may subconsciously rely on your opinions as you answer questions. To avoid doing so, you may find it helpful to remind yourself that correct answers are true *according to the passage* or *according to the author.*

Finding the framework: The passage's outline

Knowing the structure of a passage is much more important than understanding its details. Instead of trying to comprehend everything the author says, focus on how the author lays out the information.

Standard essay format includes an introduction with a thesis, two or three supporting paragraphs, and a conclusion. Many GMAT passages are excerpts from larger works, so they may not exhibit exact standard essay form, but they'll contain evidence of all three elements. As you read, determine the passage's overall point and the main points of each paragraph.

TIP

You may find it helpful to construct a mini-outline of the passage as you read it. Underneath the main theme, jot down a word or two on your noteboard that describes the type of information contained in each paragraph. So under *compare flight — house/horse,* you may list a synopsis of each supporting paragraph: *difference in wingspan, size difference — horse 3x bigger, ways flight helps house.* This outline tells you that in the first supporting paragraph, you find info about how the two flies differ in wingspan. The second supporting paragraph is where you find out how the greater size of horseflies affects their flight. And from the third supporting paragraph, you find out how the housefly's flight helps it in everyday life. Although you may not understand all the fascinating details of the author's account, you know where to go in the passage if you have to answer a detail question.

Building an outline in your head or on your noteboard helps you know where in the passage you can find answers to questions about particular details. Doing so also helps you answer any questions that ask you *how* authors develop their points.

WARNING

Even though you don't need to read and understand every detail of a passage before you answer its questions, we highly recommend that you scan the entire passage before you attempt the questions. You need an idea of what a passage is about and how it's organized before you look at the questions. Any time you save by not reading the passage first will be wasted when you have to read and reread paragraphs because you don't know where information is located or what the passage is about.

Sticking to the Subject: Types of Passages

You may think that because the GMAT measures your aptitude for MBA programs, its reading passages deal with subjects like marketing and economics. You're wrong. Although some of the passages do concern business matters, you'll also read about topics from the natural and social sciences. The GMAT wants to see how well you analyze a variety of topics, unfamiliar and familiar, so it presents you with articles about everything from the steel-making process to the quality of artifacts from the Bronze Age.

In the following sections, we explore the types of reading passages found on the GMAT.

Experimenting with natural science passages

Physical and biological sciences mean big business. Some of the areas of commerce that depend on science include pharmaceuticals, computers, agriculture, the defense industry, household products, and materials manufacturing (such as plastics and polymers). These industries, taken together, exert a huge influence on American quality of life and the nation's bottom line. Just think of this country without computers and pharmaceuticals, not to mention modern agriculture!

Although you may concede that the natural sciences are important, you may not be eager to confront a chemistry passage halfway through the GMAT verbal section. The good news is that the reading comprehension questions don't assume that you have any previous knowledge in the subject. If you do come across a reading passage on chemistry and it's been 20 years since you've studied the periodic table, relax. The answer to every question is located somewhere in the passage.

You really don't need to know a lot about a passage topic to answer the questions correctly. Although it's true that a chemistry major may read a passage about polymers more quickly than someone who never took a college chemistry course, that doesn't necessarily mean the chemistry expert will answer more questions correctly. Chemistry majors may actually be at a disadvantage because they may try to answer questions based on outside knowledge instead of using only the information stated in the passage.

WARNING

Reading comprehension questions test your reading skills, not the plethora of details you keep tucked away in your long-term memory. When you come across a passage on a subject that you're familiar with, don't rely on your outside knowledge to answer the question! Make sure the answers you choose can be justified by information contained in the passage.

REMEMBER

Natural science passages tend to be more objective and neutral than persuasive in tone. So usually the main theme of a natural science topic is *to explain, describe,* or *inform* about a scientific event.

Gathering in social circles: Social science passages

In addition to natural science passages, the GMAT presents passages about a different kind of science: social science, which includes topics like law, philosophy, history, political science, archeology, sociology, and psychology. The good news about social science passages is that their topics tend to crop up more in the news and in daily conversation than does, for example, physics! So you're more likely to be comfortable, if not necessarily familiar, with them.

Although passages about the social sciences are still mostly descriptive and informative, they're more likely to be persuasive than natural science passages, so you may see more variety in the kinds of tones these passages display.

Getting down to business passages

Business passages may be objective or persuasive and are generated from fields like economics, marketing, resource management, and accounting, among others. Finally, topics you're familiar with! You can forgo the archeology of New Zealand or an anatomy lesson on the long-horned beetle. This is business, your chosen field of study. At least it's a topic you're clearly interested in. You'll probably breeze right through most of these passages. But don't let familiarity with the topic serve as an excuse to slack off. You need your powers of concentration for every passage topic.

WARNING

If the passage is on a familiar subject, don't fall into the trap of using your own information to answer questions. Being familiar with a passage topic is an advantage, but only if you approach each question reminding yourself that the correct answer is based on information in the passage and not on what you studied last semester in your marketing courses or discussed last week in your sales meeting.

Approaching Reading Comprehension Questions

The GMAT verbal section has 23 questions, and you're allotted 45 minutes to answer them. That comes out to about two minutes per question. If you spend too much time answering reading comprehension questions, you'll have less time to consider the critical reasoning questions that also comprise the verbal section. So having a system for tackling reading comprehension questions is just as important as knowing how to read through the passages. Your approach should include

>> Recognizing the type of question

>> Quickly eliminating incorrect answer choices

>> Managing questions that ask for the answer that *isn't* supported by the passage

We show you how to do all three of these things in the following sections and provide a few examples of what to look for so you know how to answer the questions correctly.

Identifying the question type

The first step in answering a reading comprehension question correctly is identifying the type of question. Most reading comprehension questions fall into one of these five categories:

>> Summarizing the main idea

>> Finding supporting information

>> Making inferences and applications

>> Evaluating logic and structure

>> Assessing the author's tone

Each of the question types requires a slightly different approach. Main idea and tone questions ask you to make determinations about the passage as a whole, and supporting information and inference questions usually ask you to home in on particular parts of the passage. For example, when you know that a question is about specific details in the passage, you can focus your attention on the portion of the passage that's relevant to the information in the question.

We share all the details about each of the five categories of reading comprehension questions in the following sections.

Getting to the point: Main-idea questions

Main-idea questions ask you to identify the primary purpose of the whole passage. Almost every passage has at least one question that asks you to identify the thesis of the passage, and often it's the first question you answer for a particular reading passage.

TIP

You can identify main-idea questions by the language they contain. Here are some examples of the ways main-idea questions may be worded:

>> The author of the passage is primarily concerned with which of the following?

>> The author's primary goal (or purpose) in the passage is to do which of the following?

>> An appropriate title that best summarizes this passage is . . .

While you read the passage, look for its main idea because you know you'll probably be asked about it. You may even want to write a sentence that briefly states the passage's primary purpose. Then, if you're asked a question about the passage's main theme, you'll look for an answer that conveys an idea similar to your statement of the author's purpose.

TIP

The best answer to a main-idea question is general rather than specific. If an answer choice concerns information that's discussed in only one part of the passage, it probably isn't the correct answer to a main-idea question. Here are some other ways to narrow down your options for main-idea questions:

>> Eliminate answer choices that contain information that comes from only the middle paragraphs of the passage. These paragraphs probably deal with specific points rather than the main theme.

>> Eliminate any answer choices that contain information that you can't find in the passage. These choices are irrelevant.

>> Look at the first words of the answer choices to see whether you can eliminate any answer choices based on the first words only. For example, if you're trying to find the best answer to the author's purpose in an objectively written natural science passage, you can eliminate answers that begin with less objective terms, such as *to argue that . . ., to criticize . . .,* and *to refute the opposition's position that. . . .*

Finding the details: Supporting information questions

Some GMAT reading comprehension questions ask you about specific statements in the passage. These questions are potentially the easiest type of reading comprehension question because the information you need to answer them is stated in the passage. You just need to find it. This information may be quantitative, such as years, figures, or numbers, or it may be qualitative, like ideas, emotions, or thoughts.

Supporting information questions are worded in many different ways, but they almost always contain some reference to the passage. For example,

>> The passage states that . . .

>> According to the passage, . . .

>> In the passage, the author indicates that . . .

TIP

To succeed on supporting information questions, read the question carefully and refer to the outline of the passage you've written on your noteboard to remind you where the passage addresses certain types of information. And keep in mind that the correct answer may paraphrase the passage rather than provide a word-for-word repeat.

Reading between and beyond the lines: Inference and application questions

Inference and application questions ask you about information that's *implied* by the passage rather than directly stated. These questions test your ability to draw conclusions, using evidence that appears in the passage. For inference questions, you're normally required to do one of these three things:

>> Identify a different interpretation of an author's statement.

>> Infer the intended meaning of a word that's used figuratively in the passage.

>> Interpret the author's statements one step beyond what is actually written.

For example, suppose you read a passage that compares the rapidity of wing beats between houseflies and horseflies. Information in the second paragraph may state that the wings of horseflies beat at 96 bps (beats per second). Information in the fourth paragraph may say that a Purple Winger is a type of horsefly. From this information, you can infer that the wings of the Purple Winger beat at a rate of 96 bps. This is an example of the third bullet: taking the author's statements one step beyond what is actually written. Note that the horsefly conclusion doesn't require that you make great leaps of logic.

TIP

When you're answering an application question, look for the choice that slightly extends the meaning of the passage. Choices that go beyond the scope of the passage are usually incorrect. Don't choose an answer that requires you to come up with information that isn't somehow addressed by the passage.

REMEMBER

Sometimes knowing a great deal about a passage's topic can be a detriment, because you may be tempted to answer questions based on your own knowledge rather than the passage itself. Simply answer the questions as they're asked, and make inferences that can be justified by information in the passage.

The GMAT loves inference questions, so expect to see a lot of them. They're easily recognizable because they usually contain either *infer* or *imply* in the question, like these examples:

>> It can be inferred from the passage that . . .

>> The passage implies (or suggests) that . . .

>> In which of the following is the role played by the cichlid most like the role played by the algae raptor discussed in the passage?

>> The author brings up . . . to suggest which of the following?

Sometimes, the GMAT highlights in yellow the portion of the passage that discusses the material in question. If the test highlights information for you, it's likely an inference question rather than a supporting information type.

Evaluating passage flow

Some reading questions focus more on the passage's structure than its contents. For these questions you analyze the passage's organization and note how information flows from one idea to another. Questions that call on your ability to follow the author's logic include wording similar to the following:

>> Which of the following best describes the organization of the passage?

>> What purpose does the third paragraph serve?

>> Which of the following would best support the scientist's theory in the second paragraph?

TIP

Some of these logic questions may resemble the wording of and require the approach to critical reasoning questions, so following the techniques presented in Chapter 8 may help you answer these reading questions.

Feeling moody: Questions about the author's tone

As you read the passage, be sure to look for clues to the author's tone as well as purpose. You're bound to see questions that ask you to gauge how the author feels about the topic. Tone questions commonly ask you to figure out the author's attitude or complete the logical flow of the author's ideas. The author may be neutral, negative, or positive and may have different attitudes about different types of information within the same passage. It's up to you to determine the nature and degree of the author's feeling from the language used in the passage. With practice, you'll figure out how to distinguish between an enthusiastic author and one who's faking enthusiasm to mock the subject of the passage.

You can recognize questions about tone by the way they're worded. Here are some examples of how tone questions may appear on the GMAT:

>> The author's attitude appears to be one of . . .

>> With which of the following statements would the author most likely agree?

>> The tone of the passage suggests that the author is most skeptical about which of the following?

When making determinations about the author's tone, consider the passage as a whole. You may find one or two examples of negative comments in an article that is otherwise overwhelmingly positive about a subject. Don't make the mistake of quickly categorizing the passage from a few words that happen to catch your attention. Instead, determine the main idea of the passage and the author's purpose (you need to do this to answer other questions, anyway) and use that information to help you discern the author's tone. For example, if an author's purpose is to argue against a particular point of view, critical words regarding the proponents of that viewpoint reveal an overall critical attitude. However, you wouldn't say the same about an author of a passage that supports a viewpoint overall but includes one or two criticisms about some supporters of the viewpoint.

Tone questions may point you to a specific portion of a passage, or they may be about the entire passage. Even if a question does reference a specific part of the text, it'll do so in relation to the passage as a whole. For example, you can usually answer a question that asks you why an author chose to use certain words in a particular sentence only within the context of the entire passage. So if you know the main idea, author's purpose, and tone of the entire passage, you should be able to effectively deal with questions about the use of a particular word or phrase in one part of the passage.

Eliminating answer choices

One of the most effective ways of moving through reading comprehension questions is to eliminate incorrect answer choices. That's because you're looking for the best answer choice, not necessarily the perfect answer choice. Sometimes, you'll have to choose the best choice out of five pretty great choices, and other times you'll choose from five really crummy ones. Because the definitive answer usually won't pop right out at you, you have to know how to eliminate obviously wrong choices. Chapter 2 gives you general tips for eliminating answer choices. In this section, we show you how to apply those techniques specifically to reading comprehension questions.

Much of the time, you can eliminate wrong choices without having to refer back to the passage. As long as you carefully read the passage and have a good idea of the main theme, the author's purpose in writing the selection, and the author's tone, you should be able to recognize some wrong answers immediately.

Some common wrong answers include the following:

>> **Choices that concern information that isn't found in the passage:** Some answer choices contain information that's beyond the scope of the passage. Even if the information in these choices is true, you can't choose them. You have to choose answers based on what's stated or implied in the passage. Eliminate these choices, no matter how tempting they may be.

>> **Choices that contradict the main theme, author's tone, or specific information in the passage:** After you've read through the passage, you should be able to quickly eliminate most of the choices that contradict what you know about the passage.

>> **Choices that counter the wording of the question:** You can also eliminate some answer choices by paying careful attention to the wording of the question. For example, a question may ask about a *disadvantage* of something discussed in the passage. If one of the answer choices lists an advantage instead of a disadvantage, you can eliminate that choice without thinking too much about it. Or a question may ask you to choose which answer the author is most optimistic about. If one of the things listed is something the author is negative about, you can eliminate that choice.

The GMAT may try to entice you with answer choices that deal with information directly stated in the passage but don't relate to the actual question at hand. Don't choose an answer just because it looks familiar. Make sure it actually answers the question.

>> **Choices that contain *debatable* words:** Question any answer choice that uses absolutes. Examples are *all, always, only, complete, first, never, every,* and *none.* An answer choice that contains a word that leaves no room for exception is probably wrong. The GMAT makers don't want you calling them up complaining that you know of a circumstance where, say, not all fire engines are red. Beware: Usually the rest of an answer choice that includes a debatable word sounds pretty good, so you may be tempted to choose it.

Don't automatically eliminate an answer choice that contains a debatable word. If information in the passage justifies the presence of *all* or *none* in an answer choice, it may be right. For example, if a passage tells you that all horseflies beat their wings at a rate of 96 bps, the choice with *all* in it may be accurate.

Dealing with exception questions

Most questions ask you to choose the one correct answer, but some questions are cleverly disguised to ask for the *one* false answer. We call these gems *exception questions.* You'll recognize these questions by the presence of a negative word, usually *except* or *not.* When you see these words capitalized in a question, you know you're looking for the one answer choice that *doesn't* satisfy the requirements of the question.

You won't see many exception questions on the GMAT, but when you do see that negative word, take a moment to make sure you know exactly what the question is asking. Don't get confused or rush and automatically choose the first choice that looks good. *Remember:* The question is asking for the *one* answer out of five that's false or not part of the information stated or implied in the passage.

Exception questions aren't that difficult if you approach them systematically. Determining that an answer definitely isn't discussed in the passage takes time. You have to carefully look through the passage for the choice and *not* find it — then check again just to be sure. But a better way does exist: Instead of determining that an answer isn't discussed, eliminate the four true answers, which leaves you with the one false (and, therefore, correct) answer.

Identifying those choices that *do* appear in the passage is much easier than determining the one choice that isn't in the passage. After you've identified the four correct answers (remember to use your erasable noteboard to keep track), you can click on the one false answer as the choice for that question.

Take a look at two exception questions based on a fairly difficult natural science passage.

This passage is excerpted from *The Earth Through Time,* 7th Edition, by Harold L. Levin (John Wiley & Sons, Inc.):

> Geologists have proposed the term *eon* for the largest divisions of the geologic time scale. In chronologic succession, the eons of geologic time are the Hadean, Archean, Proterozoic, and Phanerozoic. The beginning of the Archean corresponds approximately to the ages of the oldest known rocks on Earth. Although not universally used, the term *Hadean* refers to that period of time for which we have no rock record, which began with the origin of the planet 4.6 billion years ago. The Proterozoic Eon refers to the time interval from 2,500 to 544 million years ago.

The rocks of the Archean and Proterozoic are informally referred to as Precambrian. The antiquity of Precambrian rocks was recognized in the mid-1700s by Johann G. Lehman, a professor of mineralogy in Berlin, who referred to them as the "Primary Series." One frequently finds this term in the writing of French and Italian geologists who were contemporaries of Lehman. In 1833, the term appeared again when Lyell used it in his formation of a surprisingly modern geologic time scale. Lyell and his predecessors recognized these "primary" rocks by their crystalline character and took their uppermost boundary to be an unconformity that separated them from the overlying — and therefore younger — fossiliferous strata.

The remainder of geologic time is included in the Phanerozoic Eon. As a result of careful study of the superposition of rock bodies accompanied by correlations based on the abundant fossil record of the Phanerozoic, geologists have divided it into three major subdivisions, termed eras. The oldest is the Paleozoic Era, which we now know lasted about 300 million years. Following the Paleozoic is the Mesozoic Era, which continued for about 179 million years. The Cenozoic Era, in which we are now living, began about 65 million years ago.

EXAMPLE

The passage uses all the following terms to describe *eons* or *eras,* except

(A) Archean

(B) Paleozoic

(C) Holocene

(D) Phanerozoic

(E) Cenozoic

The terms in this passage may be unfamiliar to you, but if you read the passage carefully, you should be able to get a general sense of what it's talking about. For this exception question, which tests you on unfamiliar terms, the best way to approach the question is to consult the text and eliminate the four terms that it uses to describe eons or eras.

TIP

First, scan the answer choices so you have an idea of the words you're looking for. Then begin at the top of the passage and look for words that resemble the answer choices. You should be especially aware of any lists that occur in the text, because exception questions often focus on lists. It's very difficult for test-makers to come up with a good exception question without a list.

The passage contains three lists. The first one appears in the first paragraph. It names eons of geologic time. The question refers to eons, and uses four terms that certainly resemble the answer choices. Consult this first list and eliminate any choices that appear on it. The terms *Archean* and *Phanerozoic* appear, so you can eliminate Choices (A) and (D). In the second paragraph, you see the term *Precambrian* (which isn't an answer choice) and a list of geologists who have mentioned Precambrian rocks. The second paragraph doesn't help with this question, so move quickly to the third paragraph.

The third paragraph also provides a list of eras that are part of the Phanerozoic eon. In this list, you see the terms *Paleozoic, Mesozoic,* and *Cenozoic. Paleozoic* is Choice (B), and *Cenozoic* is Choice (E), so you can eliminate both of these terms. Therefore, the correct answer to this exception question is Choice (C), *Holocene,* which isn't mentioned in the passage and, in fact, is neither an eon nor an era but the epoch in which you're living!

Here's another exception question based on the same passage.

Which of the following terms is not used in the passage to describe rocks that are more than 544 million years old?

(A) Precambrian

(B) Cenozoic

(C) Primary Series

(D) Archean

(E) Proterozoic

This question is more difficult because all the terms appear in the passage, but one of them doesn't apply to rocks that are more than 544 million years old. Begin in the same way you did for the previous question, by scanning the answer choices so you know the kinds of words you're looking for.

When you find a term, don't automatically eliminate it. In this example, you must confirm that it refers to rocks more than 544 million years old before you can cross it off.

WARNING

The list in the second sentence of the first paragraph doesn't help because it has no corresponding dates for the eons. The next sentence, however, says that *Archean* rocks are the "oldest known rocks on Earth." You can probably eliminate Choice (D), but keep reading to be sure. The last sentence of the paragraph says that Proterozoic rocks are 544 million to 2,500 million (2.5 billion) years old. And because Archean rocks are older than that, you can eliminate both Choices (D) and (E).

At the beginning of the second paragraph, you discover that both Archean and Proterozoic rocks are referred to as *Precambrian.* Because both types of rock are older than 544 million years, you can also eliminate Choice (A). Finally, in the very next sentence, you find out that Precambrian rocks are also called *Primary Series* rocks, so you can eliminate Choice (C). Choice (B) is the correct answer.

You'd also know that Choice (B) is the correct answer if you happened to look at the last sentence of the passage. That sentence tells you that the Cenozoic era started just 65 million years ago. The question asks for the rocks that are *not* older than 544 million years. Clearly, Cenozoic rocks are, at most, 65 million years old. So Choice (B) must be the one.

You can definitely skip the elimination process if you happen to stumble onto the right information, but that haphazard method won't work for all exception questions. You're better off approaching the question by eliminating the four answers that you find in the passage or that satisfy the criteria and locating the exception by process of elimination.

TIP

Exception questions can take some time, but they're among the easier reading comprehension questions because often the answers are right there in the text! So don't get in a hurry and make a mistake. Relax and use the proper approach, and you'll do exceptionally well.

Reading Comprehension Practice Questions with Answer Explanations

To practice the approach to answering reading comprehension questions, try your hand at these practice questions. Read the passages and answer the questions, using the techniques we've discussed in this chapter. When you're finished, read through the answer explanations that follow.

Reading comprehension practice questions

In this practice section, we provide you with three passages, one of each of the subject types you'll see in the GMAT verbal reasoning section. Try to answer the following 10 questions within the 19.6-minute minimum average pace needed to finish all 23 verbal section questions before the 45 minutes are up. For each question, choose the best answer from the five options.

The GMAT won't label answer choices with letters as we have here to make our explanations easier to follow. To choose an answer on the computerized test, you'll simply click on the radio button next to the choice.

Answer Questions 1–3 based on the following passage.

> For most Americans and Europeans, this should be the best time in all of human history to live. Survival — the very purpose of all life — is nearly guaranteed for large parts of the world, especially in the "West." This should allow people a sense of security and contentment. If life is no longer as Thomas Hobbes famously wrote, "nasty, brutish, and short," then should it not be pleasant, dignified, and long? To know that tomorrow is nearly guaranteed, along with thousands of additional tomorrows, should be enough to render hundreds of millions of people awe-struck with happiness. And modern humans, especially in the West, have every opportunity to be free, even as they enjoy ever-longer lives. Why is it, then, that so many people feel unhappy and trapped? The answer lies in the constant pressure of trying to meet needs that don't actually exist.
>
> The term "need" has been used with less and less precision in modern life. Today, many things are described as needs, including fashion items, SUVs, vacations, and other luxuries. People say, "I need a new car," when their current vehicle continues to function. People with many pairs of shoes may still say they "need" a new pair. Clearly, this careless usage is inaccurate; neither the new car nor the additional shoes are truly "needed."
>
> What is a need then? The *Oxford English Dictionary* defines the condition of "need" as "lack of means of subsistence." This definition points the way toward an understanding of what a need truly is: A need is something required for survival. Therefore, the true needs of life are air, food, water, and, in cold climates, shelter. Taken together, this is the stuff of survival. Because the purpose of life is to survive — or more broadly, to live — then these few modest requirements are all that a modern human truly needs. Other things make life exciting or enjoyable, and these are often referred to as "the purpose of life" — but this is surely an exaggeration. These additional trappings are mere wants and not true needs.

1. Which of the following most accurately states the main idea of the passage?

   (A) Modern Americans and Europeans feel unhappy and trapped because they don't distinguish true needs from mere wants.

   (B) There are no human needs, and all so-called needs are merely wants.

   (C) Human needs can never be satisfied in this life and, therefore, people will always be unhappy.

   (D) The satisfaction of human needs has resulted in nearly universal happiness for people in the United States and Europe.

   (E) There is no difference between needs and wants; the desire for wealth and power is just as real as the need for food and shelter.

2. According to the author, which of the following is an example of a fulfillment of a need?

(A) Adding a roof to block moonlight from shining on a rudimentary sleeping structure built on a tropical island

(B) Creating a pair of slippers from deer hide to protect one's bare feet from being cut by sharp rocks and stones

(C) Traveling several miles through dense foliage to obtain a particular berry, known for its sweetness and antioxidant properties, to accompany one's regular bland diet of rice and beans

(D) Climbing a steep rock face for the exhilaration and sense of accomplishment

(E) Digging a hole to locate a new water supply after one's prior single source of refreshment has run out

3. Which of the following best defines the way the first paragraph of the passage is organized?

(A) The author poses a question and provides context and then suggests an answer to the question.

(B) The author presents an argument and develops that argument by referencing a famous quote that reiterates the point that precedes it.

(C) The author presents an argument and then supports that argument by defining an essential term.

(D) The author compares life in one area of the world to life in another area of the world and shows how one way of thinking about life is better than the other.

(E) The author poses a rhetorical question and explains why modern humans are incapable of answering that question.

Answer Questions 4–6 based on the following passage.

A logarithmic unit known as the decibel (dB) is used to represent the intensity of sound. The decibel scale is similar to the Richter scale used to measure earthquakes. On the Richter scale, a 7.0 earthquake is ten times stronger than a 6.0 earthquake. On the decibel scale, an increase of 10 dB is equivalent to a tenfold increase in intensity or power. Thus, a sound registering 80 dB is ten times louder than a 70 dB sound. In the range of sounds audible to humans, a whisper has an intensity of 20 dB; 140 dB (a jet aircraft taking off nearby) is the threshold of immediate pain.

The perceived intensity of sound is not simply a function of volume; certain frequencies of sound appear louder to the human ear than do other frequencies, even at the same volume. Decibel measurements of noise are, therefore, often "A-weighted" to take into account the fact that some sound wavelengths are perceived as being particularly loud. A soft whisper is 20 dB, but on the A-weighted scale, the whisper is 30 dBA. This is because human ears are particularly attuned to human speech. Quiet conversation has a sound level of about 60 dBA.

Continuous exposure to sounds over 80 dBA can eventually result in mild hearing loss, while exposure to louder sounds can cause much greater damage in a very short period of time. Emergency sirens, motorcycles, chainsaws, construction activities, and other mechanical or amplified noises are often in the 80 to 120 dBA range. Sound levels above 120 dBA begin to be felt inside the human ear as discomfort and eventually as pain.

Unfortunately, the greatest damage to hearing is done voluntarily. Music, especially when played through headphones, can grow to be deceptively loud. The ear becomes numbed by the loud noise, and the listener often turns up the volume until the music approaches 120 dBA. This level of noise can cause permanent hearing loss in a short period of time, and in fact, many young Americans now have a degree of hearing loss once seen only in much older persons.

4. The primary purpose of the passage is to

(A) argue for government mandates that decibel levels produced by headphones be reduced.

(B) compare the scale used to measure intensity of sound to the scale used to measure the strength of earthquakes.

(C) describe the way that sound intensity is measured and explain its effect on human hearing.

(D) define which volume levels and sound exposure times are safe for humans and which are harmful.

(E) warn readers about the harmful effects of continuous exposure to sounds over 80 dBA.

5. The author mentions that "emergency sirens, motorcycles, chainsaws, construction activities, and other mechanical or amplified noises" fall in the 80 to 120 dBA range. It can be inferred from this statement that these noises

(A) are unwanted, outside intrusions common in urban life.

(B) can cause hearing loss with constant exposure.

(C) are more dangerous to hearing than sounds of the same dBA level from headphones.

(D) are loud enough to cause immediate pain.

(E) have no negative impacts.

6. The second paragraph of the passage states, "Decibel measurements of noise are therefore often 'A-weighted' to take into account the fact that some sound wavelengths are perceived as being particularly loud. A soft whisper is 20 dB, but on the A-weighted scale the whisper is 30 dBA." Therefore, for any particular sound, the A-weighted decibel level differs from the unweighted decibel level in that

(A) the A-weighted number is 10 points higher than the unweighted number.

(B) the A-weighted number is based on the way the noise is perceived in the human ear.

(C) the unweighted number is always higher than the A-weighted number.

(D) the A-weighted number is measured by more accurate instruments.

(E) only on the unweighted scale does a 10 dB increase in sound equal a tenfold increase in intensity.

Answer Questions 7–10 based on the following passage.

This passage is an excerpt from *Microeconomics Theory and Applications,* 9th Edition, by Edgar K. Browning and Mark A. Zupan (Wiley):

In 1980, Washington, D.C., city officials, hard-pressed for tax revenues, levied a 6 percent tax on the sale of gasoline. As a first approximation (and a reasonable one, it turns out), this tax could be expected to increase the price of gasoline by 6 percent. The elasticity of demand is a key factor in the consequences of this action, because the more sharply the sales of gasoline fall, the less tax revenue the city will raise. Presumably, city officials hoped that gasoline sales would be largely unaffected by the higher price. Within a few months, however, the amount of gasoline sold had fallen by 33 percent.* A 6 percent price increase producing a 33 percent quantity reduction means the price elasticity was about 5.5.

The sharp sales drop meant that tax revenue was not increased. Further indications were that when consumers had fully adjusted to the tax, tax revenues would actually decrease. (There had been a 10 cent per gallon tax before the 6 percent tax was added, so although the 6 percent levy was raising revenue, the gain was largely offset by the loss in revenue from the initial 10 cent tax following the reduction in sales.) This was not a general increase in gasoline prices but a rise only within the D.C. city limits. Gasoline sold in the District of Columbia is a narrowly defined product that has good substitutes — gasoline sold in nearby Virginia and Maryland. Higher gasoline prices in the District of Columbia, when the prices charged in Virginia and Maryland are unchanged, indicate high elasticity in the market.

No economist would be surprised at the results of this tax, but apparently city officials were. Observed one city councilman: "We think of ourselves here in the District as an island to ourselves. But we've got to realize that we're not. We've got to realize that Maryland and Virginia are right out there, and there's nothing to stop people from crossing over the line." The 6 percent gasoline tax was repealed five months after it was levied.

*"Barry Asks Gasoline Tax Repeal," *Washington Post,* November 2, 1980, p. A1.

7. The author is primarily concerned with doing which of the following?

    (A) Arguing for increased gas taxes

    (B) Arguing against increased gas taxes

    (C) Ridiculing all local government officials

    (D) Advancing a particular ideology

    (E) Explaining certain principles of supply and demand

8. It can be inferred from the passage that *elasticity* in the last sentence of the second paragraph refers to

    (A) fluctuations in the price of gasoline in Washington, D.C.

    (B) fluctuations in the price of gasoline in Virginia and Maryland.

    (C) changes in the amount of tax collected at 6 percent.

    (D) changes in the number of vehicles in the region.

    (E) fluctuations in the demand for gasoline sold in Washington, D.C.

9. For which of the following reasons does the second paragraph of the passage mention the original gas tax of 10 cents per gallon?

    (A) To show that Washington, D.C., residents were already overtaxed

    (B) To distinguish between a straight 10 cent per gallon tax and a percent tax

    (C) To explain why residents should not be subjected to different kinds of taxes

    (D) To contrast the 10 cent tax that was included in the pump price and the 6 percent sales tax that was added after the sale

    (E) To show that with a sufficient decrease in gasoline sales, the city would actually lose money despite the higher tax

10. The passage suggests that a reason the tax increase failed to raise tax revenues in the District of Columbia is that

    (A) District of Columbia consumers decreased the amount of fuel they purchased and limited their overall vehicle usage.

    (B) the amount of gas consumed by District of Columbia residents in their commute to nearby states was sufficiently negligible to justify purchasing fuel outside the city limits.

    (C) consumers in the District of Columbia were upset that city council members would decrease fuel taxes to increase tax revenues.

    (D) as a result of the tax increase, residents of Virginia and Maryland discontinued making gas purchases in the District of Columbia.

    (E) District of Columbia city council members failed to convince legislators in nearby states to increase their fuel taxes.

Answer Explanations

1. **A.** First, identify the question type. This one's pretty easy because it contains the phrase *main idea* right in the question. You're dealing with a main-idea question, so the answer concerns the general idea and purpose of the passage and is probably found in the first or last paragraphs of the passage.

   Eliminate any choices that go beyond the scope of the information discussed in the passage. You recall that the passage distinguished *true needs* from *mere wants*. Choice (C) says, "Human needs can never be satisfied in this life. . . ." The reading passage never mentions anything about needs not being satisfied in this life. You may or may not agree with the statement in Choice (C), but you can eliminate it because it discusses ideas that aren't covered in the passage.

   Next, look for choices that contradict what you remember from reading through the passage. Choice (B) states that "there are no human needs." The passage specifically lists human needs of food, water, shelter, and so on. So, Choice (B) has to be wrong. You may also recall that this list of needs is included in a section in which the author distinguishes between needs and wants. Choice (E) says that there's "no difference between needs and wants," you know that the passage says otherwise, so you can eliminate that option.

   You're left with Choices (A) and (D). If you have trouble choosing between them, consult the passage. Concentrate on the first paragraph, which says that although Americans and Europeans should be happy, many are "unhappy and trapped." You can, therefore, eliminate Choice (D).

   Choice (A) should be the correct answer. But take a moment to reread Choice (A) to make sure it makes sense as the main idea of the passage. Choice (A) says, "Modern Americans and Europeans feel unhappy and trapped because they don't distinguish true needs from mere wants." This statement agrees with the author's questioning of the reasons behind modern unhappiness found in the first paragraph and the author's distinguishing of needs from wants in the last paragraph.

2. **E.** The author describes a need as "something required for survival" and lists the true needs as "air, food, water, and, in cold climates, shelter." Eliminate answer choices that don't have something to do with air, food, water, and shelter. Climbing a rock face for the fun of it likely falls within the author's definition of a want because it makes life "exciting or enjoyable." So, you can eliminate Choice (D). As nice as it would be to maintain your pedicure with a nice pair of soft deer-hide slippers, foot apparel doesn't fall within the author's criteria for survival. (Apparently, in the author's world, clothing is optional!) Cross off Choice (B).

   You're left with Choice (A), which concerns shelter; Choice (C), which deals with food; and Choice (E), which regards water. Each of the remaining answer choices addresses one of the author's categories of needs, so it's up to you to determine which is required for survival. Although it would be nice to sleep peacefully without the interruption of pesky moonlight, the roof in Choice (A) is more likely a want than a need. The author clarifies that shelter is a need in cold climates, not tropical islands. Because Choice (C) tells you that the berry seekers already have a regular diet of rice and beans, you know they're not searching for the berry for survival purposes. The berry isn't necessary for survival, so it's unlikely that it fits the author's idea of a need.

   By process of elimination, you settle on Choice (E) as the best answer. The purpose of the hole excavation is to find one of the author's required elements for survival: water. And you know that the exercise is urgent because the hole-digger has no other source for water.

WARNING

Don't be fooled by the reference to *refreshment* in Choice (E). You may think that refreshment pertains to a want rather than a need, but the author tells you that water is necessary. Therefore, you can conclude that refreshment that refers to water is also necessary.

3. **A.** Examine the way the author introduces the point in the first paragraph of the passage. The first several sentences explain that modern humans should be happy because their daily survival is virtually guaranteed. The author inserts the Hobbes quote about how rough life used to be to show that modern life has improved considerably. The author then wonders, given how good we have it, why modern humans are unhappy. The paragraph's ending statement is the author's answer to this question. Find the answer that best describes this organization.

Choice (D) and Choice (E) are pretty easy to eliminate. The author provides an answer to the question, so modern humans aren't incapable of answering it, and Choice (E) can't be right. The author references the "West" but doesn't compare western thinking to the way people think about life in other parts of the world. Choice (D) is wrong.

You may be tempted by Choice (B). The first paragraph has a famous quote, but that quote about the nastiness of life doesn't restate the prior point that people should feel secure and content. Choice (C) may also sound good at first, but it describes the organization of the entire passage rather than just the first paragraph. The author doesn't define a need until the last paragraph.

WARNING

When you're asked to evaluate the organization of reading content, make sure you know the parameters of the portion you're supposed to consider.

The best answer has to be Choice (A). The first several sentences provide background for the author's question about why modern humans aren't happy. Then the author answers the question by stating that humans aren't happy because they don't know what a need is.

4. **C.** This passage is almost exactly 350 words, so it's as long as any passage on the GMAT is going to get. Don't let the unfamiliar scientific concepts worry you. You're probably familiar with the term *decibel*, but you may have never encountered the *A-weighted decibel* or *dBA*, as it's abbreviated. Focus on the main point of the passage, which is to describe dBAs and how human ears perceive them, and what type of information appears in each paragraph so that you can approach this main-idea question systematically:

- First, check out the first word of each answer choice to find obvious incorrect answers. The tone of the passage is primarily objective and descriptive, so an answer that begins with *argue* is likely wrong. If you read Choice (A) further, you know you can eliminate it. The author doesn't mention anything about government mandates.

WARNING

Natural science passages are usually objective and informative. Their primary purpose is rarely to argue in favor of or against a particular position.

- Next, eliminate answer choices that deal with information found in only one area of the passage. The scales mentioned in Choice (B) appear only in the first paragraph, so a comparison of them can't be the purpose of the passage. The author discusses the harmful effects of exposure to sound only in the last two paragraphs, so Choice (E) isn't the primary purpose. For the same reason, you can likely eliminate Choice (D). While the author does indeed define the sound exposure levels and times that are safe for humans and does warn readers about the harmful effects of sound exposure, neither Choice (E) nor Choice (D) provides the overall reason for the passage.

- Finally, choose the answer that incorporates information from the passage as a whole. Choice (C) brings together the information in the first two paragraphs (how sound intensity is measured) and the information in the last two (how sound intensity affects humans). Therefore, it's the best answer.

5. **B.** The word *infer* in the question gives you a fairly obvious clue to the type of question you're dealing with. Again, you can rely on the process of elimination to answer it.

Begin by eliminating those choices that rely on outside information. This passage focuses on noise levels and health effects. The passage doesn't mention societal concerns, such as the intrusive impacts of a plethora of noise in urban life. Therefore, you can cross out Choice (A). All the other choices have something to do with noise levels and health, so don't eliminate them yet.

Next, look for choices that contradict what you know about the passage. One of the author's purposes in writing the passage is to warn young people of the hearing loss associated with headphone use (or abuse). To say that the noises mentioned in the question are *more* dangerous than noises at the same decibel level from headphones would be contradictory. Because Choice (C) is inconsistent with what you find out from the passage, you can eliminate it.

You can use the information in the question to narrow down your choices. The question indicates that the noises mentioned are in the 80 to 120 dBA range. Even if you don't remember all the specifics of the passage, you probably remember that noises over 100 dBA are very loud. You may even remember that 120 dBA is the threshold for feeling discomfort in the ear. It's, therefore, not logical to say, as Choice (E) does, that noises in this range would have *no* health effects. Noises that loud have some impact on the ear!

You can also eliminate Choice (E) because it contains an implicit debatable word. *No impacts* in this answer choice suggests *none*, and answer choices that contain the word *none* are almost always wrong because *none* doesn't allow for any exceptions. If the answer were worded a little differently to say "may have no negative impacts," it could be correct. Short exposure to noise may, in fact, have no impact.

You're left with just two answer choices. If you happen to remember that 140 dB is the threshold for immediate pain, you can answer the question without having to refer back to the text. However, if you have any doubt, take a few seconds to be sure.

The last sentence of the first paragraph indicates that 140 dB is the threshold of immediate pain, and in the third paragraph, you read that 120 dBA can "eventually lead to pain." Therefore, you can eliminate Choice (D), so Choice (B) is probably the answer. Glancing at the passage confirms that it indicates that constant exposure to sounds over 80 dBA can result in hearing loss.

6. **B.** On the computerized test, the question would refer to a highlighted part of the passage on the screen instead of quoting it, but for our purposes, we use the quotation. This question asks you to evaluate information in the passage.

You can eliminate Choice (E) because the passage doesn't mention a difference between a 10 dB increase and a 10 dBA increase. Choice (D) also refers to information not covered in the passage. Nowhere does the reading suggest that instruments used to measure A-weighted decibels are more accurate; it just indicates that sounds are measured differently with the A-weighted scale. Cross out Choice (D). Likewise, Choice (C) is incorrect because it directly contradicts prominent information from the reading. A whisper registers a higher number on the A-weighted scale, so Choice (C) can't be correct.

The two choices that are left, Choices (A) and (B), both provide correct information, but only one answers the question. A whisper does register 30 dBA on the A-weighted scale, as opposed to 20 dB on the normal decibel scale, so Choice (A) provides good information. But if you refer back to the passage, you find that some wavelengths are heard more clearly than others. The passage specifically states that the reason for the A-weighted scale is to take into account those noises that are perceived better by the human ear, which is how the

A-weighted scale differs from the unweighted scale. Because sounds other than a whisper may have more or less than 10 points difference between their A-weighted and unweighted numbers, Choice (B) is a better answer than Choice (A).

7. **E.** When you're answering a question about an author's purpose, looking at the beginning words of each answer choice can be helpful. The author doesn't appear to be particularly argumentative or condescending in this piece, so you can probably eliminate Choices (A), (B), and (C) right off the bat. Additionally, Choice (C) contains the debatable word *all.* The author doesn't talk about *all* local officials in D.C., much less *all* local officials in general.

This leaves Choices (D) and (E). You can eliminate Choice (D) because the author doesn't advance "a particular ideology." Instead, the author is stunned that the city council didn't know the basic theory of supply and demand. Choice (E) is the best answer of the five.

To double-check your answer, read through the answers you eliminated based solely on first words. Choice (A) is clearly wrong because the author shows that increased taxes actually resulted in decreased revenues. Choice (B) seems more logical because the author is showing the problems with the gas tax increase in Washington, D.C. But if you check the passage, you'll notice that the author never advocates for lower taxes in the passage. The author explains why the gas tax failed in the unique case of Washington, D.C., but that isn't enough to make Choice (B) the primary purpose for writing the passage. The author is primarily concerned with explaining the principles of supply and demand, using the Washington, D.C., gas tax as a case study.

8. **E.** That this question is an inference question is pretty obvious. Be careful not to make an inference that goes beyond the scope of what's stated in the passage.

Eliminate incorrect answer choices. Because this is an inference question, it may be hard to recognize answer choices that use outside knowledge. The point of inferring is, after all, to extend the reasoning beyond what's actually written. But one of the choices strays too far from the information in the passage. Choice (D) mentions changes in the number of vehicles in the region, but the passage says nothing about people getting rid of their cars or not driving through D.C. in reaction to the increase in the price of gas. Eliminate Choice (D).

Choice (B) is inconsistent with the passage as a whole, so you can also cross it off. The passage is about price increases in Washington, D.C., and specifically not about price increases in Maryland and Virginia. This leaves you with three possible answers, each of which could fit with the term *elasticity* in this passage. You need to go back and reread the sentence that's referenced in the question and also reread the surrounding sentences to understand the sentence's context.

The sentence clearly doesn't apply to "the amount of tax collected at 6 percent," so you can cross out Choice (C). The sentence does mention changes in price in D.C., yet if you read the entire second paragraph carefully, especially the last two sentences, you'll see that the author discusses lower demand in D.C. because of good substitutes: gas in Maryland and Virginia. The paragraph states outright that prices have gone up in D.C. — but this is an inference question, which means you're looking for an implication. It's not the prices that are elastic, which means Choice (A) is wrong. *Elasticity* must refer to the demand for gas, because low price and demand are positively related. So Choice (E) is the best answer to this difficult question.

TIP

Don't forget to consider the context of the passage beyond the specific sentence and paragraph mentioned in the question. A valuable clue to this question can be found in the third sentence of the first paragraph, which states that "The elasticity of demand is a key factor." This indicates that *elasticity* as used in the passage will probably be associated with *demand.*

9. **E.** This evaluation question asks for the reason the author mentions something, and the passage doesn't directly state the reason.

As usual, start by eliminating obviously incorrect answer choices that don't deal with the subject matter of the passage. The author doesn't mention residents being overtaxed or undertaxed; the article just mentions gas prices and shifting demand. So you can eliminate Choice (A). Choice (D) is incorrect because the passage doesn't mention collecting the taxes differently or at different times. The article makes no effort to distinguish between the straight 10 cent tax and the percentage tax, so you can also cross out Choice (B).

This leaves you with just two possible answers, Choices (C) and (E). Quickly referring to the second paragraph of the passage reveals that before the authors mention the 10-cent tax, they indicate that lower demand may actually result in lower tax revenue. To show how this could be true, the authors mention that the city was previously collecting 10 cents on each gallon. When less gasoline was sold, the city lost this revenue. Choice (E) is a better answer than Choice (C) because it pinpoints the authors' reasons for mentioning the earlier tax.

10. **B.** To answer this inference question, note that the tax increase was implemented with the intent to increase tax revenue. The passage states that tax revenues didn't increase essentially because city officials didn't account for the elasticity in the market. Consumers found equal, less-expensive substitutes in nearby gas stations outside the D.C. city limits.

TIP

Eliminate answer choices that are blatantly wrong. Choice (C) presents information that's contrary to the details of the passage. City officials didn't *decrease* fuel taxes; they increased them. You can easily narrow your choices to four.

Choice (A) provides an explanation for the decreased revenues. If consumers limited their overall gas consumption, tax revenues would fall. This isn't the reason the author suggests, however. The passage doesn't say that D.C. residents stopped buying fuel altogether. It suggests that they stopped buying fuel in D.C. and started buying it in Virginia and Maryland. Furthermore, D.C. residents may actually have been consuming more gas than usual rather than less because they were driving longer distances to fuel up. Eliminate Choice (A).

REMEMBER

Just because an answer choice makes logical sense doesn't mean it's correct. The answer has to make sense given the information in the passage.

You can also cross off Choices (D) and (E) from the list. Both answers require you to infer information that's beyond the scope of the passage. You don't know anything about the fuel-buying habits of Virginia and Maryland residents, nor can you imagine that D.C. officials tried to work with officials in neighboring states. In fact, the passage states that D.C. officials were surprised that their constituents bought gas elsewhere, so it's unlikely that they had the forethought to negotiate with other governments.

The remaining answer is Choice (B). If D.C. residents went outside of the city limits to purchase fuel, the overall cost of the trip must have been more cost effective than buying gas within the city. Otherwise, they would have continued to purchase fuel in D.C.

Chapter **8**

Thinking This Through Logically: Critical Reasoning

You're taking the GMAT to go to business school, not to get a PhD in philosophy, so you're probably wondering why you need to be tested in logic and critical reasoning. Don't worry — answering the critical reasoning questions on the GMAT doesn't require any knowledge of formal logic. You won't be constructing syllogisms or using fancy Latin words, like *ad hominem,* for logical fallacies. The GMAT verbal section contains questions that test you on informal logic, which is a lot like the kind of reasoning you use to decide between a chocolate frosted doughnut and a bran muffin when the office pastry cart passes by. We fill you in on this logic (for the GMAT, not the pastry cart) in this chapter. The people who run the admissions offices at business schools want to make sure their future students can think through situations clearly and carefully. That's where the critical reasoning questions come in.

About half of the 23 questions in the GMAT verbal section are critical reasoning questions. This question type tests your ability to analyze an argument. The good news is that you analyze arguments all the time, even though you may not know you're doing so. When you see a commercial advertising a new product that claims it'll make your life better, you probably question that claim. If a weight-loss drug helped someone lose 50 pounds, you ask, "Is that a typical result?" If four out of five dentists recommend a chewing gum, you say, "Did they ask only five dentists?" When a mutual fund boasts of its performance, you ask, "Is that better than the market average?" You'll use this same kind of thinking to ace the critical reasoning questions on the GMAT.

Focusing on "Critical" Concepts: An Overview

Critical reasoning questions consist of an argument, a question, and five answer choices, of which only one is correct. You'll encounter short passages from a variety of sources, such as speeches, advertisements, newspapers, and scholarly articles. You may see an argument like this: "The local sales tax must be raised to fund city services. Admittedly, this increased sales tax will impose a greater hardship on the poorest citizens. But if the sales tax is not increased, all city services for the poor will have to be cut." The paragraph reflects the type of arguments you encounter in the news every day.

In the following sections, we clue you in on what to expect when you approach a critical reasoning question on the GMAT — from the length and format of the argument, to the type of questions you'll be asked, to how to figure out the correct answer.

Understanding the structure of the questions

Each critical reasoning question has essentially the same structure. The question usually begins with a two- to five-sentence paragraph that contains the argument. The question contains all the information you need to answer the question. Don't rely on any outside information! Even if you happen to be an expert in the area a question covers, don't rely on your expertise to answer the question.

The short argument paragraph is followed by a question. The questions usually fall conveniently into one of a few types. The question may ask that you weaken or strengthen an argument, draw a conclusion, analyze the structure of an argument, or identify an unstated assumption the author makes. We examine each of these question types in the section, "Getting from Point A to Point B: Types of reasoning," later in this chapter.

Each question has five possible answer choices, which are often long, sometimes even longer than the argument or question. For this reason, you'll spend most of your time for each question examining the answer choices.

TIP

As with most GMAT questions, you can quickly eliminate one or two of the answers that are obviously wrong. The remaining answers will be more difficult to eliminate, so spend your time analyzing these better answer choices.

Figuring out how to answer the questions

To break down a critical reasoning question, follow these three steps:

1. **Read the question.**

2. **Read the argument paragraph, focusing on the specific information you need to know to answer the question.**

3. **As you read the argument, look for inconsistencies and/or assumptions in the logic.**

The best way to tackle a critical reasoning question is to read the question first to determine its type. The later section, "Thinking Inside the Box: Question Types," shows you how to distinguish critical reasoning question types. When you first read the question, don't read all the answer choices; doing so takes way too much time and clutters your thinking. You need to concentrate on only the information you need to find to answer the question.

After you figure out what kind of question you're dealing with, you can read the paragraph very carefully. Be sure to locate the conclusion of the argument. The conclusion may come at the beginning, middle, or end of the paragraph. When you've identified the conclusion, you can better understand the rest of the paragraph. As you read the paragraph, look for inconsistencies or gaps in the argument that may help you answer the question. Isolating the argument's premises, assumptions, and conclusion helps you determine the method of reasoning.

WARNING

The argument paragraph usually isn't too complicated, and therefore you may be tempted to read it too quickly. Force yourself to read slowly and carefully so you don't skim over the word or words that provide the keys to the argument. If you read thoroughly enough, you'll be able to eliminate some — or even most — of the answer choices. When you're down to two possible answers, you can then easily refer back to the text to make sure you choose the correct answer.

Making a Case: Essentials of Informal Logic

You can score well on the GMAT critical reasoning questions without knowing the elements of informal logic, but if you understand a few terms and concepts, you can score even higher. You really just need to know the two basic components of a logical argument and a few methods of coming up with a conclusion, which we outline in the following sections.

Fighting fair: The elements of an argument

A logical argument consists of premises and a conclusion, and when you're analyzing arguments, identifying what parts are premises and what makes up the conclusion can help. The *premises* give the supporting evidence that you can draw a conclusion from. You can usually find the *conclusion* in the argument because it's the statement that you can preface with *therefore*. The conclusion is often but not always the last sentence of the argument. For example, take a look at this simple argument:

All runners are fast. John is a runner. Therefore, John is fast.

The premises in the argument are "All runners are fast" and "John is a runner." They provide the supporting evidence for the conclusion that John is fast, which is the sentence that begins with *therefore*. Not all conclusions in the GMAT critical reasoning arguments will begin with *therefore* or other words like it (such as *thus* and *so*), but you can try adding *therefore* to any statement you believe is the conclusion to see whether the argument makes sense. We give you plenty of sample arguments in this chapter so you can use them to practice identifying premises and conclusions.

Getting from Point A to Point B: Types of reasoning

Each logical argument has premises and a conclusion, but not every argument comes to a conclusion in the same way. For the purposes of the GMAT, you should be familiar with two basic types of logical reasoning: deductive and inductive (which we explain further in the next sections). You use both types of reasoning all the time, but now you can apply definitions to your logical genius.

SURE SOUNDS GREEK TO ME: ORIGINS OF LOGICAL THOUGHT

Legend has it that a Greek philosopher named Parmenides in the 5th century BC had plenty of time on his hands while living in a Greek colony off the west coast of Italy. So he whiled away the hours contemplating logical thought and became one of the first Westerners to record his findings. He penned a philosophical poem in which an unnamed goddess instructs him in the ways of determining truth about the universe. His poem explored the contrast between truth and appearance and portrayed truth to be firm and steadfast, whereas appearance (the way mortals usually think) was unstable and wavering. Parmenides's work influenced other great Greek thinkers, like Plato, Aristotle, and Plotinus.

Unfortunately, you won't have a goddess to guide you through the critical reasoning questions of the GMAT, but you can rely on Aristotle's method of developing syllogisms to examine GMAT arguments. He is credited as the father of formal logic, which is the basis for this famous syllogism: "All humans are mortal; Socrates is human; therefore, Socrates is mortal."

Elementary, my dear Watson: Deductive reasoning

In *deductive reasoning*, you come up with a specific conclusion from more general premises. The great thing about deductive reasoning is that if the premises are true, the conclusion must be true! The following is an example of a deductive reasoning argument:

> All horses have hooves. (General premise)
>
> Bella is a horse. (More specific premise)
>
> Therefore, Bella has hooves. (Very specific conclusion)

If the premise that all horses have hooves is true, and if Bella is, in fact, a horse, then it must be true that Bella has hooves. The same holds true for all examples of deductive reasoning. Here's another example:

> All who take the GMAT must work through a quantitative section. (General premise)
>
> You're taking the GMAT. (More specific premise)
>
> Therefore, you have to work through a quantitative section. (Very specific conclusion)

This example shows the relationship between the truth of the premises and that of the conclusion. The first premise is categorically true: The GMAT requires you to work through a quantitative section. The second premise, however, may not be true. Certainly, you're thinking of taking the GMAT or you wouldn't be reading this book, but you may still decide not to take the test. This possibility doesn't affect the logic of the argument. Remember, in deductive reasoning, the conclusion must be true *if* the premises are true. If you take the test, you have to work through a quantitative section, so this argument is valid.

REMEMBER

When you analyze deductive reasoning arguments for the GMAT, the only way you can prove that a conclusion is true is by showing that all premises are true. The only way to prove that a deductive reasoning conclusion is false is to show that at least one of the premises is false.

Perhaps I'm just generalizing: Inductive reasoning

In deductive reasoning, you draw a specific conclusion from general premises. With *inductive reasoning*, you do just the opposite; you develop a general conclusion from specific premises or observations. Inductive reasoning differs from deductive reasoning in that the conclusion in an inductive reasoning argument could be false even if all the premises are true. With inductive reasoning, the conclusion is essentially your best guess. That's because an inductive reasoning argument relies on less complete information than deductive reasoning does. Consider this example of an inductive argument:

> Bella is a horse and has hooves. (Specific premise)
>
> Smoky is a horse and has hooves. (Specific premise)
>
> Nutmeg is a horse and has hooves. (Specific premise)
>
> Shadow is a horse and has hooves. (Specific premise)
>
> Therefore, it is likely that all horses have hooves. (General conclusion)

Because inductive reasoning derives general conclusions from specific examples, you can't come up with a statement that "must be true." The best you can say, even if all the premises are true, is that the conclusion can be or is likely to be true.

TIP

Inductive reasoning arguments come in all sorts of flavors, but the folks who create the GMAT tend to favor three types: analogy, cause and effect, and statistical. To excel on the GMAT, you want to get very familiar with these three methods of inductive reasoning:

» **Analogy arguments:** An analogy argument tries to show that two or more concepts are similar so that what holds true for one is true for the other. The strength of the argument depends on the degree of similarity between the persons, objects, or ideas being compared. For example, in drawing a conclusion about Beth's likes, you may compare her to Alex: "Alex is a student, and he likes rap music. Beth is also a student, so she probably likes rap music, too." Your argument would be stronger if you could show that Alex and Beth have other similar interests that apply to rap music, like hip-hop dancing or fashion. If, on the other hand, you show that Alex likes to go to dance clubs while Beth prefers practicing her violin at home, your original conclusion may be less likely.

» **Cause-and-effect arguments:** A cause-and-effect argument concludes that one event is the result of another. These types of arguments are strongest when the premises indicate that the alleged cause of an event is the most likely one and that no other probable causes exist. For example, after years of football watching, you may conclude the following: "Every time I wear my lucky shirt, my favorite team wins; therefore, wearing my lucky shirt causes the team to win." This example is weak because it doesn't take into consideration other, more-probable reasons (like the team's talent) for the wins.

» **Statistical arguments:** Arguments based on statistical evidence rely on numbers to reach a conclusion. These types of arguments claim that what's true for the statistical majority is also true for the individual. But because these are inductive-reasoning arguments, you can't prove that the conclusions are absolutely true. When you analyze statistical arguments on the GMAT, focus on how well the given statistics apply to the circumstances of the conclusion. For example, if you wanted people to buy clothing through your website, you might make this argument: "In a recent study of the preferences of consumers, 80 percent of shoppers surveyed spent more than six hours a day on the Internet; therefore, you'll probably prefer to buy clothes online." You'd support your conclusion if you could show that a positive correlation occurs between the amount of time people spend on the Internet and a preference for buying clothing online. If you can't demonstrate that correlation, the statistics regarding time spent on the Internet have little to do with predicting one's preference for online shopping.

To do well on the critical reasoning questions, you need to recognize premises and conclusions in arguments, determine whether the argument applies deductive or inductive reasoning (most will be inductive), and, if the argument is inductive, figure out the method the author uses to reach the conclusion. As you can induce, knowing a little about logical reasoning is essential to scoring well on the GMAT!

Thinking Inside the Box: Question Types

When you were growing up, you probably experienced social groups or cliques. These groups were often defined by shared interests, behaviors, or backgrounds. Some of the common groups included those who enjoyed sports, those who were more laid-back, those who excelled academically (that was your group!), and various other categories. These labels were helpful because they gave you clues that allowed you to better understand how to interact with someone who was a member of a particular group. For instance, you likely knew better than to pick a fight with a talented athlete, and you might have found it easy to bond with an individual who was laid-back. Well, we categorize GMAT questions for the same reason. After you figure out a critical reasoning question's type, you know just how to deal with it. Most of the critical reasoning questions you'll encounter on the GMAT fit into one of the following five categories:

>> **Strengthening or weakening arguments:** The argument presents premises and a conclusion and asks you to evaluate the answer choices to determine which one would best strengthen or weaken the author's conclusion.

>> **Drawing conclusions from premises:** The argument paragraph consists of a bunch of premises but doesn't provide a conclusion. Your job is to choose the best conclusion for the argument.

>> **Seeking assumptions:** This more-subtle type of question requires you to discover an essential premise of the argument that the author doesn't state directly.

>> **Making inferences:** For these less-common question types, you have to surmise information that isn't directly stated, usually about one of the premises rather than the conclusion.

>> **Finding the method of reasoning:** In these questions, you'll be asked to find an argument in the answer choices that uses the same method of reasoning as the original given argument.

Because each question type has a best way to handle it, recognizing what type of question you're dealing with before you try to answer it is important. That's why you read the question before you tackle the argument. You'll immediately know what you need to look for when you read the argument from the wording of the question.

Stalking Your Prey: How to Approach Each Question Type

Knowing the types of questions you'll face is valuable only if you know the specialized strategies for dealing with each one. The following sections give you the tips you need to make approaching each of the question types second nature. You get some practice questions, too, so you'll know just what to expect when you take the actual GMAT.

Strengthening or weakening arguments

Critical reasoning questions that ask you how to best support or damage an argument are some of the easiest to answer, which is a good thing because they appear the most frequently. You probably analyze ideas every day and think of evidence to attack or defend those ideas. Because you already have the skill to evaluate arguments, it doesn't take much work for you to modify that skill to fit this specific GMAT question format. This question category has two subtypes: One asks you to strengthen an argument, and the other asks you to weaken it. You'll recognize these questions because they include words that mean to strengthen or weaken (like *support*, *bolster*, or *impair*), and they almost always contain an "if true" qualifier.

Here are a couple samples of the ways the questions could be worded:

>> Which of the following statements, if true, would most seriously weaken the conclusion reached by the business owners?

>> Which of the following, if true, provides the most support for the conclusion?

WARNING

Nearly all these questions contain the words *if true*, but not all questions that have *if true* in them are strengthening- or weakening-the-argument types. To make sure an "if true" question is really a strengthening or weakening question, look for the identifying language that asks you to either strengthen or weaken the argument.

Here are three simple steps to follow when approaching strengthening- or weakening-the-argument questions:

1. Read the question carefully so you know exactly what you'll be strengthening or weakening.

In most cases, you'll be asked to strengthen or weaken the conclusion of the main argument. But in less-frequent cases, you may be asked to support or impair a different conclusion, like the view of the author's opponent.

2. Examine the argument to find the premises and conclusion and to determine what method of reasoning the author uses to reach the conclusion.

Usually the author uses inductive reasoning, so you'll need to figure out whether the argument relies on analogy, statistics, or cause and effect to arrive at the conclusion. In the following sections, we tell you what to look for in each type of reasoning.

3. Evaluate the answer choices to determine which choice best fits with the author's conclusion and method of reasoning.

Assume all the answer choices are true and then determine which one best either supports or undermines the specific conclusion addressed in the question.

WARNING

Always assume that all the answers to strengthening- or weakening-the-argument questions are true. Almost all these questions include the words *if true* in them to remind you that you're supposed to assume that each answer choice presents a true statement. Don't fall into the trap of trying to evaluate whether answer choices are true or false! Your only job is to determine whether the choices help or hurt the argument. This means that a statement like "humans do not breathe air" could be a correct answer choice even though you know it's not true. Perhaps you're supposed to weaken the conclusion that a company must pump air into an underwater habitat for humans. If humans don't breathe air, pumping in air may not be necessary. Make sure you don't dismiss any answer choices simply because you know they aren't usually true.

Analyzing analogy arguments

Analogy arguments rely on the similarity of the two persons, things, or ideas being compared. Therefore, if the author uses an analogy to reach a conclusion, answer choices that show similarities between the compared elements will support the conclusion, and choices that emphasize the differences between the elements will weaken the conclusion. Take a look at this example of an analogy argument.

EXAMPLE

Hundo is a Japanese car company, and Hundos run for many miles on a gallon of gas. Toyo is also a Japanese car company; therefore, Toyos should get good gas mileage, too.

The author's conclusion would be best supported by which of the following?

(A) All Japanese car manufacturers use the same types of engines in their cars.

(B) British cars run for as many miles on a tank of gas as Hundos do.

(C) The Toyo manufacturer focuses on producing large utility vehicles.

(D) Toyo has been manufacturing cars for more than 20 years.

(E) All Japanese cars have excellent service records.

Recognizing the premises and conclusion in this argument is simple. The author states directly that Hundo cars are Japanese and get good gas mileage and that Toyo cars are Japanese; therefore, Toyos also get good gas mileage. Your job is to find the answer that perpetuates the similarity between Hundos and Toyos.

TIP

You can generally eliminate answer choices that introduce irrelevant information, such as Choices (B), (D), and (E). The author compares Japanese cars, so what British cars do has nothing to do with the argument. The length of time that Toyo has been in business tells you nothing about how similar its cars are to Hundo's. And the question is talking about gas mileage, not service records, so don't spend too much time considering Choice (E).

Choice (C) tells you the focus of Toyo producers, but it doesn't give you any information about how that compares to Hundo, so the best answer is Choice (A). If all Japanese manufacturers supply their cars with the same engines and Hundo and Toyo are both Japanese manufacturers, it's more likely that Toyos will achieve a gas mileage similar to that experienced by Hundos.

Considering cause-and-effect arguments

Questions that ask you to evaluate arguments often apply cause-and-effect reasoning. If the argument uses cause and effect to make its point, focus on the causes. Almost always, the correct answer to a question that asks you to strengthen the conclusion is an answer choice that shows the cause mentioned is the most likely source of the effect. The best answer for a question for which you have to weaken the argument points to another probable cause of the effect. Here's how you'd apply this reasoning to a sample question.

EXAMPLE

Average hours of television viewing per American have rapidly increased for more than three decades. To fight the rise in obesity, Americans must limit their hours of television viewing.

Which of the following, if true, would most weaken the author's conclusion?

(A) A person burns more calories while watching television than while sleeping.

(B) Over the last 30 years, the number of fast-food restaurants in America has increased.

(C) Americans spend most of their television time watching sporting events rather than cooking shows.

(D) Television viewing in Japan has also increased over the past three decades.

(E) Studies show that the number of television commercials that promote junk food has risen over the past ten years.

To tackle this question, first identify the conclusion you're supposed to weaken and the premises the author states or implies to reach that conclusion. The conclusion is pretty easy to spot. The last thought of the argument is that Americans must limit their hours of television viewing to curb the rise in obesity. The author makes this judgment using the following evidence:

>> The author directly states that the number of television viewing hours has increased over the last 30 years.

>> According to the author, the number of obese Americans has also increased.

>> The author implies that television viewing causes obesity.

To weaken the argument that Americans have to reduce their television watching, you have to find the answer choice that shows that there's another cause for the rise in obesity.

You may have been tempted to select Choice (A) because it shows that television watching may be less fat-producing than another activity, sleeping. But it doesn't give you another reason for the rise in obesity. Choice (A) could be correct only if it showed that Americans were sleeping more than they were 30 years ago. It doesn't, so move on.

On the other hand, stating that during the same time period, the number of fast-food restaurants also increased introduces another possible cause of obesity and weakens the conclusion that Americans have to stop watching so much TV to get slimmer. Maybe it's the popularity of fast food that's the culprit! Choice (B) is a better answer than Choice (A), but read through all the possibilities before you commit. Choice (C) is wrong because there's nothing in the argument that suggests that the type of television Americans watch affects their obesity; nor does Choice (C) show that viewing patterns have changed over the last three decades. Choice (D) is also out because it doesn't correlate what's happening in Japan with what's happening in America. You don't know whether Japanese citizens weigh more now than they did 30 years ago, so the information in Choice (D) is useless.

If the question had asked you to strengthen the conclusion, Choice (E) would be a good option. It shows a reason that increased television watching could cause obesity. But the question asks you to weaken the conclusion, so Choice (B) is the best answer. It's the only one that shows that another cause could be to blame for the rise in obesity.

Taking a stab at statistical arguments

If you see statistics used to promote an argument, you're looking for an answer that shows whether the statistics actually relate to the topic of the conclusion. If they do, you'll strengthen the conclusion. On the other hand, an answer choice that shows the statistics are unrelated to the conclusion significantly weakens that conclusion. The following is an example of a statistical argument critical reasoning question you could find on the GMAT.

EXAMPLE

In a survey of 100 pet owners, 80 percent said that they would buy a more expensive pet food if it contained vitamin supplements. Consequently, CatCo's new premium cat food should be a top-seller.

Which of the following best demonstrates a weakness in the author's conclusion?

(A) Some brands of cat food contain more vitamin supplements than CatCo's does.

(B) CatCo sells more cat food than any of its competitors.

(C) Some of the cat owners surveyed stated that they never buy expensive brands of cat food.

(D) Ninety-five of those pet owners surveyed did not own cats.

(E) Many veterinarians have stated that vitamin supplements in cat food do not greatly increase health benefits.

Because the argument hinges on statistics, eliminate answers that don't directly address the statistical evidence. Those surveyed stated that they'd pay more for pet food with vitamin supplements, but they didn't provide information on whether the amount of vitamin supplements was important. So even though Choice (A) may entice you, it isn't the best answer because it doesn't address the statistics used in the argument. Choice (B) doesn't regard the survey results, either, and it supports the conclusion rather than weakens it. The argument has nothing at all to do with veterinarians, so Choice (E) can't be right. Only Choices (C) and (D) deal with the survey the author uses to reach the conclusion that CatCo's premium cat food will be a big seller.

TIP

You can eliminate answer choices that show an exception to the statistical evidence. Exceptions don't significantly weaken a statistical argument.

Therefore, Choice (C) is wrong and Choice (D) is the best answer because it demonstrates a weakness in the statistics the author uses to support the conclusion. The preferences of dog or bird owners isn't a good indicator of the habits of cat owners.

Dabbling in deductive-reasoning arguments

Rarely will you see a strengthen- or weaken-the-argument question that uses deductive reasoning to reach a conclusion. It's just too hard to come up with challenging answer choices for weakening deductive arguments, because the only way to weaken them is to question the accuracy of the evidence, and correct answers are pretty easy to spot. The only way to strengthen a deductive argument is to reinforce the validity of the premises, which seems sort of silly. Even though GMAT creators don't want to make things too easy for you, one or two deductive arguments may crop up. To weaken an argument with a conclusion that must be true, look for an answer choice that shows that one of the premises is untrue. For example, you may see a question with the following argument:

All horses have tails. Nutmeg is a horse. Therefore, Nutmeg must have a tail.

The only way to weaken this argument is to question one of the two premises. Answer choices like "Scientists have recently developed a breed of horses that has no tail" or "Although Nutmeg looks like a horse, she's really a donkey" would weaken the conclusion.

Delving into drawing conclusions

Another common critical reasoning question type tests your ability to draw logical conclusions (or hypotheses). The GMAT gives you a series of premises (the evidence), and you choose an answer that best concludes the information. Questions that ask you to draw conclusions from premises may be worded like this:

>> Which of the following conclusions is best supported by the preceding information?

>> Assuming the preceding statements are true, which of the following must also be true?

>> The experimental results support which of the following hypotheses?

As you read through the premises, think of a logical conclusion of your own. Then look through the answer choices to see whether one listed comes close to what you've thought up.

TIP

The key to correctly answering drawing-conclusions questions is to look for an answer choice that addresses all the information contained in the premises. Eliminate any choices that are off topic or incomplete. A conclusion that addresses only part of the information may be plausible, but it probably isn't the best answer. For example, consider the following premises:

> Five hundred healthy adults were allowed to sleep no more than five hours a night for one month. Half of the group members were allowed 90-minute naps in the afternoon each day; the remaining subjects were allowed no naps. Throughout the month, the subjects of the experiment were tested to determine the impact of sleep deprivation on their performance of standard tasks. By the end of the month, the group that was not allowed to nap suffered significant declines in their performance, while the napping group suffered more moderate declines.

The best conclusion for these premises would have to address all the following:

>> The nightly sleep deprivation of healthy adults

>> The allowance for naps for half of the study group

>> The smaller decline in performance of standard tasks for the group who took naps

Any conclusion that fails to address all three points isn't the best conclusion. For example, the statement "Sleep deprivation causes accumulating declines in performance among healthy adults" wouldn't be the best conclusion because it fails to address the effect of naps. A better conclusion would be "Napping helps reduce the declines in performance caused by nightly sleep deprivation among healthy adults."

WARNING

You'll often see more than one plausible conclusion among the answer choices. Your task is to identify the best choice. Don't fall for the trap of choosing an answer that just restates one of the premises. Answer choices that restate a premise may entice you because they echo part of the information in the argument, but the best choice must contain an element of each of the pieces of information presented in the question.

The process is pretty simple, really. Try this sample question to see for yourself.

EXAMPLE

Over the last eight years, the Federal Reserve Bank has raised the prime interest rate by a quarter-point more than ten times. The Bank raises rates when its Board of Governors fears inflation and lowers rates when the economy is slowing down.

Which of the following is the most logical conclusion for the preceding paragraph?

(A) The Federal Reserve should be replaced with regional banks that can respond more quickly to changing economic conditions.

(B) The Federal Reserve has raised the prime rate in recent years to try to control inflation.

(C) The economy has entered a prolonged recession caused by Federal Reserve policies.

(D) The monetary policy of the United States is no longer controlled by the Federal Reserve.

(E) The Federal Reserve has consistently raised the prime rate over the last several years.

You know from the language that this is a drawing-conclusions question, so you don't have to look for a conclusion in the argument. Just read through the premises and formulate a quick conclusion, something like "Because the Federal Reserve has raised interest rates many times over the last eight years, it must fear inflation."

Eliminate answer choices that aren't relevant or that contain information not presented by the premises. The argument says nothing about regional banks or the termination of the Federal Reserve's control over U.S. monetary policy, so you can disregard Choices (A) and (D). Then get rid of any choices that don't take all premises into consideration. Choice (E) just reiterates the first premise, so it's wrong. You're left with Choices (B) and (C), but Choice (C) contradicts the information in the premises. The problem says the Federal Reserve responds to the economy, not the other way around, so it'd be wrong to say the Federal Reserve causes a recession. Choice (B) is clearly the best answer. It takes into consideration the information that the Federal Reserve has raised rates and that raising rates is its response to inflation.

WARNING

Be careful to avoid relying on outside knowledge or opinions when answering drawing-conclusions questions. You may have studied the Federal Reserve Bank and have opinions about monetary policy. Choices (A), (C), and (D) reflect some possible opinions about the Federal Reserve. Don't get trapped into choosing an answer because it supports your opinion.

Spotting those sneaky assumptions

Some GMAT critical reasoning questions ask you to identify a premise that isn't there. For these types of questions, the author directly states a series of premises and provides a clear conclusion, but in getting to that conclusion, the author assumes information. Your job is to figure out what the author assumes to be true but doesn't state directly in drawing the conclusion to the argument. Seeking-assumptions questions may look like these:

>> The argument in the preceding passage depends on which of the following assumptions?

>> The conclusion reached by the author of the preceding passage is a questionable one. On which of the following assumptions did the author rely?

>> The preceding paragraph presupposes which of the following?

TIP

Words like *assume, rely, presuppose, depend on*, and their derivatives usually indicate seeking-assumptions questions. Remember, these questions ask you to look for the ideas the author relies on but doesn't state.

As you read seeking-assumptions questions, look for information that's necessary to the argument but isn't stated by the author. In these questions, the author always takes for granted something on which the entire argument depends. You just need to identify what that is. To do so effectively, choose an answer that links the existing premises to the conclusion. The assumption you're seeking always bears directly on the conclusion and ties in with one or more premises, often with the last premise. Therefore, the best answer often contains information from both the last premise and the conclusion.

EXAMPLE

Women receive fewer speeding tickets than men do. Women also have lower car insurance rates. It is clear that women are better drivers than men.

The preceding conclusion is based on which of the following assumptions?

 I. Men and women drive cars equal distances and with equal frequency.

 II. Having lower car insurance rates indicates that one is a better driver than those who have higher rates.

 III. Speeding tickets are equally awarded for violations without any gender bias on the part of police officers.

(A) I only

(B) III only

(C) I and III only

(D) II and III only

(E) I, II, and III

As always, read the question first. Because it references assumptions, we bet you figured out pretty quickly that it's a seeking-assumptions question.

Next, read through the argument and try to figure out the assumption or assumptions the author makes in reaching the conclusion that women are better drivers. The author moves from the premises to the conclusion pretty quickly and assumes that fewer speeding tickets and lower car insurance rates indicate better driving skills. The author also assumes that men and women have equal driving experiences. Use this information to examine each of your options.

Look at Statement I first. It fits with your second observation that men and women experience equal driving situations, so eliminate any answer choices that *don't* include Statement I. This means that you can get rid of Choices (B) and (D), which leaves you with Choices (A), (C), and (E).

TIP

Before you continue reading through your options, examine the remaining answer choices. You'll see that it's best to examine Statement II next, because if it's true, you won't even have to read Statement III; you'll know the answer is Choice (E). You have to read Statement III only if you determine that Statement II isn't an assumption. (For more about strategies for answering Roman numeral questions, see Chapter 2.)

The information in Statement II links the author's last premise, that women have lower insurance rates, to the conclusion that women are better drivers. Thus, Statement II is also correct. You can eliminate Choices (A) and (C), and by process of elimination, the answer must be Choice (E). If you read through Statement III, you'll confirm that it, too, is an assumption the author makes about men and women having an equal playing field in the driving game.

TIP

If you find seeking-assumption questions to be tricky, try arguing the opposite position. For example, in the sample question, you could've taken the opposing view, that men are better drivers. This means you'll be looking for ways to undermine the conclusion. If you assume the premises to be true, the best way to attack the conclusion is to show that the author assumes things that aren't true. For example, you may argue that men have more accidents because they drive more, they get more tickets because police are less forgiving with male speeders, and they have higher car insurance rates because they drive more-expensive cars. Those counterarguments expose the author's assumptions!

Using your noggin to make inferences

Critical reasoning inference questions ask you to make an inference (using inductive reasoning) based on the argument in the passage. Making-inferences questions are pretty easy to recognize because they usually include the word *infer*, such as the following examples:

>> Which of the following statements can be correctly inferred from the preceding passage?

>> Which of the following can be inferred from the preceding statements?

The key to answering these questions correctly is to know that they usually ask you to make an inference about one of the premises in the argument rather than about the entire argument or the conclusion. Because these questions usually deal with the premises and not the conclusion, you should choose an answer that makes a plausible inference about one or more of the premises. Like the correct answer choices for the drawing-conclusions questions, the best answers to this type of question don't go beyond the scope of the information provided in the paragraph. Here's what one looks like.

EXAMPLE

The highest-rated television shows do not always command the most advertising dollars. Ads that run during shows with lower overall ratings are often more expensive because the audience for those shows includes a high proportion of males between the ages of 19 and 34. Therefore, ads that run during sporting events are often more expensive than ads running during other types of programs.

Which of the following can properly be inferred from the preceding passage?

(A) Advertisers have done little research into the typical consumer and are not using their advertising dollars wisely.

(B) Sports programs have higher overall ratings than prime-time network programs.

(C) Advertisers believe males between the ages of 19 and 34 are more likely to be influenced by advertisers than are other categories of viewers.

(D) Advertising executives prefer sports programs and assume that other Americans do as well.

(E) Ads that run during the biggest sporting events are the most expensive of all ads.

You know you're dealing with an inference question before you read through the argument because you've read the question first and it contains the word *inferred*. Focus on the premises of the argument as you read it. Then look through the answer choices and eliminate any that don't address one of the premises or that present inferences that require additional information.

The argument says nothing about advertising research or whether the particular advertising practice is wise, so you can eliminate Choice (A) immediately. You're stretching beyond the scope of the information if you infer that advertisers are unwise. Likewise, Choice (D) mentions the preferences and assumptions of advertisers, but none of the premises discuss advertisers, so you can get rid of Choice (D). The inference in Choice (E) relates to the conclusion rather than any of the premises, so you can probably eliminate it right away. Furthermore, just because sporting events ads are "often more expensive" than other ads doesn't necessarily mean that they're always the most expensive. This leaves you with Choices (B) and (C).

Choice (B) contradicts information in the argument. The author implies that some sporting events have lower overall ratings even though they have higher advertising rates. You're left with Choice (C). You need an explanation for the information in the second sentence that states that advertising is often more expensive for lower-rated shows viewed by males who are between 19 and 34 years old. This practice would be logical only if males of these ages were more susceptible to advertising than other groups. It makes sense that Choice (C) is the correct answer.

WARNING

Remember to check your outside knowledge about the critical reasoning subjects at the door! You may know that Super Bowl ads are the most-expensive ads, which may tempt you to pick Choice (E). Using your own knowledge rather than what's expressly stated in the test questions will cause you to miss questions that someone with less knowledge may answer correctly.

Pondering the paradox

A few critical reasoning questions test your ability to resolve paradoxes or apparent inconsistencies. They present a potential conflict and ask you to choose the answer that contains the piece of information that helps explain why the apparent conflict is not in fact a conflict at all.

The following list includes some examples of questions that test apparent inconsistencies:

>> Which of the following, if true, most helps to resolve the apparent paradox?

>> Which of the following, if true, most helps to explain the apparent inconsistency in the school's policy?

>> Which of the following, if true, explains why the birds do not fly away from their predators?

>> Which of the following, if true, most helps to resolve the apparent conflict described above?

>> Which of the following, if true, most helps to reconcile the experts' belief with the apparently contrary evidence described above?

You answer these questions by reading the passage to figure out which facts seem to be at odds. Then try to come up with an idea that would reconcile the inconsistency and make the paradox disappear. You probably won't be able to envision the exact answer before reading the choices, but you can come up with something in the ballpark.

Here's an example of a question that asks you to resolve an apparent inconsistency.

EXAMPLE

Skydiving experts have noted that improvements in gear and training techniques have led to fewer fatalities than occurred in the sport's earlier years. However, fatalities among very experienced skydivers, who use the most modern gear equipped with a device that automatically opens the reserve parachute if the skydiver has not opened the main parachute by a certain altitude, have held steady for the last 12 years.

Which one of the following, if true, most helps to resolve the apparent inconsistency in this passage?

(A) Most skydivers prefer not to buy improved gear because it costs too much.

(B) Experienced skydivers favor tiny parachutes that fly at high velocities and that must be landed precisely, which makes them more likely to hit the ground at an uncontrolled high speed, even under an open parachute.

(C) Not all jumpers choose to use the device that automatically opens their reserve parachute for them.

(D) The U.S. Parachute Association's recommended minimum opening altitude for reserve parachutes has increased over the last 12 years.

(E) Most inexperienced skydivers rent gear from drop zones instead of owning their own gear.

Read the question. The passage contains an apparent inconsistency. Despite advancements in safety, skydiving fatalities have not decreased among experienced skydivers. This fact is surprising because experienced skydivers use modern gear that guarantees that their parachutes will open. An open parachute must not be the only guarantee of a safe landing. If experienced skydivers are dying despite open parachutes, their fatalities must result from another cause. Snipers aren't picking them off from the ground, so they must be dying on landing. Perhaps experienced skydivers land differently from novices. See what the answer choices have to offer.

» Choice (A) doesn't explain the specific paradox related to the fates of experienced skydivers. The buying habits of other, less experienced skydivers are irrelevant.

» Choice (B) does explain the results; experienced skydivers land differently and more dangerously than novices do, which could explain why the safer parachutes aren't leading to fewer deaths.

» Choice (C) is also irrelevant because it doesn't pertain specifically to the experienced skydivers who are at the heart of the paradox.

» Choice (D) makes the inconsistency even more apparent. If the reserve parachutes activate at higher altitudes, fewer fatalities should result.

» Choice (E) doesn't explain anything about fatalities. It may explain why inexperienced and experienced skydivers use different gear, but it doesn't explain why experienced skydivers die despite having good, high-tech, perfectly functioning equipment.

Choice (B) is the correct answer.

Making your way through method-of-reasoning questions

Method-of-reasoning questions are the rarest form of GMAT critical reasoning question types. This type of question either directly asks you what type of reasoning the author uses to make an argument or, more often, asks you to choose an answer that uses the same method of reasoning as the argument. You may see method-of-reasoning questions phrased like these:

» Which of the following employs the same method of reasoning as the preceding argument?

» The author's point is made by which method of reasoning?

» David's argument is similar to Ari's in which of the following ways?

The two types of method-of-reasoning questions may seem different, but each of them asks you to do the same thing: to recognize the type of reasoning used in the argument.

REMEMBER

For the purposes of the GMAT, the methods of reasoning are as follows:

» Deductive, which is reaching a specific conclusion from general premises

» Inductive, which is drawing a general conclusion from specific premises and includes the following methods:

- Analogy, which shows that one thing is sufficiently similar to another thing such that what holds true for one is true for the other

- Cause and effect, which shows that one event resulted from another

- Statistics, which uses population samples (surveys) to reach conclusions about the population as a whole

Questions that ask you to specifically choose what kind of reasoning the author uses are straightforward, so we focus on the other type of question, which asks you to choose an answer that mimics the reasoning method of the given argument. When you know you're dealing with this type of question, you just need to focus on the way the author makes the argument to make sure you choose an answer that follows the logic most exactly.

WARNING

Don't choose an answer just because it deals with the same subject matter as the given argument. These choices are often traps to lure you away from the answer that more exactly duplicates the author's logic but addresses another topic.

It doesn't matter whether the argument makes sense. If the given argument isn't logical, pick an answer choice that isn't logical in the same way.

TIP

You may focus on the method of reasoning better if you substitute letters for ideas in the argument. For example, say you're presented with this argument: "Balloons that contain helium float. Jerry's balloon doesn't float, so it contains oxygen rather than helium." You could state this logic with letters like this: "All A (helium balloons) are B (floaters). C (Jerry's balloon) isn't B (a floater), so C isn't A." Then you can apply that formula to your answer choices to see which one matches best.

Some of the reasoning methods may be as obscure as the one in this sample question.

EXAMPLE

A teacher told the students in class, "The information that you read in your history book is correct because I chose the history book and I will be creating the test and assigning your grades."

The reasoning in which of the following statements most closely resembles that of the preceding argument?

(A) The decisions made by the Supreme Court are just because the Court has the authority to administer justice.

(B) The people who have fame are famous because they deserve to be famous.

(C) Those who play sports get better grades because of the link between the health of the body and the health of the mind.

(D) Because my favorite teacher chooses to drive this kind of car, I should as well.

(E) Of 100 professors surveyed, 99 agree with the conclusions reached by the scientist in his paper on global warming.

Reading the question first tells you that you'll have to analyze the way the author reaches the conclusion in the argument. As you read, you find that this illogical cause-and-effect argument states that information is correct because someone in a position of authority (the teacher) says so, so you need to find an equally illogical argument based on power and authority.

Because this is a cause-and-effect argument, you can eliminate any choices that don't use cause and effect to reach a conclusion. All choices contain an element of cause and effect except Choice (D), which presumes an analogy between a favorite teacher and the writer, and Choice (E), which uses statistical evidence. (Note that just because Choice [D] also concerns a teacher doesn't automatically make it the correct answer.) Disregard Choices (D) and (E) and examine the other three choices.

Among Choices (A), (B), and (C), the only choice that uses power to justify a cause-and-effect relationship is Choice (A). Choice (B) is faulty because it uses circular reasoning, which means it uses its conclusion as a premise, instead of using power to advance its position. Choice (C) doesn't work because its logic isn't necessarily faulty. Instead, it relies on a logical correlation between physical health and intellectual prowess. Therefore, Choice (A) is the answer that most nearly matches the kind of reasoning in the original argument.

Critical Reasoning Practice Questions and Answer Explanations

With practice, you'll probably find that critical reasoning questions become some of the easiest question types to master in the GMAT verbal section. To master your approach, work through these practice questions and read through the answer explanations.

Critical reasoning practice questions

This set of 11 critical reasoning practice questions offers a preview of what to expect from this verbal reasoning question type, which assesses your ability to analyze arguments. To mimic the approximate amount of time you'll have to answer critical reasoning questions on the actual exam, try to answer these 11 questions in about 21.5 minutes. Answer each question based on the passage that precedes it, and choose the best answer from the five answer choices provided.

REMEMBER

Don't expect to see letters before the answer choices on the computerized GMAT. Each answer will have a radio button next to it that you select by clicking on it. We've put letters next to the answer choices in this practice section to make it easier to discuss the choices in the explanations that follow the questions.

1. It seems that Americans are smarter than they were 50 years ago. Many more Americans are attending college now than in the past, and the typical entry-level job in business now requires a college degree.

   Which of the following statements, if true, would most seriously weaken the argument in the preceding paragraph?

   (A) High school courses are more rigorous now than they were in the past.

   (B) Tuition at colleges and universities has more than tripled in the past 25 years.

   (C) High school class sizes have gotten smaller, and computers have introduced a more individualized curriculum.

   (D) Businesses are not requiring as high a level of writing or math skills as they did in past decades.

   (E) Many of the skills and concepts taught in high school 50 years ago are now taught in college.

   Questions 2 and 3 are based on the following argument.

   Rachel: The legal drinking age in America should remain at 21, because teens have not yet reached an age where they are able to consume alcohol responsibly. Additionally, the actions of 18-year-olds are more likely to be imitated by teens aged 15 to 17 than are the actions of those who are significantly older, so lowering the drinking age to 18 would also result in increased alcohol consumption by younger teens trying to emulate the actions of their older peers.

   Mackenzie: The drinking age in America should be lowered to 18, because keeping it at 21 has not only failed to curb teen drinking but has encouraged those teens who *do* drink to do so in private, uncontrolled environments where they are more prone to life-endangering behavior. Many youths in European countries drink from an early age, and those countries have substantially fewer alcohol-related problems than we do in America.

2. Which of the following, if true, would most significantly weaken Mackenzie's argument?

   (A) The idea that Europeans and other nations with low or no minimum drinking ages do not have alcohol-related problems is a myth.

   (B) If Americans are allowed to give their lives for this country at age 18, then they should be considered old enough to make the proper decision as to what to put in their bodies.

   (C) More American high school students drink now than they did decades ago, when the drinking age was lower.

   (D) In European culture, youths are taught at an early age that it is acceptable to either abstain from alcohol entirely or drink in moderation and that it is never acceptable for them to abuse alcohol, regardless of their age.

   (E) European youths are just as likely as American youths to drink in private, uncontrolled environments.

3. Rachel's argument is based on which of the following assumptions?

   (A) Those who have reached the age of 21 are able to consume alcohol more responsibly than those who are 18.

   (B) When European teenagers consume alcohol, they do so in public, controlled environments.

   (C) Teens who are 15 to 17 years old are more impressionable than those who are aged 18 or older.

   (D) The impressionability of one's actions on others should not be a consideration when deciding the legal age to consume alcohol.

   (E) Consuming alcohol in private, uncontrolled environments is not more dangerous than consuming alcohol in more public environments, such as bars or restaurants.

4. A recent census of all American females revealed that the current average age that females in America marry is 27. The average age that females have their first child is also 27. According to a census taken 20 years ago, the average ages that females married and had their first child were 23 and 25 years, respectively.

   If the information recorded in the two censuses is true, which of the following must also be true about American females?

   (A) Currently, more females are having their first child before they marry than they did 20 years ago.

   (B) On average, females are currently waiting longer to have their first child than they did 20 years ago.

   (C) Females today are more likely to complete their education before getting married and having children than they were 20 years ago.

   (D) On average, females had larger families 20 years ago than they have today.

   (E) Twenty years ago, most females waited at least two years after they were married to have their first child.

5. Continuous technological advances are critical to many types of business, because they allow machines to do the work previously done by humans — and they don't have to be compensated. Banking executives are always looking for ways to cut costs, so they support a heavy emphasis on automated technology in the workplace. Yet what customers look for most in their banks is to be recognized by their teller and feel a sense of familiarity and friendliness upon entering, so the reliance of banks on machines should be minimized, rather than exacerbated.

Which of the following best outlines the main idea of the argument?

(A) Banks should reduce their dependence on technology.

(B) Bank patrons desire personal attention.

(C) Machines can work faster than humans.

(D) Bank executives are a greedy bunch.

(E) Bank automation is inevitable.

6. A school board candidate has indicated that cheating through the use of cellphones in the classroom is on the rise this year and has proposed a ban on cellphones in schools altogether. School officials cite only a marginal increase in the number of students who cheat this year in comparison to the last two years, so this is just a ploy to make voters think a quality education is a top priority.

Which of the following, if true, best strengthens the conclusion of the preceding argument?

(A) The school board candidate has continuously voted down proposals to increase the budget for area schools.

(B) The school board candidate has continuously voted in favor of budget increases for area schools.

(C) This year, schools in the district have smaller class sizes and better student/teacher ratios than they have had in past years.

(D) The ratio of teachers to number of students has decreased significantly over the past several years because of a growth in number of students district-wide without a concomitant rise in the number of teachers to accommodate the increase.

(E) The school board candidate has a daughter who attends a school in the district, and the candidate does not want the daughter to own a cellphone.

7. Springfield is the first city to ban fast-food advertisements marketed specifically toward children. Although eating fast food has been linked to weight gain, banning these advertisements will do little to curb childhood obesity, and it should be the job of the parent, not the government, to tell children what to eat.

The argument would be most weakened if which of the following were true?

(A) Families are increasingly relying on the fast-food industry for financial reasons and will continue to frequent these establishments on their own terms, regardless of their children's preferences.

(B) Studies indicate that, generally speaking, adults tend to be more influenced by advertising than children.

(C) If children learn that adults are trying to limit their fast-food intake, they will want to consume fast food even more.

(D) Those opposed to fast-food marketing geared toward children are welcome to buy airtime for their cause, too.

(E) Watching an advertisement has been shown to increase one's desires for a product, particularly when the product is a food item.

8. Patients who feel they have a good relationship with their doctors generally show more improvement in their health than those who lack a connection with their doctors. Patients who like their doctors show improved emotional well-being, are less anxious about their symptoms, and are more likely to follow doctors' advice.

Which one of the following, if true, would provide the most support for the argument?

(A) Patients are more likely to take legal action against a doctor for malpractice if they believe that the doctor failed to establish a connection with them during their office visits.

(B) Recently, medical schools and health insurers have taken measures to improve doctor-patient communication.

(C) Doctors who work in stressful environments are much less likely to take the time to connect with patients than doctors in more relaxed settings.

(D) The average physician spends about 15 minutes with each patient during routine office visits.

(E) A large number of studies have confirmed that the more anxious patients are, the more protracted their recovery from a medical condition is.

9. The legislature is considering a law banning the use of cellphones by people who are driving a moving car. Drivers texting and talking while driving are distracted by their phone conversations and can't give their full attention to driving their vehicles. Banning the use of cellphones by drivers will make the roads safer.

The argument depends on assuming which one of the following?

(A) A study by a sociologist has shown that the use of cellphones is occasionally a contributing factor in traffic accidents.

(B) The proper role of the legislature is to enact laws that protect the safety of drivers and passengers in automobiles.

(C) Drivers who hold their cellphones in their hands are more distracted than drivers who use a hands-free headset or speakerphone while driving.

(D) Because drivers talking and texting on cellphones are distracted, they are more prone to getting into accidents.

(E) Many drivers engage in behavior that distracts them from their driving, such as eating, adjusting the radio, reading maps, and talking on cellphones.

10. Many Americans do not take all the vacation time to which they are entitled. There are several reasons for this: They feel that they are indispensable at work, they fear the resentment of co-workers, or they dread discovering that their workplaces can actually function perfectly well without them. This is a mistake; vacation time gives workers a chance to rest, recover, and gain perspective that in turn can lead to more creativity and better performance at work.

The claim that many Americans don't take all the vacation time to which they are entitled plays which one of the following roles in the argument?

(A) It is a recommendation of a policy that the American workplace should implement.

(B) It is evidence of the author's claim that vacation time gives workers a chance to rest.

(C) It is the conclusion of the argument.

(D) It is a statement of a principle that the author wishes all people would observe.

(E) It is a statement of fact about which the author expresses an opinion.

11. A large Southern state university has changed its teaching practices. Formerly, instructors without PhDs taught most introductory courses; now professors with PhDs will teach all introductory classes. That means the average class size will increase from 44 students per class to 600 per class, but overall the students' learning experience should improve.

Which one of the following is an assumption required by this argument?

(A) Requiring professors with PhDs to teach all introductory classes will mean that the university must hire more faculty with doctorates.

(B) Students tend to participate in smaller classes more than they do in large lectures, even when the lectures are supplemented by weekly discussion sections.

(C) Major private universities already have implemented a format in which professors with PhDs teach all introductory classes as large lectures.

(D) A class taught by a PhD, even in a lecture format with hundreds of students, is a better learning environment than a smaller class taught by an instructor without a PhD.

(E) Services that rank colleges and universities usually consider the percentage of classes taught by PhDs when computing rank.

Answer Explanations

1. **E.** Read the question first so you know what to focus on in the passage. Because this question asks you to weaken the argument, you know you need to figure out what the conclusion is and what kind of reasoning the author uses in moving from the premises to the conclusion.

   When you examine the argument, you may notice that the conclusion actually comes first. The author concludes that Americans are smarter than they were 50 years ago and does so by contrasting current college participation and entry-level job requirements with those of the past. The method of reasoning is similar to analogy, except instead of showing similarities between Americans now and 50 years ago, the author shows the differences. To weaken the conclusion that Americans are smarter today, you need to find the answer choice that shows that things really aren't all that different today than they were 50 years ago.

   First, eliminate answer choices with irrelevant information. Neither college tuition rates nor class size and curriculum have anything to do with levels of intelligence, so Choices (B) and (C) are wrong. Plus, you're looking for an answer that shows that things aren't much different between now and yesterday, and Choices (B) and (C) accentuate the difference.

   Then, get rid of any answer that tends to strengthen rather than weaken the conclusion that Americans are smarter. More-difficult high school courses seem to indicate that Americans may indeed be smarter, so disregard Choice (A). This leaves you with Choices (D) and (E), and your job is to choose the one that shows that now and then aren't all that different. Not only does Choice (D) demonstrate a difference between the eras, but it also refutes the premise that businesses are looking for the higher skill levels of a college education.

   The correct answer must be Choice (E). If skills that were part of the high school curriculum 50 years ago are now offered in college, actual education hasn't changed all that much from then to now. Americans must now attend college to acquire the high school skills of earlier times, and businesses need to require college degrees to make sure their employees have the same skills that high school students had in the past. If the skill levels are the same, Americans aren't really any smarter than they were 50 years ago.

   REMEMBER

   You must know precisely what point a paragraph is arguing before you can strengthen or weaken that argument. Take the time to understand the premises, conclusion, and method of reasoning so you can quickly eliminate answer choices and accurately select the best answer. When you really understand the argument, attacking or defending it is fairly easy.

2. **E.** First, a quick review of Mackenzie's argument indicates that she is in *favor* of lowering the drinking age, not opposed, so you can quickly eliminate any answer choices that include support for doing so, such as Choices (B) and (C), because those choices actually strengthen Mackenzie's argument.

   Now, determine which of the remaining options *best* weakens Mackenzie's argument that the legal drinking age should be lowered. The remaining answers focus on Mackenzie's premise that because European countries have lower drinking ages and fewer problems with alcohol, lowering the drinking age in America would likewise lead to fewer alcohol-related problems. She makes her argument based on an analogy between Europe and America, so weaken her contention by showing that Europe and America are substantially similar in their approach to teenage drinking. It may sound surprising to weaken an analogy with a similarity, but in this case Mackenzie's analogy seeks to liken the alleged present state of affairs in Europe to the supposed future state of affairs in America if the American drinking age is lowered. Showing a similarity between present-day Europe and present-day America can therefore weaken the argument that a change in the drinking age will reduce alcohol-related problems in America.

Mackenzie doesn't say that European countries have *no* alcohol-related problems, just that there are fewer, so Choice (A) is irrelevant to her argument. Choice (D) provides a concrete difference between European and American culture that reveals why European teens tend to be more responsible than American teens when it comes to alcohol consumption, so this is an answer choice that seems to lend support to Mackenzie's argument that a lower drinking age won't result in less-responsible drinking among American teens. On the other hand, Choice (E) reveals a similarity between European and American youth, which best serves to weaken Mackenzie's analogy between the lower drinking age in Europe and the proposed lower drinking age in America. If both European and American youths drink in private, uncontrolled environments despite the difference in the drinking ages of the two cultures, it's unlikely that changing the drinking age in America will affect the behavior that Mackenzie claims is dangerous (drinking in private). Choice (E) is correct.

3. **A.** Rachel argues for retaining the current legal drinking age of 21. She bases her conclusion on the premises that younger drinkers are more likely to influence the behavior of 15- to 17-year-olds and that teens haven't reached an age where they can drink alcohol responsibly.

To find the correct answer to questions that ask for an assumption, look for the answer choice that links one or more of the premises to the conclusion. Eliminate answer choices that don't relate to at least one of the premises of the argument.

Choices (B) and (E) relate to one of Mackenzie's premises, so it's unlikely that they would reveal one of Rachel's assumptions. Cross out those two answers on your noteboard.

You can also check off Choice (D) because it contradicts Rachel's premise that the effect an 18-year-old's alcohol consumption can have on younger peers is an important consideration in determining the legal drinking age. It's also unlikely that Choice (C) is correct because Rachel doesn't make comparisons regarding the impressionability of teens based on their ages. Her premise is that younger teens are more likely to be influenced by 18-year-olds than 21-year-olds. Furthermore, Choice (C) doesn't link one of Rachel's premises to her conclusion in the way that Choice (A) does.

If Rachel concludes that the legal drinking age must remain at 21 because younger drinkers don't consume alcohol responsibly, she must think that 21-year-olds have achieved some level of responsibility that's greater than those who are younger. Choice (A) links the relevance of one of Rachel's premises (a lower level of responsible drinking) to her conclusion that people who are younger than 21 shouldn't be able to legally consume alcohol. So the correct answer is Choice (A).

4. **B.** This question asks you to come up with a conclusion based on the information in the paragraph.

Notice that the question asks you for what *must* be true rather than what *could* be true. So you can cross out any answers that aren't absolutely true given the data in the paragraph.

All you know from the paragraph is the average marrying age for females today and 20 years ago and the average age that females have their first child today compared to 20 years ago. The paragraph says nothing about the number of children females have or had, so you can easily wipe Choice (D) out of contention. Furthermore, the paragraph provides no explanation for why the data has changed over the years, so you can't know the reason that the average age has increased. So Choice (C) can't be right.

Don't choose an answer based on an assumption or your own experience. The paragraph merely reports data instead of commenting on it, and it treats the age of marrying and having one's first child as two separate statistics. You can't make assumptions about how the two sets of data are related.

That means that Choice (A) doesn't have to be true. Just because the average age for marrying and having a first child are currently the same doesn't mean that more American females are having their first child before they marry. For example, the increased marrying age could be the result of females who marry when they're older and have no children. Eliminate Choice (E) for the same reason. You can't assume from these limited statistics that the females who are 23 when they marry are the ones who are having their first child at 25. There are too many other variables in the population.

The only thing you know for sure is that, because the average age for having a first child has risen over the last 20 years, on average, females are having their first child at a later age than they did 20 years ago. Choice (B) is the only answer that must be true.

5. **A.** Asking for the main point of an argument is another sneaky way of getting you to pick out the conclusion. This paragraph makes it easy for you because the conclusion follows the *so* in the last sentence: Banks should rely less on machines. The first sentence of the argument equates machines with technological advances, which means that you can say that the main point is that banks should rely less on technology, Choice (A).

Choices (C), (D), and (E) require you to make assumptions that aren't supported by the argument. Because you read newspaper headlines, you may think that Choice (D)'s assertion about the avarice of bank executives is a foregone conclusion, but, alas, it isn't mentioned in the argument. (You should also have been alerted by the debatable word *inevitable* in Choice [E].) The paragraph does suggest that bank patrons want personal attention (Choice [B]), but this statement is a premise rather than the conclusion. So the correct answer is Choice (A).

6. **D.** The first step to answering any question that asks you to strengthen a conclusion is to figure out exactly what that conclusion is. In this case, the paragraph argues that the candidate's proposal to ban cellphones in schools is a campaign strategy to make voters think that the candidate cares about the quality of education. The argument is based on the statistic that the increase in the number of students who cheat has been insignificant. To support the author's argument, find the answer that best supports the contention that cheating really hasn't increased all that much.

Eliminate choices that don't pertain to the author's argument. You can disregard Choices (A) and (B). The argument is concerned with the implications surrounding a cellphone ban, not the candidate's position on a budget increase. You're assuming too much (or relying on your own opinion) to make a determination of whether the candidate's vote for or against a budget increase has anything to do with education quality.

Choice (E) indicates that a reason other than cheating may be the reason the candidate wishes to impose the cellphone ban, but that absurd personal reason doesn't support the author's argument that the candidate is proposing the ban for political reasons.

The answer must be either Choice (C) or Choice (D). Both deal with the number of actual students in the district, so they may reflect on the validity of the candidate's claim that cheating has increased and the author's claim that it hasn't. Having smaller class sizes tells you nothing about the overall number of students. The district could have hired more teachers to accommodate the same number of students. The only answer that relates to the cheating statistic is Choice (D). The marginal increase in cheating could be due to an increase in number of students rather than an increase in cellphone cheating, which supports the author's argument that the candidate's reason for banning cellphone use is unfounded.

7. **E.** The implication is that the advertising ban is designed to curb childhood obesity. The author states that this ban won't work, which suggests that the author thinks that the fast-food advertisements don't cause childhood obesity. To weaken this argument, show that the advertisements do indeed lead to obesity. If it's been proven that watching an ad increases one's desire for something, then banning the ads *would* reduce the desire for fast food that produces weight gain in children. Choice (E) weakens the author's argument by showing that the advertisement ban will indeed curb childhood obesity. Choice (A) seems to strengthen the author's argument, and Choices (B), (C), and (D) deal with tangents that don't relate to whether the advertisement would be effective in curbing childhood obesity. The correct answer is Choice (E).

8. **E.** The argument claims that patients do better when they feel a connection to their doctors; the premises are three factors that result from liking one's doctor. To support this argument, you need to find statements that link those factors with health improvements. Choice (A) doesn't help. It illustrates the danger of people not liking their doctors but doesn't prove the point that patients who like their doctors are healthier. Choice (B) may suggest that improving doctor-patient communication is desirable, but it doesn't specifically link improved communication to improved patient health. Choice (C) presents a reason for poor doctor-patient communication but doesn't show how that affects patient health. Choice (D) provides evidence of how the average doctor doesn't have a good relationship with patients, but it doesn't show the results of good doctor-patient rapport. Choice (E) does support the conclusion by linking one effect of liking a doctor (less anxiety) to a greater improvement in health. Choice (E) is correct.

9. **D.** You're looking for an assumption. Assumptions connect the premises to the conclusion. The conclusion that if drivers can't use cellphones, the roads will be safer is based on the evidence that drivers on phones are distracted; the author assumes that distracted drivers are unsafe drivers. (Yes, that's obvious, but the author doesn't explicitly say what the connection is, so it's an assumption.) Choice (A) is tricky and could be a possible answer if you were asked to support the legislator's argument, but information about the results of a specific cellphone use study is way too specific to be the legislator's assumption. Assumptions are rarely based on particular statistical data. See whether you can find a better answer. Choice (B) is wrong; the author probably does assume that this is the legislature's job, but this assumption isn't necessary to the specific argument connecting distraction and road safety. Choice (C) doesn't work; the author isn't concerned with distinctions among types of cellphones users. Choice (D) is something the author assumes — it explains the connection between cellphones and distracted drivers and dangerous roads. Choice (E) contains mostly irrelevant details about other behaviors, and to the extent it addresses drivers on cellphones, it just repeats evidence the argument already explicitly states. Choice (D) is the best answer.

10. **E.** The claim in the question is a statement of fact in the first sentence that the author explores more thoroughly, concluding with the statement that it's a mistake. The author is not suggesting that it's a good thing, so Choices (A) and (D) are wrong. It's not evidence, so Choice (B) is wrong. The actual conclusion is that refraining from taking vacation is a mistake, so Choice (C) is wrong. The claim is a statement of fact that provides the background information for the author's opinion about what Americans should do with their vacation time, so Choice (E) is correct.

11. **D.** The author concludes that having classes taught by PhDs instead of instructors improves students' learning experience. This assumption suggests that PhDs, even in very large classes, are somehow better at teaching than instructors in smaller ones. Choice (A) isn't the author's assumption. In fact, the reference to increased class sizes suggests that the university won't be hiring more faculty. Choice (B) contradicts the author's conclusion by suggesting that student participation is a good thing. Choice (C) is interesting information but isn't essential to the conclusion about the practices of the particular Southern state university in the argument, especially because it doesn't mention students' learning experiences. Choice (D) looks like the right answer. The author's belief in the superiority of a class taught by a PhD is evident, which explains the conclusion that the change would benefit students. Choice (E) explains why the university may want to increase classes taught by PhDs, but it doesn't explain how that would benefit students. Choice (D) is correct.

IN THIS CHAPTER

» Practicing reading comprehension
and critical reasoning questions

» Finding out why right answers
are right and wrong answers are
wrong

Chapter **9**

Bringing It Together: A Mini Practice Verbal Section

L ike the real GMAT verbal section, the mini practice test in this chapter presents a mixture of the two types of verbal questions. It contains nine reading comprehension questions and nine critical reasoning questions. The total of 18 questions makes this mini verbal test a little shorter than the 23-question GMAT verbal section. To get more practice, take the full-length practice exams included with this book.

Although we can't simulate a computer in this book, don't let that deter you. Just mark the answers right in the book, and try not to look at the answer key until *after* you've answered the questions. We designate each answer choice with a letter to make it easier to reference it in the answer explanations, but on the actual computerized exam, you'll simply click the radio button that precedes each answer choice to mark your answer.

TIP

To best mimic the computer experience during this mini practice test, answer each question in sequence and don't go back and change any of your answers after you've moved on to the next question. At the actual exam, you won't have a test booklet to write in, so try not to write anything except your answers on the pages of this book. To keep your notes and record eliminated answers, use scratch paper to simulate the noteboard you'll use on test day.

TIP

Take the time to read through the answer explanations at the end of the chapter, even for the questions you get right. The explanations apply the techniques covered in chapters 7 and 8 of this book and show you why a certain answer is a better choice than the others.

Working Through Verbal Reasoning Practice Questions

If you're the competitive type and want to subject yourself to a timed test, give yourself about 35 minutes to complete the 18 questions in this section.

REMEMBER

Here's a quick review of the directions for the two types of verbal reasoning questions that appear in this mini practice test (and on the real GMAT):

>> **Reading comprehension questions:** Choose the best answer to every question based on what the passage states directly or indirectly.

>> **Critical reasoning questions:** Pick the answer choice that best answers the question about the argument provided.

1. A study of energy consumption revealed that homeowners living within 100 miles of the Gulf of Mexico used less energy from November 1 to April 30 than did homeowners in any other region of the United States. The same study found that from May 1 to October 31, those same homeowners used more energy than any other homeowners.

   Which of the following, if true, would most contribute to an explanation of the facts above?

   (A) People who own homes near the Gulf of Mexico often own second homes in cooler locations, where they spend the summers.

   (B) Air conditioning a home is a more energy-efficient process than heating a similarly sized home.

   (C) Homes near the Gulf of Mexico require very little heating during the warm winters, but air conditioners must run longer in the summer to cool the warm, humid air.

   (D) The average daily temperature is lower year-round near the Gulf of Mexico than in other areas of the United States.

   (E) Because of the large number of refineries located in the Gulf region, the price of energy there is less than in any other area of the country.

2. A conservation group is trying to convince Americans that the return of gray wolves to the northern United States is a positive development. Introduction of the wolf faces significant opposition because of the wolf's reputation as a killer of people and livestock. So that the wolf will be more acceptable to average Americans, the conservation group wants to dispel the myth that the wolf is a vicious killer.

   Which of the following, if true, would most weaken the opposition's claim?

   (A) Wolves are necessary for a healthy population of white-tailed deer because wolves kill the weaker animals and limit the population to sustainable numbers.

   (B) In a confrontation, black bears are much more dangerous to humans than wolves are.

   (C) Wolves are superb hunters, operating in packs to track down their prey and kill it.

   (D) There has never been a documented case of a wolf killing a human in the 500-year recorded history of North America.

   (E) Wolves occasionally take livestock because domestic animals are not equipped to protect themselves the way wild animals are.

Questions 3–6 refer to the following passage.

This passage is excerpted from *The Big Splat, or How Our Moon Came to Be,* by Dana Mackenzie, PhD (John Wiley & Sons, Inc.):

It is hard for us to imagine today how utterly different the world of night used to be from the daylight world. Of course, we can still re-create something of that lost mystique. When we sit around a campfire and tell ghost stories, our goose bumps (and our children's) remind us of the terrors that night used to hold. But it is all too easy for us to pile in the car at the end of our camping trip and return to the comfort of our incandescent, fluorescent, floodlit modern word. Two thousand, or even two hundred, years ago there was no such escape from the darkness. It was a physical presence that gripped the world from sunset until the cock's crow.

"As different as night and day," we say today. But in centuries past, night and day really were different. In a time when every scrap of light after sunset was desperately appreciated, when travelers would mark the road by piling up light stones or by stripping the bark off of trees to expose the lighter wood underneath, the Moon was the traveler's greatest friend. It was known in folklore as "the parish lantern." It was steady, portable, and — unlike a torch — entailed no risk of fire. It would never blow out, although it could, of course, hide behind a cloud.

Nowadays we don't need the moon to divide the light from the darkness because electric lights do it for us. Many of us have never even seen a truly dark sky. According to a recent survey on light pollution, 97 percent of the U.S. population lives under a night sky at least as bright as it was on a half-moon night in ancient times. Many city-dwellers live their entire lives under the equivalent of a full moon.

3. The primary purpose of this passage is to

   (A) compare and contrast nighttime in the modern world with the dark nights of centuries past.

   (B) explain why the invention of the electric light was essential to increasing worker productivity.

   (C) lament the loss of the dark nights and the danger and excitement that moonless nights would bring.

   (D) describe the diminishing brightness of the moon and the subsequent need for more electric lights.

   (E) argue for an end to the excessive light pollution that plagues 97 percent of the U.S. population.

4. When the author says, "Many city-dwellers live their entire lives under the equivalent of a full moon," he is essentially saying that

   (A) city-dwellers will never be able to truly appreciate the mystique and beauty of a truly dark night.

   (B) there is no longer a need for moonlight because artificial light is sufficient.

   (C) city-dwellers are missing out on much of the beauty of the natural world.

   (D) the amount of artificial light that shines in cities is enough to produce the same amount of light as a full moon.

   (E) it is easier to view the moon from cities than from rural areas.

5. The passage mentions all the following as possible ways for travelers to find the path at night *except*

   (A) piles of light-colored stones

   (B) the moon

   (C) a torch

   (D) railings made of light wood

   (E) trees with the bark stripped off

6. The author includes the statistic "97 percent of the U.S. population lives under a night sky at least as bright as it was on a half-moon night in ancient times" to primarily emphasize which of the following points?

   (A) Modern humans have the luxury of being able to see well at night despite cloud cover or a moonless night.

   (B) Most modern people cannot really understand how important the moon was to people in centuries past.

   (C) Americans are unique among the people of the world in having so much artificial light at night.

   (D) A full moon in ancient times was brighter than modern electric lights, which are only as bright as a half-moon.

   (E) Light pollution is one of the most important problems facing the United States in the 21st century.

7. In 1995, the federal government gave states the right to set their own speed limits. Several states immediately increased their speed limits to 70 miles per hour, and some even abolished limits entirely. In most cases, this result has not been a problem; the overall rate of accidents per driver has not increased since the speed limits were raised. At the same time, however, highway accident fatalities have increased 6 percent.

   Which one of the following, if true, most helps to resolve the apparent discrepancy described here?

   (A) Teenage drivers are the most likely to exceed speed limits, and their driving skill is not yet equal to the task of avoiding high speed accidents.

   (B) Accidents that occur at a higher speed are much more likely to be fatal than those at lower speeds.

   (C) State governments are not as concerned with highway safety as the federal government was in the days of a federally mandated speed limit.

   (D) In the 1970s, more people drove smaller, compact cars that got good gas mileage but were incapable of maintaining a high speed.

   (E) Drivers today are often distracted by their cellphones, and built-in navigation and entertainment features of their vehicles, which makes them more likely to get into accidents.

   Question 8 refers to the following exchange.

   Tom: The unemployment rate has dropped below 5 percent, and that is good news for America. A lower unemployment rate is better for almost everyone.

Shelly: Actually, a low unemployment rate is good for most workers but not for everyone. Workers are certainly happy to have jobs, but many businesses are negatively affected by a low unemployment rate because they have fewer applicants for jobs, and to expand their workforce, they have to hire workers they would not usually hire. The wealthiest Americans also privately complain about the inability to get good gardeners, housecleaners, and nannies when most Americans are already employed. So a low unemployment rate is not, in fact, good for America.

8. Shelly's conclusion that "a low unemployment rate is not, in fact, good for America" relies on the assumption that

(A) what is bad for businesses owners and the wealthy is bad for America.

(B) fluctuations in the unemployment rate affect the number of applicants for job openings.

(C) wealthy Americans rarely employ other Americans as housecleaners or nannies.

(D) business owners always want what is best for their workers even when it negatively impacts the bottom line.

(E) low unemployment hurts some workers because they would prefer to stay at home and collect unemployment checks.

9. A particular company makes a system that is installed in the engine block of a car and, if that car is stolen, relays the car's location to police via satellite. The recovery rate of stolen cars with this device is 90 percent. This system helps everyone because it is impossible for a thief to tell which cars it is installed on. For these reasons, insurance companies try to encourage customers to get this system by offering lower rates to those who have the system. Competing systems include brightly colored steel bars that attach to the steering wheel and loud alarms that go off when the car is tampered with. These systems simply encourage thieves to steal different cars, and when cars with these devices are stolen, the police rarely recover them.

Which of the following is the most logical conclusion to the author's premises?

(A) Insurance companies should give the same discount to car owners who have any protective system because their cars are less likely to be stolen.

(B) The police shouldn't allow car owners to install the loud sirens on their cars because everyone simply ignores the sirens anyway.

(C) Car owners with the system that relays location to the police should prominently advertise the fact on the side window of their cars.

(D) Thieves should simply steal the cars with loud alarms or bright steel bars because those cars probably wouldn't also have the more effective system installed.

(E) Insurance companies should give less of a discount, or no discount at all, to the siren and steering-wheel systems because they aren't as effective as the relay system.

10. Companies X and Y have the same number of employees working the same number of hours per week. According to the records kept by the human resources department of each company, the employees of company X took nearly twice as many sick days as the employees of company Y. Therefore, the employees of company Y are healthier than the employees of company X.

Which of the following, if true, most seriously weakens the conclusion?

(A) Company X allows employees to use sick days to take care of sick family members.

(B) Company Y offers its employees dental insurance and company X doesn't.

(C) Company X offers its employees a free membership to the local gym.

(D) Company Y uses a newer system for keeping records of sick days.

(E) Both companies offer two weeks of sick days per year.

Questions 11–15 refer to the following passage.

This passage is excerpted from *Brand Name Bullies: The Quest to Own and Control Culture,* by David Bollier (John Wiley & Sons, Inc.):

For millennia, the circulation of music in human societies has been as free as the circulation of air and water; it just comes naturally. Indeed, one of the ways that a society constitutes itself as a society is by freely sharing its words, music, and art. Only in the past century or so has music been placed in a tight envelope of property rights and strictly monitored for unauthorized flows. In the past decade, the proliferation of personal computers, Internet access, and digital technologies has fueled two conflicting forces: the democratization of creativity and the demand for stronger copyright protections.

While the public continues to have nominal fair use rights to copyrighted music, in practice the legal and technological controls over music have grown tighter. At the same time, creators at the fringes of mass culture, especially some hip-hop and remix artists, remain contemptuous of such controls and routinely appropriate whatever sounds they want to create interesting music.

Copyright protection is a critically important tool for artists in earning a livelihood from their creativity. But as many singers, composers, and musicians have discovered, the benefits of copyright law in the contemporary marketplace tend to accrue to the recording industry, not to the struggling garage band. As alternative distribution and marketing outlets have arisen, the recording industry has sought to ban, delay, or control as many of them as possible. After all, technological innovations that provide faster, cheaper distribution of music are likely to disrupt the industry's fixed investments and entrenched ways of doing business. New technologies allow newcomers to enter the market and compete, sometimes on superior terms. New technologies enable new types of audiences to emerge that may or may not be compatible with existing marketing strategies.

No wonder the recording industry has scrambled to develop new technological locks and broader copyright protections; they strengthen its control of music distribution. If metering devices could turn barroom singalongs into a market, the music industry would likely declare this form of unauthorized musical performance to be copyright infringement.

11. Which of the following most accurately states the main idea of the passage?

   (A) Only with the development of technology in the past century has music begun to freely circulate in society.

   (B) The recording industry is trying to develop an ever-tighter hold on the distribution of music, which used to circulate freely.

   (C) Copyright protection is an important tool for composers and musicians who earn their living from their music.

   (D) Technology allows new distribution methods that threaten to undermine the marketing strategies of music companies.

   (E) If music is no longer allowed to flow freely through the society, then the identity of the society itself will be lost.

12. Given the author's overall opinion of increased copyright protections, what is his attitude toward "hip-hop and remix artists" mentioned in Paragraph 2?

(A) wonder that they aren't sued more for their theft of copyright-protected music

(B) disappointment that they don't understand the damage they are doing to society

(C) envy of their extravagant lifestyle and increasing popularity

(D) approval of their continued borrowing of music despite tighter copyright controls

(E) shock at their blatant sampling of the music of other artists

13. According to the passage, new technology has resulted (or will result) in each of the following *except*

(A) new locks on music distribution

(B) newcomers competing in the music market

(C) better music

(D) democratization of creativity

(E) faster, cheaper distribution of music

14. The author of the passage would likely agree most with which of the following statements?

(A) Small-time musicians do not benefit from strict copyright protections in the same manner as record companies do.

(B) Copyright protections are designed to let music artists keep more of the money they earn through their talent.

(C) Recording companies are largely undeserving of their greedy reputations.

(D) Recording companies embrace new technologies because they help encourage the spread of music.

(E) Copyright protections encourage creativity among musicians because the artists must find new ways to share their music with the masses.

15. The final sentence of the passage seems to imply what about the executives of the record industry?

(A) They have found ways to make money from any performance of any music at any time.

(B) They are boldly leading the music industry into a new technological era of vastly increased profits.

(C) They want their music to be performed as often as possible by the maximum number of people to create greater exposure for artists.

(D) They don't actually like music or know anything about music and are attempting to limit the society's exposure to music.

(E) No performance of music anywhere is safe from their attempts to control the distribution of all music.

16. New laws make it easier to patent just about anything, from parts of the human genome to a peanut butter and jelly sandwich. Commentators are concerned about the implications of allowing patents for things that can hardly be described as "inventions." However, the U.S. Patent and Trademark Office believes that allowing for strong copyright and patent protections fosters the kind of investment in research and development needed to spur innovation.

Which of the following can be properly inferred from the preceding statements?

(A) It was not possible in the past to patent something as common as a peanut butter and jelly sandwich.

(B) The U.S. Patent and Trademark Office is more interested in business profits than in true innovation.

(C) Investment in research and development is always needed to spur innovation.

(D) The human genome is part of nature and shouldn't be patented.

(E) Commentators who are concerned about too many patents aren't very well informed.

17. The process of "gerrymandering," or manipulating voter-district boundaries so that one party gains a considerable advantage in a district over another, is making the modern political climate more divisive than ever. It ensures that people with likeminded ideals end up densely packed in the same districts, and those people then elect officials who also share those likeminded ideals.

These elected officials are less prone to compromise, and this creates an unnecessary and harmful divide between parties.

Assuming all the following statements are true, which would most significantly weaken the argument made above?

(A) Gerrymandering sets up an unfair advantage by creating some districts that are nearly guaranteed to vote for a particular party, thereby freeing up more time and resources for that party to campaign elsewhere.

(B) People with likeminded ideals have an innate desire to live alongside others who share similar belief systems, regardless of their political affiliation.

(C) All elected officials are typically strong in their convictions.

(D) When people with likeminded ideals live in the same district, they tend to continuously elect politicians with very similar beliefs.

(E) Gerrymandering can be executed by both political parties.

18. In a recent survey, one out of six Americans were shown to have vision problems, which is a notable increase over the past two decades. The amount of time Americans spend in front of computer and television screens has risen sharply, and to reduce the number of Americans suffering from vision issues, the amount of screen exposure must also be reduced.

Which of the following, if true, would most substantially weaken the author's conclusion?

(A) Increased screen time is directly correlated with vision problems.

(B) The connection between screen time and vision problems is not entirely clear.

(C) Screen time has increased globally and not just in America.

(D) Americans can reduce their risk of vision problems caused by too much screen time by dimming the screen and using a larger font.

(E) The majority of Americans with vision problems are older people, and the percentage of people over age 60 has steadily increased over the past 20 years.

Understanding What's Right with Answer Explanations

You can check your answers to the practice questions by reading through the following explanations. To get the most benefit, read through every explanation, even the ones for the questions you answered correctly.

1. **C.** This critical reasoning question asks you to explain the facts in the passage by providing a piece to the cause-and-effect pattern. With cause-and-effect questions, you select the answer choice that could logically cause the effects noted in the premises. So, for this problem, you have to decide which of the five choices helps explain why Gulf Coast homes use little energy in the winter *and* a great deal of energy in the summer. Without even looking at the answer choices, you may conclude that the Gulf Coast climate is milder than other parts of the nation in the winter and perhaps hotter in the summer. The correct answer probably addresses that issue.

   You can eliminate Choice (A) because if most Gulf Coast residents spend the summer elsewhere, their vacant homes would use less energy during summer months rather than more. This answer would produce the opposite effect of that explained in the argument. Choice (B) would also produce the opposite effect of that found in the argument. Another important reason for eliminating Choice (B) is that it doesn't provide a way of comparing energy use in the Gulf region to energy use in the rest of the country, which is the real issue in this argument.

   Choice (C) sounds like the answer we imagined before reading through the choices. It explains why the Gulf region would have lower energy use in winter and higher use in summer, which may explain why it's different from the rest of the country as a whole. Although Choice (C) is probably the correct answer, read through the remaining two choices just to be sure.

   Choice (D) doesn't work because a region that's cool year-round would have high energy consumption in the winter for heat and low consumption in the summer. And you can eliminate Choice (E) because the argument is about energy consumption, not energy price. So the correct answer is Choice (C).

2. **D.** This critical reasoning question asks you to weaken the *opposition's* statement that the wolf is vicious, so look for a statement that shows that the wolf isn't a danger to people or livestock. Begin by eliminating answers that don't address the appropriate conclusion. Choice (A) deals with the beneficial impact of wolves on the ecosystem but doesn't talk about their propensity toward viciousness to humans or livestock, so eliminate it. You can also eliminate Choice (C) because the hunting prowess of the wolf isn't the issue, and this choice may actually strengthen the contention that wolves are dangerous. Choice (E) also doesn't weaken the conclusion in question; it argues that wolves may threaten livestock. This leaves you with Choices (B) and (D). Choice (B) compares the danger posed by wolves with the danger posed by black bears. Even if a wolf is less dangerous than a bear, that doesn't mean a wolf isn't dangerous. The best answer is Choice (D), because it provides a statistic that weakens the opposition's argument that wolves are dangerous to humans.

3. A. For a primary-purpose reading comprehension question, you're looking for the reason the author wrote the passage.

REMEMBER

Focus on the passage as a whole and not on any particular portion. You usually can find clues to the main theme and the author's purpose in the first and last paragraphs.

The main idea of this passage is that night was very different in centuries past than it is in current times, and the author's purpose is to show how this is true. So look for an answer that reflects this purpose.

TIP

You can start by eliminating answers based on their first words. The words *compare and contrast, explain,* and *describe* reflect the author's purpose, but *lament* and *argue* imply more emotion on the part of the author than is displayed in the passage, so eliminate Choices (C) and (E). Worker productivity has nothing to do with showing how our ancestors perceived night differently, so you can eliminate Choice (B). Choice (D) is simply wrong; the author doesn't maintain that the moon is actually getting darker, just that it's become overshadowed by electric lights. So that leaves Choice (A) as the correct answer.

4. D. Arguably the biggest clue to Choice (D) lies in the second-to-last sentence, when the author references a "recent survey of light pollution" in cities. This implies that there is so much visible light in cities that residents need no longer "mark the road by piling up light stones or by stripping the bark off of trees to expose the lighter wood underneath" to light their way to their destination. It's always wise to consider all the other possible answer choices, though, just to make sure. Choices (A) and (C) are somewhat similar, in that they both intimate that city-dwellers are missing out on the beauty of nature and the world around them. This doesn't appear to be the focus of the passage, however; the passage is more focused on how people used to make up for the lack of light and how they no longer need to do so to function after dark. So, you can probably eliminate both options. Choice (E) doesn't make a lot of sense; it is probably easier to get a good look at the moon in a rural area, where tall buildings, pollution, and so on are less likely to block your view. You're down to either Choice (B) or (D). The two choices seem similar, but of the two, Choice (D) is the stronger option. The last sentence provides that artificial light is "equivalent" to moonlight, which is more synonymous to the "same amount" of illumination in Choice (D) than "sufficient" in Choice (B).

5. D. This specific information exception question asks you to refer to the text to eliminate answers that *are* ways in the passage that travelers can find a path at night. The second paragraph specifically mentions Choice (A), light-colored stones; Choice (B), the moon; Choice (C), torches; and Choice (E), trees with the bark stripped off. Railings, Choice (D), aren't mentioned anywhere in the passage so it's the correct answer.

6. B. This question asks you about the use of a specific statistic. To answer this question correctly, keep in mind the author's purpose for writing the passage, which you've already considered in the third question. Find the choice that links the statistic to the author's purpose of comparing nighttime now and nighttime in centuries past. Eliminate Choice (C) because the author compares time periods, not modern countries. Because the passage doesn't indicate that the moon is brighter than electric lights, you can eliminate Choice (D). Although the 97 percent statistic may lead you to conclude that light pollution is a big problem, that's not the author's reason for using the statistic, so eliminate Choice (E). Choice (A) is a little more plausible, but Choice (B) is better because the author is more concerned with showing how night skies are different now than with showing that the modern well-lit sky is a luxury.

7. **B.** This critical reasoning question asks you to resolve the discrepancy that the overall rate of accidents per driver hasn't increased since states raised their speed limits, but total accident fatalities have increased. So even though the rate of accidents hasn't increased, the accidents that do occur have become more deadly, which is entirely possible. Look for an answer that connects cause (higher speeds) with effect (more fatal accidents despite fewer total accidents). Choice (A) doesn't explain the rise in fatalities because the argument doesn't mention illegal speeding, just higher legal speeds. Choice (B) looks correct. If higher speeds make accidents more deadly, then it makes sense for fatalities to rise even if total accident numbers don't. Choice (C) is wrong because the author is interested in resolving a statistical paradox rather than providing suggestions for state regulation. Choice (D) is wrong because it doesn't connect the lower speed limit with fewer fatalities. Perhaps slower cars caused fewer deaths, but the answer doesn't say that. Choice (E) is wrong because it attributes accidents to distractions rather than speed, and it doesn't distinguish between fatal and nonfatal accidents. Choice (B) is the best answer.

8. **A.** This critical reasoning question asks you to identify an assumption that Shelly relied on in making her conclusion that a low unemployment rate isn't "good for America."

   When you're asked to find an assumption, look for a statement that supports the conclusion but isn't actually stated in the argument.

   Eliminate choices that don't support the conclusion. Whether businesses favor workers over the bottom line may affect the unemployment rate, but it doesn't show how low unemployment isn't good for America, so Choice (D) is incorrect. Choice (E) doesn't support the conclusion, either. The conclusion is about what's good for America in general, not a select few disinclined workers.

   A person's assumption wouldn't contradict a stated premise, so Choice (C) can't be right. Choice (B) may support the conclusion, but it's actually stated in the given premises and, therefore, can't be an unstated assumption. Choice (A) is the correct answer because it links Shelly's premises about businesses and wealthy Americans to her conclusion about America in general.

9. **E.** This critical reasoning question requires you to draw a conclusion from the premises included in the argument.

   Look for an answer choice that addresses all the information in the premises. You can eliminate conclusions that are off topic or incomplete.

   Eliminate choices that don't include all the elements of the argument. Choices (B), (C), and (D) don't mention the insurance companies that are the subject of one of the premises. This leaves you with Choice (A) and Choice (E), which offer nearly opposite conclusions. The premises indicate that one of the reasons insurance companies like the engine-block system is that thieves don't know which cars have it installed. Choice (A) concludes that cars with any protective system, including alarms and steering-wheel bars, should get a discount because those cars are less likely to be stolen. This conclusion doesn't flow logically from the premises, however, because the reasons given for the insurance discounts are a high recovery rate of stolen vehicles and the general deterrent to all car thefts. Neither of these advantages comes from the alarms or steering-wheel bars. Choice (E) addresses all the premises and logically concludes the argument, making it the correct answer.

10. A. This critical reasoning question asks you to weaken the conclusion that the employees of company Y are healthier than the employees of company X. The author draws the conclusion that Y's employees are healthier than X's employees based on the cause-and-effect argument that more sick days mean sicker employees.

TIP

To weaken cause-and-effect arguments, look for an answer choice that shows another cause is possible for the effect.

Choice (E) doesn't distinguish between the two companies. It can't show another cause for the different number of sick days and, therefore, can't be right. Choice (D) differentiates between the two companies' record-keeping, but it doesn't explain how company Y's new records system accounts for fewer sick days. Dental insurance shouldn't affect the number of sick days, so Choice (B) doesn't work. Choice (C) doesn't address the issue of company X's greater number of sick days, so free gym memberships don't matter. The best answer is Choice (A) because it provides a reason other than employee health for the greater number of sick days that company X's employees take.

11. B. This reading comprehension question asks for the main idea of the passage.

Answers to main-idea questions are usually more general than specific in their wording.

Choices (C) and (D) each focus on sub-themes in the passage but not the main idea. Copyright protection and technology are specific subjects covered in the passage, but they don't make up the main idea, which is that the music industry is trying to control distribution of music. You can eliminate Choice (A) because it's not supported by any part of the passage. The passage clearly states that music has circulated freely in society for millennia. Choice (E) is wrong because it goes beyond what's stated in the passage. The author may well imply that without the free flow of music, society will lose its identity, but this isn't the passage's main idea. So that leaves Choice (B) as the best answer.

12. D. This reading comprehension question asks you to apply the author's attitude toward *hip-hop and remix artists* as specifically mentioned in the second paragraph to other circumstances. The real GMAT would highlight this phrase in yellow. You've already answered a question about the main idea, so you know the author is concerned about the tightening grip the recording industry has on the distribution of music. Because the hip-hop and remix artists defy the music industry, they'll likely meet with the author's approval. Although Choice (A) may express a valid opinion, you can eliminate it because it isn't supported by the passage. The author probably approves of hip-hop and remix artists, so wouldn't think they're doing damage — Choice (B) is completely off base. Envy and shock are usually too strong emotions for GMAT passages, so rule out Choices (C) and (E). The correct answer is Choice (D).

13. C. Here's another specific information reading comprehension question looking for an exception. Examine the text and eliminate the answers you find there. The one that remains is your correct answer. In connection with technology, the passage mentions Choice (A), new locks on music distribution, in the second paragraph; Choice (B), newcomers competing in the market, in the third paragraph; Choice (D), democratization of creativity, in the first paragraph; and Choice (E), faster, cheaper distribution of music, in the third paragraph. The author certainly doesn't mention better music. So Choice (C) is correct.

14. A. This reading comprehensive question addresses the author's attitude in the passage. If you picked Choice (B), you may not have read closely enough, or you may have stopped reading right after the author refers to copyright protections as ". . . a critically important tool for artists in earning a livelihood from their creativity," because the author then goes on to lament how such protections tend to benefit the recording companies more than the artists. As for Choice (C), because a key point made by the author throughout the passage is that recording companies are, in fact, greedy, and will do just about anything to make and keep as much money as possible, you can easily eliminate that answer. Choice (D), too, can be eliminated with relative ease, as the author makes several references to the fact that record companies do just the opposite of embracing new technologies. They instead seek to "ban, delay, or control" them for their own benefit. Choice (E) can also be knocked out of contention because the author doesn't go into whether artists are finding "new ways to share their music with the masses," instead the piece discusses how copyright protections are intended to help recording companies maintain control of music distribution to the fullest extent possible. Choice (E) also refers to the artist's creative ways to avoid technological and legal controls rather than the creativity associated with producing the artwork itself. Choice (A) is your best option, justified by the author's statement that "the benefits of copyright law in the contemporary marketplace tend to accrue to the recording industry, not to the struggling garage band."

15. E. For this reading comprehension inference question, you need to determine what the final sentence implies about recording-industry executives. The final sentence mentions that if it were possible, executives would try to stop unauthorized singalongs. This shows that the author thinks that executives will go to any length to control the distribution of music. Choices (B) and (C) paint the executives in a positive light, which is certainly not warranted by the last sentence. You can also eliminate Choice (D) because the last sentence has nothing to do with whether executives like or dislike music. Choice (A) is closer, but the sentence doesn't talk about making money from singalongs so much as stopping them altogether. That makes Choice (E) the correct answer.

16. A. This critical reasoning question asks you to draw an inference from the passage. Inference questions generally focus on a premise rather than on a conclusion. The passage implies that the patent office wants to promote invention, so Choice (B) doesn't work. Choices (D) and (E) express opinions that aren't presented in the passage. Although you may agree that the genome shouldn't be patented or that people who are concerned about patents aren't well informed, the question doesn't ask you for your opinion.

WARNING

Don't choose answer choices to critical reasoning questions just because you agree with them. Base your answers on the opinions stated or implied by the paragraph.

Because Choice (C) contains the word always, this choice leaves no room for exception and can't be a logical inference. That leaves Choice (A) as the correct answer.

17. B. This critical reasoning question asks you to identify the statement that would most significantly weaken the argument presented in the question. Choice (A) sounds more like an additional argument *in favor* of gerrymandering creating an "unnecessary and harmful divide between parties," so that answer can't be right since it strengthens rather than weakens the original argument. The same can be said for Choice (D); if folks are electing very similar politicians in their districts and those politicians share the same ideals, this would likely contribute to the divide between parties and help eliminate the political "middle." Choice (E) is irrelevant; that both sides can take part in gerrymandering doesn't mean they do or that they do at the same time. So, that argument also falls flat. You've narrowed the options down to either Choice (B) or (C). Of the two, Choice (B) is the stronger option. It presents an alternative to gerrymandering as the reason that certain districts tend to elect people from the same party over and over again, which arguably contributes to a sharper divide between parties. Choice (B) is your best bet.

18. **E.** This critical reasoning question asks you to identify the statement that would most substantially weaken the author's conclusion. Choice (E) is best because it presents a logical, alternative explanation for the statistics surrounding Americans with vision problems. It isn't screen time that causes the spike in problems but, instead, a large population of aging Americans. Choice (A) would strengthen rather than weaken the initial argument, so you know that one can't be right. Choice (B) is a possibility, but you can assume the GMAT is probably looking for something a bit more definite. Choice (C) is irrelevant; the argument is specific to *American* vision problems, so it doesn't matter how much time people in other parts of the world spend looking at screens. Choice (D), too, is irrelevant. What people do to reduce vision issues doesn't call into question the role of screen time in vision problems. Choice (E) is the correct response.

4

Conquering the Quantitative Section

Dust off your basic math skills with a review of fundamental operations, fractions, and exponents.

Take a trip down memory lane with good old algebra, including quadratic equations and functions.

Cover the ins and outs of statistics and probability — including data interpretation, combinations and permutations — and sets, from the essential concepts of mean, median, and mode to more complex considerations of standard deviation and calculations of probability.

Take a mini GMAT quantitative test to show off your fresh skills.

IN THIS CHAPTER

» **Refreshing your memory on types of numbers and basic operations**

» **Getting the skinny on bases, exponents, and radicals**

» **Keeping order of operations in mind**

» **Grabbing your share of fractions, decimals, and percents**

» **Making comparisons by using ratios and proportions**

» **Bringing numbers down to size with scientific notation**

Chapter **10**

Getting Back to Basics: Numbers and Operations

T hose of you who majored in math in college probably look at the math section of the GMAT like an old friend. Those of you who haven't stepped into a math class since high school are more likely dreading it. You know who you are! Don't worry, this chapter takes you back to the beginning with a review of the concepts you've learned through the years but may have temporarily forgotten. In this chapter, you see problems that test your knowledge of the math building blocks, such as number types, basic operations, exponents and radicals, fractions, and ratios. These concepts form the foundation of more complicated math problems, so this stuff is important to know. For example, you could end up with a completely wrong answer if you solve for real numbers when the question asks for integers. Some GMAT-takers may end up kicking themselves (and that looks just plain odd) for missing relatively simple problems because they were unfamiliar with some basic terminology. To avoid this unfortunate (and awkward) position, make sure you're well-heeled in math basics.

Just Your Type: Kinds of Numbers

Since the Stone Age, humans have found it necessary to rely on numbers to get through daily living. In hunter-gatherer cultures, the people made notches in bones to count, for example, the number of days in a lunar cycle or perhaps to indicate how long the nomadic tribe spent in a particular location until it found food. But through the millennia, humankind soon realized that numbers could become large and unwieldy. Hence, the advent of number classifications and operations!

Although understanding modern mathematical operations might have strained the cognitive abilities of prehistoric humans, it'll surely be easier for you after you complete this review. For the GMAT, you need to know the more everyday types of numbers, such as integers, rational numbers, real numbers, and prime numbers. And you should at least be aware of some of the less commonly known types, such as irrational and imaginary numbers.

>> **Integers:** Numbers that belong to the set of all positive and negative whole numbers with 0 included. Integers can't be fractions or decimals or portions of a number. Integers include –5, –4, –3, –2, –1, 0, 1, 2, 3, 4, and 5 and continue infinitely on either side of 0. Integers greater than 0 are the *natural numbers* or *positive integers.* Integers less than 0 are the *negative integers.* **Note:** Take care when working with 0. It's neither positive nor negative.

>> **Rational numbers:** Numbers that can be expressed as quotients (or fractions) of two integers, where no divisor (or denominator) is zero. Rational numbers comprise all positive and negative integers, zero, fractions, and decimal numbers that either end or repeat. For example, the fraction $\frac{1}{3}$ can be expressed as $0.33\overline{33}$. Rational numbers don't include numbers like π or radicals like $\sqrt{2}$ because the decimal equivalents of these numbers don't end or repeat. They're *irrational numbers.*

>> **Real numbers:** All numbers that you normally think of as numbers. Real numbers encompass all integers, rational numbers, and irrational numbers. Real numbers correspond to points on a number line, either positive, negative, or zero; and all points on the number line correspond to real numbers. Real numbers are also those numbers employed for measurements such as the weight of an object or the temperature recorded on a given day. So, when the GMAT asks you to give an answer expressed in terms of real numbers, just solve the problem as you normally would.

>> **Imaginary numbers:** Numbers that aren't real numbers. An imaginary number is a number like $\sqrt{-1}$. Think about it: You know that when you square any positive or negative real number, the result is a positive number. This means you can't find the square root of a negative number unless the root is simply not a real number. So imaginary numbers include square roots of negative numbers or any number containing i, which represents the square root of –1. Thankfully, the GMAT doesn't contain questions that test your knowledge of imaginary numbers.

>> **Consecutive Integers:** A sequence of two or more integers, such as 25, 26, and 27, in which each integer is one unit greater than the previous one. Consecutive integers can be positive, negative, or a mix of both, depending on the starting point. You can represent consecutive integers by n, $n+1$, $n+2$, and so on, where n is an integer.

>> **Prime numbers:** All the positive integers greater than 1 whose only positive divisors are themselves and 1; 1 isn't a prime number. The smallest prime number is 2, and it's also the only even prime number. This doesn't mean that all odd numbers are prime numbers, though. Also, 0 can never be a prime number because it's not positive; and, furthermore, you can divide 0 by every natural number there is. To determine prime numbers, consider this series: 2, 3, 5, 7, 11, 13, 17, 19, 23, 29, and so on. What makes these numbers unique is that the only two positive factors for each of these numbers are 1 and the number itself. Every integer greater than 1 is either prime or it can be expressed as a unique product of prime factors. For example, $15 = 3 \times 5$, and $100 = 2 \times 2 \times 5 \times 5$.

TIP

You probably won't encounter this term on the GMAT, but in case it comes up at cocktail parties, you should know that positive integers other than 1 that aren't prime numbers are *composite numbers*. A composite number has more than two different positive factors, so it's the product of more than simply itself and the number 1. Zero (like the number 1) is neither prime nor composite.

Questions regarding prime numbers appear fairly frequently in GMAT math sections. Here's a sample of one you may see.

EXAMPLE

Which of the following expresses 60 as a product of prime numbers?

(A) $2 \times 2 \times 3 \times 5$

(B) $2 \times 2 \times 15$

(C) $2 \times 3 \times 3 \times 5$

(D) $2 \times 3 \times 5$

(E) $1 \times 2 \times 5 \times 6$

This question tests your knowledge of prime numbers. Because the correct answer has to be a product of prime numbers, eliminate any choice that contains a composite (or non-prime) number. So, Choices (B) and (E) are out (even though the product of both is 60) because 15, 1, and 6 aren't prime numbers. Then, eliminate any answers that don't equal 60 when you multiply them. Choice (C) is 90, and Choice (D) is 30, so the answer must be Choice (A). It's the correct answer because it contains only prime numbers whose product equals 60.

It's Not Brain Surgery: Basic Operations

Now that you're a bit more comfortable with some terms, it's time to take a stab at manipulating numbers. Figuring out how to do operations, which we discuss in the following sections, is pretty simple, almost as simple as 1-2-3. It doesn't take a brain surgeon to open your mind to endless possibilities.

Adding, subtracting, multiplying, and dividing

You're probably pretty familiar with the standard operations of addition, subtraction, multiplication, and division. But even these math basics have some tricky elements that you may need to refresh your memory on.

Putting two and two together: Addition

Adding is pretty simple. Addition is just the operation of combining two or more numbers to get an end result called the *sum*. For example, here's a simple addition problem: $3 + 4 + 5 = 12$

Addition also has two important properties that you may remember from elementary school: the associative property and the commutative property. Understanding these simple concepts for the GMAT math questions is important:

» **Associative property:** The *associative property* states that the order in which you choose to add three or more numbers doesn't change the result. It shows how numbers can group differently with one another and still produce the same answer. So regardless of whether you add 3 and 4 together first and then add 5 or add 4 and 5 together followed by 3, you still get an answer of 12.

$$(3+4)+5 = 12$$
$$3+(4+5) = 12$$

» **Commutative property:** The *commutative property* states that it doesn't matter what order you use to add the same numbers. Regardless of what number you list first in a set of numbers, they always produce the same sum. So $2+3 = 5$ is the same as $3+2 = 5$.

Depleting the supply: Subtraction

Subtraction, as you probably know, is the inverse of addition. You take away a value from another value and end up with the *difference*. So, if $3+4 = 7$, then $7-3 = 4$.

In subtraction, order *does* matter, so neither the associative property nor the commutative property applies. You get completely different answers for $3-4-5$, depending on what method you use to associate the values. Here's what we mean:

$$(3-4)-5 = -6$$

but

$$3-(4-5) = 4$$

The order of the values counts in subtraction, too. For example, $3-4$ isn't the same as $4-3$ ($3-4 = -1$, but $4-3 = 1$).

Increasing by leaps and bounds: Multiplication

Think of multiplication as repeated addition with an end result called the *product*: 3×5 is the same as $5+5+5$ They both equal 15.

On the GMAT, you may see several signs that represent the multiplication operation. A multiplication sign can be designated by $\times$ or simply with a dot, like this: And in many instances, especially when variables are involved (for more about variables, see Chapter 11), multiplication can be indicated by just putting the factors right next to each other. So, ab means the same thing as $a\times b$, and $2a$ is the same as $2\times a$. One or more of these back-to-back factors may appear in parentheses: $2(3)$ means 2×3, and so does $(2)(3)$.

Multiplication is like addition, in that the order of the values doesn't matter. So, it obeys the commutative property:

$$a\times b = b\times a$$

And the associative property:

$$(a\times b)\times c = a\times(b\times c)$$

Another property associated both with multiplication and addition is the *distributive property.* It basically means that *multiplication distributes over addition.* So, you may encounter this problem:

$$a(b+c)=$$

You solve it by distributing the *a* to *b* and *c*, which means that you multiply *a* and *b* to get *ab* and then *a* and *c* to get *ac*, and then you add the results together like this: $a(b+c)=ab+ac$.

Sharing the wealth: Division

Finally, there's division, which you can consider to be the inverse of multiplication. With division, you split one value, the *dividend,* into equal parts determined by another number, the *divisor.* The end result is the *quotient.* So, whereas $3 \times 5 = 15$, $15 \div 5 = 3$, and $15 \div 3 = 5$. If the division is exact, meaning there is no remainder, then the dividend (15 in the last expression) is a *multiple* of the divisor (3 in the last expression), and the dividend is said to be *divisible* by the divisor. If the dividend cannot be divided evenly by the divisor, there will be a *remainder.* For example, when 35 is divided by 8, the quotient is 4 and the remainder is 3.

Division Algorithm: If an integer *m* is divided by a positive integer *d*, the result is a unique integer *q* (the *quotient*) and unique integer r (the *remainder*), where $0 \le r < d$ and $m = dq + r$. In addition, $r = 0$ if and only if *m* is a multiple of *d*.

As in subtraction, order matters, so division doesn't follow either the commutative or associative properties.

REMEMBER

Division by 0 is undefined; so, 0 as a divisor is not allowed.

The division sign may be represented by a fraction bar. For more info on fractions, see "Splitting Up: Fractions, Decimals, and Percents," later in this chapter.

REMEMBER

A balancing act: Operations with even and odd numbers

We're pretty sure you know that *even numbers* are integers divisible by 2: . . . −4, −2, 0, 2, 4, 6, 8, 10, and so on. And *odd numbers* are those integers that aren't divisible by 2: . . . −3, −1, 1, 3, 5, 7, 9, 11, and so on.

You're probably with us so far, but what's important to remember for the GMAT is what happens to even or odd numbers when you add, subtract, or multiply them by one another.

Here are the rules regarding evens and odds for addition and subtraction:

>> If two integers are both even or both odd, then their sum and their difference is even.

>> If you add or subtract an even integer and an odd integer, your result is an odd integer.

Here's what you should know about multiplying even and odd integers:

>> If any of the factors in a product of integers is even, then the product itself is even.

>> If every factor in a product of integers is odd, then the product itself is odd.

Division rules are a little more complex because the quotients aren't always integers; sometimes they're fractions. Here are a few rules to know:

>> When you divide an even integer by an odd integer, you get an even integer or a fraction.

>> An odd integer divided by another odd integer results in an odd integer or a fraction.

>> An even integer divided by another even integer can result in either an odd or even quotient, so that's not very helpful.

>> When you divide an odd integer by an even one, you always get a fraction; because fractions aren't integers, the quotient for this scenario is neither odd nor even.

TIP

You may be wondering why you need to know these rules. Here's why: Memorizing them can be a big timesaver when it comes to eliminating answer choices. For example, if you have a multiplication problem involving large even numbers, you know you can eliminate any odd-number answer choices without even doing the math! Here's a sample question that shows you just how valuable knowing the rules can be.

EXAMPLE

If a and b are different prime numbers, which of the following numbers must be odd?

(A) ab

(B) $4a + b$

(C) $a + b + 3$

(D) $ab - 3$

(E) $4a + 4b + 3$

To solve this number theory question, think of numbers for a and b that represent their possible values. Then substitute these values into the answer choices to eliminate all that can be even. When considering values for a and b, make sure to include 2 because it's the only even prime number. Neither 1 nor 0 is an option because neither is prime.

Substitute 2 for a or b in Choice (A), and you see that it can be even because the rules tell you that any time you multiply an even number by another number, you get an even number. You also know that Choice (B) can be even because 4 (an even number) times any number is an even number. If $b = 2$ and you added that to $4a$, you'd be adding two even numbers, which always gives you an even sum. Again, if $b = 2$ in Choice (C), then a would have to be an odd prime number. You add a (odd) to b (even) to get an odd sum. Then you add that odd number to the odd number 3, which results in an even number. Choice (D) can be even if both a and b are odd. An odd number times an odd number is an odd number. When you subtract an odd number, like 3, from another odd number, you get an even number.

By process of elimination, the answer must be Choice (E). It doesn't matter whether a or b in Choice (E) is even or odd; $4a$ and $4b$ will always be even, because anytime you multiply an even number by another number, you get an even number. When you add two evens, you get an even number, so $4a + 4b$ is an even number. And because an even number plus an odd number is always odd, when you add that even result to 3, you get an odd number, always. The correct answer is Choice (E).

Checking out the real estate: Fundamental concepts of real numbers

In addition to basic operations, the GMAT expects you to have a solid grasp of fundamental concepts of real numbers. These include understanding comparative relationships such as less than and greater than, comprehending absolute value, and performing computations with positive and negative numbers.

Not all things are equal: Comparing real numbers

On a number line, numbers that lie to the left of zero are negative and numbers that lie to the right of zero are positive. For any two numbers on the number line, the number to the left is less than the number to the right. For example, $-5 < -2 < -1.5 < 3$ and $3 < \pi < 4$.

To say that a number x is between -2 and 3 means that $x > -2$ and $x < 3$; that is, $-2 < x < 3$. If x is "between -2 and 3, inclusive," then $-2 \le x \le 3$.

Absolutes do exist: Absolute value

To simplify things, just think of the absolute value of any known real number as that same number without a negative sign. It's the distance between the number and 0 on the number line. The absolute value is denoted by enclosing the number within absolute value bars (| |), so the absolute value of 3 is written mathematically as $|3|$. And because the number 3 sits three spaces from 0 on the number line, $|3| = 3$. Likewise, because -3 sits three spaces from 0 on the number line, its absolute value is also 3: $|-3| = 3$. Examples of absolute values of numbers are $|4| = |-4| = 4$, $\left|-\frac{5}{6}\right| = \left|\frac{5}{6}\right|$, and $|0| = 0$.

REMEMBER The absolute value of any nonzero number is positive.

WARNING The GMAT loves to trip you up when dealing with multiple numbers and absolute values. Remember that absolute value pertains only to the value contained within the absolute value bars. So, if you see a negative sign outside the bars, the resulting value is negative. For example, $-|-3| = -3$ because although the absolute value of -3 is 3, the negative sign outside the bars makes the end result a negative.

TIP When you're working with variables in absolute-value expressions, remember that there is likely more than one solution for the variable because the value within the absolute value bars may be positive or negative, as demonstrated by this sample problem.

EXAMPLE Which of the following is the complete set of solutions for x when $|x - 3| = 6$?

(A) $\{9\}$

(B) $\{-9, 9\}$

(C) $\{-3, 9\}$

(D) $\{3, 9\}$

(E) $\{-9, -3, 3\}$

To find one solution for x, remove the absolute-value bars and then solve for x:

$$|x - 3| = 6$$
$$x - 3 = 6$$
$$x = 9$$

You know 9 is a solution for x, so you can eliminate Choice (E) because it doesn't contain 9. You can't end with Choice (A), though; you have to consider that the value within the absolute value bars could be negative. To accomplish this feat, multiply the terms between the bars by -1 and then solve for x:

$$|x - 3| = 6$$
$$-1(x - 3) = 6$$
$$-x + 3 = 6$$
$$-x = 3$$
$$x = -3$$

Because the value enclosed in the absolute-value bars may be either negative or positive, x may be either -3 or 9. Choice (C) is the complete set of solutions.

Half empty or half full: Positive and negative numbers

Positive and negative numbers have their own set of rules regarding operations, and they're even more important to remember than those for even and odd integers. Here's what you need to know for multiplying and dividing:

» When you multiply or divide two positive numbers, the result is positive.

» When you multiply or divide two negative numbers, the result is also positive.

» Multiplying or dividing a negative number by a positive number gives you a negative result (as does multiplying or dividing a positive number by a negative number).

As you may expect, you need to know some things about adding and subtracting positives and negatives:

» When you add two positive numbers, your result is a positive number.

» When you add two negative numbers, the resulting sum is negative.

» When you add a positive number to a negative number, the result is positive when the number with the largest absolute value is positive and negative when the number with the largest absolute value is negative.

» If you subtract a negative number from another number, you end up adding the positive version of the negative number to the other number. For example, $x - (-3)$ is the same thing as $x + 3$.

Using Little Numbers for Big Values: Bases and Exponents

Because multiplication can be thought of as repeated addition, you can think of positive integer exponents as indicating repeated multiplication. This means that 4^3 is the same as $4 \times 4 \times 4$ or 64. In the example, you refer to 4 as the *base*, the superscript 3 as the *exponent*, and 4^3 as an *exponential expression*. If you include a variable into this mix, such as $4b^3$, the base becomes b and the 4 becomes the *coefficient*. In our example, b^3 is multiplied by the coefficient 4.

As my old high school algebra teacher used to scream (usually when he caught his students napping): "The power governs only the number immediately below it!" (that is, the base). So, the exponent doesn't affect the coefficient. Only the base gets squared or cubed or whatever the exponent says to do.

This rule brings up some fascinating properties regarding positive and negative bases and even and odd exponents:

» A positive number taken to an even or odd power remains positive.

» A negative number taken to an odd power remains negative.

» A negative number taken to an even power becomes positive.

TIP

What all of this means is that any number taken to an even power either remains or becomes positive, and any number taken to an odd power keeps the sign it began with. Another interesting tidbit to digest is that any term with an odd power that results in a negative number will have a negative root, and this is the only possible root for the expression. For example, if $a^3 = -125$, then $a = -5$. That is, the cube root of -125 is -5.

On the other hand, anytime you have an exponent of 2, you have two potential roots, one positive and one negative, for the expression. For example, if $a^2 = 64$, then $a = 8$ or -8. So, 64 has two possible square roots: either 8 or -8.

In the following sections, we outline a few rules for adding, subtracting, multiplying, and dividing exponents. We also clue you in on how to figure out the powers of 0 and 1 and what to do with fractional and negative exponents.

Adding and subtracting with exponents

The only catch to adding or subtracting with exponents is that the base and exponent of each term must be the same. So, you can add and subtract like terms such as $4a^2$ and a^2 like this: $4a^2 + a^2 = 5a^2$ and $4a^2 - a^2 = 3a^2$. Notice that the base and exponent remain the same and that the coefficient is the only number that changes in the equation.

Multiplying and dividing with exponents

The rules regarding multiplying and dividing with exponents are pretty numerous, so to keep them straight, we've set up Table 10-1 for you. The table describes each rule and gives you an example or two.

TABLE 10-1 **Rules for Multiplying and Dividing with Exponents**

Rule	Examples
To multiply exponential expressions with the same bases, add the exponents and keep the same base.	$a^2 \times a^3 = a^5$
If the expressions contain coefficients, multiply the coefficients as you normally would.	$4a^2 \times 2a^3 = 8a^5$
When you divide two exponential expressions with the same bases, just subtract the exponent of the divisor term from the exponent of the dividend term and keep the same base.	$a^5 \div a^2 = a^3$
Any coefficients are also divided as usual.	$9a^5 \div 3a^3 = 3a^2$
To multiply exponential expressions with different bases, first make sure the exponents are the same. If they are, multiply the bases and maintain the same exponent.	$4^3 \times 5^3 = 20^3$; $a^5 \times b^5 = (ab)^5$
Follow the same procedure when you divide exponential expressions with different bases but the same exponents.	$20^3 \div 5^3 = 4^3$; $(ab)^5 \div a^5 = b^5$
When you raise a power to another power, multiply the exponents and keep the same base.	$\left(5^4\right)^5 = 5^{20}$; $\left(a^3\right)^5 = a^{15}$
If your expression includes a coefficient in parentheses, take it to the same power.	$\left(2a^2\right)^3 = 8a^6$

Figuring out the powers of 0 and 1

Exponents of 0 and 1 have special properties that you'll have to commit to memory:

>> The value of a base with an exponent of 0 (such as 7^0) is always 1 with the exception that 0^0 is undefined.

>> The value of a base with an exponent of 1 is the same value as the base ($3^1 = 3$).

Dealing with fractional exponents

If you see a problem with an exponent in fraction form, consider the top number of the fraction (the *numerator*) as indicating a power and the bottom number (the *denominator*) as indicating a root. So, to solve $256^{\frac{1}{4}}$, simply take 256 to the first power (because the numerator of the fraction is 1), which is 256. Then take the fourth root of 256 (because the denominator of the fraction is 4), which is 4, and that's your answer. (Find out more about roots in the "Checking Out the Ancestry: Roots" section later in this chapter.) Here's what it looks like mathematically:

$$256^{\frac{1}{4}} = \sqrt[4]{256^1} = \sqrt[4]{256} = 4$$

The GMAT may also present you with a variable base and a fractional exponent. You handle those the same way, like this:

$$a^{\frac{2}{3}} = \sqrt[3]{a^2}$$

This is what you get when you take a to the second power and then find its cube root.

Working with negative exponents

A negative exponent works like a positive exponent with a twist. A negative exponent takes the positive exponent and then flips the base and exponent around so that together they become the reciprocal (see the section, "Defining numerators, denominators, and other stuff you need to know about fractions," later in this chapter), like this:

$$3^{-3} = \frac{1}{3^3} = \frac{1}{27}$$

WARNING

When you work with negative exponents, don't fall for the trick of assuming that the negative exponent somehow turns the original number into a negative number. It ain't gonna happen! For example, $3^{-3} \neq -27$ or $\frac{1}{-27}$.

To see how the GMAT may test exponents, check out a sample problem.

EXAMPLE

If $8^{2x-3} = 1$, what is the value of x?

(A) 0

(B) 1.5

(C) 2

(D) 8

(E) 10.5

The trick to mastering this problem is to remember that a nonzero number to the power of 0 is equal to 1. So, for the expression to equal 1, 8^{2x-3} must equal 8^0. When you know that $8^{2x-3} = 8^0$, you know $2x - 3 = 0$. Solve for x.

$$2x - 3 = 0$$
$$2x = 3$$
$$x = \frac{3}{2}$$
$$x = 1.5$$

The simple answer to this perhaps initially confusing problem is Choice (B). If you picked Choice (C), you may have thought the exponent was equal to 1 instead of 0.

Checking Out the Ancestry: Roots

If you like exponents, you'll *love* roots, which are often presented as *radicals*. Roots are sort of the opposite of exponents. The square root of a number is a number that you square to get that number. So, because you can square 3 or -3 to get 9, the two square roots of 9 are 3 and -3. What could be simpler?

There are as many roots as there are powers. Most of the time, the GMAT has you work with square roots, but you may also see other roots. That won't intimidate you, though. If you come upon a cube root or fourth root, you'll recognize it by the radical sign, √. For even roots of positive numbers, the radical sign returns only the positive root of the number. Thus, $\sqrt{9} = 3$.

For example, the cube root of 27 is expressed as $\sqrt[3]{27}$. This expression asks what number, when raised to the third power, equals 27. Of course, the answer is 3 because $3^3 = 27$.

TIP

Radicals, even the seemingly ugly ones, can often be simplified. For example, if you come up with an answer of $\sqrt{98}$, you're not done yet. Just think of the factors of 98 that are perfect squares. You know that $2 \times 49 = 98$, and 49 is a perfect square: $7^2 = 49$. Put these factors under the radical sign: $\sqrt{49 \times 2}$. Now you can extract the 49 from the square root sign because its positive square root is 7. The result is $7\sqrt{2}$. Here's how you may see this situation on the GMAT.

EXAMPLE

If $\sqrt[n]{512} = 4\sqrt[n]{2}$, then $n = ?$

(A) $\frac{1}{4}$

(B) $\frac{1}{2}$

(C) 1

(D) 4

(E) 8

You can solve this equation most easily by simplifying the radical. The nth root of 512 is equal to 4 times the nth root of 2. Consider the factors of 512: $2 \times 256 = 512$, so $\sqrt[n]{512} = \sqrt[n]{256 \times 2}$, which also equals $4\sqrt[n]{2}$. $\sqrt[n]{256 \times 2} = \sqrt[n]{256} \times \sqrt[n]{2}$, so, then you know that $\sqrt[n]{256} = 4$, which is the same as saying $4^n = 256$. Because $4 \times 4 \times 4 \times 4 = 256$, $n = 4$, and Choice (D) is the correct answer.

Roots obey the same rules as exponents when it comes to performing operations. You can add and subtract roots as long as the roots are of the same order (that is, square root, cube root, and so on) and the same number. Here are a couple of examples:

$$5\sqrt{7} + 6\sqrt{7} = 11\sqrt{7}$$
$$11\sqrt{a} - 6\sqrt{a} = 5\sqrt{a}$$

When you need to multiply or divide radicals, make sure the roots are of the same order (such as all square or all cube roots) and you're good to go! For multiplication, just multiply what's under the radical signs, like this:

$$\sqrt{9} \times \sqrt{3} = \sqrt{27}$$

Divide what's under the radical signs like this:

$$\sqrt{9} \div \sqrt{3} = \sqrt{3}$$

And here's how a question about operations with radicals may appear on the GMAT.

EXAMPLE

$\sqrt{16+9} = ?$

(A) 5

(B) 7

(C) $12\frac{1}{2}$

(D) 25

(E) 625

WARNING

Pay attention to the values underneath the radical. In this question, the line of the square root symbol extends over the entire expression, so you're supposed to find the square root of $16 + 9$, not $\sqrt{16} + \sqrt{9}$. It's a subtle but major difference!

First, add the values under the radical sign: $16 + 9 = 25$. The square root of 25 is 5, so Choice (A) is the correct answer. If you chose 7, you determined the square root of each of the values before you added them together. For 7 to be the correct answer, your problem should have been written with two separate square root signs, $\sqrt{16} + \sqrt{9}$.

Order of Operations: Please Excuse My Dear Aunt Sally

Basic arithmetic requires that you perform operations in a certain order. Okay, so maybe you don't have an aunt named Sally, but this section's title is a helpful mnemonic for the order you use when you have to perform several operations in one problem. What that means is that if you have an expression that contains addition, subtraction, multiplication, division, exponents (and roots), and parentheses to boot, it helps to know which operation you perform first, second, third, and so on.

The acronym *PEMDAS* (Please Excuse My Dear Aunt Sally) can help you remember to perform operations in the following order:

>> **P**arentheses (or other grouping symbol such as brackets, braces, and fraction bars)

>> **E**xponents (and roots)

>> **M**ultiplication and **D**ivision, from left to right

>> **A**ddition and **S**ubtraction, from left to right

Here's an example:

$$20(4-7)^3 + 4\left(\frac{9}{3}\right)^2 = x$$

First, evaluate what's inside the parentheses:

$$20(-3)^3 + 4(3)^2 = x$$

Then evaluate the exponents:

$$20(-27) + 4(9) = x$$

Then multiply from left to right:

$$-540 + 36 = x$$

Finally, do the addition and subtraction from left to right:

$$-504 = x$$

Splitting Up: Fractions, Decimals, and Percents

Fractions, decimals, and percents are interrelated concepts; they all represent parts of a whole. You'll likely need to convert from one form to the other to solve several problems on the GMAT math.

Fractions are really division problems. If you divide the value of a by the value of b, you get the fraction $\frac{a}{b}$. So $1 \div 4 = \frac{1}{4}$.

To convert the fraction to a decimal, you simply perform the division indicated by the fraction bar: $\frac{1}{4} = 0.25$.

To convert a decimal back to a fraction, you first count the digits to the right of the decimal point; then divide the original number over a 1 followed by the same number of zeroes as there were digits to the right of the decimal. Then you simplify. So $0.25 = \frac{25}{100} = \frac{1}{4}$; $0.356 = \frac{356}{1,000} = \frac{89}{250}$.

Changing a decimal to a percent is really pretty easy. Percent simply means *out of one hundred*, or times $\frac{1}{100}$. To perform the conversion, you move the decimal two places to the right. Then you write the resulting number as a percent. For example, $0.25 = 25\%$, and $0.925 = 92.5\%$.

To turn a percent back into a decimal, you follow the procedure in reverse. You move the decimal point two spaces to the left and lose the percent sign, like this: $1\% = 0.01$.

TIP

The GMAT probably won't specifically ask you to express answers in all three formats (fractions, decimals, and percents), but you need to know that answer choices can appear in any one of the three formats when you're dealing with percentage problems.

You may encounter a GMAT problem that asks you to find something like the portion of garbage that's paper when you know that out of 215 million tons of garbage, about 86 million tons of the total garbage are paper products. You should be able to express the answer as a fraction, decimal, or percent.

As a fraction: $\frac{86}{215}$ or $\frac{2}{5}$; as a decimal: $\frac{2}{5} = 2 \div 5 = 0.4$; and as a percent: $0.4 = 40\%$

Dealing with decimals

If you're a pro at computing with whole numbers, then you totally have the skills to handle decimals, too. In a nutshell, here's how:

To add or subtract decimals line up their decimal points, and then add or subtract as with whole numbers.

To multiply two decimals, ignore the decimal points and multiply as with whole numbers. The number of decimal places in the product is the total number of decimal places in the two numbers being multiplied.

To divide two decimals, first move the decimal points of the two numbers equally many digits to the right until the divisor is a whole number, and then divide as with whole numbers.

Delving into fractions

GMAT questions may refer to the parts of a fraction. The *numerator* is the number on top and represents the part of the whole. The *denominator* is the number on the bottom and represents the whole. The horizontal line that separates the numerator and denominator is the *fraction bar.*

To better understand these terms, picture a cherry pie sliced into eight equal pieces (see Figure 10-1) and a hungry family of seven, each of whom has a slice after dinner (or before dinner if they're sneaky).

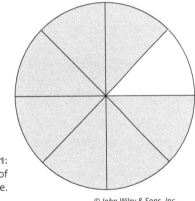

FIGURE 10-1:
Fraction of
a pie.

© *John Wiley & Sons, Inc.*

The shaded pieces of pie show how much of the dessert was gobbled up by the family; the unshaded piece shows what's left of the pie when the family is finished.

To put this pie into terms of a fraction, the total number of equal pieces in the pie to begin with (the whole) represents the denominator, and the number of pieces that were eaten (the part of the whole) is represented by the numerator. In this case, the number of pieces that were eaten made up $\frac{7}{8}$ of the total pie, so 7 is the numerator and 8 is the denominator. To look at the scenario another way, you can say that the fraction of pie that was left is $\frac{1}{8}$ of what you started with.

Here are a few other fraction definitions you should be familiar with:

> » **Proper fractions:** Fractions where the numerator is less than the denominator. Examples of proper fractions are $\frac{3}{4}$ and $\frac{13}{15}$.
> » **Improper fractions:** Fractions where the numerator is either greater than or equal to the denominator. An example is $\frac{15}{2}$.
> » **Mixed fractions:** Another way of formatting improper fractions is with a whole number and a proper fraction, such as $1\frac{2}{3}$, which is shorthand for $1 + \frac{2}{3}$.
> » **Reciprocal:** The flip-flop of a fraction. The numerator and denominator switch places. So, the reciprocal of $\frac{3}{5}$ is $\frac{5}{3}$. To get the reciprocal of a whole number, you simply divide 1 by your number. So, the reciprocal of 5 is $\frac{1}{5}$. The reciprocal of a variable a is $\frac{1}{a}$, just as long as $a \neq 0$.
> » **Equivalent fractions:** Two fractions that represent the same number. For example, $\frac{18}{24}$ and $\frac{21}{28}$ are equivalent because they both represent the number $\frac{3}{4}$. In each case, you reduce the fraction to its simplest terms by dividing both the numerator and denominator by their *greatest common factor* (gcf). The gcf of 18 and 24 is 6 and the gcf of 21 and 28 is 7.

TIP

When you work with fractions on the GMAT, you may have to substitute mixed fractions for improper fractions and vice versa. You'll find that changing a mixed fraction into an improper fraction before you perform operations is often easier. To change a mixed fraction to an improper fraction, you multiply the whole number by the denominator, add the numerator, and put that value over the original denominator, like this:

$$2\frac{2}{3} = \frac{8}{3}$$

You multiply the whole number (2) by the denominator (3) to get 6; add the numerator (2) to 6, which gives you 8; and place that value over the original denominator of 3.

To convert an improper fraction to a mixed number, you divide the numerator by the denominator and put the remainder over the denominator, like this:

$$\frac{31}{4} = 7\frac{3}{4}$$

First, you divide 31 by 4: 4 goes into 31 seven times with a remainder of 3 ($4 \times 7 = 28$ and $31 - 28 = 3$). Put the remainder over the original denominator, and place that fraction next to the whole number, 7.

TIP

Another thing you should know about fractions is how to simplify them. You may be thinking that fractions are simple enough, that it just can't get any easier. Simplifying a fraction means reducing it to its simplest terms. You make the larger terms smaller by dividing both the numerator and denominator by the same value. Here's an example of reducing or simplifying a fraction:

$$\frac{12}{36} \div \frac{12}{12} = \frac{1}{3}$$

The greatest common factor of 12 and 36 is 12. When you divide the fraction by $\frac{12}{12}$, it's the same as dividing by 1. And any number divided by 1 equals the original number. You know that $\frac{1}{3}$ has the same value as $\frac{12}{36}$. It's just in simpler terms.

Adding and subtracting fractions

Because fractions involve parts of whole numbers, they're not as easy to add together as $2+2$. To add or subtract fractions with the same denominator, all you do is either add or subtract the numerators and put that value over the original denominator, like this: $\frac{2}{7} + \frac{4}{7} = \frac{6}{7}$; $\frac{6}{5} - \frac{4}{5} = \frac{2}{5}$.

WARNING

Be careful when you're asked to add or subtract fractions with different denominators. You can't just add or subtract the numerators and denominators. You have to change the fractions to equivalent fractions that have the same denominator. So, first, you determine the *least common denominator* (lcd). For example, if you see $\frac{2}{3} + \frac{1}{9}$, you know you have to change the denominators before you add.

To determine the lcd, consider values that are divisible by both 3 and 9. When you multiply 3 by 9, you get 27. So, both 3 and 9 go into 27, but that's not the smallest number that both 3 and 9 go into evenly. Both 3 and 9 are factors of 9, so the lcd is 9 rather than 27.

Convert $\frac{2}{3}$ to $\frac{6}{9}$ by multiplying the numerator and denominator by 3. The second fraction already has a denominator of 9, so you're ready to add:

$$\frac{6}{9} + \frac{1}{9} = \frac{7}{9}$$

Multiplying and dividing fractions

Multiplying fractions is easy. Just multiply the numerators to get the product's numerator, and multiply the denominators to get the product's denominator. Reduce if you have to:

$$\frac{4}{5} \times \frac{5}{7} = \frac{20}{35} = \frac{4}{7}$$

TIP

An easier and faster (and faster is better on the GMAT) way to perform this task is to simply cancel out the fives that appear in the denominator of the first fraction and the numerator of the second one, like so:

$$\frac{4}{\cancel{5}} \times \frac{\cancel{5}}{7} = \frac{4}{7}$$

Dividing fractions is pretty much the same as multiplying them except for one very important initial step. Here's what you do to divide two fractions:

1. **Find the reciprocal of the second fraction (that is, turn the second fraction upside down).**

2. **Multiply (yes, multiply) the numerators and denominators of the resulting fractions.**

Here's an example:

$$\frac{2}{7} \div \frac{3}{5} = \frac{2}{7} \times \frac{5}{3} = \frac{10}{21}$$

To test your knowledge of how to perform operations with fractions, the GMAT may present you with a straightforward computation, such as the following.

EXAMPLE

$$\frac{1}{2}+\left(\frac{3}{8}\div\frac{2}{5}\right)-\left(\frac{5}{6}\times\frac{7}{8}\right)=$$

(A) $\frac{1}{8}$

(B) $\frac{15}{16}$

(C) $\frac{17}{24}$

(D) $2\frac{1}{6}$

(E) $\frac{5}{6}$

To solve this problem, you need to know how to perform all four operations with fractions. Be sure to follow the order of operations. (See the earlier section, "Order of Operations: Please Excuse My Dear Aunt Sally," for details.)

First, compute the operations inside the first set of parentheses:

$$\left(\frac{3}{8}\div\frac{2}{5}\right)=\frac{3}{8}\times\frac{5}{2}=\frac{15}{16}$$

Then, figure out the value of the second set of parentheses:

$$\left(\frac{5}{6}\times\frac{7}{8}\right)=\frac{35}{48}$$

Now the equation looks like this:

$$\frac{1}{2}+\frac{15}{16}-\frac{35}{48}=$$

The least common denominator of 2, 16, and 48 is 48. To convert the denominator in the first fraction to 48, multiply the fraction by $\frac{24}{24}$:

$$\frac{1}{2}\times\frac{24}{24}=\frac{24}{48}$$

To convert the denominator in the second fraction to 48, multiply by $\frac{3}{3}$:

$$\frac{15}{16}\times\frac{3}{3}=\frac{45}{48}$$

Now you can compute the expression:

$$\frac{24}{48}+\frac{45}{48}-\frac{35}{48}=\frac{34}{48}$$

That's not one of your answer options, so you need to simplify the fraction. Divide both the numerator and denominator by 2 to get $\frac{17}{24}$, which is Choice (C).

Knowing how to perform operations with fractions comes in handy for percent problems, too.

EXAMPLE

What is 75% of $7\frac{1}{4}$?

(A) $\frac{37}{130}$

(B) $5\frac{3}{4}$

(C) $5\frac{7}{16}$

(D) $7\frac{3}{4}$

(E) $21\frac{3}{16}$

This question asks you to determine a percent of a fraction. Note that the answers are in fraction form rather than decimal form, which means you need to work out the problem so it ends up as a fraction rather than a decimal.

Whenever you see the word *of* between two numerical quantities in a word problem, you know it means multiply. Therefore, you're finding the product: $75\% \times 7\frac{1}{4}$. Converted to a fraction, 75 percent is $\frac{75}{100} = \frac{3}{4}$, so you're figuring out the answer to $\frac{3}{4} \times 7\frac{1}{4}$. Converting $7\frac{1}{4}$ from a mixed fraction gives you $\frac{29}{4}$, so the answer is $\frac{3}{4} \times \frac{29}{4} = \frac{87}{16}$.

Convert to a mixed fraction: $\frac{87}{16} = 5\frac{7}{16}$. The answer is Choice (C).

TIP

You can easily eliminate Choices (D) and (E). Obviously, 75% of $7\frac{1}{4}$ has to be less than $7\frac{1}{4}$.

Calculating percent change

Percent change is the amount a number increases or decreases expressed as a percent of the original number. For example, if a store normally sells tennis shoes for $75 and has them on sale for $60, what is the percent change of the markdown? To get the percent decrease, simply take the difference in price, which is $15, and divide that number by the original price:

$$15 \div 75 = 0.2 = 20\%$$

WARNING

Pay careful attention when figuring percent change. For example, if the store then increases the marked down price by 20%, you may think the price returns to its original value. But that's not right. If you increase the lower price of $60 by 20%, you get a $12 increase. The price goes from $60 to just $72: $60 \times 0.2 = \$12$; $\$60 + \$12 = \$72$.

How can that be? The reason the numbers don't seem to add up is that when you drop the price the first time, you take 20% of $75, which is a bigger number to take a percent from than the lower sale price.

So, what percent of the marked-down price of $60 must you increase the price by in order to get the original price of $75? To find out, take the difference in price, $15, and determine what percent that is of the sale price of $60:

$$15 \div 60 = \frac{15}{60} = \frac{1}{4} = 0.25 = 25\%$$

So, it's a 25% increase from $60 to $75.

TIP

If you know what the percent increase or decrease of an original number is and want to find out how that increase or decrease changes the original number, keep these two important details in mind:

» To find the result of a percent increase, multiply the original number by 1 plus the rate as a decimal.

» To find the result of a percent decrease, multiply the original number by 1 minus the rate as a decimal.

So, if you increase 100 by 5%, you multiply 100 by $(1+0.05)$:

$$100 \times (1+0.05) = 100 \times 1.05 = 105$$

If you decrease 100 by 5%, you multiply 100 by $(1-0.05)$.

$$100 \times (1-0.05) = 100 \times 0.95 = 95$$

Try a sample percent change problem.

EXAMPLE

A file cabinet that originally cost $52 is on sale for 15 percent off. If the sales tax on office furniture is 5 percent of the purchase price, how much is the total cost of the file cabinet at its sale price?

(A) $7.80

(B) $40.00

(C) $44.20

(D) $46.41

(E) $48.23

This word problem asks you how to deal with two percentages, the subtraction of the percentage discount and the addition of the percentage sales tax. First, calculate the discount.

You can figure 15% in your head by knowing that 10% of 52 is 5.20 and half of that (5%) is 2.60, so the discount is $7.80. Now subtract the discount from the original price: $52.00 - $7.80 = $44.20. The discount price for the cabinet is $44.20.

You still need to calculate the sales tax, so don't choose Choice (C)! You know that 5% of 44.20 is half of 4.42 (10%), or 2.21. You add $2.21 to $44.20. The only answer that ends in 1 is Choice (D). You can do the math to verify your guess, but Choice (D) is the correct answer: $44.20 + $2.21 = $46.41. Not a bad price for some much-needed organization!

Taking it further: Repeated percent change

Now suppose you want to show a percent change repeated over a period of time, such as when you need to figure out how much interest accrues on a bank account after several years. To do so, you take the formula for percent change a step further.

Suppose you have $100 in a bank account at the end of 2013, and you want to know how much money will be in that same account at the end of 2023 at an annual interest rate of 5 percent (if you make no withdrawals or additional deposits). No fair pulling it out when the stock market is making a bull run! One way to figure this out is by using the percentage increase formula. The first step looks something like this:

$$100 \times (1+0.05) = 105$$

Thus, you have $105 at the end of the first year.

WARNING

Don't make the mistake of thinking that all you have to do is multiply by 10 and you have $1,050 after 10 years. You wish! This type of question will trap anyone who isn't paying attention every time.

To get the correct answer, tweak the formula a bit by adding an exponent. The exponent will be the number of times the original number changes. The formula looks like this, where n is the number of changes:

$$\text{Final Amount} = \text{Original Number} \times (1 + \text{Rate})^n$$

Plug the numbers into the formula and solve:

$$100 \times (1 + 0.05)^{10} = x$$
$$100 \times 1.05^{10} = x$$
$$100 \times 1.6289 = x$$
$$162.89 = x$$

Therefore, after 10 years, you'd have $162.89 in the bank.

To show a repeated percent decrease over time, you'd use this similar formula:

$$\text{Final Amount} = \text{Original Number} \times (1 - \text{Rate})^n$$

Making Comparisons: Ratios and Proportions

A ratio is the relation between two like numbers or two like values. A ratio may be written as a fraction ($\frac{3}{4}$), as a division expression ($3 \div 4$), or with a colon ($3:4$), or it can be stated as "3 to 4."

Because a ratio can be regarded as a fraction, multiplying or dividing both terms of a ratio by the same number doesn't change the value of the ratio. So $1:4 = 2:8 = 4:16$. To reduce a ratio to its lowest terms, simplify the ratio as you would a fraction. (See the earlier section, "Delving into fractions.")

Ratios often crop up in word problems. Suppose an auto manufacturer ships a total of 160 cars to two dealerships at a ratio of 3 to 5. This means that for every three cars that go to Dealer 1, five cars ship to Dealer 2. To determine how many cars each dealership receives, add the terms of the ratio, or $3 + 5$, to get the total number of fractional parts each dealership will get: $3 + 5 = 8$. The first dealership will receive $\frac{3}{8}$ of 160 cars, or $\frac{3}{8} \times 160$, which equals 60. The second dealership receives $\frac{5}{8}$ of 160 cars, or 100.

TIP

As long as the total number of *items* in a ratio problem can be evenly divided by the total number of fractional parts, you can find the total number of items that are attributable to each part.

A *proportion* is a statement that two ratios are equal. It may be written as the proportion sign :: or with an equal sign. You can read 1:4 :: 2:8 or $\frac{1}{4} = \frac{2}{8}$ as "1 is to 4 as 2 is to 8."

The first and last terms in a proportion are the *extremes*, and the second and third terms are the *means.* If you multiply the means together and multiply the extremes together and then compare the products, you find that the products are the same:

$$1 \times 8 = 2 \times 4$$

Anytime you know three terms of a proportion, you can find the missing term: first, by multiplying either the two means or the two extremes (depending on which are known), and then dividing the product by the remaining term. This is commonly known as *cross-multiplying*. If you know 7:8 :: *x*:104, you can solve for *x* by using cross-multiplication

$$\frac{7}{8} = \frac{x}{104}$$
$$8x = 7(104)$$
$$8x = 728$$
$$x = 91$$

Be sure to keep the order of the terms of your ratios and proportions consistent. For example, if your proportion is "3 is to 4 as 5 is to *x*," you must set up the problem like this:

$$\frac{3}{4} = \frac{5}{x}$$

rather than this:

$$\frac{3}{4} = \frac{x}{5}$$

Here's what a GMAT ratio problem may look like.

If the ratio of 4*a* to 9*b* is 1 to 9, what is the ratio of 8*a* to 9*b*?

(A) 1 to 18

(B) 1 to 39

(C) 2 to 9

(D) 2 to 36

(E) 3 to 9

At first, this problem may appear to be more difficult than it actually is. If 4*a* to 9*b* is a 1 to 9 ratio, then 8*a* to 9*b* must be a 2 to 9 ratio, because 8*a* is 2 times 4*a*. If 4*a* equals 1, then 8*a* must equal 2. The answer, therefore, has to be Choice (C).

Playing the Numbers: Scientific Notation

Scientific notation is a simple way to write out humongous (technical term) or teensy weensy (another technical term) numbers so they're more manageable. You express a number in scientific notation by writing it as the product of a number and a power of 10. Simply move the decimal point so all digits except one are to the right of the decimal point; then multiply that decimal number times 10 raised to an exponent that equals the number of places you moved the decimal point. If you're working with a large number and you moved the decimal point to the left, the exponent is positive:

$$1,234,567 = 1.234567 \times 10^6$$
$$20 \text{ million} (20,000,000) = 2.0 \times 10^7$$

To display very small numbers in scientific notation, you move the decimal point to the right so one value is to the left of the decimal point. When you move the decimal point to the right, the exponent is negative. In this example, the decimal point moved six places to the right:

$$0.0000037 = 3.7 \times 10^{-6}$$

Here's how the GMAT may test you on scientific notation.

The number of organisms in a liter of water is approximately 6.0×10^{23}. Assuming this number is correct, about how many organisms exist in a covered Petri dish that contains $\frac{1}{200}$ liters of water?

(A) 6.9

(B) 3.0×10^{21}

(C) 6.0×10^{22}

(D) 3.0×10^{23}

(E) 1.2×10^{26}

This question uses many words to ask you to the find the answer to $\frac{6.0 \times 10^{23}}{200}$. If a liter of water contains a certain number of organisms, $\frac{1}{200}$ liter of water would contain the same number of organisms divided by 200. Try not to let the wording of the question confuse you.

So, if 6.0 divided by 200 equals 0.03, the answer is 0.03×10^{23}, but that's not scientific notation because the decimal point is in the wrong place. Move the decimal point two places to the right and decrease the power by two (remember that when you move the decimal point to the right, the exponent is negative, so you subtract). The answer is Choice (B), 3.0×10^{21}.

Chapter **11**

Considering All the Variables: Algebra

Ah, algebra, the vibrant and creative realm of mathematics that uses variables to stand for unspecified numbers. With its extensive range of techniques, algebra enables you to manipulate variable expressions, unravel equations and solve complex problems, identify patterns, and analyze mathematical relationships.

Perhaps, that description may sound like mumbo-jumbo to you, but the idea is that algebra is based on the operations of arithmetic in which variables (usually letters) stand for numbers. For example, you use algebra to solve equations and to find the numerical value of a variable. A familiar situation for which this comes into play is when you encounter the instruction, "Solve the equation for x."

The algebra concepts tested on the GMAT do not extend beyond what is usually covered in a first-year algebra course, so you're at no disadvantage if you've never taken Algebra II. But many GMAT math problems involve basic algebra, and this chapter provides what you should know to excel on all of them.

Defining the Elements: Algebraic Terminology

In the following sections, we provide some key definitions to know. Although the GMAT doesn't explicitly ask you to define certain terminologies such as *variable, constant,* or *coefficient,* it does expect you to know these concepts when they crop up in the questions.

Braving the unknowns: Variables and constants

You'll see a lot of *variables* in algebra problems. They're the symbols that stand for numbers. Usually, the symbols take the form of letters and represent specific numeric values. True to their name, variables' values can change depending on the equation they're in.

Think of variables as symbols representing distinct entities. For example, if a store charges different prices for apples and peaches and you buy two apples and four peaches, the clerk can't ring them up together by simply adding $2+4$ to get 6. That strategy would be flawed because the two fruits are not the same price. So, to express the transaction in algebraic terms, you use variables to stand in for the price of apples and peaches, something like $2a$ and $4p$.

In contrast, *constants,* as their name implies, are numbers with values that don't change in a specific problem. All the real numbers are constants. Each has a definite, fixed value. Letters may also be used to refer to constants, but they don't change their value in an equation as variables do (for example, a, b, and c stand for fixed numbers in the formula $y = ax^2 + bx + c$).

Coming together: Terms and expressions

A *numerical expression* is any constant or combination of two or more constants joined by explicit or implied operational symbols. For example, 200, 4.5, $\frac{4 \times 25}{2 \times 5}$, $0.75(2{,}000) + 2{,}000$, $\frac{50\pi}{30\pi}$, and $\pi(4)^2$ are numerical expressions.

An *algebraic expression* is a meaningful combination of one or more variables joined by one or more ordinary operations of arithmetic, with or without constants (explicitly) included. It is a symbolic representation of a number. For example, $7x$, axy, $5x + 3$, $3abc$, $(x-3)^2 - 9$, $ax^2 + bx + c$, $\frac{10}{t-25}$, $8x^3 - 12x^2 + 6x - 1$, and $3xy - y^2 + x$ are algebraic expressions.

An algebraic expression can be *evaluated* by substituting values of the variables in the expression. For example, if $x = -2$ and $y = 3$, then $3xy - y^2 + x$ can be evaluated as

$$3(-2)(3) - (3)^2 + (-2) = -18 - 9 - 2 = -29.$$

A *term* is any combination of one or more variables or constants that you can multiply or divide to form a single unit in an expression. In algebraic expressions, terms are separated by addition. For example, the algebraic expression $ax^2 + bx + c$ has three terms. The first term is ax^2, the second term is bx, and the third term is c. When subtraction is involved in an algebraic expression, be mindful that terms are separated by *addition.* Thus, the terms of the algebraic expression $8x^3 - 12x^2 + 6x - 1$ are $8x^3$, $-12x^2$, $6x$, and -1. This is the case because, by the definition of subtraction, $8x^3 - 12x^2 + 6x - 1 = 8x^3 + \left(-12x^2\right) + 6x + (-1)$. The terms $8x^3$, $-12x^2$, and $6x$ are variable terms, and -1 is the constant term in the expression.

Although an expression can contain just one term, it's more common to think of expressions as combinations of two or more terms. So, in the apples and peaches scenario presented earlier, you can write an expression for the cost of two apples and four peaches as $2a + 4p$.

In a term that is a product of two or more factors, the *numerical coefficient,* or simply *coefficient,* is the numerical factor, or the product of the numerical factors, in that term. In $2a + 4p$, the variables are a and p, and the numbers 2 and 4 are the coefficients of the variables. This means that the coefficient of the variable a is 2 and the coefficient of the variable p is 4. If no coefficient is explicitly written, then the numerical coefficient is understood to be 1. Thus, the coefficient of xy^2 is 1.

In an algebraic expression, terms involving the same variable, even if they have different coefficients, are *like terms.* For example, in the expression $3x + 4y - 2x + y$, $3x$ and $-2x$ are like terms because they both contain the single x variable; $4y$ and y are also like terms because they both contain the y variable and only the y variable. All constant terms are like terms.

REMEMBER

For like terms, the variables must be exact matches with the same powers; for example, $3x^3y$ and x^3y are like terms, but x and x^2 aren't like terms, and neither are $2x$ and $2xy$.

You can combine (add/subtract) like terms together, but you can't combine unlike terms. So, in the expression $3x + 4y - 2x + y$, you can subtract the terms with the common x variable: $3x - 2x = x$. And you can add the like terms with the common y variable: $4y + y = 5y$ (y is understood to be $1y$). All this combining results in the final expression of $x + 5y$, which is a much simpler expression to work with. We work with many more algebraic expressions in the section, "Maintaining an Orderly Fashion: Algebraic Operations," later in this chapter.

Knowing the nomials: Kinds of expressions

On the GMAT, you'll work with various monomials and polynomials. These algebraic expressions comprising single or multiple terms are an integral part of the exam.

A *monomial* consists of a single term, which when simplified is a constant, a variable, or a product of a numerical coefficient and one or more variables, where each variable is raised to a nonnegative integer power, such as $4x$, $6x^2y$, and x^3z^2. The *degree of a monomial* is the sum of the exponents of its variables. Thus, the degree of $4x$ is 1, the degree of $6x^2y$ is 3, and the degree of x^3z^2 is 5.

Poly means many, so we bet you've already figured out that a *polynomial* is an algebraic expression that is the sum of monomials, such as $6x^2y + 2xy^2$, $x + 5y$, and $8x^3 - 12x^2 + 6x - 1$. Polynomials can have more specific designations, depending on how many terms they contain. For example, as previously noted, a *monomial* is a polynomial of exactly one term, such as $-12x^2$. A *binomial* is a polynomial of exactly two terms, such as $a + b$ or $2x + 3$. And a *trinomial* is a polynomial of exactly three terms, like $4x^2 - 8x - 5$. Polynomials can have any number of terms, but for the GMAT, you don't need to know specific names to describe polynomials beyond three terms.

TIP

Often of interest, are polynomials that are the sum of several terms that contain different powers of the same variable.

The *degree of a polynomial* is the same as the greatest of the degrees of its monomial terms after the polynomial has been simplified. The binomial $2x + 3$ is a *first-degree* (or *linear*) *polynomial in x* since the highest power of x is 1. The trinomial $4x^2 - 8x - 5$ is a *second degree* (or *quadratic*) *polynomial in x* since the highest power of x is 2.

REMEMBER

A famous trinomial that you should be very familiar with for the GMAT is the expression known as a *quadratic polynomial*, which is the trinomial expression $ax^2 + bx + c$, where a, b, and c are constants with $a \neq 0$.

We discuss this very important expression in the "Solving quadratic equations" section, later in this chapter.

Maintaining an Orderly Fashion: Algebraic Operations

Symbols like $+$, $-$, $\times$, and $\div$ are common to arithmetic and algebra. They symbolize the operations you perform on numbers. Arithmetic uses numbers with known values, such as $5 + 7 = 12$, in its operations (visit Chapter 10 for more on basic arithmetic operations), but algebraic operations deal with unknowns, like $x + y = z$. This algebraic equation can't produce an exact numerical value because you don't know what x and y represent, let alone z. But that doesn't stop you from solving algebra problems as best you can with the given information. In the following sections, we show you how to add, subtract, multiply, and divide expressions with unknowns.

Adding to and taking away

From arithmetic, you know that 3 dozen plus 6 dozen is 9 dozen, or

$$(3 \times 12) + (6 \times 12) = (9 \times 12)$$

In algebra, you can write a somewhat similar equation by using a variable to stand in for the dozen: $3x + 6x = 9x$. And you can subtract to get the opposite result: $9x - 6x = 3x$.

TIP

Remember to combine positive and negative numbers according to the rules of arithmetic (see Chapter 10 if you need a refresher). The sum of two or more positive numbers in an expression is positive. Similarly, the sum of two or more negative numbers in an expression is negative. If you add a positive and a negative number, it's as though you're subtracting with the answer taking the sign of the number with the greater absolute value. In particular, if you add a positive number and its opposite negative number, the sum is 0.

For example, to tackle the expression $7x + (-10x) + 22x$, you find the sum of the two positive numbers ($7x$ and $22x$) and then subtract the value of the negative number (because adding a negative is the same as subtracting a positive), like this:

$$7x + (-10x) + 22x =$$
$$29x - 10x =$$
$$19x$$

That's fine for adding and subtracting like terms, you may say, but what about working with unlike terms? You can't combine terms with different symbols or variables the same way you can when the symbols are the same. For instance, look at this example:

$$7x + 10y + 15x - 3y$$

WARNING

If you were to simply combine the whole expression by adding and subtracting without accounting for the different variables, you'd come up with a wrong answer, something like 29xy. (And you can bet the GMAT will offer this incorrect expression as one of the answer choices to try to trap you.) Instead, you first separate the x terms from the y terms and add and subtract to get something more manageable, like this:

$$7x + 15x = 22x$$
$$10y - 3y = 7y$$

which gives you this final expression:

$$22x + 7y$$

TIP

If you want to get tricky and add two or more expressions, you can set them up just as you would an addition problem in arithmetic. Remember, only like terms can be combined this way.

$$
\begin{array}{r}
3x + 4y - 7z \\
2x - 2y + 8z \\
-x + 3y + 6z \\
\hline
4x + 5y + 7z
\end{array}
$$

Here's how an algebra problem may look on the GMAT.

For all x and y, $\left(4x^2 - 6xy - 12y^2\right) - \left(8x^2 - 12xy + 4y^2\right) = ?$

(A) $-4x^2 - 18xy - 16y^2$

(B) $-4x^2 + 6xy - 16y^2$

(C) $-4x^2 - 6xy - 8y^2$

(D) $4x^2 - 6xy + 16y^2$

(E) $12x^2 - 18xy - 8y^2$

The easiest way to approach this problem is to distribute the negative sign to the second expression (see the later section, "Distributing terms") and combine the two expressions with like terms by following these steps:

1. **Distribute the negative sign (multiply each term in the second expression by –1).**

Remember that subtracting is the same as adding the opposite of a number. So, your problem is really $\left(4x^2 - 6xy - 12y^2\right) + -1\left(8x^2 - 12xy + 4y^2\right)$. Distributing the negative sign changes the second expression to $-8x^2 + 12xy - 4y^2$, because a negative times a positive makes a negative and two negatives make a positive.

2. **Combine the expressions with like terms together:**

$4x^2 - 8x^2 - 6xy + 12xy - 12y^2 - 4y^2$

3. **Add and subtract like terms:**

$4x^2 - 8x^2 = -4x^2$

$-6xy + 12xy = 6xy$

$-12y^2 - 4y^2 = -16y^2$

4. **Put the terms back into the polynomial:**

$-4x^2 + 6xy - 16y^2$

So, the answer is $-4x^2 + 6xy - 16y^2$, which is Choice (B). If you chose any of the other answers, you either distributed the negative sign improperly or you added and subtracted the like terms incorrectly.

Eliminate wrong answers as you combine terms. For instance, once you determine that the first term is $-4x^2$, you can eliminate Choices (D) and (E).

After you've combined like terms, double-check that you've used the correct signs, particularly when you change all the signs like you did in the second expression. The other answer choices for the sample problem are similar to the correct choice. They're designed to trap you in case you make an addition or subtraction error. Add and subtract carefully, and you won't fall for these tricks.

Multiplying and dividing expressions

Multiplying and dividing two or more variables works just as though you were performing these same operations on numbers with known values. So, if $2^3 = 2 \times 2 \times 2$, then $x^3 = x \times x \times x$. Likewise, if $2^2 \times 2^3 = 2^5$, then $x^2 \times x^3 = x^5$. Similarly, if $2^6 \div 2^4 = 2^2$, then $y^6 \div y^4 = y^2$.

The process is pretty simple for monomials, but polynomials may be a little more complicated. In the next sections, we explore the different methods for multiplying and dividing polynomials.

Distributing terms

You can distribute terms in algebra just like you do in arithmetic. For example, when you multiply a binomial by a number, you multiply each term in the binomial by the number. In this example, you multiply each term inside the parentheses by $4x$:

$$4x(x-3) = 4x^2 - 12x$$

With division, you do the same operation in reverse. It's important to mention that, in algebra, division is commonly indicated by the fraction bar. To perform the division, divide each term in the numerator by $4x$:

$$\frac{16x^2 + 4x}{4x} = \frac{16x^2}{4x} + \frac{4x}{4x} = 4x + 1$$

Here's an example of a GMAT question in which you use distribution to answer.

For all x, $12x - (-10x) - 3x(-x + 10) =$

(A) $10x$

(B) $-3x^2 - 10x$

(C) $3x^2 - 52x$

(D) $3x^2 + 8x$

(E) $3x^2 - 8x$

This question tests your ability to add, subtract, and multiply terms in an algebraic expression.

1. **Use distribution to multiply $(-x + 10)$ by $-3x$:** $-3x(-x + 10) = 3x^2 - 30x$

Now the equation looks like this: $12x - (-10x) + 3x^2 - 30x$

2. **Combine the terms that contain just x:** $12x + 10x - 30x = -8x$

Now you have: $3x^2 - 8x$

So, the answer is Choice (E): $3x^2 - 8x$.

Stacking terms

One easy way to multiply two polynomials is to stack them on top of one another. Suppose you have this problem: $(x^2 + 2xy + y^2)(x - y)$.

You can stack this expression just like an old-fashioned multiplication problem. Just remember to multiply each of the terms in the first line by each term in the second line.

$$
\begin{array}{r}
x^2 + 2xy + y^2 \\
x - y \\
\hline
x^3 + 2x^2y + xy^2 \\
- x^2y - 2xy^2 - y^3 \\
\hline
x^3 + x^2y - xy^2 - y^3
\end{array}
$$

Line up like terms during the first round of multiplication so they match up before you add the partial products.

The GMAT may ask you to divide a polynomial by a monomial. Simply divide each term of the polynomial by the monomial. Here's how you'd divide in the expression $\dfrac{60x^4 - 20x^3}{5x}$:

$$\frac{60x^4 - 20x^3}{5x} = \frac{60x^4}{5x} - \frac{20x^3}{5x} = \left(12x^{4-1}\right) - \left(4x^{3-1}\right) = 12x^3 - 4x^2$$

Taking a shine to the FOIL method

You can multiply two binomials by using the *FOIL* method. FOIL is an acronym for *first, outer, inner, last*, which indicates the order that you multiply the terms from one binomial by the terms of the second binomial before adding their products. Look at this example:

$$(4x - 5)(3x + 8) =$$

1. Multiply the first terms (**4x** and **3x**) of each binomial: $4x \times 3x = 12x^2$

2. Multiply the outer terms (**4x** and **8**): $4x \times 8 = 32x$

3. Multiply the inner terms (**3x** and **-5**): $3x \times -5 = -15x$

4. Add these two products at this point because they're like terms: $32x - 15x = 17x$

5. Multiply the last terms (**-5** and **8**) of each binomial: $-5 \times 8 = -40$

6. Combine all the results to form the final product: $12x^2 + 17x - 40$

You may recognize this expression as a quadratic polynomial, which we discussed in the earlier section, "Knowing the nomials: Kinds of expressions."

TIP

To save time on the GMAT, you should commit the following factors and their special products to memory:

$$(x + y)^2 = x^2 + 2xy + y^2$$
$$(x - y)^2 = x^2 - 2xy + y^2$$
$$(x + y)(x - y) = x^2 - y^2$$

So, if you're asked to multiply $(x + 3)(x + 3)$, you know without using FOIL that the answer is $x^2 + 2(3x) + 9$ or $x^2 + 6x + 9$. Also, $(x - 3)(x - 3) = x^2 + -6x + 9$ or $x^2 - 6x + 9$. And $(x + 3)(x - 3) = x^2 - 9$.

If you're able to keep track of the terms, you can use FOIL to multiply terms in the proper order without taking the time to stack them. The FOIL method comes in handy for solving GMAT problems like the next one.

When the polynomials $3x + 4$ and $x - 5$ are multiplied together and written in the form $3x^2 + kx - 20$, what is the value of k?

EXAMPLE

(A) 2

(B) 3

(C) −5

(D) −11

(E) −20

This question asks you for the coefficient of the middle term of the quadratic expression formed by multiplying $3x + 4$ and $x - 5$. Remember with FOIL, you multiply the first, outer, inner, and last. The problem gives you the product of the first terms: $3x^2$. The product of the last terms is also there: −20. Because the problem provides the products of the first terms and last terms, all you have to do to get the middle term is to multiply the outer and inner terms of the two expressions and then add them together.

1. **Multiply the outer terms:** $3x \times -5 = -15x$

2. **Multiply the inner terms:** $4 \times x = 4x$

So, the middle term of the quadratic is $-15x + 4x = -11x$. The coefficient k must equal −11, which is Choice (D).

Knowing binomial factors with variables and their special products can help you solve similar problems that have the same form, but no variables, such as this one:

EXAMPLE

What is the value of $\left(2 + \sqrt{3}\right)\left(2 - \sqrt{3}\right)$?

(A) −1

(B) 0

(C) 1

(D) $2\sqrt{3}$

(E) $4\sqrt{3}$

You may look at this question and think "Gee, I wish I had a calculator to help me add and subtract the stuff in the parentheses." But then you may notice that this problem looks a lot like $(x + y)(x - y)$, which yields the difference of x^2 and y^2, or $x^2 - y^2$, as the product when multiplied. In this problem, x is the constant 2 and y is the constant $\sqrt{3}$; but that shouldn't be a worry. It all works out fast and easy as shown here:

1. **Square 2:** $(2)^2 = 2 \times 2 = 4$

2. **Square $\sqrt{3}$:** $\left(\sqrt{3}\right)^2 = \sqrt{3} \times \sqrt{3} = 3$

3. **Write the difference of the two squares and simplify the result:** $4 - 3 = 1$

   Thus, $\left(2 + \sqrt{3}\right)\left(2 - \sqrt{3}\right) = 4 - 3 = 1$. The answer is Choice (C) — no calculator needed.

Extracting Information: Factoring Polynomials

Factors are the numbers you multiply together to get a product. So, factoring a value means you write that value as a product of its factors. For the GMAT, you should know how to pull out the common factors in expressions and the two binomial factors in a quadratic polynomial. We show you how to do both in the following sections.

Something in common: Finding common factors

To simplify polynomials for complex problems, extract their common factors by dividing each term by the factors that are common to every term. You can think of the process as the inverse of distributing terms. For example, to find the common factors of the terms in the expression $-14x^3 - 35x^6$, follow these steps:

1. **Consider the coefficients.**

   Because –7 is common to both –14 and –35, take this factor out of the expression by dividing both terms by –7. Then put the remaining expression in parentheses next to the common factor: $-7\left(2x^3+5x^6\right)$.

2. **Now look at the variables.**

   Because x^3 or a multiple of it is common to both terms, divide both terms in parentheses by x^3, multiply x^3 by the other common factor (–7), and put the remaining expression in parentheses: $-7x^3\left(2+5x^3\right)$.

   Hence, $-14x^3-35x^6 = -7x^3\left(2+5x^3\right)$.

Two by two: Factoring quadratic polynomials

The GMAT also expects you to know how to factor quadratic polynomials. To accomplish this task, you must perform the FOIL operations in reverse to come up with a couple of binomial factors that look something like this: $(x\pm a)(x\pm b)$.

For example, look at the following quadratic polynomial:

$$x^2+5x+6$$

To find its factors, draw two pairs of parentheses: ( )( ). The first terms of the two factors must be x and x because x^2 is the product of x and x. So, you can insert x as the first term in each pair of parentheses. You know that the operation in both terms must be addition because both the middle and last terms of the quadratic expression are positive:

$$(x+\ )(x+\ )$$

To find the second terms for the two factors, ask yourself which two numbers have a product of 6 (the third term of the quadratic) and add up to the number 5 (the coefficient of the quadratic's second term). The only two factors that meet these two criteria are 2 and 3. The other pairs of factors of 6 (6 and 1, –6 and –1, –2 and –3) don't add up to 5. So, the binomial factors of the quadratic equation are $(x+2)$ and $(x+3)$. Thus, $x^2+5x+6=(x+2)(x+3)$.

TIP

Because you do just the reverse of what you do when you multiply binomials using the FOIL method, you can use the FOIL method to make sure the binomial factors result in the original quadratic when you multiply them together.

There's a timesaving way to factor binomials that are made up of a difference of two squares, such as x^2-4. Factors for these types of quadratic polynomials (known as the difference of two squares) result in the following form: $(x+a)(x-a)$

The variable x is the square root of the first term, and a is the positive square root of the second term. So, $x^2-4=(x+2)(x-2)$.

This factoring technique is quite easy to memorize and can help you answer some algebra questions much more quickly than if you were to take the time to carry out long calculations. For example, if you're asked to perform the multiplication $(x+5)(x-5)$, you could use the FOIL method to figure out the answer, but spotting that the correct answer will be the difference of two squares is much faster. You know the correct answer is x^2-25 without performing time-consuming calculations.

Likewise, if you need to factor $x^2 - 25$, all you do is determine the square root of x^2 and the positive square root of 25 and enter those results into the factoring form for the difference of two squares. You know right away that the factorization is $(x+5)(x-5)$.

When you can break down quadratic polynomials into factors, you'll be able to solve numerous quadratic equations. For more about how to do this, see the section, "Solving quadratic equations," later in this chapter.

Knowing how to factor quadratic polynomials can help you more efficiently factor similar polynomials of higher degree, such as this one:

Factor $9x^6 - 25y^4$.

EXAMPLE

(A) $\left(3x^3 + 5y^2\right)^2$

(B) $\left(3x^3 - 5y^2\right)^2$

(C) $\left(4.5x^3 + 12.5y^2\right)^2$

(D) $\left(4.5x^3 + 12.5y^2\right)\left(4.5x^3 - 12.5y^2\right)$

(E) $\left(3x^3 + 5y^2\right)\left(3x^3 - 5y^2\right)$

Notice that this problem looks a lot like the difference of two squares. So, all you do is determine the square root of $9x^6$ and the square root of $25y^4$ and enter those values into the factoring form for the difference of two squares:

1. **Determine the square root of $9x^6$:** $\left(9x^6\right)^{\frac{1}{2}} = 3x^3$

2. **Determine the square root of $25y^4$:** $\left(25y^4\right)^{\frac{1}{2}} = 5y^2$

3. **Enter the results into the factoring form for the difference of two squares:**
$9x^6 - 25y^4 = \left(3x^3 + 5y^2\right)\left(3x^3 - 5y^2\right)$

Thus, the answer is Choice (E).

Minding Your Ps and Qs: Functions

Some of the GMAT math questions involve functions. Simply put, functions are relationships between two sets of numbers; each number you put into the formula gives you only one possible answer. Functions may sound complicated, but they're really pretty simple. A function problem looks something like this:

Given $f(x) = 2x^2 + 3$. What is $f(2)$?

We explore the terminology of functions and how to find the domain and range of functions in the following sections.

Standing in: Understanding function terminology

Before we show you how to solve function problems, you need to know a few definitions. Table 11-1 gives you the terms we use when we discuss functions.

TABLE 11-1 Defining Terms for Functions

Term	Definition
Function	A rule that assigns each member of one set of numbers to a corresponding *unique* member of another set.
Independent variable (input)	In the function $y = f(x)$, x is the independent variable.
Dependent variable (output)	In the function $y = f(x)$, y is the dependent variable.
Domain	The set of all possible values of the independent variable.
Range	The set of all possible values of the dependent variable.

Functions on the GMAT are usually (but, not always) displayed with lowercase letters such as *f, g,* or *h.* For example, *f(x)* indicates the function of *x,* and it simply means "*f* of *x.*"

Don't let this technical language confuse you. Think of a function as a process *f* that takes an input number *x* and produces from it an output number, which is found by substituting the input value into $f(x)$. In simple terms: $f(\text{input}) = \text{output}$. In any function, there can be no more than one output for any given input. However, more than one input can produce the same output. For example, if $h(x) = |x + 5|$, then $h(-6) = |-6 + 5| = |-1| = 1$ and, also, $h(-4) = |-4 + 5| = |1| = 1$.

Basically, to *evaluate a function*, all you must do is substitute the indicated value for *x* into the function.

WARNING

Don't think that the parentheses in the function notation mean multiplication like they do in algebraic operations. The expression *f(x)* doesn't mean $f \times x$.

To see how functions work, consider the earlier example:

Given $f(x) = 2x^2 + 3$. What is $f(2)$?

The initial expression means that the *f* function rule is "Square *x,* multiply the result by 2, and then add 3." To evaluate *f(2),* you just substitute 2 for *x* in the expression and solve.

$$f(2) = 2(2)^2 + 3 = 2(4) + 3 = 8 + 3 = 11$$

So, when *x* is 2, *f(x)* is 11. The substitution of 2 for *x* in the expression can be written as $f(2) = 11$. Then *f(2)* is called the "value of *f* at $x = 2$." That's all there is to it! The function notation is just a fancy way of telling you to perform a substitution.

Here's another example like one you might see on the GMAT.

EXAMPLE

If $g(x) = 2x^2 + 17$, what is *g(12)*?

(A) 12

(B) 17

(C) 100

(D) 288

(E) 305

The *g* function rule is "Square *x,* multiply the result by 2, and then add 17." If you quickly consider the situation, you can eliminate Choices (A), (B), and (C) right away. When you substitute 12 for *x* in the function, you square 12, which is 144. The answer then results from multiplying by 2 and adding 17 to that number, so you know the final result will be greater than 100. Furthermore, the answer in Choice (D), 288, is just 2×144. You still must add 17, so the answer probably isn't Choice (D) either. Without much calculation, you can eliminate enough answers to determine that Choice (E) is correct. But to do the calculations, just substitute 12 for x and solve:

$$g(12) = 2(12)^2 + 17 = 2(144) + 17 = 288 + 17 = 305$$

The answer is definitely Choice (E).

That was a pretty simple problem. But functions can get more complicated on the GMAT. Check out this example.

If $f(x) = (x - 2)^2$, what is $f(2x - 2)$ equal to?

(A) $4x^2 - 4$

(B) $4x^2 + 4$

(C) $4x^2 - 8x + 16$

(D) $4x^2 - 16x + 16$

(E) $4x^2 - 16x - 16$

Don't try to do this one in your head. Begin by plugging in $(2x - 2)$ for x. Then solve.

$$f(2x - 2) = [(2x - 2) - 2]^2 = (2x - 4)^2 = 4x^2 - 16x + 16$$

So, the correct answer is Choice (D).

Taking it to the limit: Domain and range of functions

The *domain of a function* is the set of all numbers that can possibly be an input of the function, the x in $f(x)$. The *range of a function* is the set of all numbers that can possibly be an output of the function, the value for $f(x)$. In other words, if you think of the domain of a function as the set of all input values that you can put into that function, the range is the set of all possible output values that can come out of it. Domain and range questions aren't difficult, but you need to be aware of some basic rules to determine the proper limits of the domain and range.

Mastering the territory: Domain

Unless a problem specifies otherwise, the domain of a function includes all real numbers for which the function is defined and can produce meaningful outputs. Here are some reasons for exclusion of a number from the domain of a function:

>> The output would result in division by zero, such as in a fraction with a denominator of 0, because then the output would be undefined.

>> The output would result in an even-numbered root of a negative number. Even-numbered roots of negatives aren't real numbers because any number that's squared or has an even-numbered power can't result in a negative number.

For example, there's no real number such as $\sqrt{-4}$ because there's no one real number whose square is a negative 4. No matter whether you calculate $(-2)(-2)$ or $(2)(2)$ the product always equals positive 4. This occurs because squaring a positive number or a negative number always yields a positive product.

To see how the first rule affects domain, look at this function:

$$f(x) = \frac{x+4}{x-2}$$

Normally, the domain of a function can contain an unlimited number of x values. In the preceding example, though, the function rule is a fractional expression with the variable x in the denominator. Because your denominator can't add up to 0, the denominator, $x-2$, can't equal 0, which implies that x can't equal 2. Therefore, the domain of $f(x) = \frac{x+4}{x-2}$ is all real numbers except 2, which you can shorten to $\{x \neq 2\}$. That's all there is to it!

Here's a function that relates to the second rule:

$$g(n) = 3\sqrt[4]{n+2}$$

In this function, you have an even-numbered radical sign with the variable n within it. You know that the root of an even-numbered radical, in this case, the 4th root, can't be a negative number. Otherwise, you wouldn't have a real number as your final answer. Therefore, the number under the radical sign can't be less than 0. So, this means $n \geq -2$. The result is that the domain of the function $g(n)$ is $\{n \geq -2\}$.

The GMAT may test your knowledge of domain with a problem such as the following.

EXAMPLE

Determine the domain of the function $f(x) = \frac{4}{x^2 - x - 2}$.

(A) $\{x \neq -1, 2\}$

(B) $\{x \neq 1, -2\}$

(C) $\{x = -1, 2\}$

(D) $\{x = -4, 2\}$

(E) $\{x \neq -4, 2\}$

This problem involves simple algebra. You know the denominator can't equal 0, so set the trinomial in the denominator equal to 0 and solve for x to find out what x can't be. We show you how to solve trinomials later in the "Solving quadratic equations" section.

$$x^2 - x - 2 = 0$$
$$(x+1)(x-2) = 0$$
$$x+1 = 0; \; x = -1$$
$$x-2 = 0; \; x = 2$$

WARNING

You're not finished! If you picked Choice (C) as your answer, your factoring would have been absolutely right, but your answer would be absolutely wrong. Answer Choice (C) gives you only the values for x that make the denominator equal to 0. You're trying to find the values that make the denominator *not* equal to 0.

So, the correct answer is Choice (A); x can be any real number other than -1 and 2 because if x were equal to -1 or 2, the denominator would be 0, and the value would be undefined. If you chose Choice (B), you switched the signs of the factors. If you chose Choices (D) or (E), you found the correct factors of the denominator but mistakenly divided the numerator by each root of the denominator.

Roaming the land: Range

Just as the domain of a function is limited by certain laws of mathematics, so, too, is the range. Here are the rules to remember when you're determining the range of a function:

» An absolute value of a real number can't be a negative number.

» An even exponent or power can't produce a negative number.

» A square root radical can't return a negative number.

Check out some situations where these rules come into play. Look at the following functions:

$$f(x) = |x|$$
$$g(x) = x^2$$
$$h(x) = \sqrt{x}$$

Each of these functions can result only in an output that's a positive number or 0. So in each case, the range of the function is greater than or equal to 0. Here's a question that puts the range rules to work.

EXAMPLE

What is the range of the function $g(x) = 1 - \sqrt{x-2}$?

(A) $g(x) \geq -2$

(B) $g(x) \leq -2$

(C) $g(x) \geq 2$

(D) $g(x) \geq -1$

(E) $g(x) \leq 1$

TIP

First, make sure the square root radical represents a real number. The value inside the square root radical symbol has to be equal to or greater than 0. So, x must be equal to or greater than 2, because any value less than 2 would make the value inside the radical a negative value. And, as you know, square roots of negative numbers are not real numbers. To check the possible outputs, consider that no matter what value of x is the input from the restricted domain (which includes only values that are greater than or equal to 2), $\sqrt{x-2}$ is nonnegative. Therefore, the output of $g(x) = 1 - \sqrt{x-2}$ always equals $1 - (\text{a nonnegative number})$, which is always less than or equal to 1. So, the correct answer is Choice (E).

WARNING

Getting confused and looking for the domain when you should be finding the range is very easy. If you chose Choice (C), you solved for the domain of x. If you chose Choices (A) or (B), you're hung up trying to make the number under the radical a positive number. If you chose Choice (D), you simply don't know how to solve for range, so be sure to review this section.

Getting in line: Sequences and series

A *sequence* is a function whose domain consists of only positive integers. For example, $a(n) = n^2$ for $n = 1, 2, 3, \ldots$ is an *infinite sequence*, whose domain is all positive integers. The sequence $a(n)$ is denoted a_n. The value of this sequence at $n = 3$ is $a_3 = 3^2 = 9$. It is customary to describe a sequence by listing its terms in the order in which they correspond to the positive integers as $a_1, a_2, a_3, \ldots, a_n, \ldots$ as follows: $1, 4, 9, \ldots, n^2, \ldots$. This sequence has *initial term* $a_1 = 1$ and its nth term is $a_n = n^2$. A *finite sequence of length k* is the function whose domain is the set of the first k positive integers.

Here is a typical GMAT question that asks you to find the next term in a sequence. For questions like these, your best approach is to look for a pattern.

What is the next number in the sequence 2, 5, 10, 17, 26, . . .?

(A) 34

(B) 37

(C) 38

(D) 40

(E) 42

To find the pattern look for differences between consecutive terms:

$$5 - 2 = 3; 10 - 5 = 5, 17 - 10 = 7; 26 - 7 = 9$$

The differences are 3, 5, 7, and 9. Notice that these differences between consecutive terms are increasing by 2 each time. Apply this pattern to find the next difference: $9 + 2 = 11$. To find the next number in the sequence, add the difference (11) to the last number (26):

$$26 + 11 = 37, \text{Choice (B)}.$$

A *series* is the sum of the terms of a sequence. The sum of the first k terms of a sequence is a *partial sum*. It is written as $\sum_{i=1}^{k} a_i = a_1 + a_2 + \ldots + a_k$, where the letter i is the *index*, the lower limit is 1, and the upper limit is k. For example, the partial sum of the first three terms of the sequence based on the function $a(n) = n^2$ is $(1)^2 + (2)^2 + (3)^2 = 1 + 4 + 9 = 14$.

Putting On Your Thinking Cap: Problem Solving

You may be wondering how the GMAT tests your knowledge of algebra concepts. Well, wonder no more. The following sections present you with many of the ways you'll use algebra to solve GMAT math problems.

Isolating the variable: Linear equations with one unknown

A *linear equation* with one unknown is a first-degree, one-variable equation, meaning that it contains one variable whose highest power is 1. Plainly, these equations are fairly basic. In its simplest form, a linear equation with one variable x is expressed as $ax + b = c$, where x is the variable and a, b, and c are constants with $a \neq 0$.

Linear equations, each with one variable, that share a common solution, are *equivalent equations*. For example, the equations $2x - 5 = 3$ and $2x = 8$ have the same unique solution: $x = 4$.

To solve a linear equation with one unknown means to find the value of the unknown that *satisfies the equation* (that is, that makes the equation true when substituted for the unknown in the equation). To solve a linear equation with one unknown do the following:

Isolate the variable in the equation you're trying to solve, which means you work to get it all by itself on one side of the equation. To accomplish this task, perform identical mathematical operations to each side of the equation. It's important to keep in mind the following two rules:

>> Adding or subtracting the same number from each side of the equation does not change the equality.

>> Multiplying or dividing each side of the equation by the same *nonzero* number does not change the equality.

Decide what operation to do based on what has been done to the variable. Basically, your goal is to undo what's been done. As you proceed, exploit the fact that addition and subtraction undo each other; and, similarly, multiplication and division undo each other.

TIP

This process essentially transforms the original equation into an equivalent equation that has the form: variable = solution (or solution = variable).

This easy question asks you to solve a linear equation: If $4x + 10 = -38$, what is the value of x?

Solve for x by isolating the variable on one side of the equation:

1. **Eliminate 10 from the left side of the equation by subtracting it from each side.**

   (Remember that if you do something to one side of the equation, you need to do the same thing to the other side. Otherwise, your math teacher is liable to rap you on the knuckles with a slide rule.) Here's what happens when you subtract 10 from each side:

   $$4x + 10 - 10 = -38 - 10$$
   $$4x = -48$$

2. **Divide each side by 4, and you have your answer.**

   $$\frac{4x}{4} = \frac{-48}{4}$$
   $$x = -12$$

   Hence, the value of x is –12.

You tackle division problems the same way. So, if you're asked to solve for x in the problem $\frac{x}{4} = -5$, you know what to do. Isolate x to the left side of the equation by multiplying each side of the equation by 4:

$$\frac{x}{4} \times 4 = -5 \times 4$$
$$x = -20$$

TIP

If the equation includes multiple fractions, you can simplify things and save precious time by eliminating the fractions. Just multiply each fraction by the *least common denominator* (which is the lowest positive whole number that each fraction's denominator divides into evenly). For example, you may have to solve for x in a problem like this:

$$\frac{3x}{5} + \frac{8}{15} = \frac{x}{10}$$

The lowest number that 5, 15, and 10 go into evenly is 30, so that's your least common denominator. Multiply each fraction by a fraction equivalent to 1 that will give you 30 in the denominators, like this:

$$\left(\frac{3x}{5} \times \frac{6}{6}\right) + \left(\frac{8}{15} \times \frac{2}{2}\right) = \left(\frac{x}{10} \times \frac{3}{3}\right)$$

$$\frac{18x}{30} + \frac{16}{30} = \frac{3x}{30}$$

Now you can eliminate the fractions by multiplying each side of the equation by 30:

$$18x + 16 = 3x$$

Then just solve for x:

$$18x + 16 = 3x$$
$$18x + 16 - 16 = 3x - 16$$
$$18x = 3x - 16$$
$$18x - 3x = 3x - 16 - 3x$$
$$15x = -16$$
$$\frac{15x}{15} = \frac{-16}{15}$$
$$x = -\frac{16}{15}$$

Being absolutely positive: Absolute value equations

To solve an equation involving an absolute value, be mindful that the expression inside the absolute value bars can be positive or negative. This situation results in two equations, each of which you must solve independently.

Suppose you are asked to solve the equation $|x - 3| = 5$.

This equation results in the two equations: $x - 3 = 5$ and $-(x - 3) = 5$

Solving $x - 3 = 5$ yields $x = 8$ as a solution, and solving $-(x - 3) = 5$ (which implies $-x + 3 = 5$) yields $x = -2$ as a solution. Thus, the original equation has two solutions: $x = 8$ and $x = -2$.

TIP

When setting up the negative possibility, use parentheses around the whole expression inside the absolute value bars.

Getting in sync: Simultaneous equations

Solving for x is simple when it's the only variable in a linear equation, but what if your equation has more than one variable, say x and y? When you have another linear equation that contains at least one of the variables, you can solve for either variable. These two equations are *simultaneous equations*. The *solution* is a pair of values, one for x with one for y that makes both equations true when substituted for x and y, respectively.

TIP

If two equations are to be solved together, the solution must satisfy both equations simultaneously.

For two linear equations with two variables, if the equations are equivalent, there are infinitely many solutions to the equations. For example, $x - 3y = 2$ and $2x - 6y = 4$ are equivalent. (Note that the second equation is 2 times the first equation.) Thus, there are infinitely many solutions to these two equations such as these pairs: $x = 2$ with $y = 0$, $x = 0$ with $y = -\frac{2}{3}$, and $x = 5$ with $y = 1$.

If the equations are not equivalent but one *contradicts* the other (both cannot be true at the same time), there is no solution. For example, $x - 3y = 2$ and $2x - 6y = 10$ have no simultaneous solution because $x - 3y = 2$ implies that $2x - 6y = 4$, which contradicts the second equation. Thus, no values of x and y can simultaneously satisfy both equations. (Note that the coefficients of the second equation are 2 times the corresponding coefficients of the first equation.)

If the equations are neither equivalent nor contradictory, you can determine exact values for the two variables.

REMEMBER

For either equivalent or contradictory equations, the ratios of corresponding coefficients of the variables are equal.

There are several methods of solving two linear equations with two variables. One way is to solve by substitution: You just solve one of the equations for one of the variables and then plug the answer into the other equation and solve.

Here's a simple example:

If $4x + 5y = 30$ and $y = 2$, what is the value of x?

Because the second equation tells you that y is 2, just substitute 2 for the value of y in the first equation and you're on your way:

$$4x + 5y = 30$$
$$4x + 5(2) = 30$$
$$4x + 10 = 30$$
$$4x = 20$$
$$x = 5$$

That's all there is to it! Thus, the solution is $x = 5$ with $y = 2$.

TIP

You also can solve simultaneous linear equations by stacking them. This method works when you have as many equations as you have possible variables to solve for. So, you can stack these two equations because they each contain the same two variables:

$$6x + 4y = 66$$
$$-2x + 2y = 8$$

Your goal is to find a way to remove one of the variables. Here's how:

1. **Examine the equations to determine what variable you can eliminate through addition or subtraction.**

   If you multiply the entire second equation by 3, you can eliminate the x variable terms in both equations because $3(-2x) = -6$, and $6x - 6x = 0$. Just be sure to multiply each term in the second equation by the same value. So, the second equation becomes $-6x + 6y = 24$.

2. Stack the equations, combine like terms, and solve for *y*.

$$6x + 4y = 66$$
$$\underline{-6x + 6y = 24}$$
$$0 + 10y = 90$$
$$y = 9$$

3. Plug the value of one variable into one of the equations and solve for the other value.

You've found that $y = 9$, so substitute 9 for the value of *y* into one of the equations to solve for *x*.

$$-2x + 2y = 8$$
$$-2x + 2(9) = 8$$
$$-2x + 18 = 8$$
$$-2x = -10$$
$$x = 5$$

Therefore, the solution to the simultaneous equations is $x = 5$ with $y = 9$.

For linear equations that are neither equivalent nor contradictory, you can determine a unique simultaneous solution provided the number of separate linear equations is the same as the number of distinct variables they contain. This certitude can help you efficiently answer certain data sufficiency questions, such as this example.

EXAMPLE

What is the value of *x*?

(1) $2x - 9y = 28$

(2) $4y - 3x = 42 + y$

(A) Statement (1) *alone* is sufficient, but Statement (2) alone is not sufficient.

(B) Statement (2) *alone* is sufficient, but Statement (1) alone is not sufficient.

(C) *Both* statements *together* are sufficient, but *neither* statement *alone* is sufficient.

(D) *Each* statement *alone* is sufficient.

(E) Statements (1) and (2) *together* are *not* sufficient.

You can't solve for *x* using either of the statements by itself. The best you can do is solve for *x* in terms of *y* in either case. So, the answer is either Choice (C) or (E). Without lifting a pencil, you know that the answer is Choice (C); the statements are sufficient together. The two distinct equations each contain the same two variables and are neither equivalent nor contradictory, which you can quickly confirm by checking the ratios of corresponding *x* and *y* coefficients — so, the conditions are met to reach an exact value for *x*. You shouldn't use your limited time to actually solve for *x* during the exam, but we'll take you through the process in case you aren't convinced.

1. Combine like terms in Statement (2):
$$4y - 3x = 42 + y$$
$$-3x + 3y = 42$$

2. Multiply all terms in the resulting equation by 3 so you can eliminate the *y* terms when you stack the two equations:
$$3(-3x + 3y = 42)$$
$$-9x + 9y = 126$$

3. **Stack the equations and solve:**

$$2x - 9y = 28$$
$$\underline{-9x + 9y = 126}$$
$$-7x = 154$$
$$x = -22$$

For two linear equations with two variables:

>> If the two equations have a unique solution, their graphs are two lines which intersect at the point that is their common solution.

>> If the two equations are equivalent, their graphs coincide and there are infinitely many solutions.

>> If the two equations are contradictory, their graphs are two parallel lines that don't intersect and there is no solution.

See the section, "Seeing is Believing: The Coordinate Plane," later in this chapter, for a discussion of graphing linear equation as lines in the coordinate plane.

Not playing fair: Inequalities

An *inequality* is a statement such as "x is less than y" or "x is greater than or equal to y."

In addition to the symbols for add, subtract, multiply, and divide, mathematics also applies standard symbols to show how the two sides of an equation are related. You're probably pretty familiar with these symbols, but a little review never hurts. Table 11-2 gives you a rundown of the symbols you'll deal with on the GMAT.

TABLE 11-2 **Mathematical Symbols for Equality and Inequality**

Symbol	Meaning
=	Is equal to
≠	Is not equal to
≈	Is approximately equal to
>	Is greater than
<	Is less than
≥	Is greater than or equal to
≤	Is less than or equal to

These are some of the more common symbols used in algebra to signify equality and inequality.

Performing operations with linear inequalities

You treat linear inequalities in one variable a lot like linear equations in one variable. Isolate the variable to one side and perform the same operations on each side of the inequality. The only difference is that if you multiply or divide by a negative number, you need to reverse the direction of the inequality sign. The set of all real numbers that are solutions of an inequality is its *solution set.* So, here's how you solve this simple inequality:

$$-2x \le 10$$
$$x \ge -5$$

Here is a GMAT candidate:

EXAMPLE

Solve $3x + 9 < 5x - 7$.

(A) $x < -8$

(B) $x < -4$

(C) $x > -8$

(D) $x > 4$

(E) $x > 8$

Here's how to solve it.

1. **Write the original equation:** $3x + 9 < 5x - 7$

2. **Subtract 9 from each side:** $3x < 5x - 16$

3. **Subtract 5x from each side:** $-2x < -16$

4. **Divide each side by -2 and reverse the inequality symbol:** $x > 8$, Choice (E).

Working with intervals of numbers

A (*finite*) *interval* is a range of numbers between two given endpoints, where one, both, or neither of the endpoints may be included in the interval. You can use inequalities to show an interval of numbers. For example, the GMAT may show the interval of numbers between -6 and 12 as a *double inequality*, like this: $-6 < x < 12$.

This double inequality means that x must simultaneously be greater than -6 and less than 12.

To show the interval between -6 and 12 including -6 and 12, you use the $\le$ sign, like this: $-6 \le x \le 12$

You can add or subtract values within an interval. For example, you can add 5 to each part of $-6 < x < 12$ to get this double inequality:

$$-6 + 5 < x + 5 < 12 + 5$$
$$-1 < x + 5 < 17$$

And you can perform operations between different intervals, such as $4 < x < 15$ and $-2 < y < 20$. To find the sum of these two intervals, follow these steps:

1. **Add the least values of each interval:** $4 + (-2) = 2$

2. **Add the greatest values of each interval:** $15 + 20 = 35$

3. **Create a new interval with the sums:** $2 < x + y < 35$

This result means that the sum $x + y$ is between 2 and 35.

Here's an example of how the GMAT may ask you to deal with inequalities.

EXAMPLE

If $x^2 - 1 \le 8$, what is the smallest real value x can assume?

(A) -9

(B) -6

(C) -3

(D) 0

(E) 3

This problem asks you to determine the least real value of x if $x^2 - 1$ is less than or equal to 8.

REMEMBER

Before you begin, it is essential that you know that $\sqrt{x^2} = |x|$. This is the case because the *square root radical* ($\sqrt{}$) always returns the nonnegative *principal square root* of a number. Since you don't know whether x is positive or negative, you use the absolute value bars to guarantee a nonnegative result. For example, $\sqrt{3^2} = |3| = 3$ and $\sqrt{(-3)^2} = |-3| = 3$.

Now, for the problem at hand. Solve the inequality for x.

1. Write the original inequality: $x^2 - 1 \le 8$

2. Isolate x^2 by adding 1 to each side of the inequality: $x^2 \le 9$

3. Take the square root of each side of the inequality: $\sqrt{x^2} \le \sqrt{9}$

4. Simplify: $|x| \le 3$

Which indicates that $-3 \le x \le 3$ (See "Solving absolute value inequalities" in the section that follows for a rule that applies.) Thus, the least real value of x is -3, Choice (C).

To make sure you're right, you can eliminate answer choices by using common sense. For example, -9 in Choice (A) would make $x^2 - 1$ equal 80, and -6 in Choice (B) would make $x^2 - 1$ equal 35. So, neither Choices (A) nor (B) can be a solution for x. In Choice (D), 0 is a possible value for x, but it isn't the least solution, because you know that -3 is less than 0. Choice (E) can't be right because it's greater than two other possible solutions, -3 and 0. So Choice (C) is the correct answer.

Solving absolute value inequalities

Solving absolute value inequalities requires that you remember a couple of rules:

Given a variable x (or a linear expression in x) and a real number $a \ge 0$,

If $|x| < a$, then $-a < x < a$; and

If $|x| > a$, then $x < -a$ or $x > a$.

REMEMBER

These two rules remain valid if you replace $<$ with $\le$ and $>$ with $\ge$ throughout.

Okay, give this one a whirl!

Solve $|x - 5| < 7$.

Here's how to do it.

1. Write the original equation: $|x - 5| < 7$

2. Write the equivalent double inequality: $-7 < x - 5 < 7$

3. **Add 5 to each part to isolate _x_:** $-7 + 5 < x - 5 + 5 < 7 + 5$

4. **Simplify:** $-2 < x < 12$

Here's another one to delight you!

Solve $|x + 3| \geq 2$.

Find the solution like this.

1. **Write the original equation:** $|x + 3| \geq 2$

2. **Write the equivalent inequalities:** $x + 3 \leq -2$ or $x + 3 \geq 2$

3. **In both, subtract 3 from each side to isolate _x_:** $x + 3 - 3 \leq -2 - 3$ or $x + 3 - 3 \geq 2 - 3$

4. **Simplify:** $x \leq -5$ or $x \geq -1$

Solving quadratic equations

All right! Let's dive into the wonderful world of quadratic equations! Why should you care about quadratic equations? Well, it turns out that they are quite handy when you want to solve all sorts of real-life problems.

A *quadratic equation* in the variable x is one that you can write in the standard quadratic form $ax^2 + bx + c = 0$, where a, b, and c are constants with $a \neq 0$ and x is a variable that you have to solve for. Specifically, a is the numerical coefficient of x^2, b is the numerical coefficient of x, and c is the constant term. Notice that all nonzero terms are on one side of the equation, and 0 is the only term on the other side.

For example, $2x^2 = 0$, $x^2 - 4 = 0$, and $3x^2 - 6x + 5 = 0$ are quadratic equations in standard form.

If a quadratic equation is not in standard form, you can use algebraic manipulation to get all nonzero terms on one side and 0 on the other side. For example, in standard form $x^2 + x = 6 + 2x$ is $x^2 - x - 6 = 0$, $-4x + 4 = -x^2$ is $x^2 - 4x + 4 = 0$, and $(x + 4)(2x - 3) = 0$ is $2x^2 + 5x - 12 = 0$.

The *solution set* of a quadratic equation is the set containing its *roots*. A quadratic equation has at most two distinct real roots; and, in some cases, it has no real root.

Factoring to find _x_

The procedure for solving a quadratic equation by factoring relies on the *zero product property* of real numbers: If the product of two quantities is zero, then at least one of the quantities is zero.

To solve a quadratic equation by factoring do the following: First, make sure it's in standard form; next, factor the nonzero side into two binomials just like you did earlier in the section, "Two by two: Factoring quadratic polynomials"; then set each factor containing the variable equal to zero; finally, solve each of the resulting linear equations. The solutions to these simpler equations are the *solutions* of the original equation.

The GMAT may give you a quadratic equation like this one, and ask you to solve for x:

$$x^2 - 6x + 5 = 0$$

To factor the trinomial on the left side, identify a pair of numbers with a product of 5 and a sum of -6.

The two pairs of factors of 5 are 1 and 5 and -1 and -5. To get a sum of -6, you need to go with the negative values. Doing so gives these two binomial factors: $(x-1)$ and $(x-5)$. So, the resulting equation is $(x-1)(x-5)=0$.

Now set each of the binomial factors equal to 0. You can do so because, by the zero product property, you know that at least one of the factors must equal 0 if their product is 0: $x-1=0$ or $x-5=0$

Solve the resulting linear equations: The solutions are $x=1$ and $x=5$; or the solution set is $\{1,5\}$.

Voila! The roots of the equation are now evident: 1 and 5. Substituting either 1 or 5 for x into the original equation, makes the equation true.

REMEMBER

Quadratic equations always have two roots (where, sometimes, a single root is repeated). On the GMAT the roots will be real numbers.

Determining solutions for the difference of two squares

Solving a quadratic equation consisting of the difference of two squares (like $x^2-a^2=0$) is a straightforward process if you remember that $x^2-a^2=(x+a)(x-a)$. Suppose the GMAT presents you with the task of solving a quadratic equation in which the difference of two squares is equal to 0. You know that all you need to do is find the square root of the first square and the positive square root of the second square, and then enter those results into the factoring form for the difference of two squares.

Suppose you are told to find the solution set for $x^2-49=0$.

To solve by factoring, all you do is determine the square root of x^2 and the positive square root of 49 and enter those results into the factoring form for the difference of two squares to obtain $(x+7)(x-7)=0$.

Next, setting each factor equal to zero and solving the resulting linear equations yields $\{-7,7\}$ as the solution set for the equation. It couldn't be easier!

Using the quadratic formula

Solving quadratic equations is easy when the solutions contain nice, round numbers. But what if the ultimate solutions have harsh-looking radicals or perhaps unwieldy fractions? For the rare GMAT occasions when you can't simply solve a quadratic equation by factoring, you may have to use the *quadratic formula*, which is a rearrangement of the standard equation: $ax^2+bx+c=0$. It looks like this:

$$x=\frac{-b\pm\sqrt{b^2-4ac}}{2a}$$

REMEMBER

Although this formula may look mighty unmanageable, it may be the only sensible way to find the solutions for quadratic equations that aren't easily factored. Here's how you'd apply the formula when asked to solve $3x^2+7x-6=0$ for x. In this equation, $a=3$, $b=7$, and $c=-6$. Plug these numbers into the quadratic formula and evaluate:

$$x = \frac{-7 \pm \sqrt{7^2 - 4(3)(-6)}}{2(3)}$$

$$x = \frac{-7 \pm \sqrt{49 + 72}}{6}$$

$$x = \frac{-7 \pm \sqrt{121}}{6}$$

$$x = \frac{-7 \pm 11}{6}$$

$$x = -\frac{18}{6} \text{ or } \frac{4}{6}$$

$$x = -3 \text{ or } \frac{2}{3}$$

The solution set is $\left\{-3, \frac{2}{3}\right\}$. Whew! Luckily, the GMAT won't give you many quadratic equations that require you to apply this formula. But you'll know what to do if you encounter one of the few.

Reading between the lines: Word problems

The GMAT tests algebra and arithmetic concepts in word problems as well as mathematical equations. In fact, word problems are more common on the GMAT than straightforward equation-solving. So you have to know how to translate the English language into mathematical expressions.

REMEMBER

To help you with the translation, Table 11-3 provides some of the more common words you'll encounter in word problems and tells you what they look like in math symbols.

TABLE 11-3 **Common Words and Their Math Equivalents**

Plain English	Math Equivalent
Added to, more than, plus, increased by, combined with, total of, sum of	Plus (+)
Minus, less than, fewer than, decreased by, diminished by, reduced by, difference between, taken away from	Minus (–)
Multiplied by, of, times, product of, twice, double, triple	Multiply (×)
Divided by, ratio of, per, out of, quotient, for every, for each, half of	Divide (÷ or /)
x percent of y	$(x \div 100) \times y$
Is, are, was, were, becomes, results in	Equals (=)
How much, how many, a certain number	Variable (x, y)

Here's an example of how you play foreign language interpreter on GMAT word problems.

EXAMPLE

On the first day of an alpine slalom competition, the total combined time of Grace's two runs was 1 minute and 57 seconds. If twice the number of seconds in her first run was 30 seconds more than the number of seconds in her second run, what was her time in seconds for the first run?

(A) 15

(B) 30

(C) 49

(D) 68

(E) 147

Focus on what you're supposed to figure out. The question asks for the time of Grace's first run in seconds. So, you know you must convert her total time to seconds so you're working in the correct units. A minute has 60 seconds, which means that Grace's total time was $60 + 57$, or 117 seconds.

You can immediately eliminate Choice (E) because Grace's first run couldn't have been longer than the sum of her two runs. Now apply your math translation skills. You have two unknowns: the time of Grace's first run and the time of her second run. Let x stand for the first unknown and y for the second.

You can solve a problem with two variables when you know two different equations that involve those two variables. So, search the problem for two equations.

For the first equation, the problem tells you that the total time of the two runs is 117 seconds. According to the English-to-math-translation dictionary, that means $x + y = 117$. You've got one equation!

You also know that 2 times ($\times$) the number of seconds in her first run (x) was (=) 30 seconds more (+) than her time for the second run (y). Translation please? $2x = 30 + y$.

After you have the two equations, you can use substitution or stacking to solve for x. For this problem, stacking is faster. Notice that $2x = 30 + y$ is the same as $2x - y = 30$. When you stack and add the two equations, you can eliminate the y variable because $y - y = 0$.

$$
\begin{aligned}
x + y &= 117 \\
2x - y &= 30 \\
\hline
3x &= 147 \\
x &= 49
\end{aligned}
$$

So, Grace ran her first race in 49 seconds, which is Choice (C). If you chose Choice (D), you solved for y instead of x. Grace's second run was 68 seconds.

Burning the midnight oil: Work problems

Work problems ask you to find out how much work gets done in a certain amount of time. Use this formula for doing algebra work problems: Production = (Rate of Work) $\times$ Time

Production means the amount of work that gets done. Because you get that quantity by multiplying two other numbers, you can say that production is the product of the rate times the time.

Here's how you'd apply the formula in a GMAT work problem.

There are two dock workers, Alf and Kendric. Alf can load 16 tons of steel per day, and Kendric can load 20 tons per day. If they each work eight-hour days, how many tons of steel can the two of them load in one hour, assuming they maintain a steady rate?

(A) 2.5

(B) 4.5

(C) 36

(D) 160

(E) 320

This question asks you to find the amount of production and gives you the rate and the time. But to calculate the rate properly, you must state the hours in terms of days. Because a workday is eight hours, one hour is $\frac{1}{8}$ of a day. Figure out how much Alf loads in one hour ($\frac{1}{8}$ of a day) and add it to what Kendric loads in one hour.

Total Production = Alf's Production + Kendric's Production

Total Production = $\left(16 \times \frac{1}{8}\right) + \left(20 \times \frac{1}{8}\right)$

Total Production = $2 + 2.5$

Total Production = 4.5

So, Alf and Kendric load 4.5 tons of steel in one hour ($\frac{1}{8}$ of a day), which is Choice (B). If you chose Choice (C), you figured out the total production for one day rather than one hour.

Going the distance: Distance problems

Distance problems are a lot like work problems. The formula for computing distance or speed problems is this: Distance = Rate × Time

Any problem involving distance, speed, or time spent traveling can be boiled down to this equation. The important thing is for you to have your variables and numbers plugged in properly. Here's an example.

EXAMPLE

Lucia can run a mile in seven minutes. How long, in seconds, does it take her to run $\frac{1}{10}$ of a mile at the same speed?

(A) 30

(B) 42

(C) 60

(D) 360

(E) 420

TIP

Before you do any calculating, you can eliminate Choice (E) because 420 seconds is 7 minutes, and you know it takes Lucia less time to run $\frac{1}{10}$ of a mile than it does for her to run a mile.

The problem tells you that Lucia's distance is $\frac{1}{10}$ of a mile. You can figure her rate to be $\frac{1}{7}$ mile per minute because she runs 1 mile in 7 minutes. The problem is asking how long she runs, so you need to solve for time. Plug the numbers into the distance formula:

Distance = Rate × Time

$$\frac{1}{10} = \frac{1}{7} \times t$$

You need to isolate t on one side of the equation, so multiply each side by 7:

$$\frac{1}{10} \times 7 = t$$

$$\frac{7}{10} = t$$

So, Lucia runs $\frac{1}{10}$ of a mile in $\frac{7}{10}$ of a minute. Convert minutes to seconds. There are 60 seconds in a minute, and $\frac{7}{10} \times 60 = 42$ seconds. The correct answer is Choice (B).

Mixing it up: Mixture problems

In a mixture problem, the amount (or value) of an ingredient in a substance before mixing equals the amount (or value) of that ingredient in the substance after mixing: Amount of Ingredient Before Mixing = Amount of Ingredient After Mixing

Here's how you'd apply this concept in a GMAT mixture problem.

EXAMPLE

What amount (in milliliters) of a 1% hydrogen peroxide solution must be added to 60 milliliters of a 6% hydrogen peroxide solution to yield a 5% hydrogen peroxide solution?

(A) 12

(B) 15

(C) 18

(D) 20

(E) 45

Let x = the amount (in milliliters) of the 1% hydrogen peroxide solution that must be added. Then $x + 60$ = the amount (in milliliters) in the final hydrogen peroxide solution.

1. Determine the amount of hydrogen peroxide before mixing: $1\%x + 6\%(60)$

2. Determine the amount of hydrogen peroxide after mixing: $5\%(x + 60)$

3. Set the two amounts equal and solve the resulting equation:

$$\text{Amount of Ingredient Before Mixing} = \text{Amount of Ingredient After Mixing}$$
$$1\%x + 6\%(60) = 5\%(x + 60)$$
$$0.01x + 0.06(60) = 0.05(x + 60)$$
$$0.01x + 3.6 = 0.05x + 3$$
$$0.6 = 0.04x$$
$$15 = x$$

Choice (B) is the correct answer.

Catching a break: Break-even problems

In break-even problems, you determine the point at which revenue equals cost: Revenue = Cost

Here's how you'd apply this idea on the GMAT.

EXAMPLE

A company manufactures and sells a certain product. The total cost, in dollars, to produce x units of the product is given by $C(x) = 3x^2 + 50x + 100$. The selling price in dollars, for each unit of the product is given by $S(x) = 6x + 30$. The company wants to determine the break-even point, which is the number of units they need to sell to cover their costs. What is the break-even point?

(A) 10

(B) 15

(C) 20

(D) 25

(E) 30

The break-even point occurs when the total revenue $(6x+30)x$ — which is the product of the selling price per unit and the number of units sold — equals the total cost $3x^2 + 50x + 100$.

To find the break-even point, set the total revenue equal to the total cost and solve for x.

$$(6x+30)x = 3x^2 + 50x + 100$$
$$6x^2 + 30x = 3x^2 + 50x + 100$$
$$3x^2 - 20x - 100 = 0$$
$$(3x+10)(x-10) = 0$$
$$3x + 10 = 0;\ x = -\frac{10}{3}$$
$$x - 10 = 0;\ x = 10$$

The break-even point represents the number of units sold, so reject the negative solution. Therefore, the break-even point is 10 units, Choice (A).

Seeing Is Believing: The Coordinate Plane

The coordinate plane is a two-dimensional system used to represent points and graphically depict relationships between them. In this section, you will revisit the definitions and formulas necessary for excelling in problem solving related to the coordinate plane.

Getting the plane truth: Coordinate plane terminology

Before you get too excited about graphical depictions, prepare yourself with an understanding of these essential terms.

>> **Coordinate plane:** The coordinate plane consists of two perpendicular real number lines intersecting at a point, called the *origin*, where points can be identified by their positions using *ordered pairs* of numbers.

>> *x*-axis: The horizontal axis in a coordinate plane. From the origin, the numbers on the axis increase in value to the right of the origin and decrease in value to the left.

>> *y*-axis: The vertical axis in a coordinate plane. From the origin, the numbers on the axis increase in value going up from the origin and decrease in value going down.

>> **Origin:** The point (0, 0) in the coordinate plane. It's where the *x*- and *y*-axes intersect.

>> **Quadrants:** The four regions formed by the intersection of the *x*- and *y*-axes.

>> **Ordered pair:** The pair of values (*x*, *y*), called *coordinates*, arranged in a specific order to represent points in the coordinate plane. The horizontal (*x*) coordinate is always listed first, and the vertical (*y*) coordinate is listed second.

>> *x*-coordinate of a point: The directed distance from the *y*-axis to the point (positive to the right and negative to the left). If it's 0, the point is on the *y*-axis.

>> *y*-coordinate of a point: The directed distance from the *x*-axis to the point (positive upward and negative downward). If it's 0, the point is on the *x*-axis.

>> **x-intercept:** The value of *x* where a line, curve, or some other function crosses the *x*-axis. The value of *y* is 0 at the *x*-intercept.

>> **y-intercept:** The value of *y* where a line, curve, or some other function crosses the *y*-axis. The value of *x* is 0 at the *y*-intercept.

>> **Slope:** The measure of a line's steepness or incline.

>> **Graph of a two-variable linear equation:** The line in the coordinate plane that consists of all the ordered pairs that are elements of the solution set of the equation.

Getting to the point? Finding the coordinates

You can identify any point in the coordinate plane by its coordinates, which designate the point's location in the plane. For example, to plot the ordered pair (2, 3) go two units to the right of the origin along the *x*-axis and from there go up three units. In Figure 11-1, point A is at (2, 3). The *x*-coordinate appears first, and the *y*-coordinate shows up second. Pretty simple so far, huh?

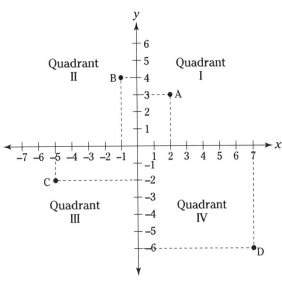

FIGURE 11-1:
Points in the coordinate plane.

© *John Wiley & Sons, Inc.*

Dividing the territory: Identifying quadrants

The intersection of the *x*- and *y*-axes forms four quadrants in the coordinate plane, which just happen to be labeled Quadrants I, II, III, and IV in a counterclockwise direction (see Figure 11-1). Here's what you can assume about points based on the quadrants they're in:

>> All points in Quadrant I have a positive *x*-coordinate and a positive *y*-coordinate.

>> All points in Quadrant II have a negative *x*-coordinate and a positive *y*-coordinate.

>> All points in Quadrant III have a negative *x*-coordinate and a negative *y*-coordinate.

>> All points in Quadrant IV have a positive *x*-coordinate and a negative *y*-coordinate.

>> All points along the *x*-axis have a *y*-coordinate of 0.

>> All points along the *y*-axis have an *x*-coordinate of 0.

Figure 11-1 also shows the location of points A, B, C, and D:

>> Point A is in Quadrant I and has coordinates (2, 3).

>> Point B is in Quadrant II and has coordinates (–1, 4).

>> Point C is in Quadrant III and has coordinates (–5, –2).

>> Point D is in Quadrant IV and has coordinates (7, –6).

The GMAT won't ask you to pick your favorite quadrant, but you may be asked to identify which quadrant a particular point belongs in.

Slip-Sliding Away: Slope and Linear Equations

The coordinate plane presents the exciting experience of visually representing linear equations in two variables, a topic you are already familiar with from the section, "Getting in sync: Simultaneous equations," earlier in this chapter. You should know the formulas for finding the slope and the slope-intercept equation. Lucky for you, we discuss these formulas in the following sections.

Taking a "peak": The slope of a line

If a line isn't parallel to one of the coordinate axes, it either slants down or slants up from left to right. The measure of the steepness of the line's slant is its *slope*. In the following sections, we explain how to find the slope of a line and explore the different types of slope in a coordinate plane.

The formula for slope

A simple way to remember the slope formula is to think, "rise over run." Here's the formula:

$$slope(m) = \frac{\text{Rise}}{\text{Run}} = \frac{\text{Change in Vertical Coordinates}}{\text{Change in Horizontal Coordinates}} = \frac{y_2 - y_1}{x_2 - x_1}$$

where (x_1, y_1) and (x_2, y_2) are two distinct points on the line and $x_1 \neq x_2$. The formula is just the ratio of the vertical change between two points and the horizontal change between those same two points. For example, the slope of the line through the points $(-1, -3)$ and $(1, 5)$ is $m = \frac{y_2 - y_1}{x_2 - x_1} = \frac{5 - (-3)}{1 - (-1)} = \frac{8}{2} = 4$.

WARNING

When you subtract the values, remember to subtract the x and y values of the first point from the respective x and y values of the second point. Don't fall for the trap of subtracting $x_2 - x_1$ to get your change in the run but then subtracting $y_1 - y_2$ for your change in the rise. That kind of backward math will mess up your calculations, and you'll soon be sliding down a slippery slope.

Types of slope

>> A line with a negative slope slants down from left to right.

>> A line with a positive slope slants up left to right.

» A horizontal line has a slope of 0 and coincides with or is parallel to the *x*-axis.

» The slope of a vertical line is undefined.

REMEMBER

If you are given two distinct points (x_1, y_1) and (x_2, y_2) on a line, you can use the definition of slope to find the equation of the line. First, calculate the slope: $m = \dfrac{y_2 - y_1}{x_2 - x_1}$. When provided with the slope value *m* and the known point (x_1, y_1), any other point (x, y) on the line must satisfy the equation $m = \dfrac{y - y_1}{x - x_1}$, which you can transform into an equivalent linear equation of your desired form.

Using the slope-intercept form for linear equations

The equation $y = mx + b$ is the *slope-intercept form* of the equation of a line.

In the slope-intercept form, the coefficient *m* is a constant that indicates the slope of the line, and the constant *b* is the *y*-intercept (that is, the point where the line crosses the *y*-axis). A line with the equation $y = 4x + 1$ has a slope of 4 and a *y*-intercept of 1. It's graph (shown in Figure 11-2) is a visual representation of all ordered pairs that are solutions to $y = 4x + 1$.

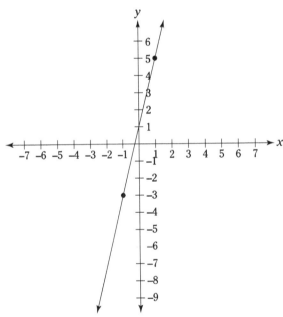

FIGURE 11-2:
The graph of
$y = 4x + 1$.

© John Wiley & Sons, Inc

The GMAT may give you an equation of a line and ask you to choose the graph that correctly shows it. You can figure out how the line should look when it's graphed by starting with the value of the *y*-intercept, marking points that fit the value of the slope, and then connecting these points with a line.

TIP

Whenever you get an equation for a line that doesn't neatly fit into the slope-intercept form, go ahead and play with the equation a little bit (sounds fun, doesn't it?) so it meets the $y = mx + b$ form that you know and love. For instance, to put the equation $\frac{1}{3}y - 3 = x$ in slope-intercept form, you simply manipulate both sides of the equation and solve for y, like this:

$$\frac{1}{3}y - 3 = x$$
$$\frac{1}{3}y = x + 3$$
$$y = 3(x + 3)$$
$$y = 3x + 9$$

The new equation gives you the slope of the line, 3, as well as the y-intercept, 9. Pretty handy! Here's a sample question to provide you with an idea of how the slope-intercept form may be tested on the GMAT.

EXAMPLE

What is the equation of a line with slope $-\frac{3}{4}$ and y-intercept 8?

(A) $4x + 3y = 32$

(B) $-3x + 4y = 16$

(C) $3x - 4y = 32$

(D) $3x + 4y = 16$

(E) $3x + 4y = 32$

REMEMBER

In the slope-intercept form, $y = mx + b$, m is the slope, and b is the y-intercept. Plug the values the problem gives you into the equation: $y = -\frac{3}{4}x + 8$

This isn't an answer choice, but all options have the same form of $ax + by = c$. So, you need to convert your equation to that form. Move the terms around by multiplying all terms on both sides by 4 and adding $3x$ to both sides, like this:

$$y = -\frac{3}{4}x + 8$$
$$4y = -3x + 32$$
$$4y + 3x = 32$$

Choice (E) is the correct answer.

IN THIS CHAPTER

» Getting a grip on group problems

» Excelling with sets and Venn diagrams

» Arranging groups with permutations and combinations

» Managing means, medians, and modes

» Scrutinizing standard deviations

» Prospering on probability problems

Chapter **12**

Manipulating Numbers: Statistics and Sets

From the time you mastered the ability to tie your shoes, you had to figure out how to work and play in groups. The GMAT tests what you know about groups of numbers, or sets. These question types are usually pretty easy, so you could probably work out the answers to most of the GMAT set questions given enough time. But, of course, you don't have all the time in the world on the GMAT, so in this chapter, we provide some shortcuts to help you answer set questions quickly.

You may find the statistics and probability questions on the GMAT a little more challenging. But don't worry: In this chapter, we go over the concepts you need to know, which include determining probability, statistical averages, and variations from the average. The statistics questions you'll encounter on the GMAT aren't particularly complex, but giving this subject your full attention will pay off.

Joining a Clique: Groups

Group problems concern populations of individuals or objects and the ways they are grouped together into categories. The questions generally ask you to either find the total of a series of groups or determine how many individuals or objects make up one of the subgroups.

You can find the answer to most group problems by using your counting skills, but counting is time-consuming, and you want to work smarter, not harder, to solve these questions. If only two groups are involved, solving the problem comes down to applying simple arithmetic using a handy rule and nothing else.

TIP

Here's the rule for solving problems involving only two groups:

Group 1 + Group 2 – Both Groups + Neither Group = Grand Total

So, if you're told that out of 110 students, 47 are enrolled in a cooking class, 56 take a welding course, and 33 take both cooking and welding, you can use the rule to find out how many students take neither cooking nor welding. Let Group 1 be the number of cooks and Group 2 be the number of welders. Let x be Neither Group, the number that take neither cooking nor welding. Plug the known values into the rule and set up an equation to solve:

Group 1 + Group 2 – Both Groups + Neither Group = Grand Total
$$47 + 56 - 33 + x = 110$$
$$70 + x = 110$$
$$x = 40$$

Of the 110 students, 40 take neither cooking nor welding. Here's an example of how group problems may appear on the GMAT.

EXAMPLE

One-third of all U.S. taxpayers may deduct charitable contributions on their federal income tax returns. Forty percent of all taxpayers may deduct state income tax payments from their federal returns. If 55 percent of all taxpayers may not deduct either charitable contributions or state income tax, what portion of all taxpayers may claim both types of deductions?

(A) $\frac{3}{20}$

(B) $\frac{9}{50}$

(C) $\frac{1}{5}$

(D) $\frac{7}{25}$

(E) $\frac{17}{60}$

Use the rule to determine the correct portion of taxpayers who may claim both deductions. Group 1 can be the $\frac{1}{3}$ who claim charitable deductions, and Group 2 can be the percentage of those who deduct state income tax payments. The Grand Total is 100% of the U. S. taxpayers. Let x be Both Groups, the portion of all taxpayers who may claim both types of deductions.

TIP

Before you begin calculating, check the answer choices. Every answer appears as a fraction. Because your final answer will be in the form of a fraction, change references to percents into fractions. Converting percents to fractions is easy; put the value of the percent over a denominator of 100.

So, 40% is the same as $\frac{40}{100}$, which reduces to $\frac{2}{5}$; 55% is the same as $\frac{55}{100}$, which equals $\frac{11}{20}$; and 100% equals 1. Plug the values into the rule and solve:

Group 1 + Group 2 – Both Groups + Neither Group = Grand Total
$$\frac{1}{3} + \frac{2}{5} - x + \frac{11}{20} = 1$$

To add and subtract fractions, find a common denominator for all fractions and then convert the fractions, so all have the same denominator (see Chapter 15 for more about performing operations with fractions). The common denominator for this problem is 60.

$$\frac{20}{60} + \frac{24}{60} - x + \frac{33}{60} = \frac{60}{60}$$

$$\frac{77}{60} - x = \frac{60}{60}$$

$$x = \frac{17}{60}$$

The correct answer is Choice (E).

WARNING

Compute accurately. Another reason for working with fractions instead of percents in this problem is that it helps you perform accurate calculations. You may be fooled into thinking that one-third of the taxpayers who can claim charitable contributions equals 33 percent of taxpayers. Although $\frac{1}{3}$ is very close to 33 percent, it isn't exactly that amount. If you used 33 percent instead of one-third, you may have calculated the group as $0.33 + 0.4 + 0.55 - x = 1$ and incorrectly chosen Choice (D). If you convert $\frac{1}{3}$ to 33 percent, you're sacrificing accuracy to save time.

Setting Up Sets

A *set* is a collection of numbers, letters, objects, or other things. The things in a set are its *elements*, or *members*. An *empty set*, or *null set*, means that nothing is in that set. GMAT questions about sets are usually fairly simple to answer as long as you know a little terminology and how to read a Venn diagram. The following sections explore all you need to know about sets.

Set terminology

The terms *union*, *intersection*, *disjoint sets*, and *subset* describe how two or more sets relate to one another through the elements they contain.

> » The *union* of two sets contains the set of all elements of both sets. For example, the union of sets $A = \{0, 1, 2, 3, 4, 5, 6, 7, 8, 9\}$ and $B = \{2, 4, 6, 8, 10\}$ is $S = \{0, 1, 2, 3, 4, 5, 6, 7, 8, 9, 10\}$.

> » The *intersection* of two sets is the set of the elements that are common to both sets. For example, the intersection of sets $A = \{0, 1, 2, 3, 5, 6, 7, 8, 9\}$ and $B = \{2, 4, 6, 8, 10\}$ is $S = \{2, 6, 8\}$.

> » *Disjoint sets* are two or more sets with no elements in common. For example, set A and set B are disjoint sets if set $A = \{0, 2, 6, 8\}$ and set $B = \{1, 3, 5, 7\}$.

> » A *subset* is a set all of whose elements are also elements of another set. If all the elements of set $B = \{2, 3, 5, 7\}$ also appear in set $A = \{0, 1, 2, 3, 5, 6, 7, 8, 9\}$, then set B is a *subset* of set A. Note: Every set is a subset of itself.

> » A Venn diagram is a visual depiction showing how two or more sets are related.

Getting a visual: Venn diagrams

The GMAT often illustrates the concept of sets with Venn diagrams, such as those presented in Figure 12-1. Venn diagrams provide visual representations of union, intersection, disjoint sets, and subsets. You can draw Venn diagrams to help you answer GMAT questions about sets.

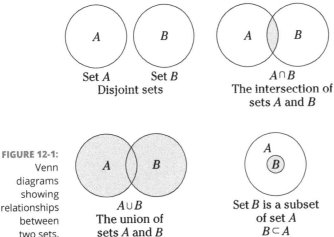

FIGURE 12-1:
Venn
diagrams
showing
relationships
between
two sets.

© John Wiley & Sons, Inc.

GMAT quantitative reasoning questions regarding sets are usually straightforward. Here's an example.

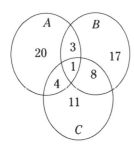

Given the Venn diagram, what are the number of elements in the intersection of sets A and B?

(A) 0

(B) 3

(C) 4

(D) 16

(E) 53

The number of elements in the intersection of sets A and B is the number of elements that are common to both sets. The portion of the diagram that represents the intersection is where the A circle and the B circle overlap. When you add the values in this intersection, you find that the number of elements that are common to both set A and set B is 4. The correct answer is Choice (C).

WARNING

If you chose Choice (B), you ignored the one element that's common to all three sets. You must include that one element, however, because it's a common element of sets A and B. Choice (E) conveys the number of elements in the union of sets A and B rather than their intersection.

Making Arrangements: Permutations and Combinations

The GMAT may test you on the number of arrangement of a set's elements (or a group's members), so you're likely to see some permutation and combination problems. When you calculate *permutations,* you figure out the number of ways set's elements can be arranged in a specific order. Determining *combinations* is similar to finding permutations, except that the order of the arrangements doesn't matter. In the following sections, we provide explanations and examples of each type of problem. But first, let's count.

Counting without listing

Suppose you're planning a fun outfit for the day. You can choose one of five different tops and one of four different pairs of pants; how do you figure out the total number of outfit combinations? Well, we have just what you need: The *multiplication principle*! It's a nifty little rule that will help you determine the total number of possibilities when you have multiple independent choices to make.

In simpler terms, the multiplication principle is all about multiplying the options together to get the total ways to make your selections. To break it down, let's say you have two tasks to complete. If there are m different ways to do the first task and n different ways to do the second task, the multiplication principle tells you that the total number of ways to complete both tasks in the order given is $m \times n$ ways.

Therefore, using the multiplication principle, you can find the total number of outfit combinations by multiplying the number of choices for each category: 5 (tops) multiplied by 4 (pants), which gives you a grand total of 20 possible outfit combinations.

And guess what! You can extend the multiplication principle to any number of tasks. So, unleash your creativity, and see how various options can be combined, whether it's choosing clothes, planning meals, or even creating passwords. Just remember to multiply those choices together, and you'll have a treasure trove of potential possibilities!

Positioning with permutations

Permutations problems ask you to determine how many arrangements are possible given a specific set of distinct numbers and a particular order for the arrangements. For example, figuring out the number of possible seven-digit telephone numbers is a permutation problem. And the answer is huge (10^7) because you have 10 possible digits (0 to 9) to fill each of the seven places. (although, some possible numbers are useless, like 000-0000.)

REMEMBER

Order matters when you set up permutations. Even though two different phone numbers in the same area code may have the same combination of numbers, such as 345-7872 and 543-7728, the numbers ring two different phones because you input them in a different order.

Consider the elements of $S = \{a, b, c\}$. You can arrange these three elements in six different ways: *abc, acb, bac, bca, cab,* and *cba.*

Even though each group contains the same elements, these groupings are completely different permutations because they convey different orderings of the three elements. Writing out the number of possible orderings of a set of three letters isn't too difficult, but what if you had to figure out the number of orderings for a set of 11 numbers? That problem would take more time than anyone would care to spend and certainly more time than you have to finish the GMAT. Luckily, you can rely on factorials to figure out permutations.

TIP

For any integer $n > 1$, *n factorial* is written $n!$ and is the product of all positive integers from 1 through n. Also, by definition, $0! = 1! = 1$. For example, $5!$ is $5 \times 4 \times 3 \times 2 \times 1 = 120$.

Instead of listing the possible permutations for the set of three letters {*a*, *b*, *c*}, use a factorial. The number of ways three different elements (the letters in the set) can be arranged in as many different orders as possible is 3!, which equals $3 \times 2 \times 1 = 6$. So, the number of possible permutations of the three letters is 6.

Suppose you have more than three elements. Maybe a photographer wants to know how many different ways to arrange five people in a single row for a wedding photo. The number of possible arrangements of the five-person wedding party is $5! = 5 \times 4 \times 3 \times 2 \times 1 = 120$.

In general, for a set *n* of distinct elements, the number of different orderings of the elements of the set is *n*!

As you can see, more possible arrangements exist as the number of objects in the arrangement increases. That's the information you need to know to answer basic permutation questions, such as the following one. Give it a shot!

Sophia is arranging four different dance trophies in a row on her bookshelf. How many different ways can she arrange the four trophies?

EXAMPLE

(A) 4

(B) 8

(C) 24

(D) 100

(E) 40,320

Because there are four trophies, the number of arrangements or permutations is $4! = 4 \times 3 \times 2 \times 1 = 24$. Thus, the correct answer is Choice (C).

WARNING

You can eliminate Choices (A) and (B) because they're too small. You know that more than four arrangements must exist, because there are four trophies. Choice (B) is 4×2, which isn't much better. In permutations, you know the number gets large in a hurry, but not as large as Choice (E), which is 8 factorial.

Permutations get a little more challenging when you have a fixed number of objects, *n*, to fill a limited number of places, *r*, and you care about the order the objects are arranged in.

For example, consider the predicament of a big-league baseball coach of a 20-member baseball team who needs to know the number of different batting orders that these 20 ball players can fill in a 9-slot batting lineup. Luckily, there's a permutation formula that will save the coach's day!

The number of permutations of *n* distinct things taken *r* at a time is written $_nP_r$. (To help you remember the formula, think of a certain public radio station that has these call letters.) The formula looks like this:

$$_nP_r = \frac{n!}{(n-r)!}$$

Substitute *n* = 20 and *r* = 9 into the formula to figure out the possible number of batting orders:

$$_{20}P_9 = \frac{20!}{(20-9)!} = \frac{20!}{(11)!}$$

The GMAT won't expect you to calculate the permutation beyond this point. Here's an example of how complex permutations may appear on the GMAT.

EXAMPLE

A lawn care company has five employees that it schedules on a given day to work the lawns of any ten possible homes. How many different ways can the company assign the five employees to the ten homes if each employee provides lawn care service for just one home?

(A) 50

(B) $\dfrac{2!}{1!}$

(C) 120

(D) $\dfrac{10!}{5!}$

(E) 10!

This question may seem counterintuitive to the formula, which calculates n number of things taken r at a time to get the number of permutations. This problem appears to be taking a smaller number of things, r (the number of employees), and finding out how many times they can be spread around a greater number of places. That's what makes this question a little tricky.

TIP

This problem may look backward, but it really follows the same formula. Rather than thinking of how to spread five workers over ten houses, think of how many ways you can arrange the ten houses over the more limited number of workers and apply the formula:

$$_nP_r = \frac{10!}{(10-5)!} = \frac{10!}{(5)!}$$

The correct answer is Choice (D). With a calculator, you can figure out that 30,240 ways exist to assign employees. If you chose Choice (A), you simply multiplied the number of workers times the number of houses. But that's not the correct calculation. Choice (C) is what you get if you calculated 5!, which isn't the complete answer. Likewise, Choice (E) is incomplete.

WARNING

Don't let Choice (B) trip you up. You can't simplify factorials like you can common fractions: $\dfrac{10!}{5!} \neq \dfrac{2!}{1!}$

If this problem was difficult for you, take heart: You won't see too many of these kinds of questions on the GMAT.

Coming together: Combinations

Combinations are a lot like permutations, only easier. You form a *combination* by extracting a certain number of persons or things from a larger total sample of persons and things. Unlike permutations, the order doesn't matter with combinations, so combinations result in fewer possibilities than permutations.

A combination problem may ask you to find how many different teams, committees, or other types of groups can be formed from a set number of persons. For example, if you're asked to select as many teams as you can from a set number of people and the order of the team members doesn't matter, you're finding the total number of combinations of different teams.

Consider how many three-member committees you can form with Tom, Dick, and Harry. Tom, Dick, and Harry don't line up in any order while they're convening, so the way you list them doesn't matter. A committee composed of Tom, Dick, and Harry is the same as a committee composed of Tom, Harry, and Dick or one composed of Dick, Tom, and Harry. So only one possible combination exists of this three-member committee. If Tom, Dick, and Harry were asked to participate in a lineup, you'd have a permutation and six different possible arrangements, but because order doesn't matter when you're forming the committee, you have only one possible combination.

You can apply a formula to figure out the number of combinations. The formula is the number of ways to choose r objects from a group of n objects when the order of the objects doesn't matter, and it looks like this:

$$_nC_r = \frac{n!}{r!(n-r)!}$$

You can see right away that this formula is different from the one for permutations. Because you have a larger number in the denominator than you'd have with a permutation, the final number will be smaller.

Suppose a pollster randomly approaches three different people from a group of five mall walkers. To figure out how many possible combinations of three different people the pollster can annoy, Substitute $n = 5$ and $r = 3$ into the combination formula:

$$_5C_3 = \frac{5!}{3!(5-3)!} = \frac{5!}{3!(2)!} = \frac{120}{6 \times 2} = \frac{120}{12} = 10$$

The factorial 5! is $5 \times 4 \times 3 \times 2 \times 1 = 120$, the factorial 3! is $3 \times 2 \times 1 = 6$, and the factorial 2! is $2 \times 1 = 2$.

Therefore, from the five mall walkers, the pollster can create ten different combinations of three people to poll.

Because you can't use a calculator in the quantitative reasoning section, GMAT combination problem solving questions won't get too complex. The test-makers won't make you perform overly complex calculations on your low-tech noteboard.

Here's an example of what you can expect from GMAT combination problem solving questions.

A group of six fourth graders are choosing foursquare teams at recess. What is the total possible number of combinations of four-person teams that can be chosen from the group of six children?

EXAMPLE

(A) 6

(B) 15

(C) 120

(D) 360

(E) 98,280

Apply the formula for combinations with $n = 6$ and $r = 4$ and see what happens:

$$_6C_4 = \frac{6!}{4!(6-4)!} = \frac{6!}{(4!)(2)!} = \frac{6 \times 5 \times 4 \times 3 \times 2 \times 1}{(4 \times 3 \times 2 \times 1)(2 \times 1)} = \frac{6 \times 5}{2 \times 1} = \frac{30}{2} = 15$$

After you perform the calculations, you find that the correct answer is Choice (B).

If you went for Choice (D), you calculated a permutation instead of a combination.

WARNING

Meeting in the Middle: Mean, Median, and Mode

At least a few GMAT math problems will require you to evaluate data sets consisting of numbers. To evaluate data correctly, you need a measure of their *central tendency*. A *measurement of central tendency* is a single numerical value that describes a data set by attempting to provide a "central" or "typical" value of the numbers in the set. Common statistical measures for describing a central tendency include the *average* or (arithmetic) *mean*, the *median*, and the *mode*.

Summing it up mean-ingfully

The average is a common and useful statistical measure of central tendency. The *average* or *mean* of a set of *n* numbers is the sum of the *n* numbers divided *by n*:

$$\text{average or mean} = \frac{\text{Sum of the } n \text{ Numbers}}{n}$$

For example, the average of the five numbers 25, 43, 40, 60, and 12 is $\frac{12+25+40+43+60}{5} = \frac{180}{5} = 36$.

TIP

You don't have to arrange the numbers in numerical order to find the average, but it's not a bad idea to do so.

You can plug known values into this formula to solve for the other values. For example, if the GMAT tells you the average of five numbers is 40, you can use the formula to figure out their sum like this:

$$40 = \frac{\text{Sum}}{5}$$
$$\text{Sum} = 40 \times 5 = 200$$

Feeling median-ly split

The *median* is the middle value or the average of the middle pair of values in an *ordered* set of data. For a small data set, you can easily determine the median using a two-step process. First, put the numbers in order, from least to greatest (or greatest to least). Next, find the value that falls exactly in the middle of the other data values. If you have an odd number of values, just select the middle value. If you have an even number of values, find the two middle values and average them. The outcome is the median. Here are two examples.

To find the median of the five numbers 25, 43, 40, 60, and 12, order them from least to greatest: 12, 25, 40, 43, 60. The median is 40, the middle number in this list.

To find the median of the six numbers 3, 15, 8, 6, 8, and 5, order them from least to greatest: 3; 5, 6, 8, 8, 15. The median is $\frac{(6+8)}{2} = \frac{14}{2} = 7$, the average of 6 and 8, the two middle numbers.

TIP

In simple terms, the median is a number that splits a list of ordered numbers into two equal parts. It should ideally have half the number above it and half below it. However, in reality, this may not always be the case.

Modeling the mode

The *mode* is the number (or numbers) that occurs with the highest frequency in a data set. A data set can have a single mode (just one number has the highest frequency), multiple modes (two or more numbers have the same highest frequency), or no mode (all numbers occur the same number of times). Here are two examples.

The mode of the list of numbers 1, 1, 2, 4, 7, 7, 7, 9 is 7 because it occurs 3 times, the highest frequency of any number in the list.

The list of numbers 51, 60, 60, 60, 72, 72, 75, 75, 75, 80 has two modes 60 and 75.

TIP

Questions about mode may contain words like *frequency* or ask you how often a value occurs. For example, you may be asked what income occurs most frequently at a certain company. If more people in the company have an income of $30,000 than any other income amount, the mode is $30,000.

Tuning into the frequencies

The number of times a value occurs in a data set is its frequency. A *frequency table* is a way to organize and present data in a tabular form. It shows the number of occurrences or frequency of each unique value in a data set. For example, look at this data set of 20 numbers:

40, 0, 0, 30, 20, 10, 10, 0, 10, 40, 10, 50, 0, 20, 0, 50, 20, 0, 0, 10

You can make a frequency table showing each unique value and its frequency:

Data Value	Frequency
0	7
10	5
20	3
30	1
40	2
50	2
Total	**20**

A frequency table simplifies the computation of statistical measures.

$$\text{Mean} = \frac{7 \times 0 + 5 \times 10 + 3 \times 20 + 1 \times 30 + 2 \times 40 + 2 \times 50}{20} = \frac{320}{20} = 16$$

$\text{Median} = \frac{10 + 10}{2} = 10$, the average of the 10th and 11th values

Mode = 0, the number with the highest frequency

You'll likely see a bunch of questions on the GMAT that ask you to figure out the central tendency of a set of values. Here's an example of one that asks about a mean.

EXAMPLE

George tried to compute the average (arithmetic mean) of his eight statistics test scores. He mistakenly divided the correct sum of all his test scores by seven and calculated his average to be 96. What was George's actual average test score?

(A) 80

(B) 84

(C) 96

(D) 100

(E) 108

The question asks you for George's average score on eight tests and gives the average of those eight scores when they're divided by seven. You know that his average must be less than 96 because you're dividing by a larger number, so you can automatically eliminate Choices (C), (D), and (E). Just use the formula for averages to determine George's average score for eight tests.

1. **Figure out the sum of all George's test scores, using what you know from his incorrect calculation:**

   $$\frac{\text{Sum}}{7} = 96$$
   $$\text{Sum} = 672$$

2. **Find George's actual average based on the sum of all his scores:**

   $$\text{Average} = \frac{\text{Sum}}{8} = \frac{672}{8} = 84$$

   The correct answer is Choice (B).

Straying from Home: Range and Standard Deviation

Besides knowing the main concepts of central tendency, you also need to know about *variability* or *dispersion* of values in statistics. The two types of dispersion you'll deal with on the GMAT are *range* and *standard deviation*, which we explore in the following sections.

Scouting out the range

The easiest measure of dispersion to calculate is the *range*. The range is the difference between the greatest and least values in the data. For example, the range of the five numbers $12, 11, -5, 13, -2$ is $13 - (-5) = 13 + 5 = 18$. Simple as that!

Watching out for wanderers: Standard deviation

Another form of dispersion to know for the GMAT is *standard deviation*. The standard deviation is a measure of how dispersed the data set is in relation to the mean. Generally, the greater the spread of the numbers away from the mean, the greater the standard deviation. Although the range (see preceding section) can give you an idea of the total spread, standard deviation is a more reliable indicator of dispersion because it considers all the data, not just the two on each end. Standard deviation is a most widely used statistical measure for quantifying the dispersion of a data set.

To find the standard deviation of the five numbers 2, 4, 5, 6, and 8, do the following steps:

1. **Calculate the mean:** $\frac{2+4+5+6+8}{5} = \frac{25}{5} = 5$

2. **Find the differences between each of the *n* numbers and the mean:**
   $(2-5) = -3; (4-5) = -1; (5-5) = 0; (6-5) = 1; (8-5) = 3$

3. **Square each difference:** $9, 1, 0, 1, 9$

4. **Find the average of the squared differences:** $\dfrac{9+1+0+1+9}{5} = \dfrac{20}{5} = 4$

5. **Determine the nonnegative square root of this average:** $\sqrt{4} = 2$

The standard deviation is 2.

TIP

Suppose you get a score of 76 on a test where the mean grade is 70 and the standard deviation of all the grades is 3. Your score is comparatively better in this situation than if you get a 76 on a different test, where the mean grade is still 70, but the standard deviation is 6. In the first situation, your score is 2 standard deviations above the mean (because $70 + 2 \times 3 = 70 + 6 = 76$), indicating you did very well relative to the others who took the test. But in the second situation, your score is only 1 standard deviation above the mean (because $70 + 1 \times 6 = 70 + 6 = 76$), indicating your score isn't as good relative to the others.

You've probably had a statistics class by this time in your career, and you probably had to calculate standard deviation in that class. The GMAT likely won't ask you to actually calculate standard deviation, but it will expect you to know how to interpret what it means.

TIP

A small standard deviation means that the data values are more tightly clustered around the mean. A large standard deviation means that the data values are more scattered away from the mean.

EXAMPLE

Here's what a standard deviation question on the GMAT may look like.

   I. {55, 56, 57, 58, 59}

   II. {41, 57, 57, 57, 73}

   III. {57, 57, 57, 57, 57}

Which of the following lists Sets I, II, and III in order from least standard deviation to greatest standard deviation?

(A) I, II, III

(B) I, III, II

(C) II, III, I

(D) III, I, II

(E) III, II, I

The set with the least standard deviation is the one that has the least total amount of deviation—in absolute terms!—from the mean, which in all three sets is 57. The values in Set III are all the same, so Set III has the least standard deviation and should be listed first. Eliminate Choices (A), (B), and (C) because they don't list Set III first. The standard deviation of the numbers in Set I is less than that of the numbers in Set II because clearly the combined absolute deviations from the mean of 55, 56, 57, 58, and 59 in Set I is less than the combined absolute deviations from the mean of 41, 57, 57, 57, and 73 in Set II. So, the set with the greatest standard deviation is Set II, which means it should be listed last. Choice (D) lists the sets in their proper order from least standard deviation to greatest standard deviation, so it's the correct answer.

Predicting the Future: Probability

Probability is the measure of how likely a particular event will occur, but figuring probability is a bit more scientific than telling fortunes and reading tarot cards. You express probability as a percent, fraction, or decimal. You'd say that the probability of an event's occurrence falls between 0 percent and 100 percent or between 0 and 1, inclusive. If the probability of an event's occurrence is 0, or 0 percent, it's *impossible* for the event to occur. If the probability is 1, or 100 percent, the event is *certain* to occur. All other events are possible but uncertain and the probability of their occurrence falls somewhere between 0 and 1, or 0 and 100 percent.

Probability questions may ask you to determine the probability of the occurrence of one event or multiple events. We show you how to determine the probability for each type of question in the following sections.

Taking a chance

Probability deals with *random experiments, outcomes,* and *events.* A *random experiment* is a chance process that gives a single result that cannot be determined beforehand. Each individual possible result is an *outcome* of the experiment. You can assume that all the possible outcomes are known before the random experiment is performed, but which of the possibilities will in fact occur is uncertain.

An *event* is a collection of outcomes from a random experiment. For situations where all possible outcomes are equally likely, the probability (*P*) that the event *E* occurs, represented by $P(E)$, is defined as

$$P(E) = \frac{\text{Number of Outcomes in } E}{\text{Total Number of Possible Outcomes}}$$

REMEMBER

Because you express probability as a fraction whose denominator is greater than or equal to its numerator, it can never be less than 0 or greater than 1. Getting both heads and tails with one flip of a coin is impossible, so the probability of that event occurring is 0. If you used a coin with heads on both sides, the probability of getting heads on one flip would be 1, because the number of possible outcomes is the same as the number of outcomes that can occur.

Fishing for a complement

The *complement* of an event *E* is the event that *E* does <u>not</u> occur. The probability that *E* does not occur is $P(\text{not } E) = 1 - P(E)$. For example, if the probability that *E* occurs is 0.6, then the probability that *E* does not occur is $1 - 0.6 = 0.4$.

Conditioning the probability

A *conditional probability* is one where partial information regarding the outcome of a random event is known.

The *conditional probability* of an event *B* given that an event *A* has already occurred is denoted $P(B|A)$, which is read as "the probability of *B* given *A*." This probability is calculated like this:

$P(B|A) = \dfrac{\text{Probability that both } B \text{ and } A \text{ occur together}}{\text{Probability that } A \text{ occurs}}$. Look at this example.

A box contains 10 chips, identical in size and shape. Six of the chips are green and four are red. Of the green chips, four are marked X and two are marked Y. Of the red chips, three are marked X and one is marked Y. Given that a chip drawn from the box is green, what is the probability that the chip is marked X?

To solve problems like this one, make a 2 ×2 table to organize the information:

	Green	Red	Total
X	4	3	7
Y	2	1	3
Total	6	4	10

Now let *A* be the event the chip is green, and *B* be the event the chip is marked X. Using the table, do the following steps:

1. **Determine the probability that the chip is marked X and is green:** $\frac{4}{10}$.
2. **Determine the probability that the chip is green:** $\frac{6}{10}$
3. **Determine the probability that the chip is marked X given that it is green:**

$$P(\text{marked X}|\text{given it's green}) = \frac{\left(\frac{4}{10}\right)}{\left(\frac{6}{10}\right)} = \frac{4}{6} = \frac{2}{3}$$

Another way to find this probability is to observe that once you know the chip is green, you don't have to concern yourself with the red chips at all. In other words, the number of outcomes is "reduced" to 6, rather than 10. There are 6 green chips, 4 of which are marked X, so the probability that the chip is marked X given that it's green is $\frac{4}{6} = \frac{2}{3}$.

Recognizing mutually exclusive events

Two events are *mutually exclusive* if they cannot occur at the same time; that is, they have no outcomes in common. For example, if you draw one marble from a box containing 10 red marbles and 5 green marbles, the event of drawing a red marble and the event of drawing a green marble are mutually exclusive because you can only get one or the other, but not both in one draw.

Gaining insight into independent and dependent events

Two events are *independent* if the occurrence of one does not affect the probability of the occurrence of the other. Knowing that one of the events has occurred does not give you any information about whether the other event will occur. For example, flipping a fair coin and rolling a fair six-sided die are independent events; the result of flipping the coin has no bearing on the outcome of rolling the die, and vice versa. Similarly, the probability of getting heads on a fair coin flip is always $\frac{1}{2}$, regardless of the outcome of the previous flip. Each coin flip is an independent event; that is, the outcome of one flip does not affect the outcome of the subsequent flips.

Two events that are not independent are *dependent:* that is, the occurrence of one impacts the probability of the occurrence of the other. A dependent event relies on another event happening first. For example, if a coin is flipped twice, the probability that both flips result in heads depends on what happens on the first flip. If the first flip is heads, the probability that both flips result in heads is $\frac{1}{2}$. On the other hand, if the first flip is tails, the probability that both flips result in head is 0. Clearly, there is no chance of getting two heads in a row if the first flip is tails.

Juggling multiple probabilities

You can find the probability of multiple events by following several rules. Table 12-1 lists and describes each rule, shows the corresponding formula, and provides an example of when you'd use it.

TABLE 12-1 Finding the Probability of the Occurrence of Multiple Events

Rule	Circumstance	Formula	Example
Special Rule of Addition	The probability of the occurrence of either of two possible events that are mutually exclusive	$P(A \text{ or } B) = P(A) + P(B)$	The probability of rolling a 5 or 6 on one roll of a fair die
General Rule of Addition	The probability of the occurrence of either of two possible events that can happen at the same time	$P(A \text{ or } B) = P(A) + P(B) - P(A \text{ and } B)$	The probability of drawing a club or a queen from a well-shuffled deck of 52 playing cards
Special Rule of Multiplication	The probability of the occurrence of two events when the two events are independent of each other	$P(A \text{ and } B) = P(A) \times P(B)$	The probability of rolling a 5 followed by a 6 on two rolls of a fair die
General Rule of Multiplication	The probability of the occurrence of two events when the occurrence of the first event affects the outcome of the second event	$P(A \text{ and } B) = P(A) \times P(B|A)$	The probability of first drawing the queen of clubs from a well-shuffled deck of 52 playing cards, not replacing it, and then drawing the jack of diamonds on the next try

Applying the special rule of addition

You use the special rule of addition to figure out the probability of rolling a die and coming up with either a 1 or a 2. You can't get both on one roll, so the events are *mutually exclusive* (which means that the events cannot occur at the same time). Therefore, the probability of rolling a 1 or a 2 in one roll is $P(A) + P(B)$:

$$P(A \text{ or } B) = \frac{1}{6} + \frac{1}{6}$$

$$P(A \text{ or } B) = \frac{2}{6}$$

$$P(A \text{ or } B) = \frac{1}{3}$$

Applying the general rule of addition

You use the general rule of addition to figure probability in the case of choosing sodas from a cooler. Imagine that three types of sodas are in a cooler. Colas are numbered consecutively 1 through 5, orange sodas are numbered 1 through 7, and grape sodas are numbered 1 through 8. Let event *A* stand for when a cola is taken out of the cooler and event *B* represent when a can with a number 4 is taken out. You want to know the probability of picking out *either* a cola *or* a can with the number 4 on it but *not* specifically a cola with the number 4 on it. Five of the 20 cans are colas, three display the number 4, and only one can is a cola with the number 4. So $P(A)$ is $\frac{5}{20}$, $P(B)$ is $\frac{3}{20}$, and $P(A \text{ and } B)$ is $\frac{1}{20}$. Plug the values into the formula and solve:

$$P(A \text{ or } B) = P(A) + P(B) - P(A \text{ and } B)$$

$$P(A \text{ or } B) = \frac{5}{20} + \frac{3}{20} - \frac{1}{20}$$

$$P(A \text{ or } B) = \frac{7}{20}$$

You can also express this probability as 0.35 or as 35%.

Applying the special rule of multiplication

The probability of multiple independent events occurring together is the product of the probabilities of the events occurring individually. For example, if you're rolling two dice at the same time, here's how you find the probability of rolling a 1 on one die and a 2 on the other:

$$P(A \text{ and } B) = \frac{1}{6} \times \frac{1}{6}$$

$$P(A \text{ and } B) = \frac{1}{36}$$

Applying the general rule of multiplication

Suppose the outcome of the second event depends on the outcome of the first event. You then invoke the general rule of multiplication. The term $P(B|A)$ is a conditional probability, where the likelihood of the second event *B* depends on the fact that event *A* has already occurred. For example, to find the probability of drawing the ace of spades from a well-shuffled deck of 52 playing cards on one try and then drawing the king of spades on the second try — with the ace out of the deck — apply the formula, like this: $P(A \text{ and } B) = P(A) \times P(B|A)$.

WARNING

The vertical line between the *B* and *A* stands for the word "given"; it doesn't mean divide! Thus, $P(B|A)$ is read "the probability of *B* given *A*."

$$P(A \text{ and } B) = P(A) \times P(B|A)$$

$$P(A \text{ and } B) = \frac{1}{52} \times \frac{1}{51}$$

$$P(A \text{ and } B) = \frac{1}{2,652}$$

We wouldn't bet against the house on that outcome! The probability of drawing the king of spades on the second draw is slightly better than the probability of drawing the ace on the first draw, because you've already removed one card from the deck on the first draw. Here's a sample of how the GMAT may test your knowledge of probability rules.

A candy machine contains gumballs: three blue, two red, seven yellow, and one purple. The machine randomly distributes one gumball for each dime. Dara has exactly two dimes with which to purchase two gumballs. What is the chance that Dara will get two red gumballs?

(A) $\dfrac{2}{169}$

(B) $\dfrac{1}{13}$

(C) $\dfrac{2}{13}$

(D) $\dfrac{1}{156}$

(E) $\dfrac{1}{78}$

TIP

You need to treat getting the two red gumballs as two events. The occurrence of the first event affects the probability of the second because after Dara extracts the first red gumball, the machine has one fewer gumball. So, you apply the general rule of multiplication.

The chance of getting a red gumball with the first dime is 2 (the number of red gumballs) divided by 13 (the total number of gumballs in the machine), or $\dfrac{2}{13}$. When Dara tries to get a second red gumball, the first red gumball is already gone, which leaves only 1 red gumball and 12 total gumballs in the machine, so the chance of getting a second red gumball is $\dfrac{1}{12}$. The probability of both events happening is the product of the probabilities of the occurrence of each event:

$$P(A \text{ and } B) = P(A) \times P(B \mid A)$$
$$P(A \text{ and } B) = \dfrac{2}{13} \times \dfrac{1}{12}$$
$$P(A \text{ and } B) = \dfrac{2}{156}$$
$$P(A \text{ and } B) = \dfrac{1}{78}$$

Choice (E) is the correct answer. Choice (A) is $\dfrac{2}{13} \times \dfrac{1}{13}$, which would look right if you didn't subtract the withdrawn red gumball from the total number on the second draw. Choice (B) is the chance of drawing one red gumball from a machine with 13 gumballs and only 1 red gumball. In this problem, $\dfrac{1}{13}$ is also the chance of drawing the purple gumball. If you picked Choice (C), you found the chance of drawing the first red gumball.

Chapter **13**

Houston, We Have a Problem: Problem Solving Questions

The GMAT quantitative section consists of 21 problem solving questions for which you are allowed 45 minutes to complete. The questions (not surprisingly!) require you to apply your mathematical skills to solve a problem. These questions are like the ones you've seen on other standardized tests, like the SAT and ACT. They present you with a question and provide five possible answer choices from which you must select the correct answer. The questions test your understanding of arithmetic, elementary algebra, and basic probability and statistics. Chapters 10, 11, and 12 provide a review of these topics. Don't freak out! The math knowledge you need to answer the questions is no more advanced than what is typically taught in secondary school.

REMEMBER

The kinds of math questions that appear on the GMAT test your ability to reason and think on your feet as you make use of the information you're given.

Be Prepared: A Practice Problem Solving Plan

Arriving at the test center with a practice problem solving plan not only provides you with a groovy little alliteration but also gives you a real edge for answering standard math questions. These techniques apply more directly to some questions than others, but learn all of them so you're prepared for all types of problem solving questions:

> » **Examine all the information the question provides to make sure you know exactly what you're asked to do.** Some problems present you with tables, graphs, and scenarios, and some

with just an expression to evaluate or an equation to solve. Don't jump into the answer choices until you've given the question a little thought. Isolate exactly what the problem asks you to solve for and what information the problem provides you. Especially for more complex questions and word problems, use your noteboard to keep track of what you know and what you have to find out.

>> **Eliminate obviously incorrect answer choices if possible.** Before you begin solving a more complex math problem, look at the answer choices to root out any clearly illogical options. You can then focus your problem solving, and you won't pick these answers later through mistaken calculations. You can find more tips for eliminating answer choices in Chapter 2.

>> **Use the information in the problem.** You can expect that GMAT problem solving question contains enough information for you to figure out the correct answer. But you need to use what you're given (including the answer choices!). Pull out the numbers and other terms in a problem and write them on your noteboard in a way that makes the numbers meaningful. Depending on the problem, you may show relationships between quantities, draw simple diagrams, or organize information in a quick table.

>> **Find the equation.** Some GMAT problems provide an equation for you. Others, such as word problems, might require you to come up with an equation using the language in the problem. Whenever you need to turn what you know into an equation, formulate the equation to solve from the information provided in the problem and write it down on your noteboard.

>> **Know when to move on.** Sometimes you may confront a question that you just can't solve. Relax for a moment and reread the question to make sure you haven't missed something. If you still don't know what to do or if you can't remember the tested concept, eliminate all the answers you can and record your best guess. You can find more suggestions for successful guessing in Chapter 2.

Let's apply the problem solving plan to a sample problem.

EXAMPLE

A survey reveals that the average income of a company's customers is $45,000 per year. If 50 customers responded to the survey and the average income of the wealthiest 10 of those customers is $75,000, what is the average income of the other 40 customers?

(A) $27,500
(B) $35,000
(C) $37,500
(D) $42,500
(E) $50,000

Scan the question to get an idea of what it's asking of you. The problem talks about surveys and averages, so it's a statistics question. It asks for the average income of 40 out of 50 customers when the average of the other 10 is $75,000 and that the average of all 50 is $45,000.

You can eliminate Choice (E) off the bat because there's no way that the 40 customers with lower incomes have an average income that's more than the average income of all 50 customers. Choice (D) is probably wrong, too, because the top ten incomes carry such a high average compared to the total average. You know the answer is either Choice (A), (B), or (C), and you haven't even gotten down to solving yet!

TIP

Quickly eliminating answers before you begin can save you from choosing an answer that comes from making a math error. Sometimes, the test-makers are tricky; they anticipate the kinds of little mistakes you'll make and offer the resulting wrong answers as distractors in the answer choices. So be sure to eliminate illogical answers before you begin a problem.

You can find the total income of all 50 customers and the total income of the wealthiest 10 customers by using the formula for averages. The average of *n* values equals the sum of the values divided by *n*. Apply the formula to find the total income for the group of 50. Then find the total income for the group of 10. Subtract the total income of the 10 from the total income of the 50 to find the total income of the 40. Then you can divide by 40 to get the average income for the group of 40. Here's how you do it:

TIP

Your calculations may be easier if you drop the three zeroes from the salaries. For this problem, shorten $45,000 to $45 and $75,000 to $75. Just remember to add the zeroes back on to your solution when you find it!

1. Find the total income for the group of 50:

The average income is $45 and the number of group members is 50, so use the formula to find the sum of all incomes (*x*):

$$\text{Average} = \frac{\text{Sum of Values}}{\text{Number of Values}}$$

$$45 = \frac{x}{50}$$
$$2,250 = x$$

2. Find the total income for the group of 10:

The average income is $75 and the number of group members is 10, so use the formula to find the sum (*y*):

$$75 = \frac{y}{10}$$
$$750 = y$$

3. Find the total income for the group of 40:

Subtract the total income of the group of 10 (*y*) from the total income for the group of 50 (*x*):
$$2,250 - 750 = 1,500$$

4. Find the average income of the group of 40:

The sum of the incomes in the group is $1,500, and the number of group members is 40, so apply the average formula:

$$\text{Average} = \frac{1,500}{40}$$
$$\text{Average} = 37.5$$

Move the decimal point three places to the right to make up for the three zeroes you excluded in your calculations, and you have your answer. The average income of the 40 customers is $37,500, which is Choice (C).

Trying Out Some Problem Solving Practice Problems

Here are a few practice questions to help you master the approach to problem solving questions in the quantitative section. When you're finished answering them, read through the answer explanations to see how you fared.

Try to answer these five practice problems in the same allotted time you'll experience on the actual GMAT (give yourself about 10 minutes 40 seconds to answer all five questions). Remember to keep track of the information you know and the information you have to figure out as you work through the problems. Use a piece of scratch paper to simulate the noteboard as you work out the answers.

1. An electronics firm produces 300 units of a particular MP3 player every hour of every day. Each unit costs the manufacturer $60 to produce, and retailers immediately purchase all the produced units. What is the minimum wholesale price (amount the manufacturer receives) per unit that the manufacturer should charge to make an hourly profit of $19,500?

   (A) $60

   (B) $65

   (C) $95

   (D) $125

   (E) $145

2. If $x \neq 0$, what is the value for x in the equation $\dfrac{2x}{4+2x} = \dfrac{6x}{8x+6}$?

   (A) -3

   (B) 1

   (C) 2

   (D) 3

   (E) 6

$$g(r) = \begin{cases} 4|r| & \text{if } r \geq 2 \\ -|r| & \text{if } r < 2 \end{cases}$$

3. Given the function g defined above, what is the value of $g(-r)$ if $r = -7$?

   (A) -28

   (B) -14

   (C) -7

   (D) 7

   (E) 28

4. In a survey of 200 students regarding pet ownership of cats and dogs, c students own at least one cat, d students own at least one dog, and b students own at least one dog and at least one cat. Write an expression that indicates how many students own neither a cat nor a dog.

   (A) $200 - c - d - b$

   (B) $200 - c - d + b$

   (C) $200 + c + d - b$

   (D) $200 - c - d$

   (E) $200 - b$

5. Luis, Maya, and Kira interviewed for jobs at companies X, Y, and Z, respectively. The probability that Luis will get a job offer from Company X is 30 percent; the probability that Maya will get a job offer from Company Y is 50 percent; and the probability that Kira will get a job offer from Company Z is 60 percent. The three companies have no connections to one another, so the job offers are mutually independent. What is the probability that Luis and Maya will get job offers, but not Kira?

(A) 6%

(B) 9%

(C) 20%

(D) 40%

(E) 120%

Answer Explanations

1. **D.** Note what the question gives and what it's asking for. It provides units per hour and cost per unit. It also tells you the total desired hourly profit. You're supposed to find the price per unit.

   The first thing to do is eliminate obviously incorrect answer choices. You know that you're looking for the wholesale price that will yield a profit (which results from price minus cost to produce) of $19,500 per hour. Because the answers given are wholesale prices, you can eliminate Choices (A) and (B). The cost to produce each unit is $60. If the company charged the same amount for the MP3 players as it spent to produce them, it would make no profit, so Choice (A) is obviously incorrect. Choice (B) isn't much better. At a profit of just $5 per unit and 300 units per hour, the firm would make only $1,500 per hour.

   You've eliminated two answer choices. Evaluate the data to find the correct answer from the remaining three. You know that 300 units are produced every hour and that those 300 units have to net a profit of $19,500. If you knew the amount of profit per unit, you could add that to the amount each unit costs to produce and get the minimum wholesale price. Set up an equation with x as the profit per unit. Remember that *per* means to *divide*:

   $$x = \frac{19,500}{300}$$
   $$x = 65$$

   The firm needs to make a profit of $65 per unit.

   You can't stop here and pick Choice (B). You're not done yet, but you know that because you've already eliminated Choice (B).

   You have to add profit to the per-unit production cost to get the final wholesale price:

   $$\$60 + \$65 = \$125$$

   Correct answer: Choice (D).

   TIP

   You could use estimation to solve this problem by rounding $19,500 up to the nearest convenient multiple of 300, which is $21,000, and then dividing 21 by 3 in your head and getting 7. This would tell you that you need a little less than $70 profit from each unit, or a little under $130 as the wholesale price (because $60 + $70 = $130).

2. **D.** Here's a relatively simple algebra question that asks you to solve for x. The only element that makes it a little complex is that you're dealing with algebraic fractions. Take a moment to consider the equation. The numerator in the fraction on the right is 3 times the numerator in the fraction on the left. Multiplying the numerator of the left-side fraction by 3 would make it equal to the numerator on the right side.

   REMEMBER

   When the numerators of two equivalent fractions are equal, their denominators are also equal, so creating equal numerators allows you to set the denominators equal to each other. Then just solve for x.

   1. **Multiply the left-side fraction by $\frac{3}{3}$:**

      This doesn't change the value of the fraction, because multiplying by $\frac{3}{3}$ is the same as multiplying by 1.

      $$\frac{2x}{4+2x} \times \frac{3}{3} = \frac{6x}{12+6x}$$

2. Set the denominators equal to each other and solve for *x*:

$$12 + 6x = 8x + 6$$
$$6x = 8x - 6$$
$$-2x = -6$$
$$x = 3$$

Correct answer: Choice (D).

You can also solve this question by cross-multiplying opposite numerators and denominators:

$$\frac{2x}{4 + 2x} = \frac{6x}{8x + 6}$$
$$2x(8x + 6) = 6x(4 + 2x)$$
$$16x^2 + 12x = 24x + 12x^2$$
$$4x^2 = 12x$$
$$x^2 = 3x$$
$$x = 3$$

Note: You can divide both sides by *x* because $x \neq 0$.

TIP

You can solve many GMAT problems by using more than one method. Go with the one that's easiest for you.

3. **E.** This problem provides what's known as a "piecewise" function in which, in this case, you use one of two different output rules depending on the value of the input. If the input is greater than or equal to 2, the output is 4 times the absolute value of the input. If the input is less than 2, the output is the negative of the absolute value of the input.

WARNING

Don't let the negative signs mess you up. If $r = -7$, then $g(-r)$ is the same as saying $g(7)$, because $-(-7)$ is 7. So the value of the input in this problem is 7.

Because 7 is greater than 2, you'll look to the first rule of the function $g(r)$. The solution to $g(7) = 4|7|$ is simply $4 \times 7 = 28$. *Correct answer:* Choice (E).

If you confuse the signs, you'll come up with the negative version of the correct answer, which is Choice (A). You get the other answer choices when you use an incorrect rule.

4. **B.** This question is a group problem that asks you to use the information given to write an expression that indicates how many students own neither a cat nor a dog.

The rule for solving two-group problems is

Group 1 + Group 2 − Both Groups + Neither Group = Grand Total

So if you're told that out of 200 students, *c* students own at least one cat, *d* students own at least one dog, and *b* students own at least one cat and at least one dog, you can use the rule to find out how many students own neither a cat nor a dog. Let Group 1 be the number of cat-only owners and Group 2 be the number of dog-only owners. Then let *n* be Neither Group, the number of students who own neither a cat nor a dog. Plug the known values into the rule and set up an equation:

Group 1 + Group 2 − Both Groups + Neither Group = Grand Total
$$c + d - b + n = 200$$
$$n = 200 - c - d + b$$

Thus, an expression that indicates how many students own neither a cat nor a dog is $200 - c - d + b$. *Correct answer:* Choice (B).

Choices (A) and (C) result if you solve the equation incorrectly. Choices (D) and (E) result if you use a wrong rule.

5. **A.** This question asks you to find the probability that Luis and Maya will get job offers, but not Kira. To determine the correct answer, consider that you have the following three events that are mutually independent:

Luis gets a job offer from Company X; this event has probability 30%.

Maya gets a job offer from Company Y; this event has probability 50%.

Kira does <u>not</u> get a job offer from Company Z; this event has probability 100% − 60% = 40%.

Now apply the special rule of multiplication to these three mutually independent events:

(30%)(50%)(40%) = (0.3)(0.5)(0.4) = 0.06 = 6%

Correct answer: Choice (A).

Choice (E) should be eliminated at first glance because probabilities cannot exceed 100%. Choice (B) results if you compute (30%)(50%)(60%), which suggests you failed to determine the probability that Kira does not get a job offer. Choices (C) and (D) result if you use some version of an addition rule.

IN THIS CHAPTER

» Honing your GMAT math skills
by working through practice
questions

» Taking a look at the answer
explanations to understand what
you did wrong — and right

Chapter **14**

Prove Your Prowess: A Mini Practice Quantitative Section

ere's a chance to test your GMAT math skills before you embark on the real adventure of taking the test. This chapter contains fewer math questions than the number you'll see on the GMAT, so it's kind of like a mini practice test. To get a better idea of the time restrictions you'll face on test day, try to complete the 14 questions in the following section in about 30 minutes. If you want to avoid the time pressure for now, feel free to just focus on answering the questions. You'll have the opportunity to time yourself again when you take the full-length practice tests included with this book.

TIP

Read through all the answer explanations (even the ones for the questions you answered correctly), because you want to make sure you know why you got the answer you did and because you may see something in the explanations that can help you with other questions.

Tackling Problem Solving Practice Questions

Here are 14 practice questions for the GMAT quantitative section. Grab your pencil, set your timer for 30 minutes, and get started. (Try not to peek at the answers until you've come up with your own.)

DIRECTIONS: For each question, select the best answer from the choices provided.

1. If $\left(\dfrac{3}{y}+2\right)(y-5)=0$, where $y \neq 0$ and $y \neq 5$, then $y =$

   (A) $-\dfrac{3}{2}$

   (B) $-\dfrac{2}{3}$

   (C) $\dfrac{2}{3}$

   (D) $\dfrac{3}{2}$

   (E) 6

2. If Esperanza will be 35 years old in 6 years, how old was she x years ago?

   (A) $41-x$

   (B) $x-41$

   (C) $35-x$

   (D) $x-29$

   (E) $29-x$

3. Sofa Haven is having "a sale on top of a sale!" The price of a certain sofa, which already had been discounted by 20 percent, is further reduced by an additional 20 percent. These successive discounts are equivalent to a single discount of which of the following?

   (A) 40%

   (B) 38%

   (C) 36%

   (D) 30%

   (E) 20%

4. In a previous year, the U.S. Census estimated that there were approximately 6.5 billion people in the world and 300 million in the United States. Approximately what percent of the world's population lived in the United States that year?

   (A) 0.0046%

   (B) 0.046%

   (C) 0.46%

   (D) 4.6%

   (E) 46%

5. To boost sales around the holidays, the government of the fictional country of Capitalitamia dictates that a citizen may purchase goods up to a total value of $1,000 tax-free but must pay a 7 percent tax on the portion of the total value in excess of $1,000. How much tax must be paid by a citizen who purchases goods with a total value of $1,220?

    (A) $14.00
    (B) $15.40
    (C) $54.60
    (D) $70.00
    (E) $87.40

6. If $\frac{180}{b} = \frac{5}{2}$; what does b equal?

    (A) 108
    (B) 99
    (C) 81
    (D) 72
    (E) 63

7. The arithmetic mean and standard deviation for a set of numbers are 9.5 and 1.5, respectively. Which of the following lies more than 2.5 standard deviations from the mean?

    (A) 5.75
    (B) 6
    (C) 6.5
    (D) 13.25
    (E) 13.5

8. On her annual road trip to visit her family in Seal Beach, California, Traci stopped to rest after she traveled $\frac{1}{3}$ of the total distance and again after she traveled $\frac{1}{4}$ of the distance remaining between her first stop and her destination. She then drove the remaining 200 miles and arrived safely at her destination. What was the total distance in miles from Traci's starting point to Seal Beach?

    (A) 250
    (B) 300
    (C) 350
    (D) 400
    (E) 550

9. If n is a positive integer and $x + 3 = 4^n$, which of the following could *not* be a value of x?

    (A) 1
    (B) 13
    (C) 45
    (D) 61
    (E) 253

GO ON TO NEXT PAGE

10. If $3^{(b-4-2c)} = 9^{(b-c)}$, what is the value of b?

(A) -4

(B) $-\dfrac{4}{3}$

(C) 0

(D) $\dfrac{4}{3}$

(E) 4

11. This stem-and-leaf plot shows the number of automobiles sold by 22 sales associates of Ace Auto Sales during the month of January. Next month, management wants to increase the average number of automobiles sold per sales associate to 35. If the number of sales associates remains at 22, on average how many additional automobiles will each sales associate need to sell next month for management to reach this goal?

Number of Automobiles Sold per Sales Associate in January	
1	2 5 7 8 8
2	2 3 3 4 5 5 5
3	2 4 4 4 8 9 9
5	0 2
6	1

Legend: 2 | 3 = 23

(A) 3

(B) 5

(C) 32

(D) 35

(E) 110

12. For all $a \neq 0$ and $b \neq 0$, $\dfrac{\left(4a^4b^3\right)^2}{2a^2b^{-2}} = ?$

(A) $8a^6b^8$

(B) $8a^6b^4$

(C) $8a^4b^7$

(D) $2a^6b^8$

(E) $2a^4b^7$

13. Akhil invests \$1,200 in a certificate of deposit (CD) that earns 1.05% in interest compounded annually, which means that he earns 1.05% of his existing money yearly. The money he makes in interest is added to his account balance and rounded to the nearest cent. After four years, the CD matures. Akhil decides to use \$400 of the funds to purchase a tablet and invest the remaining balance in another CD. How much money did Akhil invest in the second CD?

(A) \$800.00

(B) \$850.40

(C) \$851.20

(D) \$1,250.40

(E) \$1,251.20

14. If $w, x, y,$ and z are positive integers such that the ratio of w to x is 3 to 4, the ratio of x to z is 8 to 5, and the ratio of y to z is 3 to 2, what is the ratio of w to y?

(A) 5 to 9

(B) 4 to 5

(C) 5 to 4

(D) 9 to 5

(E) 16 to 5

Checking Out the Answer Explanations

1. **A.** The GMAT usually starts with a question of medium difficulty, and this one is in that range. If the product of two factors equals 0, then at least one of the factors must be 0 (by the *zero product property* of real numbers). Therefore, one of the factors in this equation must equal 0. You know it isn't the second one, because y doesn't equal 5, and y would have to equal 5 for the second term to result in 0.

   Therefore, you need to create an equation that sets the first factor equal to 0 and then solve for y. Here's what you get for the first factor:

   $$\frac{3}{y} + 2 = 0$$

   $$\frac{3}{y} = -2$$

   Cross-multiply (because $-2 = -\frac{2}{1}$) and solve:

   $$3 = -2y$$

   $$-\frac{3}{2} = y, \text{ Choice A}$$

2. **E.** If Esperanza will be 35 years old in 6 years, she is 29 right now ($35 - 6 = 29$). Therefore, to determine how old she was x years ago, simply subtract x from her current age of 29 to obtain $29 - x$, Choice (E).

3. **C.** This is a repeated percent decrease question. You can apply a formula to solve it, but a faster and easier method is to apply actual numbers to the circumstances. To simplify your life, use a nice, round figure like $100.

   If the sofa originally cost $100 but was discounted by 20%, multiply $100 by 20% (= 0.20) and subtract that from $100 to find the price after the first discount ($100 \times 0.20 = 20$, and $100 - 20 = 80$). Thus, after the first round of discounts, the sofa cost $80.

   However, the sofa was discounted an additional 20%. Now, you have to repeat the process, this time using $80 as the original price ($80 \times 0.20 = 16$, and $80 - 16 = 64$). So, after both discounts, the sofa cost $64.

   But you're not finished yet. You need to calculate the total discount. The sofa originally cost $100 and, after the series of discounts, cost $64. The discount, in dollars, is $100 - 64$, which is $36. To find the percent of the full discount, simply divide $36 by the original price of $100 to obtain $\frac{36}{100} = 0.36$ or 36%, Choice (C).

4. **D.** This question requires you to work with very large numbers, so you need to know what large numbers look like. But before you proceed, eliminate Choice (A) because it's unrealistic to think the population of the United States is 0.0046% (which is less than $\frac{1}{200}$ of one percent) of the world's population; and eliminate Choice (E) because it's equally unrealistic to think the population of the United States is 46% (which is close to 50%) of the population of the world!

   One billion = 1,000,000,000, and 1 million = 1,000,000. In other words, 1 billion is 1,000 million.

REMEMBER

Now, look at the question at hand: 6.5 billion is written as 6,500,000,000. Writing out 6 billion is obvious, and 0.5 billion is one-half of 1,000 million, which is 500 million, or 500,000,000. You write 300 million as 300,000,000. To solve for the percent, simply divide 300,000,000 by 6,500,000,000, using the fraction form:

$$\frac{300,000,000}{6,500,000,000}$$

Simplify things by canceling out eight zeros on the top and bottom. (This step is legal because you're just reducing your fraction.) Then divide 3 by 65.

You don't actually have to complete the mathematical calculation, because all the answer choices are derivatives of 46. You do need to know, though, that when you divide 3 by 65, your answer will have three places after the decimal. If you can't figure this in your head, quickly set up the division problem on your noteboard and mark where the decimal will be in your answer.

So $\frac{3}{65} = 0.046$, but the question asks for a percent. To convert the decimal to a percent, move the decimal point two places to the right and add a percent sign. The answer is 4.6%, Choice (D).

You can also use estimation to narrow down the remaining answer choices. $\frac{3}{65}$ is about $\frac{3}{60}$, which reduces to $\frac{1}{20}$, or 0.05. The answer has to be slightly smaller than 0.05 because $\frac{3}{65}$ is less than $\frac{3}{60}$. The answer that is slightly less than 0.05 is 0.046 or 4.6%.

5. **B.** The first thing that should jump out at you is that the first $1,000 of purchases is tax-free, so you don't need to consider the first $1,000. Subtract $1,000 from $1,220 to get the value of purchases that will actually be taxed: $220.

To find the amount of tax due, you multiply 220 by 7% (or 0.07), but you don't have to take the time to fully work out the calculation. To make things simple, you can estimate: 200 is close to 220, and $200 \times 0.07 = 14$, so the amount has to be just a little more than $14.

The only answer that's just a little more than $14 is Choice (B). If you take the time to multiply 220 by 0.07, you'll find that it's exactly $15.40. But because this is a test where saving time is crucial, avoid making full calculations whenever possible.

6. **D.** Solve for b:

$$\frac{180}{b} = \frac{5}{2}$$
$$5b = 360$$
$$b = 72$$

So, the correct answer is Choice (D).

7. **E.** Don't let the language of this problem scare you. You're really just applying basic arithmetic operations.

The arithmetic mean is 9.5 and the standard deviation is 1.5, so you'll use a deviation of 1.5 to find values that stray from the mean. The values that are 2.5 standard deviations from the mean are 13.25 and 5.75, which you derive by adding and subtracting 3.75 ($= 2.5 \times 1.5$) from 9.5, the mean.

So, to solve this problem, look for an answer choice that's greater than 13.25 or less than 5.75. The answer is 13.5, Choice (E).

8. **D.** To find the total distance of Traci's trip, set up an equation that expresses the sum of the three separate trip portions. Let x equal the total distance in miles. Traci stopped to rest after she traveled $\frac{1}{3}$ of the total distance, so the first part of the trip is $\frac{1}{3}x$. She stopped again after she traveled $\frac{1}{4}$ of the distance remaining between her first stop and her destination, which is the total distance she traveled minus the first part of her trip. You can represent the second part of the trip mathematically, like this:

$$\frac{1}{4}\left(x - \frac{1}{3}x\right)$$

The third part of the trip is the remaining 200 miles. Add up the three parts of the trip to set up the equation and solve for total distance:

$$x = \frac{1}{3}x + \frac{1}{4}\left(x - \frac{1}{3}x\right) + 200$$
$$x = \frac{1}{3}x + \frac{1}{4}\left(\frac{3}{3}x - \frac{1}{3}x\right) + 200$$
$$x = \frac{1}{3}x + \frac{1}{4}\left(\frac{2}{3}x\right) + 200$$
$$x = \frac{1}{3}x + \frac{1}{6}x + 200$$

TIP

At this point, you can make it easier on yourself by multiplying each expression on both sides by 6 to get rid of the fractions:

$$6x = 2x + x + 1,200$$
$$6x = 3x + 1,200$$
$$3x = 1,200$$
$$x = 400$$

Traci traveled a total distance of 400 miles, so the correct answer is Choice (D).

9. **C.** You could try to solve for n, but a faster and easier way to approach this problem is to plug each of the answer choices into the given equation and pick the one that doesn't make the expression true:

>> Choice (A) gives you 1. Plug in 1 for x in the equation: $1 + 3 = 4^n$. Doing so makes $n = 1$, which is a positive integer. Because 1 is a possible value for x, Choice (A) is wrong.

>> If you substitute 13 from Choice (B), you get $13 + 3 = 4^n$. And $13 + 3$ is 16 and $4^2 = 16$. If $n = 2$, it's a positive integer, so eliminate Choice (B).

>> For Choice (C), you substitute 45 into the equation: $45 + 3 = 4^n$. The equation comes out to $48 = 4^n$, and although it may seem like 4 could be a root of 48, it's not. There's no way n could be a positive integer when $x = 45$. Choice (C) is the correct answer. Choose Choice (C) and move on! Here's the checks for the last two answers to assure you that moving on is the right decision.

>> If you plug in 61 from Choice (D) into the equation, you get $61 + 3 = 4^n$. And $61 + 3 = 64$, which is 4^3. But 3 is a positive integer, so Choice (D) can't be right.

>> Choice (E) is 253, and $253 + 3 = 256$. And $256 = 4^4$, which would make $n = 4$, a positive integer. Choice (E) makes the equation true, so it's the wrong answer.

WARNING

Be careful when you answer questions that ask you to find the answer that *can't* be true. In these cases, if an answer choice works, you have to eliminate it rather than choose it. Keep reminding yourself of your goal.

10. A. At first glance, it appears you cannot find an exact value for *b* because the equation contains more than one variable, but none of the options is phrased as "None of these," so you know there must be a way to determine the value of *b*. First, make the bases equal:

$$3^{(b-4-2c)} = 9^{(b-c)}$$
$$3^{(b-4-2c)} = 3^{2(b-c)}$$

TIP

No option in the quantitative section is phrased as "None of these."

Then set the exponents equal to each other to discover whether you can solve for *b*:

$$b - 4 - 2c = 2(b-c)$$
$$b - 4 - 2c = 2b - 2c$$
$$b - 4 = 2b$$
$$-4 = b$$

The minute you realize that the *c* values cancel, you know that you can solve for *b*. The answer is Choice (A).

11. B. Apply the average formula to find the current month's average number of automobiles sold. To find the sum, you need to add all the values represented on the plot. This stem-and-leaf plot presents a set of values in terms of their tens and ones digits. The left column is the tens digit, and the right column is the ones digit for each of the numbers of automobiles sold. Use data to find the sum:

$$12 + 15 + 17 + (2 \times 18) + 22 + (2 \times 23) + 24 + (3 \times 25) + 32 + (3 \times 34)$$
$$+ 38 + (2 \times 39) + 50 + 52 + 61 = 660$$

Enter these numbers into the average formula:

$$\text{Average} = \frac{\text{sum of autos sold}}{\text{\# of sales associates}} = \frac{660}{22} = 30$$

At this point, you may notice that to obtain an average of 35 autos sold per sales associate, on average each sales associate needs to sell 5 additional autos.

If this isn't obvious at first, you can apply the formula again to determine the total number of additional autos the sales associates need to sell next month to achieve an average of 35 autos sold per sales associate:

$$35 = \frac{660 + x}{22}$$
$$770 = 660 + x$$
$$110 = x$$

This number is the total number of additional autos the sales associates need to sell next month to reach management's goal, but the question asks for the average number each sales associate needs to sell to achieve an average of 35 autos per sales associate. So divide 110 by 22:

$$\frac{110}{22} = 5$$

On average, each sales associate needs to sell 5 additional automobiles to reach an average of 35 autos per sales associate. The answer is Choice (B).

12. **A.** This question requires basic algebraic simplification. Because the entire numerator is squared, you first need to square every term in the parentheses. Take them one-by-one and apply process of elimination to the answer choices as you go.

$$4^2 = 16$$

Divide the coefficients of 16 and 2 to get 8 and eliminate Choices (D) and (E) because they don't have a coefficient of 8. Continue by squaring the variables in the numerator. When you take an exponent to a power, you multiply the exponents:

$$\left(a^4\right)^2 = a^8$$
$$\left(b^3\right)^2 = b^6$$

The new expression is $8\left(\dfrac{a^8 b^6}{a^2 b^{-2}}\right)$.

Divide the variables by subtracting exponents:

$$\frac{a^8}{a^2} = a^6$$
$$\frac{b^6}{b^{-2}} = b^8$$

Combine the components to get a final answer of $8a^6 b^8$, Choice (A).

Choice (B) results if you subtract the 2 from 6 when you worked with the b exponents. When you subtract a negative value, you actually add the value. Choice (C) results if you add the exponents when you square them instead of multiplying them.

13. **C.** Akhil begins with an initial CD investment of $1,200. Every year he makes 1.05% (= 0.0105) on his existing money. So after the first year, Akhil has his initial investment plus 1.05% of that investment, which is 1.0105 times the $1,200 initial investment, or $1,212.60. But the balance doesn't increase by just $12.60 the next year because Akhil makes 1.05% on the new existing balance, So after two years, he has 1.0105 times $1,212.60 instead of $1,200, which is a balance of $1,225.33. At three years, Akhil has 1.0105 times $1,225.33, or $1,238.20. One year later the CD matures after another 1.05% is added to Akhil's balance yielding $1,238.20 \times 1.0105 = \$1,251.20$.

The amount Akhil invests into a second CD is $1,251.20 less the $400 he uses to purchase the tablet: $1,251.20 - \$400 = \$851.20$. Pick Choice (C).

TIP

You can save some time by making a comparison between what Akhil earns from compounded interest to what he would earn from simple interest. Eliminate Choice (A) because $800 is the result if he earned no interest at all! The amount of compounded interest earned in a certain time period should be greater than that earned from simple interest. By multiplying $1,200 by 0.0105, you know with simple interest he earns $12.60 each year. Multiplying $12.60 times 4 give you $50.40 earned from simple interest in 4 years, which would make Akhil's balance $1,250.40. When you subtract $400 for the tablet, you learn that Akhil would have $850.40 to invest in the second CD if he had earned simple interest. Eliminate Choice (B) because he would have earned slightly more with compound interest but not so much more that you can justify choices (D) or (E). Choice (C) is the only value that fits that description!

14. B. Expressed as a fraction, the ratio of w to y is $\dfrac{w}{y}$. From the question information, you can write three proportions:

$\dfrac{w}{x} = \dfrac{3}{4}$, $\dfrac{x}{z} = \dfrac{8}{5}$, and $\dfrac{y}{z} = \dfrac{3}{2}$. From $\dfrac{w}{x} = \dfrac{3}{4}$, you have $w = \dfrac{3}{4}x$; from $\dfrac{x}{z} = \dfrac{8}{5}$, you have $x = \dfrac{8}{5}z$; and from $\dfrac{y}{z} = \dfrac{3}{2}$, you have $z = \dfrac{2}{3}y$.

Therefore,

$$w = \frac{3}{4}x = \frac{3}{4}\left(\frac{8}{5}z\right) = \left(\frac{3}{4} \times \frac{8}{5}\right)(z) = \left(\frac{3}{4} \times \frac{8}{5}\right)\left(\frac{2}{3}y\right) = \left(\frac{3}{4} \times \frac{8}{5} \times \frac{2}{3}\right)(y) = \left(\frac{\cancel{3}}{\cancel{4}} \times \frac{\cancel{8}^2}{5} \times \frac{2}{\cancel{3}}\right)(y) = \frac{4}{5}y$$

Then from $w = \dfrac{4}{5}y$, you have $\dfrac{w}{y} = \dfrac{4}{5}$. So, the ratio of w to y is 4 to 5, Choice (B).

Choice (C) is the ratio of y to w. Choices (A), (D), and (E) result if you fail to reason correctly or make a computation error.

5

Excelling on the Data Insights Section

Find out how to most effectively approach the four data insights integrated reasoning question types (table analysis, two-part analysis, graphics interpretation, and multi-source reasoning).

Review crucial analytical, critical thinking, and data-interpretation skills you need to successfully reason your way through integrated reasoning questions.

Learn about the unique format for data insights data sufficiency questions along with a tried and true methodical approach to answering them.

Chapter **15**

Four Types of Distinctive Data Insights Questions

The data insights section of the GMAT has five types of questions: table analysis, two-part analysis, graphics interpretation, multi-source reasoning, and data sufficiency. These question types are exclusive to the GMAT and possess unconventional formats. Traditionally, the four question types — table analysis, two-part analysis, graphics interpretation, and multi-source reasoning — have collectively been referred to as "integrated reasoning" questions. For convenience, we will also use the term "integrated reasoning" (or IR, for short) in our discussions when relevant. This chapter aims to familiarize you with these four data insights question types and to provide guidance on approaching each one, considering their distinctive styles and characteristics. Chapter 17 will equip you with everything you need to effectively tackle data sufficiency questions.

IR questions throw you something completely different from the five-option multiple-choice questions you're probably accustomed to. They require you to actively explore, manipulate, and extract meaningful information from multifaceted data landscapes to derive insights and make informed decisions. A lot goes on at once with these questions, and this chapter gives you the strategies you need to manage it all successfully.

Understanding What the IR Questions Are All About

To achieve success with IR questions requires you to effectively apply a blend of the critical reasoning skills assessed in the verbal reasoning section and the math skills essential for problem solving in the quantitative reasoning section to real-world scenarios. Therefore, if you have adequately prepared for the GMAT's math and verbal sections, you are likely to perform well with the IR questions. We explain the details of the IR questions and the purpose behind them in the next two sections.

Skills tested

The most common math computations in the IR questions involve these areas:

>> Basic statistics, such as average, median, mode, range, and standard deviation

>> Sets and counting methods

>> Probability, sequences, and series

>> Rates, ratios, and percents

>> Algebraic expressions, equations, and functions

You'll need to apply the following essentials of critical reasoning:

>> Basic elements of logical arguments — premises, conclusions, and assumptions

>> Complex mental processes — evaluate, infer, synthesize, and strategize

>> Critical analysis including supporting or weakening claims

>> Argument types — cause and effect, analogy, and statistical

You can review the necessary math concepts in Chapters 10, 11, and 12. Read more about evaluating logical arguments in Chapter 8.

About the question types

Each IR question type — table analysis, two-part analysis, graphics interpretation, and multi-source reasoning — requires synthesizing information from multiple sources to solve complex problems. Furthermore, more often than not, you are given more information than is needed to arrive at correct answers. You must carefully go through the provided information to discern which of it is relevant to the question posed.

WARNING

Even though you may have personal knowledge related to the topic presented, always answer IR questions based only on the information provided to you.

Almost every question has multiple parts. To get credit for answering a question correctly, you have to answer *all* its parts correctly. You don't receive partial credit for getting just one part of the question correct.

On average, you can expect to encounter a couple of each IR question type on the GMAT. However, the specific number and order of these questions may vary. Therefore, make sure you are ready to tackle all four question types during your test:

>> **Table analysis:** This three-part question type offers you a spreadsheet-like table of data. You can sort the table by one or more of its columns by clicking a column's heading from a drop-down menu. You use the data to make judgments (e.g., Yes/No; True/False) about three statements, phrases, words, numerical values, or formulas. Each of your judgments has to be correct to get credit for the question.

>> **Two-part analysis:** Based on a short written scenario of a phenomenon, situation, or mathematical problem, you make two choices that, together or separately, meet one or more conditions presented in the question. You make your two selections in the first two columns from a list of options in the third column of a three-column response table. The top row of the response table labels the columns. You must pick one correct answer in the first column and one correct answer in the second column to get credit for the question. You can pick the same answer in both columns.

>> **Graphics interpretation:** A graphic, image, or other visual representation provides all the data you need to complete the missing pieces of information in one or two statements. You must select the best choice from a drop-down menu of several answer options to record your answer for each missing piece of information. If there are two or more drop-down menus, you must select the best choices in all of them to get credit for the question.

>> **Multi-source reasoning:** These aptly named questions present you with two or three sources of information, each labeled with a tab that allows you to switch from one source to another. One or more sources will be in the form of a written passage. Other possible source types include tables, graphics, images, letters, and business documents. You click on a tab to see what information it provides. You integrate information from the sources to reach logical conclusions that provide answers to questions in either of two formats: standard five-option multiple-choice questions and three-part questions that ask you to indicate whether a statement, phrase, numerical value, or formula meets a certain condition. For the multiple-choice questions, you must select the correct choice from the five given answer options to get credit for the question. For three-part questions, you must answer all three parts correctly to get credit for the question.

TIP

Recall from Chapter 1 that the average time per question in the data insights section is 2.25 minutes (that's 2 minutes, 15 seconds), which seems generous. But don't get too excited just yet! Because almost every IR question has multiple parts, you will have to work at a steady pace to make sure you have time to answer all parts of the question. You must answer all parts correctly to get credit for the question.

We cover the steps to answering each IR question type in the section, "Approaching Each Question Type," later in this chapter.

To assist you with the mathematical computations you may need to make for data insight questions, the GMAT software provides you with a simple on-screen calculator. Whenever you need it, you click the blue box labeled CALCULATOR and something that looks like Figure 15-1 appears. You select its functions by using your mouse. Don't get too attached to it, though; the calculator is available only for the data insights section, so you won't be able to use it in the quantitative reasoning section. If you want more information on the calculator's features, see the nearby sidebar, "Using the GMAT calculator."

USING THE GMAT CALCULATOR

The calculator in the GMAT data insights section works a lot like the calculator that appears when you access the Microsoft calculator accessory. It has minimal features but everything you need to work out the calculations in the data insights section. When you click on CALCULATOR in the blue box at the top of your screen, the tool pops up. You can move it anywhere on the screen by dragging it with your mouse. It stays open until you close it by clicking the X in the upper-right corner of the tool.

The number and operation keys work just like a regular calculator. You can clear a single entry with the CE key or just the right digit with the ← key. Start over again from scratch by clicking the C key, which wipes out the entry and all its associated computations.

The MS key stores a value to the memory. You can add values to the memory with the M+ key and subtract them with the M– key. To access the value in the memory, click MR. To clear it, click MC.

The ± changes a positive value to negative and a negative value to positive. Press the + key to add, the – key to subtract, the ÷ key to divide, and the × key to multiply. Press the = key to complete a computation. The % key changes a percent to a decimal, and the √ finds the nonnegative square root of a number.

FIGURE 15-1:
The GMAT
calculator.

© John Wiley & Sons, Inc.

TIP

Because using an on-screen calculator can be awkward, you'll likely answer most IR questions more efficiently by using estimation or doing quick calculations by hand on your noteboard. Save the calculator for only the most complex or precise computations.

Approaching Each Question Type

Each of the four IR question types tests your analytical ability in a slightly different way, so your approach depends on the question format. This section outlines the important considerations for handling each type.

Table analysis

Table analysis questions present you with a table that contains several columns of data, similar to the one in Figure 15-2. As you can see, a little bit of explanatory material precedes the table, but don't waste too much time reading those words. Usually, everything you need to answer the question appears in the data table.

The *Sort By* feature at the top of the table allows you to organize the information by column heading, a capability that comes in handy when you analyze the three statements that follow the table. When you click on *Sort By,* a drop-down menu of all column headings appears. Clicking on the column heading in the menu causes the table to rearrange its data by that category. So, if you were to click on *Cuisine Type* in the drop-down menu in Figure 15-2, the table would rearrange the order of the rows alphabetically so that all the American restaurants would be listed first, followed by the Asian, Italian, Latin, Mexican, Steakhouse, and Seafood restaurants, respectively.

Using the information in the table, you decide whether the proper response to each statement is *True* or *False, Inferable* or *Not Inferable, Yes* or *No,* or some other similar either/or answer choice dictated by the specifications of the question. Then you indicate your choice by clicking on the radio button next to the appropriate answer.

During Lexington Restaurant Week, participating eateries design a three-course meal that they will offer throughout the week at a set price of either $20, $30, or $40 a person, excluding drinks (unless otherwise noted), tax, and tip, as reported on the following table.

Sort By:	Restaurant
	Cuisine Type
	Price Per Meal
	Neighborhood
	Wine Included? (Y/N)
	Average Daily Number of Meals Sold

Restaurant	Cuisine Type	Price Per Meal	Neighborhood	Wine Included? (Y/N)	Average Daily Number of Meals Sold
Bendimere's	Steakhouse	$40	Downtown	N	150
Big Ben's Bistro	American	$30	Central	Y	175
Chang's	Asian	$20	Chinatown	N	142
Frank's House	American	$20	Downtown	N	175
Hadley's on the Beach	Seafood	$40	Uptown	Y	160
Meritage	American	$40	Uptown	N	152
Ocean View	Seafood	$40	Uptown	N	151
Pesce Blue	Seafood	$40	Downtown	Y	164
The Purple Parrot	Latin	$30	Northwest	Y	134
Sorbello's	Italian	$40	Old Town	Y	175
Sushi Fusco	Asian	$30	Old Town	N	100
Thai Time	Asian	$20	Northwest	N	87
Valenzuela's	Mexican	$20	Downtown	N	113

FIGURE 15-2: Sample table analysis format.

© John Wiley & Sons, Inc.

These questions require you to manipulate data and make observations and calculations. Some of the most common calculations are statistical ones, such as percentages, averages, medians, and ratios, so table analysis questions can be some of the easiest IR questions to answer. Here's how to make sure you get them right:

>> **Jump to the question immediately.** Most of the information you need appears in the table, so you rarely need to read the introductory paragraph that comes before the table. Glance at the column headings to get an idea of the type of information the table provides, and then move promptly to the question.

>> **Read the question carefully.** You're most likely to get tripped up on these questions simply because you haven't read them carefully enough to figure out exactly what data they ask you to evaluate.

>> **Identify the relevant column heading.** Often, the key to answering a table analysis question is ordering the data properly. Quickly figure out which column provides you with the best way to arrange the data and sort by that column. For example, if you were asked for the neighborhood on the list with the most participating restaurants, you'd sort by *Neighborhood*.

>> **Make accurate computations.** Determine exactly what calculations the question requires and perform them accurately, either in your head or on the calculator. Based on Figure 15-2, for example, you could easily figure the restaurant with the greatest average daily number of meals sold by sorting by that column and glancing at the highest number. However, calculating which participating restaurant in the Downtown neighborhood brought in the greatest average

daily gross revenue may require the calculator to multiply each restaurant's price per meal by its average daily number of meals sold.

>> **Make use of your noteboard.** Keep track of more complex calculations on your noteboard. As you calculate each Downtown restaurant's average daily gross revenue, for example, record the results on your noteboard. Then you can easily compare the four values without having to memorize them.

Now apply these strategies to a sample question.

For each of the following statements, select *Yes* if the statement is true based on the information provided in Figure 15-2. Otherwise, choose *No*.

Yes	No	
○	○	A. The average price per meal for all participating restaurants in the Downtown neighborhood was approximately $30.
○	○	B. The average price per meal for participating restaurants in the Uptown neighborhood was less than the average price per meal in the Downtown neighborhood.
○	○	C. Participating restaurants that included wine with the meal in the Uptown neighborhood sold more meals on average per day than participating restaurants that did not include wine with the meal.

Statement (A) references two columns, *Price Per Meal* and *Neighborhood.* Sorting by *Neighborhood* makes more sense because it lists all Downtown restaurants together so that you may better view and compare each Downtown restaurant's price per meal. After you've sorted by *Neighborhood*, the table looks like this:

Restaurant	Cuisine Type	Price Per Meal	Neighborhood	Wine Included? (Y/N)	Average Daily Number of Meals Sold
Big Ben's Bistro	American	$30	Central	Y	175
Chang's	Asian	$20	Chinatown	N	142
Bendimere's	Steakhouse	$40	Downtown	N	150
Frank's House	American	$20	Downtown	N	175
Pesce Blue	Seafood	$40	Downtown	Y	164
Valenzuela's	Mexican	$20	Downtown	N	113
The Purple Parrot	Latin	$30	Northwest	Y	134
Thai Time	Asian	$20	Northwest	N	87
Sorbello's	Italian	$40	Old Town	Y	175
Sushi Fusco	Asian	$30	Old Town	N	100
Hadley's on the Beach	Seafood	$40	Uptown	Y	160
Meritage	American	$40	Uptown	N	152
Ocean View	Seafood	$40	Uptown	N	151

This arrangement allows you to see that two participating restaurants in the Downtown neighborhood charged $20 per meal and two charged $40 per meal. The number of $20 meals sold by both restaurants is 288, and the number of $40 meals sold at the two other restaurants is 314. To find the average A, multiply $20 by 288 and $40 by 314. Add the two products and divide by the total number of meals sold (602):

$$A = \frac{(20 \times 288) + (40 \times 314)}{602} = \frac{5,760 + 12,560}{602} = \frac{18,320}{602} \approx 30.43$$

Because $30.43 is approximately $30, you can say that the average price of a Downtown meal was approximately $30. The answer is *Yes.*

You've already figured out the second calculation for Statement (B). The average price per meal at a Downtown restaurant is about $30. You can write $D = 30$ on your noteboard to remind you. All the Uptown restaurants charged $40 per meal, so the average price per meal in Uptown is greater than the average price in Downtown. Select *No.*

Statement (C) again focuses on one neighborhood, so you don't have to resort to the table. The one restaurant that included wine in the meal price sold 160 meals on average per day, which is more than the 152 and 151 sold by the other two restaurants in the neighborhood. The answer is *Yes.*

REMEMBER

Table analysis questions may not require that you use all the data provided. For example, you didn't need to evaluate *Cuisine Type* for any of the question parts in the example question. Don't worry if you don't use the data in some columns at all. Part of the task in answering table analysis questions is knowing what data is important and what's irrelevant.

Two-part analysis

When you see a paragraph or two of information that sets you up to choose two pieces of information from a table with three columns, you know you're dealing with a two-part analysis question. The third column provides a list of possible answer choices for each part. You select the answer for the first part of the question in the first column and the answer to the second part in the second column. On the actual test, you will not be able to select more than one answer in a column. Also, in some cases, both the first and second parts could have the same answer choice.

TIP

Here are some tips to help you confidently answer two-part analysis questions:

>> **Read the explanatory paragraph carefully.** Reading the explanatory paragraph for these questions is absolutely essential. It provides the conditions you need to consider and clarifies what each part of the question asks for.

>> **Read all the answer options.** Don't attempt to answer the question without looking over the answer options first. Thoroughly consider each possibility offered in the third column.

>> **Answer using only the information provided.** Base your answers only on the information given in the question rather than your own personal knowledge of the topic.

>> **Be sure to mark your choices in the proper column.** The possible answers are in the third column, on the far-right side of the table. For the first question, choose an answer from the list by making a selection in the first column; for the second question, choose an answer from the list by making a selection in the second column.

>> **Verify that your answer selections are logical and coherent.** Check your answers against the conditions stated in the explanatory paragraph. Make sure your selections are the best among all those offered.

The GMAT usually uses the two-part analysis question type to test mathematical skills (such as figuring functions) and verbal logical reasoning abilities (such as strengthening and weakening arguments). Often the best way to figure out the answer for the math variety is to try each of the possible values to see which ones fulfill the requirements. Usually, the best way to answer the verbal type is by process of elimination.

The following two sample questions give you an example of a math two-part analysis and a verbal two-part analysis question.

REMEMBER

The GMAT won't label the answer options in the third column with letters as we have here to make our explanations easier to follow. To select an option on the computerized test, you'll simply click the radio button next to the option.

EXAMPLE

A set of four expressions consists of these three expressions $\{2n+8, n+4, 6n-2\}$ and one additional expression. From the following expressions, select the one that could be the fourth expression in the set and the one that could be the resulting average of the four expressions in the set. Make only one selection per column.

Fourth Expression of the Set	Arithmetic Mean of the Set	
○	○	A. $2n$
○	○	B. $3n + 2$
○	○	C. $3n - 2$
○	○	D. $12n + 8$
○	○	E. $48n + 32$
○	○	F. $4n + 8$

Approach this question by trying out the possible answer choices as potential fourth expressions to see which, when it's included with the given expressions, results in an average that's another of the possible answer choices.

First, evaluate the three provided expressions. All contain one-digit values that are multiplied by n with a one-digit value added or subtracted from that term. So, evaluate similar expressions, such as choices (B), (C), and (F) before you consider less similar expressions, such as choices (A), (D), and (E).

If Choice (B), $3n+2$, were the fourth expression, the average of the four expressions would be

$$\frac{(2n+8)+(n+4)+(6n-2)+(3n+2)}{4} = \frac{12n+12}{4} = 3n+3$$

Because $3n+3$ isn't one of the answer choices, you know that $3n+2$ can't be the fourth expression.

Try Choice (C), $3n-2$. If you wrote your calculations for $3n+2$ on your noteboard, you know that the first term of the average is the same because the $3n$ doesn't change.

$$\frac{(2n+8)+(n+4)+(6n-2)+(3n-2)}{4} = \frac{12n+8}{4} = 3n+2$$

This value is a possible option. When the fourth expression in the set is $3n-2$, the average of the four expressions is $3n+2$. Select Choice (C) for the first column and Choice (B) for the second. Only one possible set of answers exists, so if you're confident about your calculations, you don't have to consider the other options. Submit your answer and move on.

EXAMPLE

Joseph: Health insurance premiums are growing at an alarming rate. This is, in part, because many hospitals and clinics bill for unnecessary diagnostics and tests that inflate the subsequent amount that insurers pay out to them. These expenses are then passed on to consumers in the form of increased insurance premiums. Therefore, reducing the number of unnecessary tests performed by hospitals and clinics will effectively curb the rise in health insurance premiums.

Ronald: Often, the unnecessary diagnostics that you speak of are the result of decisions made by doctors on behalf of their patients. Doctors usually choose the diagnostics that allow them to bill insurers for more money but may not necessarily benefit the patient in a meaningful way or influence the course of treatment chosen. As a result, in order to succeed in reducing the number of unnecessary tests, patients should be allowed to decide which course of diagnostics they would like to undergo.

In the following table, identify the unique assumption upon which each argument depends. Make only one selection in each column: one in the first column for the best representation of Joseph's assumption in his argument and one in the second column for the best representation of Ronald's.

Joseph	Ronald	
○	○	A. Doctors are generally able to determine with great reliability which diagnostic procedures and tests will yield the most effective results.
○	○	B. Tests and diagnostic procedures make up a significant portion of the bills that are sent to insurers.
○	○	C. Insurance companies in other industries, such as auto and home, have been able to reduce costs by reducing the number of unnecessary repairs and replacements on claims for automobiles and homes.
○	○	D. Patients are not as likely as doctors to choose the most expensive diagnostics and tests.
○	○	E. Health insurance premiums have increased twice as fast in the past 5 years as they have over an average of the past 25 years.

Whereas the sample math two-part analysis question required you to figure out the answers to both parts at the same time, this verbal reasoning sample question is more easily handled one column at a time. First, consider the assumption that's most likely part of Joseph's argument. Then consider the one that pertains to Ronald's.

REMEMBER

An assumption is usually a statement that links the premises of an argument to its conclusion. For details on evaluating arguments, see Chapter 8.

Following are the premises of Joseph's argument:

>> Hospitals and clinics are billing health insurance companies for unnecessary and expensive tests.

>> This practice has caused health insurance companies to pay inflated rates to hospitals and clinics.

>> The result is that health insurance companies are compensating by raising consumers' health insurance premiums.

Based on these premises, Joseph concludes that reducing unnecessary tests will significantly control the rise in health insurance premiums.

To find the assumption that provides a link between the cessation of the unnecessary tests and a significant effect on increasing healthcare premiums, begin by narrowing your options. Joseph doesn't mention doctors in his argument, so you can eliminate choices (A) and (D). Choice (E) addresses healthcare premiums but not unnecessary tests, so it's out. Choice (C) concerns other insurance industries, so it has nothing to do with Joseph's argument about healthcare premiums. The best option for Joseph is the assumption that unnecessary tests make up a significant portion of insurance billing. If they make up just a small portion, eliminating tests wouldn't have a significant impact on the rising cost of healthcare premiums. Mark Choice (B) in the column for Joseph.

Now evaluate Ronald's argument. Here are his premises:

>> Doctors order unnecessary tests to increase their earnings.

>> Patients should be able to choose their tests.

>> Putting the decision regarding diagnostics and tests in the patients' control would reduce the number of unnecessary tests.

So you're looking for the assumption that links patients' decisions to fewer unnecessary tests.

Notice that Ronald doesn't address healthcare premiums at all, so you can confidently eliminate Choice (E). Choice (B) is out because it doesn't relate to patients' decisions. Choice (C) doesn't work for the same reason that it doesn't work for Joseph. Ronald's argument concerns only healthcare. Of the two remaining options (choices [A] and [D]), only Choice (D) relates to patients' decisions. Only if patients make decisions differently than doctors do would putting patients in control lessen the number of unnecessary tests. So you mark Choice (D) in the column for Ronald.

Graphics interpretation

Not surprisingly, graphics interpretation questions require that you interpret a graphic or other image. You may see line graphs, bar graphs, pie charts, scatter plots, Venn diagrams, and other data representation. Based on the information displayed in the graphic, you fill in two separate blanks by selecting the best option from a drop-down menu for each blank. (In the example question later in this section, we include the answer options in parentheses.) You have to complete both blanks correctly to get credit for one graphics interpretation question.

The information you need to fill in the blanks comes primarily from the graphic, so make sure you know how to read graphics. Chapter 16 provides a review of the most common GMAT graphics to refresh your memory.

TIP

Here are some other tips to help you efficiently move through graphics interpretation questions:

>> **Read any text that accompanies the graphic.** Text around the graphic may clarify its purpose. It also might provide information that you need to select a correct answer.

>> **Analyze the graphic to determine exactly what information it provides and how.** Observe the labels and examine numerical increments carefully.

>> **Click on Select One to view all the answer options.** To see the possible answers in the drop-down menu for each blank, you have to click on the box that says Select One. Filling in the blank is much easier when you're limited to just the several available choices. Don't attempt to answer the question without seeing the answer choices first.

>> **Eliminate illogical answer choices.** Approach the two parts of a graphics interpretation question much like you would a standard multiple-choice question. Eliminate obviously incorrect options and use your reasoning skills to select the best answer from the remaining choices.

>> **Make estimations.** The data in graphics are rarely precise, so most of your calculations are estimates or approximations that you can work out on your noteboard or in your head rather than on the calculator.

Here's a sample graphics interpretation question to consider.

EXAMPLE

Scientists, health professionals, and life insurance agents are interested in examining the percentage of people in a population who will live to a certain age. One way to measure this information is to look at the percentage of the population who have died after a certain number of years. The following graph displays the results of such a study.

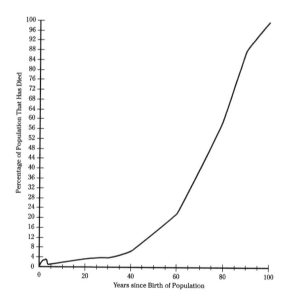

Approximately _____ (10, 40, 60, 80) percent of the population lives to at least 80 years of age. A person who was a member of the study population would still have an 80 percent chance of being alive at around a maximum age of _____ (15, 35, 55, 80) years.

Filling the first blank in the question tests your graph-reading skills. Find 80 years of age on the horizontal axis. Move your finger from the 80-year mark upward on the graph until you reach the plotted curve. Move your finger to the left to see that at 80 years, about 60 percent of people have died. Don't stop there and choose 60 percent, however. The question asks for how many are alive at the 80-year mark. Subtract 60 from 100 to get that approximately 40 percent of the population live to at least 80 years. The correct answer is 40 percent.

To complete the second blank, make sure you look at the answer choices first. Because the statement concerns the *maximum* value, consider higher ages first. The oldest option is 80, but it's very unlikely that 80 percent of people are alive at age 80, so try the next highest age, 55. Move along the graph until you reach 55 years. At 55 years of age, 20 percent have died, leaving a maximum of 80 percent alive. Ages above 55 can't be right, so 55 is the correct answer.

If you start with the first option of 15 years, you may be misled. Note that the graph shows you that at about 15 years of age, less than 5 percent of people have died, which means that more than 95 percent of the population are still alive. That's more than 80 percent, but the statement regards the *maximum* age where 80 percent of the population is still kicking, so 15 can't be correct.

Multi-source reasoning

Multi-source reasoning questions present two or three sources of information, labeled with tabs, each providing a distinct aspect of a given situation. The scenarios covered in these questions encompass a wide range of topics. You might encounter scientific phenomenon like black holes or plant photosynthesis, or you may be tasked with applying data to business-related situations, such as hiring decisions or event planning.

At least one of the tabs shows a written passage. Others may show additional written information or data presented in graphical form. You use the resources in the tabs to gather the necessary information to answer the questions posed. For example, Figure 15-3 shows the first tab for a sample multi-source reasoning scenario regarding guest reservations for a hotel's wedding block. The email in this tab sets up the situation and provides you with the guidelines for the reservation.

FIGURE 15-3: Sample multi-source reasoning format, Background Information tab.

Background Information | Contract Paragraph 3 | Guest List

The Pearson family is hosting the destination wedding of their daughter Emily and her fiancé, Matthew Voorhies. The event will take place on Saturday, September 8th, at the popular Grand Maryvale Resort, which is located on a tropical island accessible only by airplane. The resort has provided a block of rooms at a discounted rate to accommodate the wedding guests. The terms of the room discount are outlined in Paragraph 3 of the contract between the resort and Emily's father.

The Pearson and Voorhies families want to make sure that all who attend their wedding have accommodations at the resort because the island has few other hotels, and those are shabby and located far away from the resort. The resort is known to be fully booked on weekends in September. Therefore, Emily and Matthew have contacted each guest regarding their room reservation status and have recorded their statuses as of August 1st on a spreadsheet entitled Guest List.

Figure 15-4 shows what you find when you click on the second tab: language from the contract between the Pearson family and the resort.

| Background Information | Contract Paragraph 3 | Guest List |

III. For the Pearson/Voorhies Wedding, a hotel room block has been reserved at the Grand Maryvale Resort for the nights of September 7, 8, and 9. Instead of the regular room rate of $175 per night, guests who book as a part of the block for all three nights can pay a special rate of only $135 per night. Those who book for less than three nights will be charged $150 per night. Those who book rooms for the nights before or after the three nights specified by the hotel block must pay the regular nightly room rate for nights stayed beyond the three-night block discount. We can hold five rooms at a time for the attendees of the Pearson/Voorhies wedding — once the first five are filled, we will be able to release five more. We do not guarantee accommodations to wedding guests beyond these specifications.

FIGURE 15-4: Sample multi-source reasoning format, Contract tab.

© John Wiley & Sons, Inc.

Figure 15-5 shows what you find when you click on the third tab: a table showing the wedding guest list and their reservation status.

| Background Information | Contract Paragraph 3 | Guest List |

Name	Number Attending	Number of Rooms Needed	Nights Staying at Resort	Reservations Made?
The Rose Family	4	1	3	N
The Crawford Family	6	2	2	Y
The Fishers	2	1	1	Y
The Ball Family	5	2	3	Y
The Ranks Family	6	2	3	N
The Keppners	2	1	1	Y
The Albertsons	4	1	1	N
....	....	....	....	....

FIGURE 15-5: Sample multi-source reasoning format, Guest List tab.

© John Wiley & Sons, Inc.

The multi-source reasoning questions appear in one of two formats: three-part table (similar to table analysis questions) or standard five-option multiple-choice. Keep in mind that you have to answer correctly all three parts of the first format to get credit for the one question. The multiple-choice format may be one of the easiest IR questions to answer. You can use the process of elimination to narrow the answers, and you have to choose only one correct answer to get full credit for the question.

The trickiest aspect of answering multi-source reasoning questions is sifting through the plethora of information to discover what's relevant. Depending on the scenario, you may have to juggle information in tables, diagrams, articles, and so on to come up with correct answers.

TIP

Here are some pointers to help you with multi-source reasoning questions:

>> **Read the whole question carefully.** You're most likely to encounter difficulties with these questions simply due to not having carefully read them, thereby hindering your ability to figure out the specific task being asked of you.

>> **Summarize each tab.** As you read through the information in each tab for the first time, record pertinent points to help you remember which tab holds what type of data. That way you don't have to continually flip back and forth between screens as you answer questions. For example, summarize the contract details in Figure 15-4 on your noteboard with quick notations such as *9/7, 8, & 9 = $135/night; < 3 nights = $150/night; before/after 9/7 or 9/9 = $175/night.*

>> **Make connections.** After reviewing the information in each tab, synthesize facts and figures from one tab with related data from another. Make sure to record your observations on your noteboard. For example, as you examine the details in Figures 15-4 and 15-5, you can draw connections between the information in the table provided in the third tab and the room-charge specifications in the second tab. This strategy will help you figure out how much each guest will pay for resort rooms.

>> **Rely on what the test gives you.** Some of the topics in multi-source reasoning scenarios may be familiar to you. Although familiarity may make the information more accessible to you, it may also influence you to answer questions based on what you know instead of what the exam tells you. For example, you shouldn't answer any questions about the Pearson wedding sample scenario based on what you know about hotel booking from your own experience as a front-desk manager.

Here's another sample multi-source scenario with a couple of questions to help you get more acquainted with the question type. This scenario has only two tabs, each conveying an opposing opinion from two scientists on a specific scientific phenomenon.

Scientist 1

Ancient ice cores from Antarctica indicate that the concentration of carbon dioxide in the atmosphere and global mean temperatures have followed the same pattern of fluctuations in levels over the past 160,000 years. Therefore, the increase in atmospheric carbon dioxide concentration from 280 parts per million to 360 parts per million that has occurred over the past 150 years points to significant and detrimental climatic changes in the near future. The climate has already changed: The average surface temperature of the earth has increased 0.6°C in the past hundred years, with the ten hottest years of that time period all occurring since 1980. Although 0.6°C may not seem large, changes in the mean surface temperature as low as 0.5°C have dramatically affected crop growth in years past. Moreover, computer models project that surface temperatures will increase about 2.0°C by the year 2100 and will continue to increase in the years after even if concentration of greenhouse gases is stabilized by that time. If the present trend in carbon dioxide increase continues, though, carbon dioxide concentration will exceed 1,100 parts per million soon after 2100 and will be associated with a temperature increase of approximately 10.0°C over the present mean annual global surface temperature.

The observed increases in minor greenhouse gases such as carbon dioxide and methane will not lead to sizeable global warming. Water vapor and clouds are responsible for more than 98% of the earth's greenhouse effect. Current models that project large temperature increases with a doubling of the present carbon dioxide concentration incorporate changes in water vapor, clouds and other factors that would accompany a rise in carbon dioxide levels. The way these models handle such feedback factors is not supported by current scientific knowledge. In fact, there is convincing evidence that shows that increases in carbon dioxide concentration would lead to changes in feedback factors that would diminish any temperature increase associated with more carbon dioxide in the atmosphere. The climatic data for the last hundred years show an irregular pattern in which many of the greatest jumps in global mean temperature were too large to be associated with the observed increase in carbon dioxide. The overall increase of 0.45°C in the past century is well under what the models would have predicted given the changes in carbon dioxide concentration. As with the temperature models, recent increases in atmospheric carbon dioxide have not risen to the extent predicted by models dealing solely with carbon dioxide levels. The rate of carbon dioxide concentration increase has slowed since 1973. Improved energy technologies will further dampen the increase so that the carbon dioxide concentration will be under 700 parts per million in the year 2100.

Consider each of the following statements about atmospheric carbon-dioxide levels and determine whether Scientists 1 and 2 are both likely to agree by marking either *Yes* or *No:*

EXAMPLE

Yes	*No*	
○	○	A. Increasing carbon dioxide levels affect other factors.
○	○	B. Humans will never be able to stabilize atmospheric carbon dioxide levels.
○	○	C. The rate of increase in carbon dioxide levels will rise throughout the next 100 years.

Statement (A) is a nice, noncontroversial statement with which both scientists would agree. Scientist 1 stresses that rising carbon dioxide is linked to higher temperature (another factor), while Scientist 2 discusses *feedback factors*, which are factors that respond to carbon-dioxide changes and will, in turn, affect the carbon dioxide. Select *Yes* for Statement (A).

To answer Statement (B), notice that Scientist 2, who refers to improved energy technology, clearly disagrees with the statement, but so does Scientist 1, who mentions the possibility that carbon-dioxide levels will stabilize. Neither scientist would agree with Statement (B), so the answer is *No*.

Scientist 2 disagrees with Statement (C) and actually discusses a slowing down in the rate of carbon-dioxide-level increase. Because at least one of the scientists would disagree with the statement, the answer to Statement (C) is *No*.

The next question is in multiple-choice format.

Which of the following statements does only Scientist 1 support?

(A) A change in atmospheric water vapor could significantly affect global temperatures.

(B) The increase in atmospheric carbon-dioxide concentration from 280 parts per million to 360 parts per million that has occurred over the last 150 years is not expected to affect climactic change negatively in the future.

(C) Recent increases in atmospheric carbon dioxide have surpassed those predicted by temperature models dealing solely with carbon-dioxide models.

(D) Temperature fluctuations will match carbon-dioxide changes when carbon-dioxide changes are abrupt.

(E) Increases in carbon-dioxide concentration would lead to changes in feedback factors that would compound any temperature increase associated with more carbon dioxide in the atmosphere.

Focus on the information in the first tab. Scientist 1 mentions a match between carbon dioxide and temperature variations and then uses the recent large change in carbon-dioxide levels as evidence that significant changes in temperature will occur. Scientist 1 goes on to discuss how continued sharp increases in atmospheric carbon dioxide will lead to similar dramatic temperature increases. Scientist 1 implies that the recent carbon-dioxide changes have been unprecedented. The data during the past 160,000 years show a correspondence between temperature and carbon-dioxide fluctuations, but this correspondence has occurred in the absence of the dramatic changes the earth is now and soon will be experiencing. For Scientist 1 to use the fluctuation correspondence as evidence for what will soon happen, that scientist must assume that the correspondence will continue in light of current and near-future sharp changes. So Choice (D) is correct.

Choice (A) is supported by Scientist 2, and neither scientist would support choices (B), (C), or (E). In fact, Scientist 1 actually says that an increase in atmospheric carbon-dioxide concentration from 280 parts per million to 360 parts per million can cause "significant and detrimental climactic changes in the near future."

Chapter **16**

Deciphering Data in Graphics

A *graphic* is a visual representation or image that conveys information, data, or messages. Graphics can take various forms, including graphical displays like bar and line graphs, histograms,and pie charts. This chapter provides an overview of the different types of graphics commonly encountered in GMAT questions. Additionally, it offers guidance on effectively interpreting each type of graphic to maximize your efficiency in understanding the presented information. You read and interpret data provided in the graphic, and then you apply your analysis to draw conclusions about a bunch of scenarios.

Overall, graphics are an essential tool for visual representation of data, enabling you to impart tricky concepts in a way that's simple and easy to understand. So, buckle up and get ready to embark on an exciting journey of data visualization! Shall we begin?

Mastering Graphics-Focused Questions with Five Simple Steps

Regardless of the graphic you're working with in a data insights question, you'll follow a similar, five-step approach:

1. **Identify the type of graphic.**

   Graphics display data in different ways, so start by recognizing which type you're dealing with. To make this step easy, we provide detailed information on each of the most common types of graphics on the GMAT within this chapter.

2. **Read the accompanying question and determine what it asks.**

   Before you attempt to read the graphic, examine the question to figure out exactly what kind of information you need to answer it.

3. **Identify what you need to get out of the graphic to successfully answer the question.**

   Refer to the graphic to discover where it conveys the specific data you need to answer the question.

4. **Read the graphic properly.**

   Take a close look at the graphic and ensure that you comprehend its title. Examine the labels on the parts of the graphic and the legend to gain an understanding of what's being depicted.

   REMEMBER

   For bar graphs, line graphs, histograms, and scatterplots note the labels on the horizontal and vertical axes, and their measurement scales. For line graphs, look for noticeable trends such as rising or falling values and periods of inactivity. Look for clusters, gaps, and outliers.

5. **Answer the question.**

   Use the data you've carefully extracted from the graphic to come up with the correct answer to the question. Where possible, use estimation to answer questions. However, be ready to do some simple arithmetic calculations (such as compute percentages, calculate an average, and more). Make sure the numbers add up correctly. Use the online calculator as needed.

   WARNING

   Use only the information provided in the graphic and accompanying text. Do not answer based on your personal knowledge or opinion.

   The remaining sections in this chapter show you how to apply this approach to reading and interpreting a variety of graphics.

Translating Information in Tables

Tables show data organized into rows and columns, enabling you to conveniently observe and analyze accurate information. For example, a table can be an effective way of presenting average daily high and low temperatures in a given area, the number of male and female births that occur each year within a population, or the rankings of a band's top-ten hits.

The table displayed in Figure 16-1 presents the recorded scores of five gymnasts who took part in a local meet. It includes both the individual event scores and the all-around score of each gymnast. The data are precise rather than approximated, which allows you to come up with accurate analyses of the values. For example, you can see from the table that Kate just barely edged out Jess on the balance beam by a 0.005 difference in scores.

FIGURE 16-1:
Table similar to one you're likely to encounter in a data insights question.

Bayside Gymnastics Club Score Report					
Name	Vault Score	Uneven Bars Score	Balance Beam Score	Floor Exercise Score	All-Around Score
Kelsea Moore	16.250	15.500	15.100	14.985	61.835
Adrianne Rizzo	15.900	14.975	15.225	15.325	61.425
Kate McCaffery	16.000	14.600	15.000	13.995	58.595
Jess Hartley	15.875	13.966	14.995	15.000	59.836
Maggie Birney	16.100	13.920	15.100	13.870	58.990

© John Wiley & Sons, Inc.

When analyzing a table, pay particular attention to the column labels (called *headers*) as they name which variables are shown. Read carefully to differentiate values and determine, say, whether the numbers represent percentages or actual figures. For example, by taking a few moments to examine the values in the table depicted in Figure 16-1, you can ascertain that a gymnast's all-around score is the sum of that gymnast's other scores rather than their average. So, if a question asks you about a particular gymnast's average score for all events, you'd know to calculate this value instead of simply recording the given all-around score.

Not surprisingly, tables are the primary source of information in table analysis questions. These questions use tables to display data, usually a lot of it. You may also find tables in multi-source reasoning and two-part analysis questions. (Chapter 15 provides more details on answering data insights questions.)

Making Comparisons with Bar Graphs

Bar graphs (also sometimes called *bar charts*) have a variety of uses. They're especially good for comparing data and approximating values. As the name suggests, they use rectangular bars, displayed either horizontally or vertically, to visually depict various data categories. The bars are labeled at the base, indicating the different categories they represent. The height or length of each bar indicates the corresponding quantity for that category of data.

You see bar graphs most frequently on the GMAT in graphics interpretation questions, but they may also appear in multi-source reasoning and two-part analysis questions. Simple bar graphs present the relationship between two variables. More complex bar graphs show additional data by displaying additional bars or by segmenting each individual bar. We show you how to read simple and complex bar graphs in the following sections.

Simple bar graphs

Bar graphs provide an excellent way to visualize the similarities and differences among several categories of data. Even a simple bar graph, such as the one in Figure 16-2, can convey a whole bunch of information.

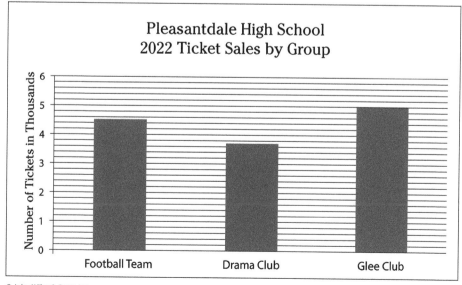

FIGURE 16-2: Simple bar graph.

© John Wiley & Sons, Inc.

The title of the bar graph in Figure 16-2 defines the overall category of information: 2022 ticket sales for Pleasantdale High School by group. You don't need a title for the horizontal axis. It's obvious from the graph's title that each bar provides the data for each school group. From the vertical axis label, you discover that the data represent number of tickets sold rather than the total revenue from those tickets. "In Thousands" means that each major horizontal gridline represents 1,000 tickets. Each of the four minor gridlines between each major gridline represents 200 tickets (the four lines divide the segments between the whole numbers into five parts, and $(1000 \div 5 = 200)$. So, the graph indicates that the number of drama club tickets sold was approximately 3,700 because the Drama Club bar ends between the third and fourth minor gridlines above the 3,000 mark. To find the total number of drama club tickets sold, add 200 for each of the three minor gridlines and half of that (100) as represented by the half space between the third and fourth minor gridlines: $3,000 + 3(200) + 100 = 3,700$.

Some GMAT bar graphs may display information for a range of values. An example appears in Figure 16-3. Based on this graph, you can figure that the minimum total number of tickets sold by all groups in 2022 was the sum of the lowest numbers for each group $(4,000 + 5,000 + 6,000)$, or 15,000 tickets. The maximum possible total of tickets sold by the three groups combined was the sum of the highest value for each category: $5,000 + 6,000 + 7,000$, or 18,000.

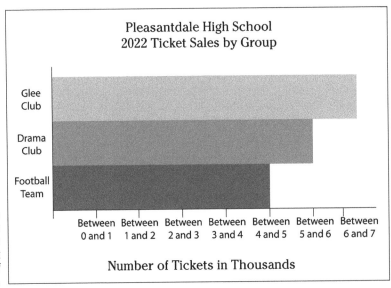

FIGURE 16-3:
Simple
bar graph
showing
ranges of
values.

Graphs with many bars

Altering the design of a bar graph allows you to convey even more information. Graphs with multiple bars reveal data for additional categories. For example, Figure 16-4 compares the ticket sales totals for the three groups by year for three years.

The legend designates which group the bars stand for. This graph allows you to easily make comparisons over the years and among the three groups. For example, it's easy to see that in 2020, glee club ticket sales were not only greater than they had been in previous years but also exceeded sales for either of the other two groups.

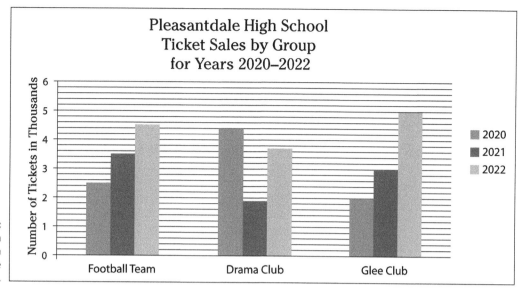

FIGURE 16-4:
Bar graph with multiple categories.

Segmented bar graphs

Graphs with segmented bars display the characteristics of subcategories. Each bar is divided into segments that represent different subgroups. The height of each segment within a bar represents the value associated with that particular subgroup. For example, Pleasantdale High can provide more specific comparisons of the ticket sales during different times of the year by using a segmented bar graph, such as the one in Figure 16-5.

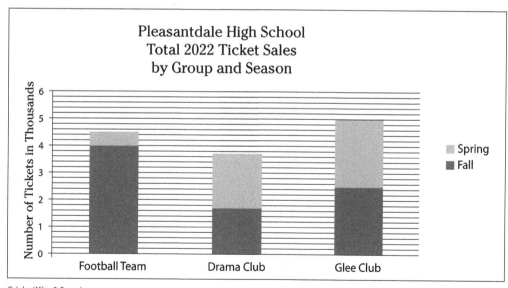

FIGURE 16-5:
Segmented bar graph with sub-categories.

You apply subtraction to read a segmented graph. The top of each bar is the total from which you subtract the designations for each subcategory. So, for the *Football Team* bar in Figure 16-5, the total number of tickets sold in 2022 was 4,500. The number of tickets sold in the fall is represented by the lower segment, which climbs up to about the 4,000 mark. The number of tickets sold in the spring is the difference between the approximate total number of tickets (4,500) and the approximate number of fall tickets (4,000), which is about 500. The graph also reveals that activity sales for the glee club and drama club occur more consistently across both seasons than for the football team, which sells many more tickets in the fall than it does in the spring.

Whenever you reference data from a bar graph, you speak in estimates. Bar graphs don't provide exact values; that's not their job. They allow you to make comparisons based on approximations.

Honing in on Histograms

A *histogram* is a special type of bar graph that summarizes data by displaying *frequencies* (or *relative frequencies*) of the data within specified *class intervals.* Class intervals are of equal length and cover from the lowest to the highest data value. The left and right endpoints for the class intervals are selected so that each data value clearly falls within one and only one class interval. The frequency of occurrence of the data values within a class interval is represented by a rectangular column. The height of the column is proportional to the frequency of data values within that interval. Unlike the bars in other bar graphs, the bars in a histogram are side-by-side (usually) with no space in between. In a *frequency histogram,* the scale for measuring the height of the bars is marked with actual frequencies (that is, raw counts). In a *relative frequency histogram,* the scale is marked with relative frequencies instead of actual frequencies. Looking at the histogram in Figure 16-6, can you determine how many students received 90 or above on the first test?

The scale on the vertical axis shows the number of students who achieved the grade. The scale is marked in multiples of 2. The top of the bar for the interval 90–99 is halfway between 4 and 6, indicating that 5 students received 90 or above on Test 1.

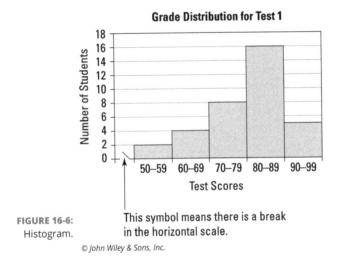

FIGURE 16-6: This symbol means there is a break
Histogram. in the horizontal scale.

© *John Wiley & Sons, Inc.*

Looking at Line Graphs

Another graph that crops up frequently in graphics interpretation questions is the *line graph.* Line graphs display information that occurs over time or across graduated measurements and are particularly effective in highlighting trends, peaks, or lows. Typically (but not always), the horizontal axis displays units of time or measurement (the independent variable), and the vertical axis presents the data that's being measured (the dependent variable).

Basic line graphs

The line graph in Figure 16-7 shows the garbage production for three cities for each of the four quarters of 2021. You can tell from the graph that Plainfield produced more garbage in every quarter than the other two cities did, and it's evident that all three cities produced less garbage in Quarter 3 than they did in the other quarters.

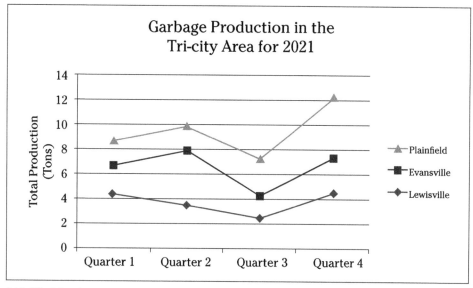

FIGURE 16-7:
Line graph.

Scatter plots

Scatter plots display the relationship between two numerical variables. These graphs display a bunch of points that show the relationship between two variables, one represented on the horizontal axis (or *x*-axis) and the other on the vertical axis (or *y*-axis). For example, the scatter plot in Figure 16-8 plots each city's population on the *x*-axis and its garbage production on the *y*-axis. Scatter plots show you trends and patterns. From Figure 16-8, you can figure out that, generally, a direct or positive relationship exists between a city's population and the amount of garbage it produces. The graph indicates that this is the case because the data points tend to be higher on the *y*-axis as they move to the right (or increase) on the *x*-axis. You can also surmise that of the 20 cities listed, more have fewer than 200,000 people than have greater than 200,000 people. That's because the graph shows a greater number of points that fall to the left of the 200,000 population line than to the right.

REMEMBER

When two quantitative variables are *positive correlated,* higher values of one are associated higher values of the other, and lower values are associated with lower values as well. If they are *negatively correlated,* higher values of one are associated with lower values of the other, and vice versa.

Scatter plots also convey trend and pattern deviations. The GMAT may provide a scatter plot with or without a *trend line.* The trend line shows the overall pattern of the data plots and reveals deviations. The scatter plot in Figure 16-8 doesn't display a trend line, so you have to imagine one. You can lay your noteboard along the graph to help you envision the trend line if one isn't provided. Figure 16-9 shows you the trend line for the garbage production graph. With the trend line in place, you can more easily recognize that the largest city in the county deviates from the trend somewhat considerably. Its garbage production is less in proportion to its population than that of most other cities in the county. You know that because its data point is considerably below the trend line.

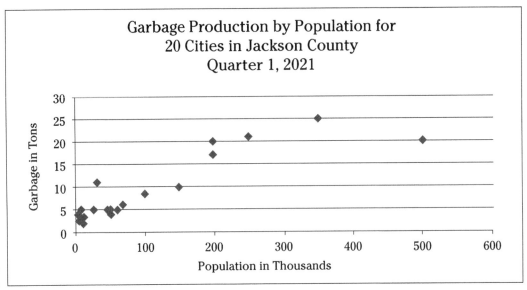

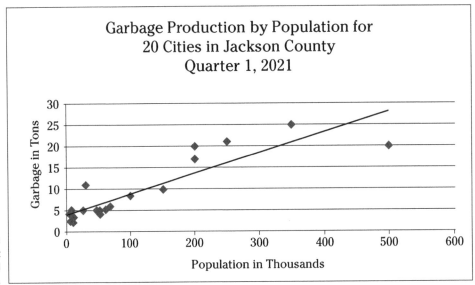

Complex scatter plots

Sometimes the GMAT crams even more information on a scatter plot by introducing another variable associated with the data. The values for this variable appear on a vertical axis on the right side of the graph. This type of graph is just a way of combining information in one graph that could appear on two separate graphs.

Figure 16-10 shows you an example of a complex scatter plot. It adds another variable (average yearly income by population) to the mix. The average annual income for each city lies on the right vertical axis. The points for one set of data have different symbols than those for the other so that you can distinguish between the two sets. The legend at the right of the graph in Figure 16-10 tells you that garbage production is represented by diamonds, and the symbol for income is a square. The trend line for the relationship between city population and average yearly income has a negative slope, which shows you that the smaller the population, the greater the average yearly income. This trend indicates an inverse relationship between city population and average yearly income.

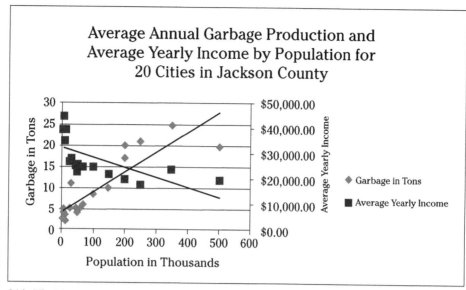

FIGURE 16-10:
Scatter
plot with
multiple
variables.

© John Wiley & Sons, Inc.

REMEMBER The GMAT may ask you to identify the relationship between two variables as positive, negative, or neutral. If the trend line has a positive slope (that is, it slants upward from left to right), the relationship is positive; if it has a negative slope (that is, it slants downward from left to right), the relationship is negative. If the trend line is horizontal or the points are scattered without any recognizable pattern, the relationship is neutral, meaning that no linear correlation exists between the variables.

WARNING When you encounter scatter plots and line graphs with more than two variables, make sure you keep your variables straight. So, if you're asked a question about garbage production, using Figure 16-10, you have to use the data represented by the left vertical axis and the diamond symbol rather than the right vertical axis and the squares.

Like bar graphs, line graphs display approximate values. Use the technique explained in the earlier section, "Simple bar graphs," to help you estimate the values associated with each data point from the axes labels and grid marks on these graphs.

Perusing Stem-and-Leaf Plots

A *stem-and-leaf plot* is a visual display of data in which each data value is separated into two parts: a stem and a leaf. For a given data value, the leaf is the last digit and the stem is the remaining digits. For example, for the data value 49, 4 is the stem and 9 is the leaf. When you create a stem-and-leaf plot, include a *legend* that explains what is represented by the stem and leaf so that the reader can interpret the information in the plot; for example, 4|9 = 49. Note that a useful feature of a stem-and-leaf plot is that the original data is retained and displayed in the plot. Usually, the stems are listed vertically (from least to greatest), and the corresponding leaves for the data values are listed horizontally (from least to greatest) beside the appropriate stem. Figure 16-11 shows an example.

According to the graphic, the range of the ages of the people who joined the health club in February is $93 - 41 = 52$ years.

**Ages of 40 People Who Joined
the Fit-Past-Forty Club in February**

Stem	Leaf
4	1 2 6 8 9
5	1 1 2 3 3 6 7 7 7 7 8 9
6	0 0 3 3 4 4 5 6 8 8 9
7	0 1 2 3 5 7 8
8	0 1
9	0 3

Legend: 4|9 = 49

FIGURE 16-11:
Stem-and-
leaf plot.

Clarifying Circle Graphs (Also Known as Pie Charts)

Circle graphs, also known as *pie charts*, show values that are part of a larger whole, such as percentages. The graphs contain divisions called *sectors*, which divide the circle into portions that are proportional to the quantity each represents as part of the whole 360-degree circle. Each sector becomes a *piece* of the *pie*; you get information and compare values by examining the pieces in relation to each other and to the whole pie.

When a graphics interpretation question provides you with a circle graph and designates the percentage values of each of its sectors, you can use it to figure out actual quantities. The circle graph in Figure 16-12 tells you that Plainfield has more Republican affiliates than Democrat and that Democrats constitute just over twice as many Plainfield residents as Independents do.

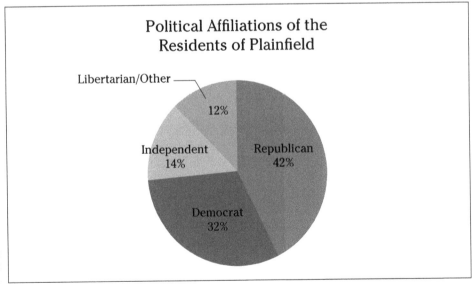

FIGURE 16-12:
Circle graph
or pie chart.

When you know one of the quantities in a circle graph, you can find the value of other quantities. For example, if a multi-source reasoning IR question provides you with both the scatter plot in Figure 16-8 and the circle graph in Figure 16-12 and tells you that the city of Plainfield is the city in Figure 16-8 with the highest population, you can use information from both graphs to discover the approximate number of Plainfield residents who are registered Democrats. The city with the largest population in Figure 16-8 has around 500,000 residents. Figure 16-12 tells you that 32 percent of Plainfield residents are Democrats. So just about 160,000 ($= 500,000 \times 0.32$) Democrats reside in Plainfield.

Venturing into Venn Diagrams

Venn diagrams, like the one depicted in Figure 16-13, consist of interconnected circles — typically, two or three in number — and are a great way to show relationships that exist among sets of data. Each circle represents a distinct data set while the overlap among the circles visually demonstrates the connections among the data.

You encounter Venn diagrams in graphics-interpretation questions. For example, the GMAT could tell you that the Venn diagram in Figure 16-13 represents the results of a survey of 100 cat and dog owners. You know from the diagram that 33 of those surveyed own cats, but no value appears for the number of dog owners. The shaded portion represents the intersection: the four members of the survey who own both cats and dogs. If you need to find the number of those surveyed who own dogs, you can't simply subtract 33 from 100 because that doesn't take into consideration the four people who own both types of pets. The total number of people in the survey who own dogs is actually (100 − 33) + 4, or 71. The number of people in the survey who own dogs only, and not cats, is 71 − 4, or 67.

Your calculations can get a little more complicated when not all the members of the general set are represented by the circles in the Venn diagram. For example, say the survey represented in Figure 16-13 was modified a bit to represent 100 pet owners instead of 100 cat and dog owners. The 100 members of the survey could own cats, dogs, or other pets. The results of this survey appear in Figure 16-14.

Based on this diagram, the GMAT could pose questions that ask for the number of people who own only cats but not dogs, the number of people who own at least one cat or one dog, or the number of those surveyed who own neither a cat nor a dog. Here's how you'd solve for these three cases:

>> The number of pet owners who own cats but not dogs is simply the quantity in the cat-owner circle that doesn't include the number in the intersection of the two circles. Of the 100 people surveyed, 29 own cats but don't own dogs.

>> The total number of cat owners is 33, which is what you get when you add the 4 cat and dog owners to the 29 owners of cats but not dogs. To find how many of the surveyed pet owners own at least a cat or a dog, you just need to add the values in each circle and add the quantity in the shaded intersection: (29 + 65) + 4 = 98. Of the 100 people surveyed, 98 own at least one cat or one dog.

>> Figuring the number of pet owners who own neither a cat nor a dog means that you're looking for the quantity that exists outside of the two circles. The number of pet owners represented inside the circles plus the number of pet owners outside of the circles is equal to 100, the total number of pet owners surveyed. You know the number of people represented by the space inside the circle; it's the same number as those who own at least a cat or a dog (98). The number of pet owners who don't have a cat or a dog is simply 100 − 98 or 2.

So to evaluate Venn diagrams correctly, keep track of the total members in the set and what they represent. Information in the question will allow you to assess whether the circles represent the total number of members or whether a subset of members resides outside of the circle, so reading carefully will allow you to accurately interpret the Venn diagram. When you've successfully figured out the general set and the subsets, extracting information from Venn diagrams is easy.

Individuals Surveyed: 100

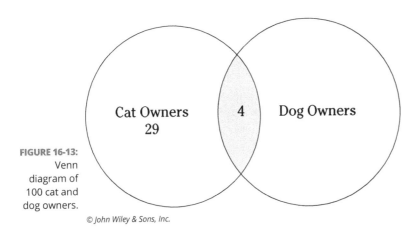

FIGURE 16-13: Venn diagram of 100 cat and dog owners.

© John Wiley & Sons, Inc.

Individuals Surveyed: 100

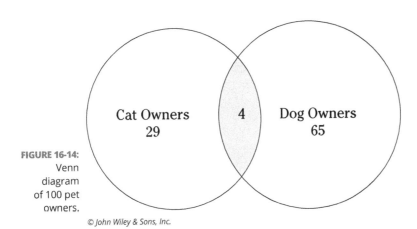

FIGURE 16-14: Venn diagram of 100 pet owners.

© John Wiley & Sons, Inc.

Chapter **17**

Enough's Enough: Data Sufficiency Questions

A s noted in Chapter 15, the data insights section of the GMAT consists of five types of questions: table analysis, two-part analysis, graphics interpretation, multi-source reasoning, and data sufficiency. The first four types were extensively discussed in Chapter 15. However, this chapter focuses specifically on data sufficiency questions, which have a distinctive format that is unique to the GMAT.

Data sufficiency questions can be manageable if you familiarize yourself with effective approaches before you encounter them on the GMAT. However, if you don't know much about these questions, getting confused and making careless mistakes is easy. Fortunately, you've decided to read this book to get a sneak peek. Thereafter, your knowledge should be more than sufficient for data sufficiency!

You Don't Need the Solution to Find the Answer

Unlike the traditional math problems you've seen throughout your life, data sufficiency questions don't actually require you to solve the problem. Instead, you have to analyze the data in two statements and determine whether at some point there is *sufficient* information for you to answer the question.

For each data sufficiency problem, you have a question and two statements, labeled (1) and (2). Your job is to decide whether each of the statements gives you enough information to answer the question using general math skills and everyday facts (such as the number of days in a week and the meaning of *clockwise*). If you need a refresher in the math concepts tested on the GMAT, review Chapters 10 through 12. And if you need help analyzing tables, graphs, and similar data representations, check out Chapter 16.

WARNING

Don't make foolish assumptions when you answer data sufficiency questions. Keep in mind that your job is to determine whether the information given is sufficient, not to try to make up for the lack of data! You're used to having to come up with an answer to every math problem, so if the statements lack just a little information, you may be tempted to stretch the data to reach a solution. Don't give in to temptation. Deal only with the information expressly as it's stated, without making unwarranted assumptions.

The five answer choices for data sufficiency questions are the same for each question:

(A) Statement (1) *alone* is sufficient, but Statement (2) *alone* is *not* sufficient.

(B) Statement (2) *alone* is sufficient, but Statement (1) *alone* is *not* sufficient.

(C) *Both* statements *together* are sufficient, but *neither* statement *alone* is sufficient.

(D) *Each* statement *alone* is sufficient.

(E) Statements (1) and (2) *together* are *not* sufficient.

The computer doesn't actually designate the answer choices with the letters A through E, but the choices appear in this order (you choose the correct one with your mouse or keyboard), and we refer to them as A, B, C, D, and E to make the discussion simpler.

It's possible that just one of the statements gives enough data to answer the question, that the two statements taken together solve the problem, that both statements alone provide sufficient data, or that neither statement solves the problem, even with the information provided by the other one. That's a lot of information to examine and apply in two minutes and fifteen seconds— the average time per question for the data insights questions! Don't worry. You can overcome brain block by following a step-by-step approach to these questions.

Steps to Approaching Data Sufficiency Questions

Take a methodical approach to answering data sufficiency questions, and follow this series of steps:

1. **Evaluate the question to make sure you know exactly what you're supposed to solve.**

   Read the initial information and the question carefully. If you can, decide what kind of information you need to solve the problem.

2. **Examine one of the statements and determine whether the data in that one statement is enough to answer the question.**

   Start with the first statement or whichever one seems easier to evaluate. Record your conclusion on the noteboard.

3. **Examine the other statement and determine whether it has enough information to answer the question.**

   While performing this step, ignore information given in the statement you started with. Record your conclusion on the noteboard.

4. **Evaluate what you've written on your noteboard.**

   - If you recorded *yes* for both statements, pick the fourth answer, which we designate as Choice (D).

   - If you recorded *yes* for (1) and *no* for (2), select the first answer, Choice (A) in this book.

- If you recorded *no* for (1) and *yes* for (2), choose the second answer, Choice (B) for our purposes.

- If you've written *no* for both statements, go on to the next step.

5. **Consider the statements together to determine whether the data given in both is enough information to answer the question.**

- If the answer is *yes,* select the third answer, Choice (C).

- If the answer is *no,* choose the last answer, Choice (E).

You can boil this method down to a nice, neat chart, like the one shown in Figure 17-1.

Data Sufficiency Answer Elimination Chart

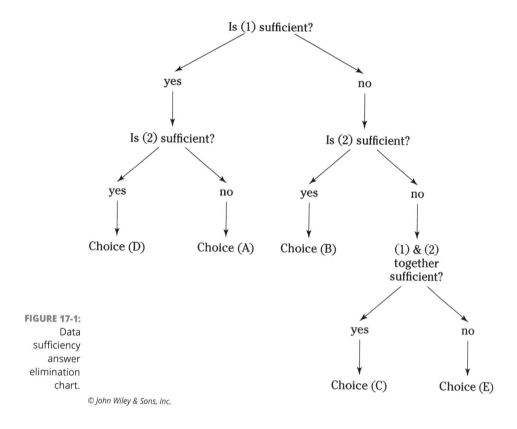

© John Wiley & Sons, Inc.

FIGURE 17-1: Data sufficiency answer elimination chart.

Don't think *too* hard about whether an answer provides sufficient information to solve a problem. Data sufficiency questions aren't necessarily designed to trick you. For example, you deal only with real numbers in these questions, and if a line graph looks slanted, it is.

TIP

A statement is sufficient to answer the question if it provides only one possible answer for the question. If the information in a statement allows for two or more answers, the statement isn't sufficient.

EXAMPLE

David and Karena were among a group of runners who were raising money for a local charity. If David and Karena together raised $900 in the charity race, how much of the money did Karena raise?

(1) David raised $\frac{4}{5}$ as much money as Karena did.

(2) David raised 5 percent of the total money raised at the event.

Use the steps and/or the chart in Figure 17-1 to solve the problem:

1. **Know what you have to solve for.**

The question asks you to figure out how much money Karena raised for charity. The question gives you the total money raised by David and Karena together ($D + K = \$900$) but doesn't specify how much David raised. Check out the statements to see whether either or both of them let you know how much David came up with. If you have David's amount, you only need to subtract it from $900 to get Karena's amount.

2. **Examine Statement (1) to determine whether it lets you solve for Karena's total.**

You determined that you needed data that would allow you to separate the money raised by Karena from that raised by David. Knowing that David raised $\frac{4}{5}$ as much money as Karena allows you to set up a formula to solve for Karena's portion. Let K stand for Karena's contribution and substitute $\frac{4}{5}K$ for D in the equation $D + K = \$900$. Your new equation is $\frac{4}{5}K + K = \$900$. This equation has only one variable, and that variable stands for how much Karena raised. Therefore, you know you can solve the problem by using just the data from Statement (1). You don't need to actually figure out what K stands for. Just write (1) is *yes* on your notebook. You know that the correct answer is either Choice (A) or Choice (D), but you have to look at Statement (2) to know which.

TIP

If a question like this one appears at the end of the section and you're pressed for time, you can guess between choices (A) and (D), knowing that you have a 50 percent chance of answering correctly without even reading Statement (2).

3. **Examine Statement (2).**

Statement (2) tells you that David raised 5 percent of the total money raised at the event. The question doesn't tell you how much total money was raised at the event, so you can't use this information to figure out how much David raised. And if you don't know how much David raised, you can't figure out how much Karena raised. Jot down (2) is *no* on the notebook. Because (1) is *yes* and (2) is *no,* the answer has to be Choice (A).

TIP

If you've read both statements and determined that either Statement (1) or Statement (2) is sufficient alone, two things are true:

➤ You're done with the question and can move on to the next one.

➤ The answer can't be Choice (C) or Choice (E).

Both Choices (C) and (E) apply to the statements when they're considered together. You don't need to consider the statements together if either statement is sufficient alone. Your only possible choices if *either* statement is sufficient are Choice (A) if only Statement (1) is sufficient, Choice (B) if only Statement (2) is sufficient, and Choice (D) if each statement alone is sufficient.

Don't evaluate whether both statements together answer the problem unless you've determined that neither is sufficient alone. The only time you consider together is when you've answered *no* to both individual statements. For instance, say the example question replaced Statement (1) with this information: "The event raised a total of $8,000." Statement (1) wouldn't be enough to answer the question. But because Statement (2) tells you that David raised 5 percent of the total event money, you can answer the question using the data from both statements. Statement (1) provides the total amount, and Statement (2) allows you to figure out how much David raised based on that amount. If you subtract that amount from $900, you'll have Karena's total.

Choice (E) would be correct if Statement (1) said, "The event raised more money this year than last year." In this case, neither statement, nor the two together, could answer the question.

Don't waste time trying to come up with the actual numeric answer if you don't have to. When you look at a question like the example, you may be tempted to solve the equation and figure out how much Karena raised. Don't give in! Finding the number just wastes precious time, and no one gives you extra credit for solving the problem! Instead, use your valuable time to solve other questions in the data insights section.

Taking on Data Sufficiency Practice Problems

The best way to master the steps for solving data sufficiency questions is to practice on sample problems. Use the following set of five questions to hone your skills. Make sure you have a piece of scratch paper nearby to simulate the noteboard. You can check your answers by reading through the explanations that follow the questions.

The GMAT allows an average of two minutes and fifteen seconds to answer each data insights question. So set your timer for 11 minutes and 15 seconds for these five data sufficiency questions to get a feel for the time limit you'll be facing on the actual test. Follow the chart in Figure 17-1 to work your way through the answer choices. If you need to refresh your memory of the answer choices before you begin, see the earlier section, "You don't need the solution to find the answer."

> **DIRECTIONS:** Each data sufficiency problem consists of a question and two statements labeled (1) and (2). Decide whether the given statements are sufficient for answering the question, and then select one of the answer choices that follow.

1. What's the value of the two-digit integer x?

   (1) The sum of the two digits is 5.

   (2) x is divisible by 5.

   (A) Statement (1) *alone* is sufficient, but Statement (2) *alone* is *not* sufficient.

   (B) Statement (2) *alone* is sufficient, but Statement (1) *alone* is *not* sufficient.

   (C) *Both* Statements *together* are sufficient, but *neither* statement *alone* is sufficient.

   (D) *Each* statement *alone* is sufficient.

   (E) Statements (1) and (2) *together* are *not* sufficient.

2. Office Solutions employs both male and female workers who work either full time or part time. What percentage of its employees work part time?

   (1) Twenty percent of the female employees at Office Solutions work part time.

   (2) Thirty percent of the workforce at Office Solutions is male.

   (A) Statement (1) *alone* is sufficient, but Statement (2) *alone* is *not* sufficient.

   (B) Statement (2) *alone* is sufficient, but Statement (1) *alone* is *not* sufficient.

   (C) *Both* Statements *together* are sufficient, but *neither* statement *alone* is sufficient.

   (D) *Each* statement *alone* is sufficient.

   (E) Statements (1) and (2) *together* are *not* sufficient.

3. Suppose a jar contains 24 tokens, each of which is blue, green, orange, or red, all identical except for color. If a token is randomly drawn from the jar, what is the probability that the token drawn is blue or orange?

   (1) The probability is $\frac{1}{2}$ that the token drawn is green or red.

   (2) The probability is $\frac{1}{3}$ that the token drawn is orange.

   (A) Statement (1) *alone* is sufficient, but Statement (2) *alone* is *not* sufficient.
   (B) Statement (2) *alone* is sufficient, but Statement (1) *alone* is *not* sufficient.
   (C) *Both* Statements *together* are sufficient, but *neither* statement *alone* is sufficient.
   (D) *Each* statement *alone* is sufficient.
   (E) Statements (1) and (2) *together* are *not* sufficient.

4. Joe uses three different modes of transportation to travel a total of 225 kilometers to visit his aunt. How many kilometers does Joe travel by bus?

   (1) Joe rides his bike 5 kilometers to the bus station where he boards the bus to take him to the train station. He then takes the train 10 times the distance he has traveled by bus.

   (2) The distance Joe travels by bike is $\frac{1}{4}$ the distance he travels by bus, and his train ride is 40 times longer than his bike ride.

   (A) Statement (1) *alone* is sufficient, but Statement (2) *alone* is *not* sufficient.
   (B) Statement (2) *alone* is sufficient, but Statement (1) *alone* is *not* sufficient.
   (C) *Both* Statements *together* are sufficient, but *neither* statement *alone* is sufficient.
   (D) *Each* statement *alone* is sufficient.
   (E) Statements (1) and (2) *together* are *not* sufficient.

5. If x and y are real numbers and $(a)^{2x}(a)^{2y} = 81$, what is the value of $x + y$?

   (1) $a = 3$

   (2) $x = y$

   (A) Statement (1) *alone* is sufficient, but Statement (2) *alone* is *not* sufficient.
   (B) Statement (2) *alone* is sufficient, but Statement (1) *alone* is *not* sufficient.
   (C) *Both* Statements *together* are sufficient, but *neither* statement *alone* is sufficient.
   (D) *Each* statement *alone* is sufficient.
   (E) Statements (1) and (2) *together* are *not* sufficient.

Answer Explanations

The following answer explanations provide not only the correct answer for the data sufficiency practice questions in the preceding section, but also additional insight into how to approach this unique question type. So be sure to read all the info provided here.

1. **C.** Apply the steps:

   1. **Find out what to solve for.**

      This short question gives you little information about *x*; all you know is that it's a two-digit integer.

   2. **Examine Statement (1).**

      Statement (1) tells you that the sum of the digits is 5. Five two-digit numbers are composed of digits that when added together equal 5: 14, 23, 32, 41, and 50. Statement (1) narrows the field of two-digit numbers down to just these five possibilities, but that's not good enough. Because you don't have a single answer, Statement (1) isn't sufficient. Write down (1) is *no* on the noteboard. You've just eliminated choices (A) and (D).

   3. **Examine Statement (2).**

      Statement (2) says that *x* is divisible by 5. You probably realize immediately that every two-digit number ending in 0 or 5 is divisible by 5, so the possibilities are 10, 15, 20, 25, and so on. Clearly, Statement (2) isn't sufficient, because $\frac{1}{5}$ of all two-digit numbers are divisible by 5. Write down (2) is *no*. You've just eliminated Choice (B).

   4. **Evaluate what you've written on your noteboard.**

      You have double *nos*, so you have to consider both statements together.

   5. **Consider the two statements together.**

      Statement (1) narrows the two-digit numbers down to five possibilities: 14, 23, 32, 41, and 50. Statement (2) narrows the list to those numbers that are divisible by 5. The only possibility from Statement (1) that ends in 0 or 5 is 50. Because 50 is divisible by 5 and the digits add up to 5, it answers the question. The two statements together provide enough information to answer the question. *Correct answer:* Choice (C).

TIP

You'll notice that, for this question, you had to find the actual answer to the question to determine whether the information was sufficient. Sometimes doing so is the quickest way to determine whether statements provide enough data. An equation may exist that you could've set up (and not solved) that would have told you that you had sufficient information. However, on questions like this one, just applying the information to the question is often simpler and quicker. Solving the actual problem is okay *if it's the quickest way to determine that you have enough information.* Just remember to stop solving the problem as soon as you determine whether the information is sufficient!

2. **E.** Here's an example of how word problems may appear as data sufficiency questions. Apply the steps in the same way you do for solving linear equations:

   1. **Find out what to solve for.**

      The question asks you to find the percentage of part-time employees at Office Solutions. You know two facts at this point: (1) Office Solutions employs a certain number of males (*m*) and a certain number of females (*f*), and (2) a certain number of employees work either full time (*F*) or part time (*P*). That undertaking creates four unknown variables. The question doesn't tell you anything about how many total people (*T*) Office Solutions employs, so you have another unknown. Here's what you know in mathematical terms: $F + P = T$ and $f + m = T$.

2. Examine Statement (1).

The first statement gives you the percentage of female part-time employees but tells you nothing about the percentage of male part-time employees. It takes care of only two of the unknown variables; you're missing half of what you need to solve the problem. Statement (1) isn't sufficient. Write (1) is *no* on the noteboard, and eliminate choices (A) and (D).

3. Examine Statement (2).

This statement concerns male employees at Office Solutions, but not females, so it's insufficient by itself. Record your finding as (2) is *no*. The answer can't be Choice (B).

4. Evaluate what you've written on your noteboard.

You have double *no*s, so consider Statement (2)'s sufficiency when paired with Statement (1).

5. Consider the two statements together.

One statement provides a percentage for females and the other offers a percentage for males. You may be on your way to finding the percentage for both.

WARNING

Read the statements carefully. You may be tempted to think that Statement (2) offers the other half of the solution, but this statement tells you the percentage of *all* males who work at the company, not just the ones who work part time.

You can't determine the total percentage of part-time workers if you don't know the ratio of male full-time to male part-time workers. Neither statement is sufficient and the two together don't cut it. *Correct answer:* Choice (E).

3. **A.** For this problem, you work with probabilities:

1. Find out what to solve for.

You're asked to find the probability that the token drawn is blue or orange.

2. Examine Statement (1).

Statement (1) gives you that the probability is $\frac{1}{2}$ that the token drawn is green or red. From this information, you know that $\frac{1}{2}$ of the tokens are green or red. Thus, $\frac{1}{2}$ of the tokens are blue or orange. So, the probability is $\frac{1}{2}$ that the token drawn is blue or orange. Problem solved! Statement (1) is sufficient. Write (1) is *yes* on your noteboard and eliminate choices (B), (C), and (E). You know that the correct answer is either choice (A) or (D), but you have to assess Statement (2) to know which.

3. Examine Statement (2).

Statement (2) gives you that the probability is $\frac{1}{3}$ that the token is orange, which tells you that $\frac{1}{3} \times 24 = 8$ of the tokens are orange. However, there is no information about how many of the remaining 16 tokens are blue, green, or red. Without additional information, you cannot obtain an exact value of the probability that the token drawn is blue or orange. Statement (2) is not sufficient. Write (2) is *no* on your noteboard. Because (1) is *yes* and (2) is *no*, the answer has to be Choice (A).

4. **D.** This data sufficiency question is essentially a simple addition problem.

1. Find out what to solve for.

You know the total distance Joe travels to his aunt's is 225 kilometers and that he takes different types of transportation, one of which is a bus. Lucky guy! The question asks for the length of Joe's bus ride. That's your unknown, so designate the number of kilometers by bus as *x*.

2. **Examine Statement (1).**

From Statement (1), you learn that the other modes of transportation are bike (*b*) and train (*t*). Great news! It also tells you the exact length of Joe's bike ride (5 kilometers) and that his train ride is 10 times his bus ride. So $t = 10x$. You can set up an equation with this information: $5 + x + 10x = 225$. The equation has only one variable, the unknown length of the bus ride. You know you can solve a linear equation with only one variable, so Statement (1) is sufficient. Write (1) is *yes* on your noteboard, and eliminate choices (B), (C), and (E).

3. **Examine Statement (2).**

Create an equation from the information in the second statement. If Joe's bike ride (*b*) is $\frac{1}{4}$ as long as his bus ride (*x*), then $b = \frac{1}{4}x$. If the train trip (*t*) is 40 times the length of the bike ride (*b*), then $t = 40b$. This gives simultaneous equations. Substitute $\frac{1}{4}x$ for *t* in the train ride equation: $t = 40\left(\frac{1}{4}x\right)$. So the equation for the bike ride plus the bus ride plus the train trip is this:

$$\frac{1}{4}x + x + 40\left(\frac{1}{4}x\right) = 225$$

This equation has only one variable, so you know you can solve for *x*. You don't have to actually solve for *x*; you just need to know that you can solve for *x*, to know that Statement (2) is also sufficient. Write (2) is *yes*. So, each statement alone is sufficient. *Correct answer:* Choice (D).

5. **A.** The last question in the practice set contains a bunch of unknown variables, so you may think you can't solve for much. You may be surprised!

1. **Find out what to solve for.**

Take a few seconds to evaluate the equation. You're given two factors with exponents, and their product is equal to a perfect square. Both factors have the same base (*a*), and both contain an exponent with a factor of 2. The problem asks you to find the sum of the other two factors in the exponents of the terms.

2. **Examine Statement (1).**

From the information in the first statement, you can substitute 3 for *a* in the equation: $(3)^{2x}(3)^{2y} = 81$

The terms have the same base, so you add the exponents when you multiply the terms: $3^{2x+2y} = 81$

Now extract the common factor in the exponent: $3^{2(x+y)} = 81$

Square 3 to get 9: $9^{(x+y)} = 81$

Because $9^2 = 81$, you know that the exponent $(x + y)$ must equal 2.

You could also find the value of $x + y$ by rewriting 81 as a base and exponent: $3^{2x+2y} = 3^4$

When the bases are equal, the exponents are equal:

$$2x + 2y = 4$$
$$x + y = 2$$

Either way, the information in Statement (1) is sufficient to tell you the value of $x + y$. Write (1) is *yes* on your noteboard, and eliminate Choices (B), (C), and (E).

3. **Examine Statement (2).**

This statement tells you that x and y are equal, so you may be tempted to draw from the information in the last statement and assume that x and y each equal 1. Well, that could be true if $a = 3$. But you no longer know that $a = 3$.

You can't carry over the information from one statement to evaluate the sufficiency of the other. It's true that x and y could each equal 1, but they could also each equal 0.5. Start fresh with each statement.

If x and y are equal, then you can substitute x for y in the equation, simplify, and solve for a:

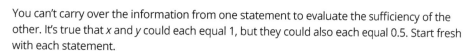

$$(a)^{2x}(a)^{2x} = 81$$
$$a^{4x} = 81$$
$$a^{4x} = 3^4$$
$$a^x = 3$$
$$a = \sqrt[x]{3}$$

Since a is equal to the xth root of 3, the possible values of x, y, a, and, of course, $x + y$, are infinite. For example, if $x = 2$, then so does y, and $a = \sqrt{3}$. If x and y each equal 3, then $a = \sqrt[3]{3}$, and so on. Because Statement (2) results in more than one value for $x + y$, it can't be sufficient to answer the question. Write (2) is *no* on your noteboard. So, Statement (1) alone is sufficient, but Statement (2) alone is not sufficient. *Correct answer:* Choice (A).

6

Practice Makes Perfect

Chapter **18**

GMAT Practice Test

If you want to perform well on the GMAT, it is essential to practice answering questions before exam day. This practice test consists of three sections: data insights, quantitative reasoning, and verbal reasoning. Each section has a time limit of 45 minutes, and you are free to complete them in any order that you choose. However, keep in mind that once you start a section, you cannot move on to the next one until the time limit ends. In total, you are required to answer 20 data insights questions, 21 quantitative questions, and 23 verbal questions within the allotted time for each.

Note: To provide a realistic simulation of your capability to digitally interact with the data insights questions on the actual GMAT, these specific questions can be accessed only in online Practice Test 1. You will find instructions for logging into the online Test Bank in the Introduction chapter.

To maximize the benefits of this practice test, take it under conditions like those you'll face on test day:

>> Find a place where you won't be distracted (preferably as far from your refrigerator as possible).

>> If possible, take the practice test at the same time of day as when you'll be taking the actual GMAT.

>> Use a timer to keep track of the time limits for each section.

>> Take no more than one 10-minute break, after either Section 1 or Section 2.

>> Indicate your answers online for Section 1 by either clicking the radio button next to your answer choice or by selecting from a drop-down menu, as necessary.

>> Mark your answers for Section 2 and Section 3 by circling the appropriate letters in the text or shading the corresponding letters on the provided bubble sheet in this chapter. (On the actual GMAT, you'll mark your answer by clicking the radio button next to your answer choice.)

>> Use a blank piece of paper to simulate the noteboard for keeping notes and making calculations.

>> When your time is up for a section, stop working.

After you finish Section 1 online, review your test and read the answer explanations. After you finish Section 2 and Section 3 in the book, turn to Chapter 19 to check your answers with the answer key and read the answer explanations — even the ones for the questions you got right. The explanations may present a way of approaching a problem that you haven't considered. The end of each explanation directs you to the chapter or chapters where you can find the information relevant to understanding that question type.

TIP

If you want to practice taking the test electronically, go to www.dummies.com/go/getaccess and use your pin code to activate the online access that accompanies the purchase of this book. (Complete instructions are in the Introduction.) You'll find this test, along with two others for even more practice. You can answer the questions digitally, and the software tabulates correct and incorrect responses. This summary provides you with a snapshot of which areas you excel in and which areas you may need to review again.

You can also download a fill-in-the-bubble answer sheet from www.dummies.com/go/relebubblesheets and use it as you take the practice test.

Answer Sheet

The test consists of three sections, though only Section 2 and Section 3 appear here in the book. (You can find the data insights questions in the online version of this practice test.) In both Section 2 and Section 3, all of the questions require you to select the best answer from among the given answer choices.

Section 2: Quantitative

1. Ⓐ Ⓑ Ⓒ Ⓓ Ⓔ   6. Ⓐ Ⓑ Ⓒ Ⓓ Ⓔ   11. Ⓐ Ⓑ Ⓒ Ⓓ Ⓔ   16. Ⓐ Ⓑ Ⓒ Ⓓ Ⓔ   21. Ⓐ Ⓑ Ⓒ Ⓓ Ⓔ
2. Ⓐ Ⓑ Ⓒ Ⓓ Ⓔ   7. Ⓐ Ⓑ Ⓒ Ⓓ Ⓔ   12. Ⓐ Ⓑ Ⓒ Ⓓ Ⓔ   17. Ⓐ Ⓑ Ⓒ Ⓓ Ⓔ
3. Ⓐ Ⓑ Ⓒ Ⓓ Ⓔ   8. Ⓐ Ⓑ Ⓒ Ⓓ Ⓔ   13. Ⓐ Ⓑ Ⓒ Ⓓ Ⓔ   18. Ⓐ Ⓑ Ⓒ Ⓓ Ⓔ
4. Ⓐ Ⓑ Ⓒ Ⓓ Ⓔ   9. Ⓐ Ⓑ Ⓒ Ⓓ Ⓔ   14. Ⓐ Ⓑ Ⓒ Ⓓ Ⓔ   19. Ⓐ Ⓑ Ⓒ Ⓓ Ⓔ
5. Ⓐ Ⓑ Ⓒ Ⓓ Ⓔ   10. Ⓐ Ⓑ Ⓒ Ⓓ Ⓔ   15. Ⓐ Ⓑ Ⓒ Ⓓ Ⓔ   20. Ⓐ Ⓑ Ⓒ Ⓓ Ⓔ

Section 3: Verbal

1. Ⓐ Ⓑ Ⓒ Ⓓ Ⓔ   6. Ⓐ Ⓑ Ⓒ Ⓓ Ⓔ   11. Ⓐ Ⓑ Ⓒ Ⓓ Ⓔ   16. Ⓐ Ⓑ Ⓒ Ⓓ Ⓔ   21. Ⓐ Ⓑ Ⓒ Ⓓ Ⓔ
2. Ⓐ Ⓑ Ⓒ Ⓓ Ⓔ   7. Ⓐ Ⓑ Ⓒ Ⓓ Ⓔ   12. Ⓐ Ⓑ Ⓒ Ⓓ Ⓔ   17. Ⓐ Ⓑ Ⓒ Ⓓ Ⓔ   22. Ⓐ Ⓑ Ⓒ Ⓓ Ⓔ
3. Ⓐ Ⓑ Ⓒ Ⓓ Ⓔ   8. Ⓐ Ⓑ Ⓒ Ⓓ Ⓔ   13. Ⓐ Ⓑ Ⓒ Ⓓ Ⓔ   18. Ⓐ Ⓑ Ⓒ Ⓓ Ⓔ   23. Ⓐ Ⓑ Ⓒ Ⓓ Ⓔ
4. Ⓐ Ⓑ Ⓒ Ⓓ Ⓔ   9. Ⓐ Ⓑ Ⓒ Ⓓ Ⓔ   14. Ⓐ Ⓑ Ⓒ Ⓓ Ⓔ   19. Ⓐ Ⓑ Ⓒ Ⓓ Ⓔ
5. Ⓐ Ⓑ Ⓒ Ⓓ Ⓔ   10. Ⓐ Ⓑ Ⓒ Ⓓ Ⓔ   15. Ⓐ Ⓑ Ⓒ Ⓓ Ⓔ   20. Ⓐ Ⓑ Ⓒ Ⓓ Ⓔ

Section 1: Data Insights

TIME: 45 minutes for 20 questions

DIRECTIONS: [For the 20 data insights questions, follow the directions provided in online Practice Test 1.]

DO NOT TURN THE PAGE UNTIL TOLD TO DO SO **STOP** **DO NOT RETURN TO A PREVIOUS TEST**

Section 2: Quantitative

TIME: 45 minutes for 21 questions

DIRECTIONS: Choose the best answer from the five choices provided.

$$\frac{10xy+15x}{2y+3}+3y=1$$

1. If $x=4$ and $y \neq -1.5$, what is the value of y?

   (A) $-\dfrac{19}{3}$

   (B) $-\dfrac{3}{19}$

   (C) $\dfrac{3}{19}$

   (D) $\dfrac{1}{3}$

   (E) $\dfrac{19}{3}$

2. A stand at a farmer's market is selling peaches individually and in cartons. An individual peach costs $1. When bought in a carton of 30, the price of each peach is discounted by 10 percent. Since it is the end of the growing season, there is a sale going on where the price is further discounted by 60 percent. What is the price of two cartons of peaches?

   (A) $9.00

   (B) $10.80

   (C) $18.00

   (D) $21.60

   (E) $32.40

3. The table shows the peak price each year for stocks from five different companies. Which stock had the greatest increase in peak price from Year 1 to Year 3?

	Year 1	Year 2	Year 3	Year 4	Year 5
OMK	$5.12	$6.86	$9.12	$6.20	$7.31
RRW	$30.51	$32.84	$45.18	$40.08	$47.12
LKP	$15.12	$25.32	$32.10	$31.12	$34.19
AWL	$130.54	$162.18	$154.96	$151.83	$183.39
TCK	$62.48	$71.31	$73.99	$79.42	$83.14

   (A) OMK

   (B) RRW

   (C) LKP

   (D) AWL

   (E) TCK

GO ON TO NEXT PAGE

4. If $y = 1$, what is the value of the following expression: $\left(4^{y+z}\right)(16)\left(4^{-z}\right)$?

   (A) 4

   (B) 16

   (C) 64

   (D) 128

   (E) 256

5. When $x \neq 0$, $\left(\dfrac{2}{x} + \dfrac{1}{3}\right)\left(\dfrac{x}{2}\right)$ can be simplified to which one of the following?

   (A) $1 + \dfrac{x}{6}$

   (B) $\dfrac{3x - 2}{3}$

   (C) $\dfrac{1}{6} + x$

   (D) $\dfrac{1}{3}$

   (E) $\dfrac{3x}{2x + 6}$

6. If $x - y = 8$ and $5x + y = -8$, then $x + y =$

   (A) -2

   (B) -8

   (C) 2

   (D) 3

   (E) 8

7. If $y = \dfrac{x}{2}$ and $x \neq 0$, which one of the following is equal to $\dfrac{y}{2x} + \dfrac{x}{4}$?

   (A) $\dfrac{4x^2 + x}{4}$

   (B) $\dfrac{x + 1}{4}$

   (C) $\dfrac{x + 4}{2x}$

   (D) $x^2 + 1$

   (E) $\dfrac{1}{4}$

8. Anthony runs a business manufacturing machine parts. If Anthony's business manufactured 80,000 machine parts last year and 88,000 machine parts this year, how many parts must the business produce next year to maintain the same percent growth from year to year?

   (A) 88,000

   (B) 88,800

   (C) 96,000

   (D) 96,800

   (E) 100,000

9. Patrick and Mel are each selling shirts at a rock concert to promote their favorite bands. It costs each of them the same amount to produce each shirt. Mel is selling her shirts for $60. If Patrick is making 20 percent more profit than Mel, and his profit is $24 per shirt, how much is Patrick charging for his shirts?

   (A) $48.00
   (B) $62.00
   (C) $64.00
   (D) $68.80
   (E) $72.00

10. If $7\left(\dfrac{x}{2}+\dfrac{x}{5}\right)=3$, what is the value of x?

   (A) $\dfrac{3}{49}$
   (B) $\dfrac{30}{49}$
   (C) $\dfrac{30}{49}$
   (D) $\dfrac{15}{7}$
   (E) $\dfrac{49}{3}$

11. Given $\dfrac{3-5x}{2}+4<\dfrac{x+2}{3}$, which one of the following describes the possible values for x?

   (A) $x<\dfrac{29}{17}$
   (B) $x<\dfrac{3}{14}$
   (C) $x<-\dfrac{29}{17}$
   (D) $x>\dfrac{29}{17}$
   (E) $x>\dfrac{1}{6}$

12. A parking lot contains ten cars. The average age of the cars is seven years. If the average age of nine of the cars is six years, what is the age of the remaining car in years?

   (A) 3
   (B) 7
   (C) 10
   (D) 16
   (E) 20

13. If Cindy ran at 7.5 miles per hour for 16 minutes, and then ran at 6 miles per hour for 10 minutes, how far in miles did she run in total?

   (A) 2.5
   (B) 2.8
   (C) 3
   (D) 3.5
   (E) 5

GO ON TO NEXT PAGE

14. If $x > 0$ and $2x^2 - 81 = 0$, what is the value of x?

(A) 4.5

(B) 6

(C) $\sqrt{40.5}$

(D) $\sqrt{45}$

(E) $\sqrt{162}$

15. Taco Fusion restaurant served a total of 60 guests for lunch today. Twenty of the guests ordered sushi, and 45 of the guests ordered tacos. If five of the guests didn't order tacos or sushi, how many of the guests ordered both?

(A) 0

(B) 5

(C) 10

(D) 15

(E) 20

16. A flag football league has ten teams. Each game in the season is between two teams from the league. If each team plays each of the other teams exactly one time, how many games are played in a season?

(A) 20

(B) 45

(C) 50

(D) 90

(E) 100

17. If one seedling grew 6 inches, while a second seedling grew 250 percent more than the first, how many inches did the second seedling grow?

(A) 6

(B) 8

(C) 12

(D) 15

(E) 21

18. Identify which one of the following expressions can be simplified to a rational number?

I. $\dfrac{\sqrt{46}\,\sqrt{46}}{(46)^2}$

II. $\left(\sqrt{46} + \sqrt{46}\right)^2$

III. $46\sqrt{46}$

(A) I only

(B) II only

(C) III only

(D) I and II only

(E) II and III only

19. The number of red dots is 4 times the number of blue dots, which, in turn is twice the number of yellow dots. What is the ratio of the number of red dots to the number of yellow dots?

(A) 8:1

(B) 4:1

(C) 1:2

(D) 1:4

(E) 1:8

20. The simultaneous solution of $(2x+1)(4x-1)=0$ and $(5x-1)\left(x-\dfrac{1}{4}\right)=0$ is $x =$

(A) $-\dfrac{1}{2}$

(B) $-\dfrac{1}{4}$

(C) $\dfrac{1}{5}$

(D) $\dfrac{1}{4}$

(E) $\dfrac{1}{2}$

21. The range of the six numbers, 20, 6, 14, 8, 28, and N is 24. What is the difference between the greatest and least possible values of N?

(A) 4

(B) 24

(C) 26

(D) 30

(E) 34

Section 3: **Verbal**

TIME: 45 minutes for 23 questions

DIRECTIONS: Follow these directions for each of the two question types:

- **Reading comprehension questions:** Choose the best answer to every question based on what the passage states directly or indirectly.

- **Critical reasoning questions:** Pick the answer choice that best answers the question about the argument provided.

Questions 1–6 refer to the following passage, which is excerpted from *Playing against Nature: Integrating Science and Economics to Mitigate Natural Hazards in an Uncertain World,* by Seth Stein and Jerome Stein (John Wiley & Sons, Inc. 2014).

Natural hazards are the price we pay for living on an active planet. The tectonic plate subduction producing Japan's rugged Tohoku coast gives rise to earthquakes and tsunamis. Florida's warm sunny weather results from the processes in the ocean and atmosphere that cause hurricanes. The volcanoes that produced Hawaii's spectacular islands sometimes threaten people. Rivers that provide the water for the farms that feed us sometimes flood.

Humans have to live with natural hazards. We describe this challenge in terms of hazards, the natural occurrence of earthquakes or other phenomena, and the risks, or dangers they pose to lives and property. In this formulation, the risk is the product of hazard and vulnerability. We want to assess the hazards — estimate how significant they are — and develop methods to mitigate or reduce the resulting losses.

Hazards are geological facts that are not under human control. All we can do is try to assess them as best we can. In contrast, risks are affected by human actions that increase or decrease vulnerability, such as where people live and how they build. We increase vulnerability by building in hazardous areas, and decrease it by making buildings more hazard resistant. Areas with high hazard can have low risk because few people live there. Areas of modest hazard can have high risk due to large population and poor construction. A disaster occurs when — owing to high vulnerability — a natural event has major consequences for society.

The harm from natural disasters is enormous. On average, about 100,000 people per year are killed by natural disasters, with some disasters — such as the 2004 Indian Ocean tsunami — causing many more deaths. Although the actual numbers of deaths in many events, such as the 2010 Haiti earthquake, are poorly known, they are very large.

Economic impacts are even harder to quantify, and various measures are used to try to do so. Disasters cause losses, which are the total negative economic impact. These include direct losses due to destruction of physical assets such as buildings, farmland, forests, etc., and indirect losses that result from the direct losses. Because losses are hard to determine, what is reported is often the cost, which refers to payouts by insurers (called insured losses) or governments to reimburse some of the losses. Thus, the reported cost does not reflect the losses to people who do not receive such payments.

1. The main idea of the first paragraph is best expressed as

   (A) the factors that make an area desirable are also those that can pose the most risk.

   (B) the Hawaiian Islands would not exist if not for powerful and explosive volcanoes.

   (C) floods, volcanoes, and earthquakes pose threats to the natural environment.

   (D) humans must learn to live with natural hazards such as volcanoes and tsunamis.

   (E) natural hazards are most prevalent in areas that are sunny and warm.

2. Which one of the following might the author of the passage consider an "indirect loss" associated with a disaster?

(A) Desecration of a library due to vandalism

(B) Damage to a school building in a fire

(C) Loss of retail clothing sales due to a mall flood

(D) Death of a ranch's livestock due to a volcanic eruption

(E) Destruction of a pavilion due to a hurricane

3. According to the passage, an important distinction between hazards and risks is

(A) risks occur naturally, while hazards arise because of human actions.

(B) hazards result from risks, and risks result from vulnerability.

(C) hazards can lead to disasters, while risks cannot.

(D) hazards are not under human control, while risks usually are.

(E) risks are harder to quantify than hazards.

4. The passage is primarily concerned with

(A) describing the causes and impacts of natural disasters.

(B) assessing the impact that disasters render on the global economy.

(C) depicting the various ways human beings may endanger themselves.

(D) raising awareness of the loss of human lives due to the severity and unpredictability of natural disasters.

(E) explaining that natural disasters are not under human control.

5. Which one of the following best describes the purpose of the fourth paragraph in relation to the passage as a whole?

(A) It uses numerical data and metrics to describe the economic impacts of natural disasters.

(B) It emphasizes how little is known about how many lives are lost in natural disasters.

(C) It outlines the differences between hazards and risks to set up information detailed in the remainder of the passage.

(D) It provides sensory details about specific recent natural disasters that may be familiar to readers to evoke an emotional response.

(E) It applies statistical data to emphasize the magnitude of damage created by natural disasters.

6. Which one of the following logically follows the information given in the passage?

(A) The number of unreported deaths in the 2010 Haitian earthquake exceeded the number of unreported deaths in the 2004 Indian Ocean tsunami.

(B) In the years 2010 and 2004, there were more deaths than average due to natural disasters.

(C) The number of deaths due to natural disasters along Japan's tectonic plate is greater on average than those experienced on islands such as Hawaii or Haiti.

(D) Economic costs are more frequently unreported than numbers of deaths in any given natural disaster.

(E) Areas of high hazard, such as Japan's Tohoku coast, may have a lower risk of natural disaster costs than areas where hazard incidents are lower.

GO ON TO NEXT PAGE

7. The size of oceanic waves is a function of the velocity of the wind and of *fetch*, the length of the surface of the water subject to those winds. The impact of waves against a coastline is a function of the size of the waves and the shape of the sea bottom. The degree of erosion to which a coastline is subject is a function of the average impact of waves and the geologic composition of the coastline.

If these statements are true, which one of the following must also be true?

(A) The degree of erosion to which a coastline is subject is related to the shape of the sea bottom.

(B) The size of oceanic waves will not fluctuate far from an average for any given stretch of ocean.

(C) The fetch of winds is related to the shape of the sea bottom.

(D) The size of oceanic waves is related to the shape of the sea bottom.

(E) The average velocity of the wind in an area plays no role in the degree of erosion to which a coastline is subject.

8. Health insurers are largely immune to the factors that are limiting profit in many sectors of the healthcare economy. Consumers have shown a willingness to pay almost any price for health insurance premiums. Capital demands, which are the responsibility of doctors and hospitals, are increasing dramatically, even as cost-containment measures, largely encouraged by the insurers and their friends in government, have forced new levels of fiscal discipline upon hospitals and doctors. Patients still need MRI scans and buildings to conduct them in, but hospitals are limited in how much they can charge patients for the use of these facilities.

Which one of the following most accurately describes the role that the statement "patients still need MRI scans and buildings to conduct them in" plays in the argument?

(A) It is a specific example of a general condition described during the argument.

(B) It is used to counter a consideration that may be taken to undermine the argument.

(C) It is used to indirectly support the claim made by the argument.

(D) It describes a social side effect of the benefit with which the argument is concerned.

(E) It introduces the conclusion that the argument intends to support.

9. Forcing businesses to furnish employees with paid leave for family concerns, such as family leave or leave to care for a sick child, is a terrible idea. If a business allows employees to take this time off, the workers will take advantage of the privilege and come to work as little as possible. This will destroy productivity and workplace morale.

Which one of the following, if true, most seriously weakens the argument?

(A) European countries guarantee employees generous family leave and paid vacation time, but the European standard of living is slightly below that of the United States.

(B) Most male workers refuse to take family leave even though it is allowed under federal law and their employers encourage it; they fear they may anger co-workers and harm their chances for promotion if they take time off for what is still seen as a frivolous reason.

(C) The Family and Medical Leave Act requires employers to grant employees 12 weeks a year of unpaid leave for family purposes; although employers save money because the leave is unpaid, they often must spend money to find a replacement for the employee who takes time off.

(D) In some workplaces, the loss of a single employee at a busy time of year can be devastating, even if that employee plans to return after a few weeks; allowing family leave can overwhelm the employees who stay on the job.

(E) Allowing employees to take leave for family matters reduces absenteeism, improves morale, and surprisingly increases productivity because the employees who are granted leave tend to work much harder and more efficiently when they come back to work.

10. Software engineers know that a poorly written application can consume more memory than it should and that running out of memory can cause an application to crash. However, if a crashing application causes the whole operating system to crash, the fault lies with the operating system.

Which one of the following, if true, is least helpful in establishing that this conclusion is properly drawn?

(A) Operating systems with generous amounts of memory are less susceptible to crashing, even when applications are poorly written.

(B) Operating systems can isolate the memory used by individual applications, even when an application uses a large amount of memory.

(C) An operating system can monitor an application's consumption of memory and act when that consumption gets too high.

(D) Techniques for programming operating systems to catch and manage memory errors are well defined and well known among programmers.

(E) Because many applications can run simultaneously under a single operating system, the operating system should have a well-defined method of managing memory consumption.

11. This museum does not grant people the right to use images of items in its collection in online publications. We are obliged to do everything in our power to ensure the continued appeal of visiting our collection in person.

The above conclusion depends on assuming which one of the following?

(A) Taking photographs of art objects, especially using a flash, can damage the objects by accelerating the fading of paint.

(B) The museum sells pictures of its collection in its gift shop, which is an important source of income for the museum.

(C) Images placed online are easily copied and reused by other people.

(D) The quality of most electronic images, especially those online, falls short of the professional standards of the museum.

(E) If people see online images of items in the museum's collection, they will no longer be interested in seeing the collection with their own eyes.

Questions 12–15 refer to the following passage, which is excerpted from *Handbook of Early Childhood Development Programs, Practices, and Policies,* by Elizabeth Votruba-Drzal (Editor) and Eric Dearing (Editor) (John Wiley & Sons, Inc. 2017).

Researchers, educators, and policymakers generally agree that school readiness is a multidimensional concept that includes cognitive, executive functioning, language, socioemotional, behavioral, and health characteristics that contribute to children's ability to adapt and thrive in school settings. These performance domains are correlated but typically are assessed and studied as independent indicators of school readiness and predictors of later achievement. Importantly, the guiding definitions of school readiness typically include skills and behaviors that are related to learning processes as well as learning outcomes, as opposed to the K–12 system, which often only emphasizes student outcomes based on children's performance on academic achievement tests.

In the area of cognition, school readiness includes both acquired knowledge or skills in a particular content area (such as knowing a certain number of letters) as well as learning/processing skills or how fast children acquire knowledge. In particular, there has been a growing emphasis on executive functioning skills and how these skills interact with other domains to promote learning in preschool classrooms. Executive functioning typically is defined as the set of skills and behaviors required to attain a goal, including working memory, attention control, attention shifting, and response inhibition. For young children, this means being able to resist distractions (e.g., pay attention to a teacher rather than talk with peers), inhibit dominant responses in emotional contexts (e.g., raise hand instead of talking while the teacher is reading a book), and prioritize and sequence information and hold onto it in memory (e.g., plan and carry out the series of steps required to line up for lunch).

In addition, school readiness includes children's language skills, including their receptive language (i.e., the ability to listen and understand language) and expressive language (i.e., the ability to communicate with others using verbal language). Children's socioemotional skills are also an important component of school readiness and include behaviors such as cooperation with teachers and peers and developing social relationships, as well as behavior problems, including aggression or poor regulation. There are also a set of skills referred to as approaches to learning, which reflect children's curiosity, flexibility, attention, persistence, and engagement. The physical health domain includes motor development, such as development of fine and gross motor skills, and healthy behavior practices. Collectively, all of these skills are theorized to affect children's learning opportunities and their acquisition of new skills and behaviors in the classroom setting.

12. According to the passage, being able to resist distractions is a form of

   (A) socioemotional growth.

   (B) executive functioning.

   (C) behavioral growth.

   (D) motor development.

   (E) cognitive growth.

13. The author of the passage makes the distinction between the guiding principles of school readiness and those observed by the K–12 system to

   (A) emphasize that school readiness regards the process as much as the results.

   (B) demonstrate the failings of the K–12 system.

   (C) explain why the guiding principles of school readiness are superior to those used at K–12 settings.

   (D) emphasize the author's opinion about the importance of student outcomes.

   (E) explain how cognition factors into a child's degree of success in a school setting.

14. The passage indicates that attention to which one of the following school readiness skills has increased in recent years?

   (A) responding accurately on standardized achievement tests

   (B) using verbal language to communicate ideas to others

   (C) cooperating with peers and managing aggressive behaviors

   (D) paying attention to the teacher

   (E) ensuring that students consume a healthy breakfast

15. It can be inferred from the passage that children who collaborate successfully with their teachers and other students have strong

(A) motor skills.

(B) receptive language skills.

(C) expressive language skills.

(D) executive functioning skills.

(E) socioemotional skills.

16. Career counselor: Many large international companies have changed their practices regarding international assignments. They are placing much more emphasis on helping spouses of expatriate employees to adjust to the foreign environment. This has reduced premature returns by 67 percent.

Which one of the following is an assumption upon which the career counselor's argument depends?

(A) Spousal and marital difficulties were formerly responsible for many premature returns from foreign assignments.

(B) When employees are placed in a foreign assignment for a year or less, their families see the assignment as an adventure.

(C) Expatriate employees work long hours and travel a great deal, and their children make new friends at school, but spouses often have no friends and no work to support them while they are abroad.

(D) The majority of international assignments today last for less than a year, but ten years ago, 70 percent of them lasted much longer than one year.

(E) Many companies now offer expatriate spouses language training, career guidance, and assistance in finding homes and schools.

17. Scientists have discovered a gene that controls whether an individual is monogamous. They took a gene from the monogamous prairie vole and implanted it into its more promiscuous relative, the meadow vole. Thereafter, the meadow voles with the new gene became monogamous.

Which one of the following, if true, would provide the most support for the argument's conclusion?

(A) Studies on humans and other mammals have shown that receptors for the hormone vasopressin play a role in autism, drug addiction, and the formation of romantic attachments.

(B) Prairie voles typically form lifelong partnerships, which scientists have linked to an increased number of receptors for the hormone vasopressin.

(C) Meadow voles live in a harsher environment than prairie voles and cannot afford to pass up opportunities to mate as often as possible.

(D) The scientists used a harmless virus to capture the gene and transfer it into the meadow voles.

(E) The meadow voles that had the prairie vole gene implanted in them were released into and observed in the same habitat in which they had previously lived.

18. Physician: Scottish researchers have developed a test that allows them to predict at what age a woman will experience menopause. The scientists use a model that compares a woman's ovaries to "average" ovaries to see whether her ovaries are aging faster or more slowly than average. They have discovered that the size of ovaries is directly related to the number of eggs they contain, which in turn is directly related to fertility. This discovery will significantly influence women's decisions on when to have children.

The physician's conclusion follows logically if which one of the following is assumed?

(A) Women with smaller ovaries tend to have less success with assisted reproduction techniques, such as in vitro fertilization.

(B) Most women experience menopause around the age of 50, but their fertility starts to decline at the age of 37.

(C) Women who want to have children increasingly seek to delay doing so for many varied reasons.

(D) The test cannot tell women how likely they are to conceive in the years just prior to menopause.

(E) Every woman is born with several million eggs in her ovaries, which formed while she was a fetus; the number of eggs dwindles over her lifetime, until at menopause she has 1,000 or fewer.

19. To earn a graduate equivalency diploma, students must pass tests on subjects taught in high schools, proving that they have mastered them to the degree assumed of high school graduates. It makes sense for students to drop out of high school and earn GEDs. A GED takes much less time to earn than a high school diploma and provides evidence that students have learned everything they would have learned in high school.

Which one of the following, if true, most seriously weakens the argument?

(A) Some GED-prep programs incorporate enrichment activities into their test preparation, such as taking students to art exhibits and theatrical performances.

(B) Most colleges and universities consider a GED equivalent to a high school degree for admission purposes.

(C) Many successful businesspeople dropped out of high school and earned a GED.

(D) Employers assume that high school graduates generally have a much higher level of mastery of academic subjects than those who earn GEDs.

(E) Many GED students are slightly older than high school students, and they often hold jobs in addition to studying to pass the GED tests.

Questions 20–23 refer to the following passage, which is excerpted from *Beyond Cybersecurity: Protecting Your Digital Business*, by James M. Kaplan, Tucker Bailey, Derek O'Halloran, Alan Marcus, and Chris Rezek (John Wiley & Sons, Inc. 2015).

All business investments require trade-offs between risk and reward. Does the interest rate on a new bond issue adequately compensate for the risk of default? Are the potential revenues from entering a new emerging market greater than the risk that the investments will be confiscated by a new regime? Does the value of oil extracted via deep-water, offshore drilling outweigh the chance of a catastrophic accident? Tough questions must be answered by weighing up the business imperatives against a calculation of the risk — and the greater the risk, the harder it is to make the case for investment.

Technology investments are no different. They, too, have always been a trade-off between risk and return. However, for enterprise technology, increased global connectivity is raising the stakes on both sides of the equation. The commercial rewards from tapping into this connectivity are enormous, but the more tightly we are connected, the more vulnerabilities exist that attackers can exploit and the more damage they can do once inside. Therefore, when a manufacturer invests in a new product life-cycle management system, it is making a bet that the system will not enable the theft of valuable intellectual property. When a retailer invests in mobile commerce, it is betting that cyber-fraud won't critically damage profitability. When a bank invests in customer analytics, it is betting that the sensitive data it analyzes won't be stolen by cyber-criminals. The odds on all those bets appear to be shifting away from the institutions and toward cyber-attackers. They could swing decisively their way in the near future given most companies' siloed and reactive approach to cybersecurity.

Our interviews with business leaders, chief information officers (CIOs), chief technology officers (CTOs), and chief information security officers (CISOs) indicate that concerns about cyber-attacks are already affecting large institutions' interest in and ability to create value from technology investment and innovation. Potential losses, both direct and indirect, reduce the expected economic benefits of technology investments, as do the high cost and lengthy time frame required to build the defense mechanisms that can protect the organization against a growing range of attackers. In short, the models companies use to protect themselves from cyber-attack are limiting their ability to extract additional value from technology.

Concern about cyber-attacks is already having a noticeable impact on business along three dimensions: lower frontline productivity, fewer resources for information technology (IT) initiatives that create value, and — critically — the slower implementation of technological innovations.

20. The primary purpose of this passage is to

(A) identify gaps in the business world that lead to cybersecurity breaches.

(B) refute the notion that companies are failing to thwart hackers.

(C) discuss how the modern business marketplace is all about risk and reward.

(D) explain how attention to cybersecurity impacts companies' technological innovation.

(E) demonstrate how today's hackers are winning the fight against big corporations.

21. According to the passage, all of the following decrease the economic benefits of technological investment EXCEPT

(A) experiencing stolen intellectual property.

(B) realizing indirect losses.

(C) weighing business outcomes and risks.

(D) investing in cybersecurity protection technology.

(E) reacting to cyber-threats only when necessary.

22. When the authors assert that companies take a "siloed and reactive" approach to cybersecurity, they are implying that companies

(A) perform thorough research before implementing programs meant to improve cybersecurity.

(B) combat problems after they have occurred.

(C) have made strides against hackers in the ultimate battle of cybersecurity.

(D) invest too much in cybersecurity.

(E) take unnecessarily large investment risks and disregard the importance of cybersecurity.

GO ON TO NEXT PAGE

23. Which one of the following is an example of intellectual property as mentioned in the second paragraph?

   (A) works of art posted to social media

   (B) personal information, such as Social Security numbers or banking information

   (C) computers and related technological devices

   (D) customer and client lists and related contact information

   (E) an outline of a streamlined manufacturing process

Chapter 19

Practice Test Answers and Explanations

Y ou've finished the test, but you're not done yet. Reading the following explanations may be the most important part of taking the practice exam. Examine the information for the questions you missed as well as those you answered correctly. You may find tips and techniques you haven't thought of before in one of the answer explanations. If you're short on time or just want to quickly check your answers, head to the end of this chapter for an abbreviated answer key.

Section 1: Data Insights

Refer to "Section 1: Data Insights" of online Practice Test 1 to check this section. (*Note:* You can find instructions for accessing the online Test Bank in the Introduction.)

Section 2: Quantitative

1. **A.** $-\dfrac{19}{3}$

   This question gives you an equation with variables x and y, and asks you to solve for the value of y. It gives you a value of x and says that $y \neq -1.5$. Looking at the first part of the expression, you may notice that you are able to factor the numerator. Factor out the common factor of $5x$:

   $$\frac{10xy + 15x}{2y + 3} + 3y = 1$$

   $$\frac{5x(2y + 3)}{2y + 3} + 3y = 1$$

   Because you know that $y \neq -1.5$, you know that the denominator is not equal to 0, so you are able to cancel out the common factor of $(2y + 3)$. Now you have $5x + 3y = 1$.

   Rearrange the equation to solve for y:

   $$y = \frac{1 - 5x}{3}$$

   When you insert 4 for x, you arrive at the conclusion that $y = -\dfrac{19}{3}$, Choice (A).

   For more about how to solve problem solving questions, review Chapters 13 and 14. To review algebraic expressions and equations, read Chapter 11.

2. **D.** $21.60

   In this price discount problem, you will need to apply multiple price discounts to the original price of the peaches to calculate the final price. The problem tells you that each peach costs $1, so a carton of 30 peaches would therefore cost $30. But the problem says that the price is discounted by 10% when the peaches are bought in a carton of 30. If the discount is 10%, then multiply the cost of the peaches by $1 - 10\%$, which is 90%. So, two cartons of peaches would be 60 peaches, and the price would be $\$60 \times 90\% = \$54$.

   The problem tells you that there is an additional discount of 60%. To apply the additional discount, simply multiply $54 by 40% (which is $1 - 60\%$), and you get $21.60. Choice (D) is the answer.

   For more about how to solve problem solving questions, review Chapters 13 and 14. To review percentages and other fundamental math concepts, read Chapter 10.

3. **D.** AWL

   This data-interpretation question presents you with a table showing peak prices of various stocks over the course of five years. The question is asking you to find which stock had the greatest increase in peak price from Year 1 to Year 3. Looking at the peak prices for OMK, you can see that they were $5.12 in Year 1 and $9.12 in Year 3. This is an increase of $4. Use estimation to evaluate the rest of the table.

   Continuing down the table, you can see that the peak price of RRW increased by about $45.00 - \$30.00 = \$15.00$, and the peak price of LKP increased by about $\$30.00 - \$15.00 = \$15.00$.

   If you don't find an answer with a greater increase, you'll have to evaluate these two options more carefully later. But there are still two more stocks to evaluate. Looking at AWL, its peak price increased by about $\$155.00 - \$130.00 = \$25.00$. AWL is now the highest increase in peak price you've seen and is higher than TCK, which increased from around $62.00 to $74.00, an increase of only about $12.00.

Of all the stocks, the peak price of AWL, Choice (D), increased the most from Year 1 to Year 3.

For more about how to solve problem solving questions, review Chapters 13 and 14. To review price increases, read Chapter 10. For more on extracting information from tables, review Chapter 16.

4. **C. 64**

This question concerns exponents. You are given an expression and asked for the value of the expression if $y = 1$. Look for a way to make the bases of the terms the same. Because $16 = 4^2$, you can rewrite the expression as

$$4^{y+z} \times 4^2 \times 4^{-z}$$

Since exponents with the same base can be added together, you can simplify the expression to

$$4^{y+z+2-z}$$

The z terms cancel out and you are left with 4^{y+2}. You know that $y = 1$, so the expression becomes 4^3, or 64. The answer is Choice (C).

For more about how to solve problem solving questions, review Chapters 13 and 14. To review exponents and other fundamental math concepts, read Chapter 10.

5. **A. $1 + \dfrac{x}{6}$**

The first fraction involves addition, so you'll need to find a common denominator. The simplest common denominator for 3 and x is $3x$. So, multiply the first fraction by $\dfrac{3}{3}$ and the second fraction by $\dfrac{x}{x}$ to create equivalent fractions that have the common denominator. Then add:

$$\frac{2}{x} + \frac{1}{3} = \frac{6}{3x} + \frac{x}{3x} = \frac{6+x}{3x}$$

Multiply this new fraction by $\dfrac{x}{2}$:

$$\left(\frac{6+x}{3x}\right)\left(\frac{x}{2}\right) = \frac{6x + x^2}{6x}$$

Simplify:

$$\frac{6x + x^2}{6x} = \frac{6x}{6x} + \frac{x^2}{6x} = 1 + \frac{x}{6}$$

And you're done! The answer is Choice (A).

For more about how to solve problem solving questions, review Chapters 13 and 14. To review simplifying algebraic expressions, read Chapter 11.

6. **B. –8**

To find the value of $x + y$, first, find the value of x by adding the two equations to eliminate y. The equation for the first line is $x - y = 8$, and the equation for the second line is $5x + y = -8$:

$$\begin{aligned} x - y &= 8 \\ 5x + y &= -8 \\ \hline 6x &= 0 \\ x &= 0 \end{aligned}$$

When you know that $x = 0$, solve for y by substituting x into either equation:

$$5x + y = -8$$
$$0 + y = -8$$
$$y = -8$$

Therefore, $x + y = 0 + -8 = -8$, Choice (B).

For more about how to solve problem solving questions, review Chapters 13 and 14. To review solving simultaneous linear equations, read Chapter 11.

7. **B.** $\dfrac{x+1}{4}$

You are given $y = \dfrac{x}{2}$, so you can insert $\dfrac{x}{2}$ for y in $\dfrac{y}{2x} + \dfrac{x}{4}$ to get the expression solely in terms

of x: $\dfrac{y}{2x} + \dfrac{x}{4} = \dfrac{\left(\dfrac{x}{2}\right)}{2x} + \dfrac{x}{4}$. Simplify by performing division in the first fraction: $\dfrac{x}{2} \times \dfrac{1}{2x} = \dfrac{x}{4x}$,

which simplifies to $\dfrac{1}{4}$ when you cancel x from the numerator and denominator.

Then add to find the correct answer:

$$\dfrac{1}{4} + \dfrac{x}{4} = \dfrac{1+x}{4} = \dfrac{x+1}{4}$$, Choice (B).

For more about how to solve problem solving questions, review Chapters 13 and 14. To review simplifying algebraic expressions, read Chapter 11.

8. **D. 96,800**

This is a percent change problem dealing with the number of parts produced in different years. Knowing that Anthony's business made 80,000 parts last year and 88,000 parts this year, you can calculate the percent growth using the percent change formula, which is the difference between the two values divided by the original value, expressed as a percent:

$$\dfrac{\text{parts produced this year} - \text{parts produced last year}}{\text{parts produced last year}} = \dfrac{88,000 - 80,000}{80,000} = \dfrac{8,000}{80,000} = \dfrac{1}{10} = 10\%$$

To maintain 10% growth next year, the business will need to produce the same number of parts as last year + 10% more, which you can express as 110% or 1.1 of 88,000: $88,000 \times 1.1 = 96,800$, which is Choice (D).

TIP

Make sure you use the new year's value when calculating the percentage increase for the upcoming year. Choice (C) reflects an increase of 8,000 parts, but that amount is 10% of the parts made last year and only about 9.1% of the parts made this year. To maintain 10% growth, the number of additional parts made next year must be greater than this year's.

For more about how to solve problem solving questions, review Chapters 13 and 14. To review percents and percent change, read Chapter 10.

9. **C. $64.00**

This is a profit question dealing with two different merchants each selling the same product.

You can eliminate Choice (A) right away. If Patrick makes more profit than Mel, he must be charging more than $60, the price Mel charges for her shirts.

A general equation for the profit of each merchant is that profit (p) is equal to selling price (s) minus cost (c). So, $p = s - c$. You can write a profit equation for each merchant to make solving the question easier. For Mel (M), $p_M = s_M - c_M$. Because Mel is selling her shirts for $60, $s_M = 60$ and $p_M = 60 - c_M$.

For Patrick (P), $p_p = s_p - c_p$. You know that Patrick's profit is $24, so $24 = s_p - c_p$.

If Patrick makes 20% more profit than Mel, then $p_p = 120\%(p_M) = 1.2(p_M)$. Find Mel's profit by substituting $24 for p_p in the equation:

$$24 = (1.2)p_M$$
$$\frac{24}{1.2} = p_M$$
$$20 = p_M$$

After you know Mel's profit is $20 per shirt, you can find the cost of her shirt:

$$p_M = 60 - c_m$$
$$20 = 60 - c_m$$
$$-40 = -c_m$$
$$40 = c_m$$

Because you know Patrick and Mel have the same shirt cost, you can now find out how much Patrick sells his shirt for:

$$p_p = s_p - c_p$$
$$24 = s_p - 40$$
$$64 = s_p$$

Patrick sells his shirt for $64.00, Choice (C).

For more about how to solve problem solving questions, review Chapters 13 and 14. For help with translating word problems into equations and solving, read Chapter 11.

10. **B.** $\frac{30}{49}$

To solve this algebraic equation with one unknown x, begin by dividing both sides by 7:

$$7\left(\frac{x}{2} + \frac{x}{5}\right) = 3$$
$$\frac{x}{2} + \frac{x}{5} = \frac{3}{7}$$

Next, determine a common denominator for the fractions on the left side and find their sum:

$$\frac{x}{2} + \frac{x}{5} = \frac{5x}{10} + \frac{2x}{10} = \frac{7x}{10}$$

Set that sum equal to $\frac{3}{7}$ and solve for x:

$$\frac{7x}{10} = \frac{3}{7}$$
$$49x = 30$$
$$x = \frac{30}{49}$$

Choice (B) is the correct answer.

For more about how to solve problem solving questions, review Chapters 13 and 14. To review solving equations, read Chapter 11.

11. **D.** $x > \dfrac{29}{17}$

This question presents you with an inequality and asks for the possible values of x to solve the inequality. The fastest way to solve this problem is to get x by itself on one side of the inequality. An easy way of getting rid of the denominators is by multiplying the entire inequality by 6.

$$6\left(\frac{3-5x}{2}\right)+6(4)<6\left(\frac{x+2}{3}\right)$$
$$3(3-5x)+24<2(x+2)$$

Then, you can solve the resulting equivalent inequality for x:

$$3(3-5x)+24<2(x+2)$$
$$9-15x+24<2x+4$$
$$-15x+33<2x+4$$
$$-17x<-29$$
$$x>\frac{29}{17}$$

Choice (D) is the correct answer.

TIP

Recall that when you divide an inequality by a negative number, you must reverse the direction of the inequality sign, from less-than to greater-than or vice versa.

For more about how to solve problem solving questions, review Chapters 13 and 14. To review solving inequalities, read Chapter 11.

12. **D.** 16

This question deals with the average age of cars in a parking lot. It tells you that the average age of the ten cars is seven years. The equation for averages can help for this problem:
$$\text{Average} = \frac{\text{Sum}}{\text{Quantity}}$$

You know that the average age is seven years, and the quantity of cars is ten, so the sum of the ages is 70 years:
$$7 = \frac{\text{Sum}}{10}$$
$$70 = \text{Sum}$$

The problem then tells you that the average age of nine of the cars is six years. Using the same average equation, you can find that the sum of the ages of those cars is 54 years:
$$6 = \frac{\text{Sum}}{9}$$
$$54 = \text{Sum}$$

The difference in the sums is the age of the remaining car: $70-54=16$. The age of the tenth car is 16 years, Choice (D).

For more about how to solve problem solving questions, review Chapters 13 and 14. To review statistical concepts like average (that is, the arithmetic mean), read Chapter 12.

13. C. 3

This is a rate problem dealing with the speed and distance of a runner, Cindy. In rate problems, rate multiplied by time equals distance.

First, Cindy runs for 16 minutes at 7.5 miles per hour. Multiplying the rate by the time will get you the distance traveled. However, you need to convert the units so that you're only dealing with minutes.

$$\frac{7.5 \text{ miles}}{\text{hour}} \times \frac{1 \text{ hour}}{60 \text{ minutes}} \times 16 \text{ minutes} = 2 \text{ miles}$$

So, for the first portion of her run, Cindy traveled two miles. For the second portion, Cindy runs at six miles per hour for ten minutes.

$$\frac{6 \text{ miles}}{\text{hour}} \times \frac{1 \text{ hour}}{60 \text{ minutes}} \times 10 \text{ minutes} = 1 \text{ mile}$$

Therefore, Cindy ran for two miles at 7.5 miles per hour and then for one mile at 6 miles per hour, which results in a total of three miles, Choice (C).

For more about how to solve problem solving questions, review Chapters 13 and 14. To review solving distance problems, read Chapter 11.

14. C. $\sqrt{40.5}$

Solve the given quadratic equation:

$$2x^2 - 81 = 0$$
$$2x^2 = 81$$
$$x^2 = 40.5$$
$$x = \pm\sqrt{40.5}$$

Because $x > 0$, choose $x = \sqrt{40.5}$, making Choice (C) the correct answer.

For more about how to solve problem solving questions, review Chapters 13 and 14. To review solving quadratic equations, read Chapter 11.

15. C. 10

This problem is asking how many of the 60 guests at Taco Fusion restaurant ordered both tacos and sushi for lunch.

Let t be the number of guests that ordered tacos, s be the number that ordered sushi, b be the number that ordered both, and n be the number that ordered neither.

From the problem you know that there were 60 guests total and that $t = 45$, $s = 20$, and $n = 5$. The unknown is b, the number that ordered both. Use the rule for solving group problems, where Group 1 is t, the number that ordered tacos; Group 2 is s, the number that ordered sushi; Both Groups is b, the number that ordered both; Neither Group is n, the number that ordered neither; and the Grand Total is 60, the total number of guests:

Group 1 + Group 2 – Both Groups + Neither Group = Grand Total

$$t + s - b + n = 60$$
$$45 + 20 - b + 5 = 60$$
$$70 - b = 60$$
$$-b = -10$$
$$b = 10 \ .$$

Choice (C) is the correct answer.

For more about how to solve problem solving questions, review Chapters 13 and 14. To review problems involving groups and sets, read Chapter 12.

16. B. 45

This is a combination counting problem. You can determine the number of games played in a season by calculating the combination of 10 items (teams) taken 2 at a time. Using the combination formula, you have

$$_{10}C_2 = \frac{10!}{2!(10-2)!} = \frac{10!}{2!8!} = \frac{10 \times 9 \times 8!}{2 \times 1 \times 8!} = \frac{10 \times 9}{2} = \frac{90}{2} = 45, \text{ Choice (B)}.$$

For more about how to solve problem solving questions, review Chapters 13 and 14. To review counting techniques including permutations and combinations, read Chapter 12.

17. E. 21

The second seedling grew 6 inches plus 250% of 6 inches, which is 6 in + 250%(6 in) = 6 in + 2.5(6 in) = 6 in + 15 in = 21 in, Choice (E).

For more about how to solve problem solving questions, review Chapters 13 and 14. To review percents and other fundamental math concepts, read Chapter 10.

18. D. I and II only

Recall that *rational numbers* are numbers that can be expressed as the ratio of two integers, provided that the integer in the denominator is not zero. The expression in Roman I is rational because $\frac{\sqrt{46}\sqrt{46}}{(46)^2} = \frac{46}{46^2} = \frac{1}{46}$, which is rational. The correct choice must contain Roman I, so eliminate (B), (C), and (E). The expression in Roman II is rational because $\left(\sqrt{46} + \sqrt{46}\right)^2 = \left(2\sqrt{46}\right)^2 = 4 \times 46$, which is rational (you don't have to multiply it out to know it's rational, so don't!). The correct choice must contain Roman II, so eliminate Choice (A). Therefore, I and II only is the correct answer, Choice (D).

For more about how to solve problem solving questions, review Chapters 13 and 14. To review rational and irrational numbers and other fundamental math concepts, read Chapter 10.

19. A. 8:1

Let y = the number of yellow dots, then $2y$ is the number of blue dots; and $4 \times 2y = 8y$ is the number of red dots. The ratio of the number of red dots to the number of yellow dots is $\frac{8y}{y} = \frac{8}{1}$, which is the same as 8:1, Choice (A).

For more about how to solve problem solving questions, review Chapters 13 and 14. To review ratios, fractions, and other fundamental math concepts, read Chapter 10.

20. D. $\frac{1}{4}$

For each equation, set each factor equal to zero and solve for x. For the first equation, $(2x+1) = 0$ implies $x = -\frac{1}{2}$ and $(4x-1) = 0$ implies $x = \frac{1}{4}$. For the second equation, $(5x-1) = 0$ implies $x = \frac{1}{5}$ and $\left(x - \frac{1}{4}\right) = 0$ implies $x = \frac{1}{4}$. Therefore, the simultaneous solution is $x = \frac{1}{4}$, Choice (D).

For more about how to solve problem solving questions, review Chapters 13 and 14. To review solving equations, read Chapter 11.

21. **C. 26**

If N is neither the least nor the greatest of the six numbers, then the range of the numbers would be 28 − 6 = 22, which is not consistent with the question information that the range is 24. So, N is either the least of the six numbers or the greatest. If N is the least of the six numbers, then 28 − N = 24, which implies that N = 4. If N is the greatest of the six integers, then N − 6 = 24, which implies that N = 30. Thus, the two possible values for N are 4 and 30, which yields a difference of 30 − 4 = 26, Choice (C).

For more about how to solve problem solving questions, review Chapters 13 and 14. To review range and other statistical concepts, read Chapter 12.

Section 3: Verbal

1. **A. The factors that make an area desirable are also those that can pose the most risk.**

   The substantiating details in the paragraph describe situations where those factors that create desirable areas such as the Toboku coast, Florida, Hawaii, and productive farmlands are the same factors that create great destruction, so Choice (A) is the best answer.

   Choice (B) is too specific. Choice (C) mentions the destructive forces in the paragraph but not the concomitant desirability of the environments they also cause. Choice (D) requires too much speculation. The paragraph states that humans pay a price for living on Earth, but it doesn't state the requirement that they learn to live with the risks. The paragraph is less about humans and more about the kinds of natural risks on Earth. Choice (E) doesn't address all of the risks provided in the paragraph and is therefore too specific to be its main idea.

   For more on answering reading comprehension questions, review Chapters 7 and 9.

2. **C. Loss of retail clothing sales due to a mall flood**

   In the final paragraph of the passage, the authors discuss what they call direct and indirect losses. Direct losses, they note, are those that involve the destruction of physical assets; indirect losses are those that arise because of the direct ones. Choices (A), (B), (D), and (E) all involve the actual destruction of physical assets: a library, school building, livestock, and a pavilion, respectively.

   Choice (C), on the other hand, reports the loss of income due to a direct loss — a mall flood. Thus, only Choice (C) denotes an indirect loss because loss in sales isn't tangible and therefore isn't a physical asset.

   For more on answering reading comprehension questions, review Chapters 7 and 9.

3. **D. hazards are not under human control, while risks usually are**

   Skim the answer choices to determine whether any of them can be easily eliminated. Choice (B) isn't a true statement according to the information contained in the passage. The passage notes that ". . . risk is the product of hazard," which is the opposite of stating that hazards result from risks. You can also eliminate Choice (A) because it claims that risks occur naturally while hazards result from human interaction; the passage states that the opposite is true. So, you've narrowed options down to Choices (C), (D), or (E). Choice (C) makes another false statement — nowhere in the passage do the authors report that hazards, and not risks, can lead to disasters. Rather, they imply that the two together increase the risk of a disaster.

Choice (D) sounds like a serious contender, and the first two lines of the third paragraph back it up. Just to be sure, however, take a look at Choice (E). The words "harder to quantify" may jump out at you because you find them in the final paragraph, but upon more scrutiny, you can determine that the author claims that "economic impacts," not risks, are hard to quantify. Choice (D) is the best answer.

For more on answering reading comprehension questions, review Chapters 7 and 9.

4. **A. describing the causes and impacts of natural disasters**

Eliminate answers that contain information that appears in just a part of the passage rather than the whole. The authors don't discuss economic impacts until the final paragraph, so Choice (B) isn't a strong contender for the passage's primary concern. The role of human beings in risk is covered early in the passage, but the passage also discusses that some hazards are simply beyond human control, so Choice (C) isn't the best expression of the primary purpose. Choice (D), too, only tells part of the story; in addition to loss of human life, the passage discusses financial costs. Choice (E) is also inaccurate; the authors note that hazards aren't under human control, but risks, at least to some degree, are.

By process of elimination, Choice (A) is the best answer. This general summary statement incorporates information discussed in the entire passage.

For more on answering reading comprehension questions, review Chapters 7 and 9.

5. **E. It applies statistical data to emphasize the magnitude of damage created by natural disasters.**

Choice (A) is incorrect because the numerical information in the fourth paragraph relates to human lives lost rather than economic impacts. Choice (B) mentions a specific detail in the fourth paragraph, but the detail provides supporting evidence rather than the primary purpose of the paragraph. Choice (C) provides a better description of the function of the third paragraph than the fourth. And you can eliminate Choice (D) because its statement isn't true; the paragraph gives numerical data about one event rather than sensory detail about several.

Only Choice (E) offers a plausible explanation for the function of the fourth paragraph in relation to the rest of the passage. The paragraph provides statistics regarding a specific event that provides an example of the colossal destruction a natural disaster can cause.

For more on answering reading comprehension questions, review Chapters 7 and 9.

6. **E. Areas of high hazard, such as Japan's Tohoku coast, may have a lower risk of natural disaster costs than areas where hazard incidents are lower.**

The third paragraph clarifies that the highest cost risk isn't always associated with the greatest hazard. Places with less hazard risk may experience greater costs because the hazard affects more people, or the area is less prepared to withstand damage. Therefore, Choice (E) is correct.

The passage doesn't provide clear data regarding the number of reported and unreported deaths in the tsunami and earthquake disaster, so you can't definitively compare number of deaths in Choice (A). The passage says that the tsunami in 2004 caused many more deaths than average, but it doesn't say the same for the 2010 Haiti disaster, so Choice (B) is wrong. Because you don't have actual data for deaths due to natural disaster in Japan, Hawaii, and Haiti, you also can't pick Choice (C). The passage suggests that both economic costs and death totals are unreported for natural disasters, but it doesn't compare the two, so you can't justify Choice (D).

7. **A. The degree of erosion to which a coastline is subject is related to the shape of the sea bottom.**

Choice (A) makes sense because the impact of waves is related to the shape of the sea bottom, and the coast's erosion is related to the impact of waves. Choice (B) is wrong because the statements only state the factors (wind velocity and fetch) that influence wave size; there's nothing to suggest that wave size stays close to an average. Choice (C) doesn't work; if fetch is the length of the surface of the water, it shouldn't be related to the shape of the sea bottom. Choice (D) is wrong because the size of waves comes from wind and fetch, not the shape of the bottom. Choice (E) looks wrong, too. Wind velocity creates size of waves, size of waves affects impact, and impact affects erosion, so average velocity of wind playing no role in erosion doesn't make sense. Choice (A) is the best answer.

For more on answering critical reasoning questions, review Chapters 8 and 9.

8. **A. It is a specific example of a general condition described during the argument.**

The argument is that because patients need medical care and hospitals, regardless of what those services cost, hospitals and doctors rather than insurers bear the brunt of cost-containment measures; the MRI statement provides an example. Choice (A) is a good answer; the statement is a specific example of capital demands (MRIs and buildings) of the general condition of fiscal discipline described in the argument.

Choice (B) doesn't work because the MRI statement doesn't counter an attack. Choice (C) isn't as good an answer as Choice (A). The author's claim or conclusion is that health insurers are still profiting from healthcare while doctors, hospitals, and patients are being increasingly squeezed, but the MRI statement doesn't indirectly support that claim. Choice (D) doesn't work. Patients' needing treatment isn't a social side effect but a normal event that remains consistent, regardless of changing circumstances. Choice (E) is wrong; the MRI statement doesn't introduce the conclusion about the immunity of health insurers. Choice (A) is correct.

For more on answering critical reasoning questions, review Chapters 8 and 9.

9. **E. Allowing employees to take leave for family matters reduces absenteeism, improves morale, and surprisingly increases productivity because the employees who are granted leave tend to work much harder and more efficiently when they come back to work.**

To weaken the argument, look for an answer showing that allowing family leave doesn't hurt productivity or perhaps even helps it. Choice (A) doesn't affect the argument because standard of living isn't an issue, and it doesn't mention workplace productivity. Choice (B) could arguably weaken the argument because it provides evidence that workers may not abuse the privilege of leave — fathers aren't taking family leave at all, which weakens the conclusion that workers would work less if they had leave. On the other hand, if taking paternity leave angers co-workers, that strengthens the conclusion that family leave hurts workplace morale, so this isn't the best answer. Choice (C) strengthens the argument by showing that FMLA leave costs the employer money. Choice (D) also strengthens the argument by illustrating the destruction caused by one employee leaving for a while.

Choice (E) weakens the argument. If employers are worried about productivity and morale, this choice says that allowing leave increases productivity and morale. Choice (E) is the right answer.

For more on answering critical reasoning questions, review Chapters 8 and 9.

10. **A. Operating systems with generous amounts of memory are less susceptible to crashing, even when applications are poorly written.**

Okay, you want to find the four answers indicating that operating systems are responsible for the smooth functioning of applications and can somehow manage their memory problems. The best way to do this is by process of elimination. If you can find four answers that show the operating system handling applications' memory issues, then the answer that's left over should be correct. Choice (B) helps the conclusion because it shows that operating systems are responsible for handling the memory used by individual applications. Choice (C) helps because it shows that operating systems can spot overuse of memory and stop it. Choice (D) helps because it tells you that programmers should know how to program an operating system that can prevent memory errors, which means all operating systems should be able to do this. Choice (E) helps the conclusion because it describes what an efficient operating system should be able to do.

Choice (A) is the only answer that doesn't put responsibility for memory management on the operating system; adding memory to the computer evidently can let the operating system off the hook. Choice (A) is the right answer.

For more on answering critical reasoning questions, review Chapters 8 and 9.

11. **E. If people see online images of items in the museum's collection, they will no longer be interested in seeing the collection with their own eyes.**

The argument seems to assume that if people see the images online, they won't have any interest in visiting in person. Choice (A) isn't the point because the author of the argument isn't worried about damaging the images. Choice (B) doesn't work because the author doesn't mention a concern for decreased revenue. Choice (C) likely isn't the author's concern. The author isn't specifically worried about the extent of online distribution but rather its effect. Check the remaining answers to see whether you have a better option. Choice (D) isn't of concern, either, because the author doesn't mention quality issues.

Choice (E) is the best answer. The author is worried that online publication of the images will remove the incentive to visit the actual museum in person.

For more on answering critical reasoning questions, review Chapters 8 and 9.

12. **B. executive functioning.**

Answering this question is pretty cut and dried. The second paragraph indicates that learning how to resist distraction is part of what it takes for a child to recognize and work toward a goal, which is defined as — you guessed it — executive functioning. Choices (A), (C), (D), and (E) are all touched upon to some extent in the passage, but the definitive answer is Choice (B).

For more on answering reading comprehension questions, review Chapters 7 and 9.

13. **A. emphasize that school readiness regards the process as much as the results.**

The authors' key point is that school readiness is about assessing a child's ability to learn rather than relying on test results and the like to determine knowledge. When they're in a K–12 school setting, kids must demonstrate "school readiness" through the results of academic testing and grades. Choice (A) expresses this point best.

Choice (B) is wrong because although the authors note the difference between the guiding principles of school readiness and those used by K–12 school systems, nothing in the passage suggests that they consider those of the latter "failings." Choice (C) essentially makes the same argument as Choice (B), so you can knock that option from contention, too.

Eliminate Choice (D); no evidence exists that this passage is about the authors' opinion. Choice (E) is out, too. Although the authors deal with cognition in the second paragraph, this factor isn't the primary reason for making the more general distinction between school readiness and K–12 guidelines. Stick with Choice (A).

For more on answering reading comprehension questions, review Chapters 7 and 9.

14. **D. paying attention to the teacher**

In the second paragraph, the authors mention a growing emphasis on executive functioning skills in the concept of school readiness. They then define executive functions as those pertaining to working memory, attention control, attention shifting, and response inhibition. The authors give the example of paying attention to the teacher as an indication of ability to resist distractions. Because paying attention to the teacher is an indication of executive functioning, this skill has been one of those on which there has been a "growing emphasis," and Choice (D) is best.

Choice (A) is easy to eliminate; performance on achievement tests is associated with the K–12 system. The other answers relate to school readiness factors mentioned in the last paragraph and aren't included as part of executive functioning. Choice (B) is associated with language skills, Choice (C) is defined as a socioemotional skill, and Choice (E) is part of the physical health domain.

For more on answering reading comprehension questions, review Chapters 7 and 9.

15. **E. socioemotional skills**

In the final paragraph of the passage, the authors mention cooperation with teachers and peers and developing social relationships as examples of socioemotional skills, which is Choice (E).

Motor skills pertain to the physical health domain. As for Choices (B) and (C), the author places them into the language skills category. Strong executive functioning skills are discussed in detail in the second paragraph, where the authors note that these skills help kids work toward achieving specific goals. Choice (E) is the best bet.

For more on answering reading comprehension questions, review Chapters 7 and 9.

16. **A. Spousal and marital difficulties were formerly responsible for many premature returns from foreign assignments.**

If helping spouses has improved expatriate retention by such a huge amount, then unhappy spouses must have previously been responsible for lots of premature returns. Choice (A) looks like a good answer.

If unhappy spouses contributed to employees' leaving international assignments, helping spouses adjust would improve the situation. Choice (B) is wrong. If spouses are already thrilled with the international experience, their dissatisfaction is unlikely to contribute to employees' leaving their overseas posts. Choice (C) would support the argument, but it's too specific to be a necessary assumption on which the conclusion depends (there could well be other reasons why spouses are dissatisfied). Choice (D) doesn't explain why helping spouses has improved retention. Choice (E) provides an example of what companies are doing to help spouses but isn't the assumption that links the argument's premises to the conclusion. Choice (A) is the best answer.

For more on answering critical reasoning questions, review Chapters 8 and 9.

17. **E. The meadow voles that had the prairie vole gene implanted in them were released into and observed in the same habitat in which they had previously lived.**

Look for information that supports the assumption that the meadow voles' change in behavior was caused by the implanted gene. Choice (A) is wrong. The choice doesn't relate the effects of the hormone to the gene that makes meadow voles monogamous. Choice (B) explains what's up with prairie voles but not with meadow voles, and neither's genes are mentioned. Choice (C) explains why meadow voles are typically promiscuous but says nothing about whether a gene plays a part in that. Choice (D) says nothing about whether the transferred gene is the cause of the monogamous behavior.

Choice (E) provides the most support for the assertion that the scientists' work with genes was the factor that turned the formerly promiscuous meadow voles into models of monogamy because it rules out a possible other important factor that may have explained the change (different surroundings). Choice (E) is the correct answer.

For more on answering critical reasoning questions, review Chapters 8 and 9.

18. **C. Women who want to have children increasingly seek to delay doing so for many varied reasons.**

The conclusion is that predicting when menopause will occur will make a difference to women planning when to have children, which must mean that not knowing when menopause will occur makes it difficult to plan. Choice (A) is wrong because it doesn't explain why predicting menopause will help anyone. Choice (B) just provides general information about menopause.

Choice (C) may be right — it provides a reason that women would benefit from knowing when they'll experience menopause (they're delaying longer, so they need to know how long is too long to delay). Choice (D) isn't relevant because the argument is about how accurately predicting the onset of menopause affects childbearing decisions, not how likely a woman is to conceive in the years immediately prior to menopause. Choice (E) is just information about ovaries, not an explanation of how this test will help make family planning decisions. Choice (C) is the best answer.

For more on answering critical reasoning questions, review Chapters 8 and 9.

19. **D. Employers assume that high school graduates generally have a much higher level of mastery of academic subjects than those who earn GEDs.**

The argument suggests that a GED is just as good as a high school education; look for an answer that contradicts that. Choice (A) doesn't work. You don't want evidence showing the benefits of earning GEDs. Choice (B) doesn't pose a problem. If universities accept GEDs, that's more evidence that they're as good as diplomas. Choice (C) actually strengthens the argument.

Choice (D) does weaken the argument. If a GED might put one at a disadvantage in the job market, that's a reason to stay in school. Choice (E) doesn't strengthen or weaken the argument. Choice (D) is correct.

For more on answering critical reasoning questions, review Chapters 8 and 9.

20. **D. explain how attention to cybersecurity impacts companies' technological innovation.**

Perform a quick scan through the answer choices and see if any catches your eye. Of those available, only Choice (D) specifically references the relationship between cyber-attacks and technological innovation, which was a major part of the subject matter. Choice (D) is correct.

Choices (A), (B), and (E) similarly suggest that the main idea regards the hackers' success, but the passage is less about hackers and more about how companies react to hacking. And Choice (E) even suggests that hacking is heroic. Choice (C) presents the primary purpose of the first paragraph but not the entire passage. Choice (D) is the only option that incorporates ideas that appear throughout the passage.

For more on answering reading comprehension questions, review Chapters 7 and 9.

21. C. weighing business outcomes and risks

The third paragraph clearly states that indirect losses and the cost of defending against cyber-threats reduce the benefits of technology investments, so you can eliminate Choices (B) and (D). Likewise, in the second paragraph, you find evidence to support that theft of intellectual property is a risk of increased global connectivity created by technology investment, so Choice (A) is out. The last sentence of the second paragraph also suggests that the way that companies approach cyber-threats — reacting to them only when they occur — is costly and will likely result in more cyber-attacks. Therefore, Choice (E) likely decreases the benefit of investing in technology.

The passage doesn't indicate that the mere act of weighing risk and reward incurs cost, so Choice (C) is the answer that has the least chance of decreasing the potential gains of investing in technology.

For more on answering reading comprehension questions, review Chapters 7 and 9.

22. B. combat problems after they have occurred.

When the authors reference companies' "siloed and reactive approach" to cybersecurity, they do so after the discussion about how investing in technology comes with inherent cybersecurity risks. The implication is that companies take on these risks without a clear plan for protecting against them, and therefore, the hackers seem to be winning the battle against business security systems. Choice (A) incorrectly asserts that companies are performing their due diligence when it comes to trying to improve cybersecurity, so you can count this one out. Choice (C) mistakenly gives the credit to companies, so you can eliminate that one for the same reason you knocked out Choice (A). The passage doesn't quantify what constitutes "too much" investment, and regardless of whether Choice (D) is true, the passage infers that this "siloed and reactive approach" is not so much about spending money but about waiting for issues to develop rather than attempting to prepare for them. Finally, Choice (E) suggests that companies are moving full speed ahead with unnecessary technological innovations and advancements, which is contradictory to the information in the rest of the passage that suggests companies are becoming slower to innovate because of cybersecurity concerns.

Choice (B) correctly indicates that companies' reactive approach waits for problems to happen before considering the potential risks of technological investment. It's the best answer.

For more on answering reading comprehension questions, review Chapters 7 and 9.

23. E. an outline of a streamlined manufacturing process

The second paragraph specifically links intellectual property to a new product life-cycle management system. The answer that relates most directly to proprietary product information is Choice (E), information regarding a proprietary product-manufacturing process. Choice (E) is correct.

Choice (A) describes intellectual property but not that which would be leaked in a new product life-cycle management system. The other choices aren't examples of intellectual property.

For more on answering reading comprehension questions, review Chapters 7 and 9.

Answers at a Glance

Section 1: Data Insights

(Check these answers online.)

Section 2: Quantitative

1.	A	7.	B	13.	C	19.	A
2.	D	8.	D	14.	C	20.	D
3.	D	9.	C	15.	C	21.	C
4.	C	10.	B	16.	B		
5.	A	11.	D	17.	E		
6.	B	12.	D	18.	D		

Section 3: Verbal

1.	A	7.	A	13.	A	19.	D
2.	C	8.	A	14.	D	20.	D
3.	D	9.	E	15.	E	21.	C
4.	A	10.	A	16.	A	22.	B
5.	E	11.	E	17.	E	23.	E
6.	E	12.	B	18.	C		

7

The Part of Tens

IN THIS PART . . .

Discover ten question types that are easy to master.

Go beyond just mastering the GMAT and discover ten things you can do to increase your chances of getting accepted to an MBA program.

Chapter **20**

Ten Question Types You've Got a Good Shot At

With all that math, reading, and logical reasoning, you can develop a headache just thinking about the GMAT. Why can't the GMAT cut you some slack? Well, it does . . . sort of. You see, certain GMAT questions may be a little easier to answer than others. In this chapter, we lay out ten types of questions you have a greater chance of answering correctly with greater consistency so you can buy yourself a little time to use on the tougher questions in each section.

Main-Idea Reading Questions

In general, reading comprehension questions are a little easier than critical reasoning questions. For reading comprehension questions, the answers are right there on the screen; you just need to find them. One reason main-idea questions in particular are easier is that 90 percent of the passages present you with one. Identifying the main idea should become automatic, so you don't even have to refer to a passage to answer a question. And usually, three of the five answer choices are clearly off topic or too specific, so all you have to do is choose the best answer of the remaining two.

Specific Information Reading Questions

Specific information questions appear in every reading comprehension passage, so you'll get used to them. You have a great shot at these questions because the computer highlights the text that contains the answer. Just read the highlighted part of the passage (and maybe the text around it) to find the correct answer. As long as you stay focused, you should bat a thousand on these beauties!

Exception Questions for Reading Passages

Exception questions ask you to choose the answer that *isn't* stated in the passage. Usually, all you have to do is eliminate each answer choice that appears in the text. The choice left standing is the correct answer.

Critical Reasoning Questions about Strengthening or Weakening Arguments

Critical reasoning questions that ask you what strengthens or weakens the argument tend to rely on cause-and-effect relationships or analogies. If an author reaches a conclusion by cause and effect, you choose an answer that either shows other causes for the effect (to weaken the argument) or that emphasizes that no other causes for the effect exist (to strengthen the argument). To weaken analogy arguments, choose an answer that shows the compared entities are dissimilar. An answer that highlights similarities strengthens the argument.

Critical Reasoning Questions Involving Statistical Arguments

When statistics are used to promote an argument, you can eliminate answer choices that don't directly address the statistical evidence. This action narrows the number of answer choices from which to choose.

Data Sufficiency Questions

Data sufficiency questions usually take less time to answer than other data insights questions. You don't have to actually solve the problem to answer the question correctly. Just follow the step-by-step process outlined in Chapter 17 to stay focused.

Math Problem Solving Questions Involving Graphics

One of the hardest parts of a problem solving question is getting started. You may have trouble sifting through the information you get from word problems, but graphics present known information clearly. Examine the information in the graphics and solve the problem.

Math Problem Solving Questions Involving Basic Operations

Some problem solving questions present you with an equation or a simple word problem involving arithmetic, exponents, or other basic operations. You've been applying these basics since childhood, so all you have to do is read carefully!

Substitution Math Problem Solving Questions

Problem solving questions that ask you to substitute values for symbols can be simple after you understand what you're supposed to do. In most cases, you just need to exchange a value for a symbol in an otherwise simple equation.

Table Analysis Questions

The data insights questions that require you to analyze data in tables primarily test your ability to read data. Finding the correct answer is rarely based on your ability to read lengthy paragraphs or perform complex calculations. As long as you pay attention to how the table presents the data, you should sail through these questions fairly smoothly. Just don't complicate matters by reading more into these questions than you have to.

Chapter **21**

Ten Ways to Increase Your Chances of Getting into Business School

The number of business school applications continues to increase, but quantity doesn't necessarily mean quality. And the quality of your application remains your single best bet for standing out among the crowd. A great application emphasizes your academic preparation, strong work experience, and a clear sense of what you hope to gain from your quest for an MBA. This chapter highlights what you can do to make sure your application process provides what it takes to impress the decision makers.

Accumulate a Little Work Experience

You don't have to get your MBA right after you graduate. In fact, waiting and working for a while may be to your advantage. Many admissions officers like to see at least three years of managerial work experience when you apply for an MBA program so they can be sure you're cut out for a career in business. They also look for signs of competence and career progress, such as promotions, the acquisition of new skills, and increased responsibilities in the workplace.

Ace the Interview

Some programs require an interview; others may recommend one. If a business school states that an interview is optional, grab this opportunity to demonstrate your social skills and highlight your passions. To make a good impression, heed the following advice:

» Dress in business attire.

» Smile, look your interviewer in the eye, and answer questions honestly.

» Exude confidence without arrogance.

» Ask questions of the interviewer that demonstrate your knowledge of the program.

» Follow up with a thank-you note.

Apply Early

Applying early to an MBA program demonstrates strong planning skills and a significant interest in the program. Submitting your application before the rest of the crowd also increases the chances of your application getting the time and attention from admissions officers it rightfully deserves!

Apply While You're Upwardly Mobile

Business schools want go-getters, and what better time to catch someone than on the way up? Show your school of choice that you're a force to be reckoned with by highlighting any recent promotions, achievements, accolades, or anything that helps suggest that it had better snatch you up while you're in your prime before another school beats it to the punch.

Capitalize on What Makes You Unique

Don't waste too much time trying to fit into some imaginary mold of the ideal business student. Business school admissions officers are seeking students with varying life experiences and from a broad variety of backgrounds, so embrace who you are and avoid trying to present a false persona that may ultimately backfire. In fact, your non-traditional profile may make you even more desirable to a program that seeks to diversify its class.

Demonstrate Interest

Business schools want to know that if they accept you, you'll actually attend. Admissions committees equate communication with interest, so the more you reach out to them, the more interested they'll be in you. Contact your admissions representative regularly with pertinent questions. Just make sure you don't become a pest!

Focus on Fit

Just as you want to know what school is the best fit for you, admissions officers seek the students who are the best fit for them. Do your research about what a particular school is known for and what sorts of skills and personality traits it embraces, and tailor your application, essay, and interview accordingly. You can find out a lot about a particular business school's personality by researching its website, searching the Internet for articles about the program and its graduates, and visiting the campus.

Get the Right Recommendations

Business school applicants commonly fixate so much on the essay process that they diminish the importance of securing solid recommendations. Don't undervalue the crucial role of recommendations. Choose supervisors who know you well, both personally and professionally. Admissions officers focus on how well your reference knows your strengths and weaknesses. Find someone who can expound on how well you interact with others and provide evidence of your academic prowess and leadership abilities.

REMEMBER

The person who knows you best is more likely to be your direct supervisor than the company CEO.

Study for the GMAT

Your GMAT score matters. The test was designed to determine how well you'll likely do in an MBA program in comparison to a plethora of other applicants, so scoring sky-high on the GMAT can place you head and shoulders above the rest of the crowd. Use this book's step-by-step instruction for each area of the test to help you prepare, and be sure to take the practice tests to help you identify areas where you could benefit from a bit of a refresher.

Write a Memorable Admissions Essay

When crafting your admissions essay, keep in mind that the admissions committee already knows your facts and figures — what you studied, where you worked, and your scores on the GMAT. The point of the essay is to give application readers a glimpse of the *real* you — what makes you stand out from the crowd, what motivates you, what you have overcome, and what you want to achieve in life. Keep in mind that admissions committees are reading thousands of responses to the same questions, so avoid falling into the trap of writing what you *think* they want to hear and instead shift your focus to self-revelation through vivid details and thoughtful anecdotes.

Index

stem-and-leaf plots, 255–256
strategies
  for guessing, 18
  importance of completing each section, 19
  relaxation techniques, 26–27
  review and edit feature, 18
  time-management, 19–21
studying, for GMAT, 315
subsets, 193
substitution math problems, 311
subtraction
  about, 138
  in algebra, 160–161
  with exponents, 143
  of fractions, 150
supporting information questions, 75

T

table analysis, 232, 234–237, 311
tables, translating information in, 248–249
Technical Support (website), 3
terms
  about, 158–159
  distributing, 162
  stacking, 162–163
testing center, 9
time limits, 13–14
time-management strategies, 19–21
timing, for applying to business schools, 32
Tip icon, 2
trinomial, 159
two-part analysis, 232, 237–240

U

union, of two sets, 193

V

variables
  about, 158
  isolating, 171–173
Venn diagrams, 193–194, 257–258

verbal section
  about, 38, 119
  answers to practice questions, 58–61, 66, 127–132
  practice questions, 46–49, 120–126
  practice test, 282–290, 299–305, 306
verbal skills, testing with GMAT, 13
vertical lines, 188
Vitruba-Drzal, Elizabeth (author)
  Handbook of Early Childhood Development Programs, Practices, and Policies, 285–288

W

Warning icon, 2
wasting time, on hard questions, 26
websites
  Cheat Sheet, 3
  GMAT, 4, 9
  Technical Support, 3
word problems, 181–182
work experience, 313
work problems, 182–183
writing effective essays, for business school applications, 33–34

X

x, factoring to find, 179–180
x-axis, 185
x-coordinate of a point, 185
x-intercept, 186

Y

y-axis, 185
y-coordinate of a point, 185
y-intercept, 186
yourself, pacing, 20–21

Z

zero (0), power of, 144
Zupan, Mark A. (author)
  Microeconomics Theory and Applications, 9th Edition, 83–84

About the Authors

Lisa Zimmer Hatch, M.A., and **Scott A. Hatch, J.D.,** have prepared teens and adults since 1987 to excel on standardized tests, gain admission to colleges of their choice, and secure challenging and lucrative professional careers. For more than 35 years, they have created and administered award-winning standardized test preparation and professional career courses worldwide for live lecture, online, and other formats through more than 500 universities worldwide.

Scott and Lisa have written the curriculum for all formats, and their books have been translated for international markets. Additionally, they wrote, produced, and appeared in the landmark weekly PBS *Law for Life* series. They continue to develop new courses for a variety of careers and extend their college admissions expertise to assist those seeking advanced degrees in law, business, and other professions. Together they have authored numerous law and standardized test prep texts, including *ACT For Dummies, 1,001 ACT Practice Problems For Dummies, LSAT For Dummies,* and *Paralegal Career For Dummies* (John Wiley & Sons, Inc.).

Lisa is currently an independent educational consultant and the president of College Primers, where she applies her expertise to guiding high school and college students through the undergraduate and graduate admissions and financial aid processes and prepares students for entrance exams through individualized coaching and small group courses. She prides herself in maximizing her students' financial aid packages and dedicates herself to helping them gain admission to the universities or programs that best fit their goals, personalities, and financial resources. She graduated with honors in English from the University of Puget Sound and received a master's degree in humanities with a literature emphasis from California State University. She holds a certificate in college counseling from UCLA and is a member of and the webinar manager for the Higher Education Consultants Association (HECA) and a member of the Rocky Mountain Association of College Admissions Counselors (RMACAC).

Scott received his undergraduate degree from the University of Colorado and his Juris Doctorate from Southwestern University School of Law. He's listed in *Who's Who in California and Who's Who Among Students in American Colleges and Universities* and is one of the Outstanding Young Men of America as determined by the United States Jaycees. He was also a contributing editor to McGraw-Hill's *Judicial Profiler* series and *The Colorado Law Annotated* series published by Lawyers Cooperative Publishing. He also served as editor of the Freedom of Information Committee Newsletter and functioned as editor of several national award-winning periodicals. His current law books include *A Legal Guide to Probate and Estate Planning* and *A Legal Guide to Family Law* in B & B Legal Publication's *Learn the Law* series.

In addition to writing law books, periodical articles, television scripts, and college curricula, Scott was editor of his law school's nationally award-winning legal periodical, winner of two first-place awards from the Columbia University School of Journalism, and another first-place award from the American Bar Association. He also contributed to Los Angeles's daily newspaper, *The Metropolitan News,* was an editorial assistant during the formation of the Los Angeles Press Club's Education Foundation, and served on the Faculty of Law at the City University of Los Angeles.

Sandra Luna McCune, PhD, is professor emeritus and a former Regents professor at Stephen F. Austin State University. She's currently a full-time author and math/statistics consultant.

Dedication

Lisa Zimmer Hatch, M.A., and **Scott A. Hatch, J.D.:** We dedicate *GMAT Prep 2024 For Dummies* to our children and their families. They demonstrated patience, understanding, and editorial assistance while we wrote this book, and we're very blessed to have them in our lives.

Sandra Luna McCune, PhD: I dedicate my contribution to this work to my precious and delightful family— especially my wonderful grandchildren Richard, Tristan, Jude, Sophie, Josie, Myla, Micah, and Hailey.

Authors' Acknowledgments

Lisa Zimmer Hatch, M.A., and **Scott A. Hatch, J.D.:** This book would not be possible without the contributions of Julia Brabant, Hank Zimmer, Jackson Sutherland, Zachary Hatch, and Zoe Hatch, who provided practice test material and helpful input. We also acknowledge the input of thousands of our students who have completed our test preparation courses over the last 35 years. The classroom and online contributions offered by these dedicated and motivated learners have provided us with a significant amount of information about those subject areas that require the greatest amount of preparation for success on the GMAT.

Our project organization and attempts at wit were greatly facilitated by the editing professionals at Wiley. Our thanks go out to Elizabeth Stilwell and Chad Sievers for their patience and guidance throughout the editing process.

Finally, we wish to thank our literary agent, Margo Maley Hutchinson, at Waterside Productions in Cardiff, for her support and assistance and for introducing us to the innovative *For Dummies* series.

We thrive on feedback from our students and encourage our readers to provide comments and critiques at info@hatchedu.com.

Sandra Luna McCune, PhD: Thanks to everyone on the Editorial Team. I offer special gratitude to the incomparable duo of Elizabeth Stilwell and Colleen Diamond for their invaluable assistance. I am grateful to Grace Freedson for being the best agent I could ever imagine.

Publisher's Acknowledgments

Acquisitions Editor: Elizabeth Stilwell

Project and Copy Editor: Colleen Totz Diamond, Chad R. Sievers

Managing Editor: Kristie Pyles

Production Editor: Saikarthick Kumarasamy

Cover Image: © Ground Picture/Shutterstock

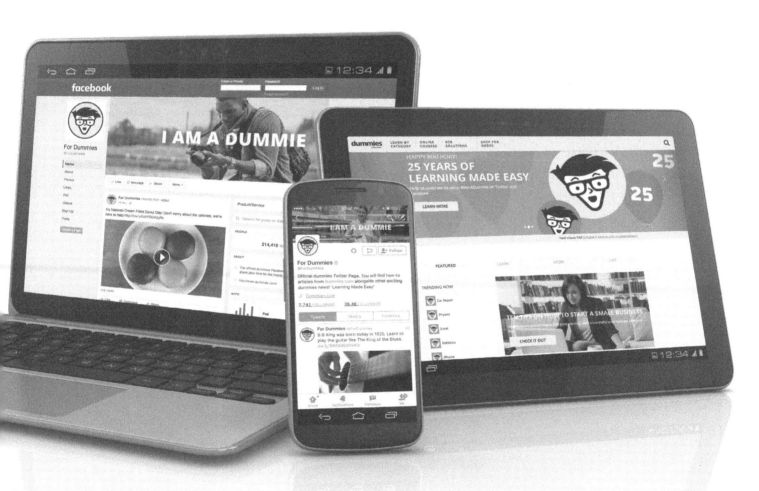

Leverage the power

Dummies is the global leader in the reference category and one of the most trusted and highly regarded brands in the world. No longer just focused on books, customers now have access to the dummies content they need in the format they want. Together we'll craft a solution that engages your customers, stands out from the competition, and helps you meet your goals.

Advertising & Sponsorships

Connect with an engaged audience on a powerful multimedia site, and position your message alongside expert how-to content. Dummies.com is a one-stop shop for free, online information and know-how curated by a team of experts.

- Targeted ads
- Video
- Email Marketing

- Microsites
- Sweepstakes sponsorship

20 **MILLION**
PAGE VIEWS
EVERY SINGLE MONTH

15
MILLION
UNIQUE
VISITORS PER MONTH

43%
OF ALL VISITORS
ACCESS THE SITE
VIA THEIR MOBILE DEVICES

700,000 NEWSLETTER
SUBSCRIPTION
TO THE INBOXES OF
300,000 UNIQUE INDIVIDUALS
EVERY WEEK

# of dummies

Custom Publishing

Reach a global audience in any language by creating a solution that will differentiate you from competitors, amplify your message, and encourage customers to make a buying decision.

- Apps
- Books
- eBooks
- Video
- Audio
- Webinars

Brand Licensing & Content

Leverage the strength of the world's most popular reference brand to reach new audiences and channels of distribution.

For more information, visit **dummies.com/biz**

PERSONAL ENRICHMENT

Staying Sharp
9781119187790
USA $26.00
CAN $31.99
UK £19.99

Facebook
9781119179030
USA $21.99
CAN $25.99
UK £16.99

Guitar
9781119293354
USA $24.99
CAN $29.99
UK £17.99

Investing
9781119293347
USA $22.99
CAN $27.99
UK £16.99

Beekeeping
9781119310068
USA $22.99
CAN $27.99
UK £16.99

Digital Photography
9781119235606
USA $24.99
CAN $29.99
UK £17.99

Meditation
9781119251163
USA $24.99
CAN $29.99
UK £17.99

Pregnancy
9781119235491
USA $26.99
CAN $31.99
UK £19.99

Samsung Galaxy S7
9781119279952
USA $24.99
CAN $29.99
UK £17.99

iPhone
9781119283133
USA $24.99
CAN $29.99
UK £17.99

Crocheting
9781119287117
USA $24.99
CAN $29.99
UK £16.99

Nutrition
9781119130246
USA $22.99
CAN $27.99
UK £16.99

PROFESSIONAL DEVELOPMENT

Windows 10
9781119311041
USA $24.99
CAN $29.99
UK £17.99

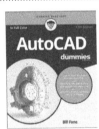

AutoCAD
9781119255796
USA $39.99
CAN $47.99
UK £27.99

Excel 2016
9781119293439
USA $26.99
CAN $31.99
UK £19.99

QuickBooks 2017
9781119281467
USA $26.99
CAN $31.99
UK £19.99

macOS Sierra
9781119280651
USA $29.99
CAN $35.99
UK £21.99

LinkedIn
9781119251132
USA $24.99
CAN $29.99
UK £17.99

Windows 10
9781119310563
USA $34.00
CAN $41.99
UK £24.99

SharePoint 2016
9781119181705
USA $29.99
CAN $35.99
UK £21.99

Fundamental Analysis
9781119263593
USA $26.99
CAN $31.99
UK £19.99

Networking
9781119257769
USA $29.99
CAN $35.99
UK £21.99

Office 2016
9781119293477
USA $26.99
CAN $31.99
UK £19.99

Office 365
9781119265313
USA $24.99
CAN $29.99
UK £17.99

Salesforce.com
9781119239314
USA $29.99
CAN $35.99
UK £21.99

Coding
9781119293323
USA $29.99
CAN $35.99
UK £21.99

dummies.com

dummies
A Wiley Brand

Learning Made Easy

ACADEMIC

9781119293576
USA $19.99
CAN $23.99
UK £15.99

9781119293637
USA $19.99
CAN $23.99
UK £15.99

9781119293491
USA $19.99
CAN $23.99
UK £15.99

9781119293460
USA $19.99
CAN $23.99
UK £15.99

9781119293590
USA $19.99
CAN $23.99
UK £15.99

9781119215844
USA $26.99
CAN $31.99
UK £19.99

9781119293378
USA $22.99
CAN $27.99
UK £16.99

9781119293521
USA $19.99
CAN $23.99
UK £15.99

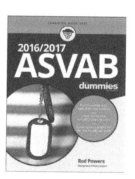

9781119239178
USA $18.99
CAN $22.99
UK £14.99

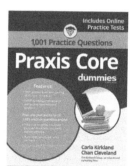

9781119263883
USA $26.99
CAN $31.99
UK £19.99

Available Everywhere Books Are Sold

dummies.com

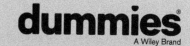

dummies
A Wiley Brand

Small books for big imaginations

9781119177173
USA $9.99
CAN $9.99
UK £8.99

9781119177272
USA $9.99
CAN $9.99
UK £8.99

9781119177241
USA $9.99
CAN $9.99
UK £8.99

9781119177210
USA $9.99
CAN $9.99
UK £8.99

9781119262657
USA $9.99
CAN $9.99
UK £6.99

9781119291336
USA $9.99
CAN $9.99
UK £6.99

9781119233527
USA $9.99
CAN $9.99
UK £6.99

9781119291220
USA $9.99
CAN $9.99
UK £6.99

9781119177302
USA $9.99
CAN $9.99
UK £8.99

Unleash Their Creativity

dummies.com